W9-BEC-592

DISCARD

Fourth Edition

The SPORTS RULES Book

Date: 3/1/19

796 HUM
The sports rules book /

Human Kinetics

with **Myles Schrag**

HUMAN KINETICS

PALM BEACH COUNTY
LIBRARY SYSTEM
3650 SUMMIT BLVD.
WEST PALM BEACH, FL 33406

Library of Congress Cataloging-in-Publication Data

Names: Human Kinetics (Organization) | Schrag, Myles, author.
Title: The sports rules book / Human Kinetics with Myles Schrag.
Description: Fourth edition. | Champaign, IL : Human Kinetics, [2019] |
   Includes bibliographical references.
Identifiers: LCCN 2018025433 (print) | LCCN 2018037848 (ebook) | ISBN
   9781492567608 (ebook) | ISBN 9781492567592 (print)
Subjects: LCSH: Sports--Rules.
Classification: LCC GV731 (ebook) | LCC GV731 .H85 2019 (print) | DDC
   796--dc23
LC record available at https://lccn.loc.gov/2018025433

ISBN: 978-1-4925-6759-2 (print)

Copyright © 2019, 2009, 2004, 1997 by Human Kinetics, Inc.

All rights reserved. Except for use in a review, the reproduction or utilization of this work in any form or by any electronic, mechanical, or other means, now known or hereafter invented, including xerography, photocopying, and recording, and in any information storage and retrieval system, is forbidden without the written permission of the publisher.

The web addresses cited in this text were current as of August 2019, unless otherwise noted.

Acquisitions Editor: Diana Vincer
Project Writers: Thomas Hanlon and Myles Schrag
Managing Editor: Anna Lan Seaman
Copyeditor: Kevin Campbell
Permissions Managers: Martha Gullo and Dalene Reeder
Senior Graphic Designer: Joe Buck
Graphic Designer: Whitney Milburn
Cover Designer: Keri Evans
Cover Design Associate: Susan Rothermel Allen
Photograph (cover): Dmytro Aksonov/E+/Getty Images
Photographs (interior): © Human Kinetics, unless otherwise noted
Photo Asset Manager: Laura Fitch
Photo Production Manager: Jason Allen
Senior Art Manager: Kelly Hendren
Illustrations: © Human Kinetics, unless otherwise noted
Printer: Data Reproductions Corporation

Printed in the United States of America   10 9 8 7 6 5 4 3 2 1

The paper in this book is certified under a sustainable forestry program.

Human Kinetics
P.O. Box 5076
Champaign, IL 61825-5076
Website: www.HumanKinetics.com

In the United States, email info@hkusa.com or call 800-747-4457.
In Canada, email info@hkcanada.com.
In the United Kingdom/Europe, email hk@hkeurope.com.

For information about Human Kinetics' coverage in other areas of the world, please visit our website: **www.HumanKinetics.com**

E7317

Fourth Edition

The
SPORTS
RULES
Book

Contents

Contributors

Adventure Racing
Craig Bycroft
Adventure Racing World Series

Alpine Skiing
Chip Knight and Paul Van Slyke
US Ski and Snowboard Association

Archery
Guy Kruger
USA Archery

Australian Football
Steve Teakle
Australian Football League

Badminton
Martin Andrew
Badminton World Federation

Basketball
Ryan Goodson

Bowling
Terry Bigham
United States Bowling Congress

Canoeing and Kayaking
Morgan House
American Canoe Association

Cheerleading
Billie Ann Caya
National Federation Rules Interpreter

Climbing (Sport)
Alex Fritz
USA Climbing National Team Coach

Cornhole
Frank Geers American
Cornhole Organization

Cricket
Jonny Singer
Marylebone Cricket Club

Cross Country
John Lofranco, Serge Thibaudeau
Athletics Canada

Cycling
Shawn Farrell
Bicycle Racing Association of Colorado

Equestrian
Sarah Gilbert
United States Equestrian Federation

Field Hockey
Steve Horgan
USA Field Hockey

Figure Skating
Mimi McKinnis
U.S. Figure Skating

Golf
Joe Foley
US. Golf Association

Handball
Vern Roberts
United States Handball Association

Ice Hockey
Matt Leaf
USA Hockey

Ju-Jitsu
Patrick Hickey
Director, USA Sport Ju-Jitsu Alliance

Karate
Patrick Hickey
President, USA Karate Federation

Kung Fu
Patrick Hickey
Director, International Kwanmukan

Lacrosse
Brian Logue
U.S. Lacrosse

Netball
Lainie Houston
Netball Australia

Pickleball
Justin Maloof
USA Pickleball Association

Racquetball
Otto E. Dietrich
USA Racquetball

Rowing
Dr. Volker Nolte
Western University

Rugby Union
Nathan Abdelnour
Rugby Canada

Shooting
Launi Meili
NCAA Rifle Coach and Olympic Gold Medalist

Skateboarding
Don Bostick
USA Skateboarding

Snowboarding
Mike Mallon
USA Snowboard and Freeski Association

Soccer
Erika True
Say Soccer

Softball
Kurt Gibson
Illinois High School Association

Speed Skating
Guy Thibault
U.S. Speedskating

Squash
Harry Smith
US Squash

Swimming and Diving
Ben Balkwill

Synchronized Swimming
Shari Darst
USA Synchro

Table Tennis
Jörg Bitzigeio
USA Table Tennis

Taekwondo
May Spence
USA Taekwondo

Team Handball
Christian Latulippe
Women's National Team Head Coach, USA
Team Handball

Tennis
Karl Davies
Unites States Tennis Association

Track and Field (Athletics)
John Lofranco, Serge Thibaudeau, Les Gramantik,
Richard Parkinson
Athletics Canada
Alfredo Villar-Sbaffi
St. Laurent Select
James Holden
Ottawa Lions

Triathlon
Deb Wilson
USA Triathlon

Ultimate
Josh Murphy
USA Ultimate

Volleyball
Paul Albright
USA Volleyball

Water Polo
Levon Dermendjian
USA Water Polo

Water Skiing
Scott N. Atkinson
USA Water Ski and Wake Sports

Weightlifting
Suzy Sanchez
USA Weightlifting

Wrestling
Mike Clayton
USA Wrestling

Introduction

Whether you binge-watch the Olympics, take part in organized activities at your local fitness center, or make up your own games with your kids on a camping trip, you surely have marveled at the seemingly infinite number of sports and physical activities, new and old, that continue to evolve. It can be intimidating to try new sports, but *The Sports Rules Book, Fourth Edition,* gives you a one-stop reference source for sports that are familiar as well as those that have been a mystery to you. *The Sports Rules Book, Fourth Edition,* is designed for sport administrators, coaches, physical education teachers, players, and fans who want to know a sport's basic rules and procedures, penalties, scoring system, playing area dimensions, and officials' signals—providing a concise yet clear overview of how a sport is played.

The reader-friendly format helps you understand the fundamental rules without getting bogged down in every minute detail. Inside you'll find overviews and rule descriptions of 64 sports popular in the United States and around the world. In addition to the 54 sports from the third edition, we have added 10 new chapters in the fourth. The additions are an acknowledgment that sports participation is as popular as ever and even more varied. The newcomers include sports that will debut at the 2020 Tokyo Olympics (surfing and speed climbing); casual backyard games (cornhole, bocce, croquet, and horseshoes); sports that have been gradually gaining in popularity for some time in recreation settings (pickleball), in the water (stand up paddle board racing), and in the remote outdoors (adventure racing); and yet another martial art (kung fu), the fifth in our collection.

You'll find historical descriptions of how each of the 64 sports was started and interesting statistics about the popularity of the sport worldwide. For accuracy, each sport's terminology and the field dimensions (metric versus English measurements) specific to the sport are maintained. You will also find a conversion chart to help you convert between metric and English measurements.

Here's what you'll find in most chapters of *The Sports Rules Book, Fourth Edition:*

- A brief introduction that touches on the sport's origin and provides an overview of the sport's main features, such as number of players, length of game, scoring, and how the game is played (When noteworthy, recent data regarding the participation in or popularity of a sport is included in the introduction.)
- A diagram and description of the playing area, when appropriate
- Useful terms that will help you understand the sport
- Descriptions of the sport's equipment
- Rules that pertain to the players and to the various aspects of the sport (e.g., pitching, batting, and base running in baseball)
- Information on the sport's officials, occasionally including drawings of their signals
- For a handful of the sports, rule modifications to help teachers and sport administrators adapt the sport to make it more appropriate for younger and less-skilled players
- Organizations to contact for more in-depth rules

You can find comprehensive officiating rules and information for most sports by writing to the National Association of Sports Officials, 2017 Lathrop Avenue, Racine, Wisconsin 53405, or by calling the association at 262-632-5448.

The Sports Rules Book, Fourth Edition, is not meant to be complete in its coverage of any sport. Most of the sports are now being played by such varied skill levels, age groups, and gender groups that such an effort would be impossible. Rather, this resource is meant to provide the basic rules and procedures of the sport and to be practical, understandable, and concise without sacrificing the essentials. You can consult it for basic questions that come up with sports you know well to make sure that you are not missing an essential rule or aspect of play. Or you can use it when you embark on a sport you are less familiar with so you can confidently articulate the basics to your class or clients for maximum enjoyment. *The Sports Rules Book, Fourth Edition,* provides you with the information necessary to teach and play everything from alpine skiing to handball to wrestling. Whether you are indoors or outdoors, on land, in the water, on ice, or on top of a mountain, this book will guide you through fundamental instruction of the basics.

Measurement Conversions

	English to metric			Metric to English
Feet	0.3048006 m/ft		Meters	3.280833 ft/m
Feet	30.48006 cm/ft		Centimeters	0.032808 ft/cm
Inches	2.540005 cm/in.		Centimeters	0.39370 in./cm
Inches	25.4000 mm/in.		Millimeters	0.0394 in./mm
Miles	1.60935 km/mi		Kilometers	0.62137 mi/km
Ounces	28.349527 g/oz		Grams	0.0352740 oz/g
Pounds	453.5924 g/lb		Grams	0.00220462 lb/g
Pounds	0.453592 kg/lb		Kilograms	2.2046223 lb/kg
Yards	0.91440183 m/yd		Meters	1.093611 yd/m

Data from C. Hodgman, S. Selby, and R. Weast (eds.), *CRC Standard Mathematical Tables,* 12th ed. (Cleveland, OH: Chemical Rubber Company [presently CRC Press, 1961).

To convert: Start with the measurement you are dealing with. Multiply by the appropriate conversion factor using all the decimal places. If there is more than one choice of conversion factor, use the one that is closest in comparison (i.e., pounds and kilograms rather than pounds and grams, or feet and meters rather than feet and centimeters). In general, round the answer to the same number of places after the decimal as you had in the original number. For example, to convert 99 pounds to kilograms, look under "pounds" in the English-to-metric column where it specifies the conversion in "kg/ lb." Multiply 99 lb by 0.453592 kg/lb, and the result is 44.905608 kg. Since you started with a whole number, you may also want to round the result to a whole number: 45 kg.

Common conversions

10 meters = 32.8 feet

100 meters = 328 feet

500 meters = 1,640 feet

10 feet = 304.8 centimeters

100 feet = 30.5 meters

10 inches = 25.4 centimeters

10 centimeters = 4 inches

20 millimeters = 0.79 inches

50 millimeters = 2 inches

10 inches = 254 millimeters

10 kilometers = 6.2 miles

5 kilometers = 3.1 miles

5 miles = 8 kilometers

5 ounces = 142 grams

100 grams = 3.5 ounces

5 kilograms = 11 pounds

500 grams = 1.1 pounds

100 pounds = 45.4 kilograms

20 yards = 18.3 meters

10 yards = 9.1 meters

Adventure Racing

AleSocci/Getty Images

Adventure racing incorporates many endurance sports and skills. Events in adventure racing are as varied as the terrain that forms the backdrop for these incredible exhibitions of strength, skill, and determination. Teams of contestants might prove their prowess mountain biking, display their ability to excel under duress while rock climbing, or even saddle up and ride to victory on horses.

Each event includes several different "legs" to form one inspiring, challenging journey. Teams succeed or fail based not only on athleticism but also due to their bonds, ability to cooperate, and stress-management techniques. It is a cliché in sports to say that no two events are alike, but in the case of adventure racing, the statement rings true. Each race pushes the contestants to overcome challenges they've never experienced before on courses that are not very comparable to one another because of the uniqueness of each event in terms of activities, ground rules, and race director's discretion. In the United States, participation in adventure racing has grown steadily over the past decade, reaching about three million in 2016. The hit reality-TV show *The Amazing Race*, produced by Mark Burnett, used some elements of the sport, and it is credited with boosting adventure racing's popularity.

Also known as expedition racing, adventure racing has a long and colorful history. Endurance races have been around for decades. In the 1980s, the Alpine Ironman, the Coast to Coast Race, the Raid Gauloises, and the Alaskan Wilderness Classic all served as foreshadowing for modern adventure racing.

Today, there are many expedition racing competitions around the world. Because they vary a great deal from one another in terms of qualification, events, length, and other details, we'll be focusing on the Adventure Racing World Series (ARWS) for the remainder of this entry. The ARWS is representative both of adventure racing in general and the scope of events it can encompass. Athletes around the world compete in their home countries and across the globe in demonstration races as well as premier qualifying races. Qualifying race winners then go on to compete in the annual Adventure Racing World Championship.

OVERVIEW

Objective: Get all team members through the specified course together, following directions in the provided course book and maps and going through all designated race checkpoints (CPs) and transition areas (TAs). Any accumulated time penalties must be taken into consideration before the winning team is determined.

Length of Events: Range from a few hours to several days. ARWS races may occur yearly, every other year, and some every 18 months. They range from 400 to 600 kilometers (249 to 373 miles) in length, and they may take three to eight days to complete. Of course, as each new course is designed, these distances and times themselves change. Part of the excitement and anticipation for each racer is discovering the new terrain, challenges, and opportunities for growth that each race provides.

Teams: Mixed-gender teams of two to five people, depending on the event. In ARWS, teams of four compete.

COURSES

Each course is unique, and courses vary from year to year. Each new course is kept secret until the start of the qualifier race. Here's a sampling of the qualifying races for ARWS.

Raid in France

With a route that is only discovered as the race progresses, Raid in France is one of the most unique expeditions. Dependent on maps (no GPS), teams have five days to cover 500 kilometers (311 miles) by rafting, hiking, kayaking, mountain biking, climbing, horseback riding, and more.

Expedition Africa

Expedition Africa is another 500-kilometer course, which allows teams to experience the unique, often harsh, and remote beauty of the African continent. Mountain biking, kayaking, and trekking take center stage in this one-of-a-kind three- to six-day adventure.

XPD

Australia's XPD bills itself as "as much an expedition as a race" and with good reason. This 550-kilometer course runs every 18 months, with each iteration being unique and located in a new, remote region of Australia. Trekking, biking, and kayaking through the formidable terrain (and encountering its equally formidable wildlife) is a challenge many racers look forward to.

Itera

The Emerald Isle is proud to host Itera, a 600-kilometer course every other year. This race focuses on speed rather than formidable challenges, which makes it an excellent first race for new and inexperienced teams. Easy accessibility from much of Europe also makes this race a regional favorite.

Expedicion Guarani

Rappelling down sheer cliffs amid cascading waterfalls, bearing witness to the last remnants of the Americas' original Atlantic forests, and exploring the steep peaks of Paraguay is a once-in-a-lifetime opportunity for many racers. This 600-kilometer course is challenging even for the most determined athletes.

Raid Gallaecia

Spain hosts Raid Gallaecia biennially, inviting competitors to enjoy the paradisiacal region surrounding Galicia. This special race is designed with balance in mind—the balance between people and nature, the balance between the physical and the technical—in order to create a special race for veterans and first-timers alike.

Cameco Cowboy Tough

Alaska isn't the only state in the United States to lay claim to hosting a qualifying race. Wyoming's wide open spaces were once the wandering grounds for America's cowboys, who were often adventurers themselves. Today, modern adventurers relish the opportunity to take part in a 500-kilometer journey through the state's famous mountains and remote high deserts.

Maya Mountain Adventure Challenge

Belize's blue waters, rugged mountains, deep canyons, and mysterious cave systems provide adventurers with a stunning backdrop for competition. This 400-kilometer race allows teams to explore one of the last and largest rainforests on the planet.

Huairasinchi

Ecuador hosts a race that takes participants across the equator and brings them into contact with a vast sampling of biological and cultural diversity. Huairasinchi celebrates the indomitable human spirit as well as the beauty of the natural world.

WORLD CHAMPIONSHIP ENTRIES

Half of the entries in the World Championship are determined by qualifying race winners. In addition to qualifier race winners, there are other opportunities for teams to join in the World Championship event. Those with an AR World Ranking (calculated using participation and scores in events over the prior year) may join the race at a discounted price; these constitute one-quarter of the available entries. Finally, the remaining entries may be purchased by teams as part of the Wild Card Entry program on a first-come, first-serve basis.

The World Championship event is hosted in a new location each year.

EQUIPMENT

Because events are so varied, there is no single equipment list for ARWS events. However, there are discipline-specific lists, zone-specific all-discipline lists, and a list of items all racers must carry regardless of zone or discipline. Here is a sampling of the latter:

- Official race bib (must be visible at all times and worn over the outermost layer)
- Whistle (used to sound an alert; must be waterproof)
- Light source (may be discipline specific, such as a bike lamp or head lamp)

- Jacket (shell layer; must be water- and wind-proof and must feature a hood)
- Base layer top (long-sleeved, moisture-wicking or quick-dry fabric; may be carried or worn)
- Base layer legs (long, fitted, moisture-wicking or quick-dry fabric; may be carried or worn)
- Base layer hat (fitted, moisture-wicking or quick-dry fabric; may be carried or worn)
- Survival/space blanket (metallic blanket for emergency use)
- Compass (magnetic, balanced to the race zone)
- Video recording device (digital camera or similar device; shockproof, waterproof)
- Cell phone (fully charged, kept off in a waterproof container for emergencies)
- Fire-starting devices (flint and steel, matches, gas lighter)
- Knife (folding blade, sharp enough to cut twine and rope)
- Course map and information, as provided by organizers
- First aid kit (adhering to ARWS regulations)
- Strobe light (white, high intensity, 360-degree light)
- GPS/emergency communication device (not for use during the race except in emergency, provided by organizers)

RULES OF COMPETITION

For many participants, adventure racing exemplifies the adage that just finishing is a victory. Teams take part in prerace preparations together and must cross the finish line as a unit. Prior to the race, all teams must meet the registration requirements as specified by the organizers. This may include meetings, equipment checks, and competency checks to ensure safety. Teams and individuals must meet the equipment requirements as laid out by ARWS for the overall competition, the zone in which they will be competing, and the disciplines in which they will be competing. Organizers may also require race-specific equipment. Course information provided by organizers specifies checkpoints and transition areas, and teams must adhere to these to complete the race successfully.

Teams must stick together, with all members close enough to visually and verbally signal one another. In most situations, no more than 100 meters should separate the first and last team members. Exceptions include one team member staying with an injured teammate while other teammates go for help, teams within the transition areas, and teams participating in specialized activities, such as orienteering, that require greater separation distances in order to complete the task. Substitutions are not allowed, but whether a team is allowed to continue if a team member drops out is at the discretion of the race director and depends on many factors, including weather, timing, ongoing support and care of the departing team member, and the well-being of remaining team members. While no unauthorized assistance may be received during the race, adventure racing maintains an ethic of support and environmental sustainability. Athletes are expected to be respectful of the course, their teammates, and their rival athletes at all times without exception. Should a team or individual experience an emergency, all other athletes who encounter this team or individual must assist. This gets taken into consideration at the end, when finish times are being recorded. All athletes must treat the course and the surrounding environment with the utmost respect.

If a team completes the course but does not do so in the manner directed by organizers, the team may be subject to disqualification, DNF (did not finish) status, UR (unranked) status, or a time penalty.

TERMS

Checkpoints (CPs) are periodic spots on the course where teams must check in with race officials to confirm progress on the course. Unmanned CPs are often used, requiring teams to record proof that they checked in via orienteering punches, electronic timing chips, and other technological or rudimentary methods.

Penalties can be assessed against a team's overall time for failure to follow the ground rules outlined prior to the race or failure to observe the spirit of the race.

Transition areas (TAs) are used to move from the completion of one event in the race to the start of another, which often includes equipment preparation and clothing changes.

OFFICIALS

Race Referees, the Race Jury, and the Race Director are responsible for adjudication of the rules. Any dispute by a team must be submitted in writing and must be submitted more than three hours before the final awards ceremony. Race organizers may add specific rules for their own courses.

ORGANIZATIONS

AR World Series
Geocentric Pty Ltd.
P.O. Box 542
Buderim, QLD 4556
Australia
http://arworldseries.com

USARA Adventure Race National Championship
979-703-5018
www.usaranationals.com

Alpine Skiing

karaboux/fotolia.com

Accounts of Alpine ski competition date back to the 6th century. Skiing competition began on a broader scale in the early 1800s; the sport was introduced to the United States in the mid-1800s by Norwegian immigrants. Early skis were made of wood and were laminated. Today's skis offer many shapes and lengths to accommodate different styles of skiing, racing, and snow conditions. Today there are more than 54 million skier and snowboarder visits (one person buying one ticket a day) each year in the United States alone. Market size is estimated at 5.8 million U.S. participants in alpine skiing, with 2.2 million of those considered frequent (10-plus days a year) skiers, according to the National Sporting Goods Association. Alpine skiing is popular not only in the United States but also in Europe and in many other countries around the world. It consists of several disciplines, including downhill, slalom, giant slalom, super-giant slalom (super-G), super combined, team, and skier-cross competitions.

OVERVIEW

In downhill, giant slalom, and super-G competitions, skiers start at intervals of 30 seconds to 2 minutes, depending on the length of the course and the demands of television. Slalom competitors begin at irregular intervals at the starter's command. Competitors must pass across the gate line (between two poles or panels) with ski tips and both feet. If a competitor loses a ski without committing a fault, the tip of the remaining ski and both feet must pass the gate line. Competitors must cross the finish line on both skis, on one ski, or with both feet (in case of a fall at the line). The time stops once any part of the competitor's equipment or body stops the electric timing.

COURSE

Each discipline in alpine skiing has various course measurements and obstacles (see figure 2.1). Specifics for each one follow.

Downhill

The vertical drop for men ranges from 350 to 1,100 meters and for women from 350 to 800 meters. (Distances vary between U.S. Ski and Snowboard Association courses and international courses.)

Men's and women's courses are marked with red gates (blue may be used to mark a women's gate on a men's course). The gate width is at least 8 meters. Courses through wooded terrain must be at least 30 meters wide. Competitors are required to take part in official training on the course, which takes place on three separate days before the event. A downhill event may consist of one run or two runs. If the event has two runs, those runs take place on the same day.

Slalom

The vertical drop for men's courses ranges from 140 to 220 meters and for women's courses from 120 to 200 meters. The gates alternate in color. Each gate must be between 4 and 6 meters wide. Successive open gates must have at least 7 meters and no more than 13 meters between them. Vertical gates must have 0.75 to 1.00 meter between them.

At major competitions, the course has a gradient of 33 to 45 percent. It may reach 52 percent in brief portions of the course. The course includes a series of turns that the competitors should be able to complete rapidly. The course must be at least 40 meters wide if two runs are set up on the same slope. It must contain both horizontal (open) and vertical (closed) gates as well as one to three vertical combinations consisting of three or four gates and at least three hairpin combinations.

The slalom start takes place at irregular intervals; on the starter's command to go, the competitor must begin within 10 seconds. Competitors take two runs on two different courses; usually both runs are taken on the same day.

Giant Slalom

The vertical drop for men's courses is 250 to 450 meters and for women's courses 250 to 400 meters. A giant slalom gate consists of four slalom poles and two panels (flags). Gates are alternately red and blue and are between 4 and 8 meters wide. Successive gates must be greater than 10 meters apart. The course normally should be at least 40 meters wide and should present a variety of turns. A giant slalom competition consists of two runs. The runs may be held on the same trail, but the gates must be changed for the second run. Both runs are usually held on the same day.

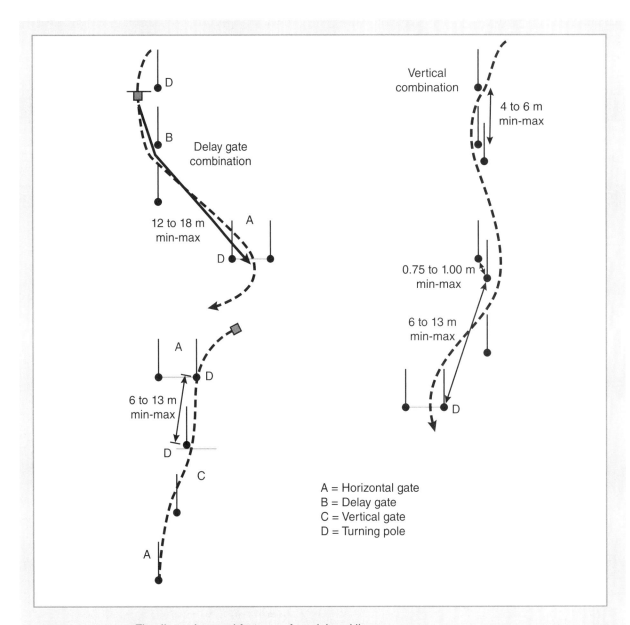

▶ **Figure 2.1** The dimensions and features of an alpine skiing course.

Reprinted by permission from International Ski Federation (FIS), *The International Ski Competition Rules* (Oberhofen/Thunersee, Switzerland: FIS, 2018), 79.

Super-G

The vertical drop for men's courses is 350 to 650 meters and for women's courses 350 to 600 meters. A gate consists of four slalom poles and two panels; gates are alternately red and blue. They must be between 6 and 8 meters wide from inner pole to inner pole for horizontal (open) gates and between 8 and 12 meters wide for vertical (closed) gates.

The required direction changes for Olympic competitions are 6 percent of the vertical drop and FIS competitions are 7 percent. The distance between the turning poles of two successive gates must be at least 25 meters. A super-G course is undulating and hilly with a minimum width of 30 meters. The competition consists of one run for each competitor.

Parallel Events

A parallel event is a competition where two or more competitors race simultaneously side by side down two or more courses that are as identical as possible. Competitions typically consist of 32 competitors, paired off as follows: 1st and 32nd; 2nd and 31st; and so on. (These placings are based on previous races.)

Each match consists of two runs; the two competitors exchange courses on the second run. The competitor with the lower total time on the two runs advances; the other is eliminated. The second round also consists of two runs. Eight skiers from this round advance to the quarterfinals; four advance to the semifinals; and two advance to the final.

The vertical drop is between 80 and 100 meters. Each course has between 20 and 30 gates; the run-time of each race should be between 20 and 25 seconds. The first gate is between 8 and 10 meters from the start. The difference between the competitors' times—not each competitor's total time—is recorded at the finish. The difference is recorded in hundredths of a second.

EQUIPMENT

Gate poles are either rigid or flex-poles. Rigid poles have a diameter of 20 to 32 millimeters and have no joints. They are made of a nonsplintering material, such as plastic, and when set they must project at least 1.8 meters out of the snow. Flex-poles have a spring-loaded hinge; they must be used for all competitions except downhills.

A turning pole is the pole that is closest to the skier's line of travel in the gate. Turning poles for slalom, giant slalom, and super-G must be flex-poles. Slalom poles are red or blue. In giant slalom and super-G competitions, two slalom poles with a panel between them make up one-half of the gate; a like pair of slalom poles makes up the other half of the gate.

TERMS

A **blocking pole plant** is a forceful placement of the ski pole's tip in the snow to help the athlete change edges on steep terrain (usually found only in slalom).

The **edge angle** is the degree of angle between a ski's edge and the snow; a greater angle creates greater resistance to the pull of gravity.

An **edge set** is the equal edging of both the inside (uphill) and outside (downhill) skis to momentarily or permanently stop one's progress.

Edging is the combination of edge angle; ankle, knee, and hip angulation; pressure and weight distribution; and steering that influences the degree of skidding (slow) or carving (fast) of the skis while turning.

A **flat ski** is one that is not edged.

The **gate line** is the imaginary shortest line an athlete can take between the gate poles. In slalom, the gate passage is correct when both ski tips and feet pass the inside gate markers in the direction of the turn. A competitor who misses a gate is disqualified.

The **inside ski** is the one that's inside the arc of the turn (often referred to as the uphill ski).

The **outside ski** is the downhill ski, performing most of the turn and carrying most of the pressure in the arc of the turn.

A **pole swing** is the preparatory movement of the ski pole forward that precedes a pole plant or a pole touch; it's often used as a timing device for turning in rhythm.

A **sideslip** occurs when the skis slide sideways, under control, down the fall line.

A **sidestep** occurs when a skier lifts one ski and moves it sideways away from the other ski, then moves the other ski next to the first ski to re-form the original parallel position.

OFFICIALS

The technical delegate, along with the competition jury, oversees the event and the officials. The chief of race is responsible for the overall race, organizing committee, and course workers. The chief of course is responsible for course preparation. The chief of timing and calculations coordinates the start and finish officials. The chief gate judge supervises the gate judges. The chief steward is in charge of safety precautions and keeping spectators off the course. A jury oversees adherence to race rules.

MODIFICATIONS

Children ages 12 to 15 may take part in an alpine competition. The maximum vertical drop is 450 meters for both boys and girls. For the maximum vertical drops and numbers of gates for children's races, see table 2.1.

TABLE 2.1

Children's Drops and Gates

Classification	Event	Vertical drop (max. meters)	Configuration of gates
U-14	Slalom	160	Maximum 4 hairpin combinations and maximum 2 vertical combination consisting of maximum 3 gates.
			Distance between turning poles of successive gates must be between 7 and 11 meters. Maximum distance to delayed gates is 15 meters. The vertical drop must be between 100 and 600 meters.
U-16	Slalom	160	Maximum 6 hairpin combinations and maximum 3 vertical combinations consisting of 3 or 4 gates.
			Must contain minimum of 1 and maximum of 3 delayed turns. Distance between turning poles of successive gates must be between 7 and 11 meters. Maximum distance to delayed gates is 15 meters. The vertical drop must be between 100 and 600 meters.
U-14	Giant slalom	350	The vertical drop must be between 200 and 400 meters. Possibility for 2 runs must be granted. Distance between turning poles must not be more than 27 meters.
U-16	Giant slalom	350	The vertical drop must be between 200 and 400 meters. Must consist of 2 runs. Distance between turning poles must not be more than 27 meters.
U-14	Super-G	250-450	8 to 12% direction changes of vertical drop. All courses used for children's SG must be homologated.
U-16	Super-G	250-450	8 to 12% direction changes of vertical drop. All courses used for children's SG must be homologated.
6U-14U	Sl/GS Kombi	140-200	There should be a minimum of 30 turns and a minimum of 5 sections.
16U-14U	GS/SG Kombi	250	10 to 12% direction changes of vertical drop on a GS homologated course.

Data from International Ski Federation (FIS), *The International Ski Competition Rules* (Oberhofen/Thunersee, Switzerland: FIS, 2004), 22.

ORGANIZATIONS

International Ski Federation
Marc Hodler House
Blochstrasse 2
CH-3653 Oberhofen/Thunersee
Switzerland
+41 (0)33 244 6161
www.fis-ski.com

U.S. Ski and Snowboard Association
P.O. Box 100
1 Victory Ln.
Park City, UT 84060
435-649-9090
http://usskiandsnowboard.org

3

Archery

Archery began as a method of defense and as a way to hunt game. It evolved into a sport by the mandates of English kings as a competition among the men who defended the crown. By the 17th century, tournaments were commonplace. In the United States, the first archery club was formed in Philadelphia in 1826.

Archery made brief appearances in the Olympic Games in the early 1900s and was readmitted to the Games in 1972 after enough countries had adopted international rules. Since 1972, technology has greatly advanced the equipment. Archery has become wedded to skiing in the sport of ski-archery and to running in run-archery.

OVERVIEW

Objective: To score the highest number of points by shooting arrows into a target marked with rings worth various points.

Scoring: Determined by where the shaft lands in the target; rings are valued from 1 to 10 points.

Number of Players: Individuals or teams of three.

Number of Arrows per Archer: 72 or 144.

Length of Range: From 15 to 90 meters, depending on the category.

Length of Contest: An agreed-on number of rounds, or ends (see "Terms").

For an end consisting of three arrows, an archer has 2 minutes to complete shooting. For an end of six, a maximum of 4 minutes is allowed. In case of equipment adjustment, such as changing a bowstring, additional time may be granted. Archers shoot in rotation and can shoot either from the longest to the shortest target or vice versa. Scores are entered for each arrow; the score is called out by the archer and checked by competitors.

RANGE

The shooting range is divided into lanes and is laid out so that shooting is usually done from south to north. Each lane has lines at right angles between the shooting line and the target; a lane can contain up to three targets. Men and women are separated by a clear lane of at least 5 meters. A waiting line is set at least 5 meters behind the shooting line. No more than four competitors may shoot at one target. Each buttress is num-bered and set at an angle of about 15 degrees from vertical. The distance is measured from the ground directly below the gold of each target to the shooting line. The center of the gold is about 130 centimeters above ground.

ARCHERS

Archery is a sport for people of all ages. Men, women, and children compete. The longest distances that archers shoot vary by category:

- Men 18+: 90 and 70 meters
- Junior boys up to age 18: 70 meters
- Women 18+: 70 and 60 meters
- Junior girls up to age 18: 70 meters
- Cadet boys and girls up to age 16: 70 meters
- Cub boys and girls up to age 14: 50 meters
- Bowman boys and girls up to age 12: 30 meters

EQUIPMENT

The target is made of straw mat or other material and has a target face of canvas, paper, or cloth. The target face has five concentric colored zones arranged from the center outward as follows: gold, red, blue, black, and white. Each color is divided by a thin line into two zones of equal width, resulting in 10 scoring zones of equal width. Diameters for 122- and 80-centimeter target faces are shown in table 3.1.

The target face is supported on a buttress, which is at least 2 centimeters larger in diameter than the target face itself. Each buttress is numbered and set at an angle of about 15 degrees from vertical. The distance is measured from the ground directly below the gold of each target to the shooting line. Any portion of the buttress that can damage an arrow is covered.

A bow consists of a handle (grip), riser, and two flexible limbs ending in a tip with a string nock. A single bowstring is used; an adjustable arrowrest is also allowed. No crossbows are allowed. A bowsight or bowmark is permitted, but only one or the other may be used at one time. A bowsight may not incorporate any magnifying lens or electronic devices to aid in sighting.

Arrows of any type may be used as long as they do not cause undue damage to the target faces or

TABLE 3.1

Diameters for Target Faces

Target zone	122 cm face (cm)	80 cm face (cm)
Inner 10	6.1	4
10	12.2	8
9	24.4	16
8	36.6	24
7	48.8	32
6	61.0	40
5	73.2	48
4	85.4	56
3	97.6	64
2	109.8	72
1	122.0	80

Data from International Archery Federation (FITA), 2008, *FITA Constitution and Rules: Book 2: Outdoor Target Archery Rules.* Available: http://www.archery. org/UserFiles/Document/FITA%20website/05%20Rules/01%20C&R%20 Book/2008RulesENG_Book2.pdf.

buttresses. An arrow consists of a shaft with a tip (point), nocks, fletching, and, if desired, cresting. Finger protectors, such as gloves, tape, tabs, or a combination of the three are permitted, but they cannot include any device that helps the athlete to hold, draw, or release the bowstring. Field glasses may be used to spot the arrows.

RULES

Following are the basic rules that pertain to shooting and scoring.

Shooting

Shooting takes place in one direction only. Archers shoot from a standing position, without support, either with their feet straddling the shooting line (one foot in front of the line, one foot behind it) or with both feet on the line.

When a signal is given to begin, archers may raise their bows and shoot. If they shoot either before the signal to start or after the signal to stop, they forfeit their highest-scoring arrow for that particular end. (In team competition, the highest-scoring arrow for any member of the team—regardless of who committed the foul—is forfeited.)

A spent arrow is not counted as a shot if any part of the arrow lies within 3 meters of the shooting line or if the target face or buttress blows over. The judges may compensate for lost time in such cases.

Shooters can receive advice or instruction while they are on the shooting line, provided this does not disturb other archers.

For safety, participants are not allowed to use a high draw (also known as sky draw), in which the judges rule, based on the position of the bow arm and the direction of the arrow at the moment the string is pulled back, that the arrow could fly beyond a safety zone if accidentally released. A judge who identifies an archer with a high draw should observe the archer several times, consult with other judges, then discuss it with the chair of judges. The judge will speak to the coach, parent, or the archer, then ask the archer to adjust the draw process. If it is not corrected, the archer may be disqualified.

Scoring

Scores are checked by competitors and, if assigned, by scorers. The score is determined by where the shaft lands in the target (see figure 3.1). No arrows are touched until the archers complete the end and all arrows for that end are scored. Scoring takes place after every end. Here are rules that cover specific occurrences:

◾ Shaft touching line: If the shaft of the arrow is touching two colors or a dividing line between two scoring zones, the higher value is awarded.

◾ Bouncing off target: Unless all arrow holes are marked when scored, subsequent arrows bouncing off or passing through the target will not be scored. If an arrow does pass through the target or bounce off another arrow, however, and its mark can be identified, it scores however many points it would have had if it had stuck in the target.

◾ Landing in another arrow: An arrow that lands in another arrow receives the same points as the first arrow.

◾ Deflecting off another arrow: An arrow that deflects off another arrow and lands in the target receives the points awarded for that portion of the target face. An arrow that rebounds off another arrow scores the point value of the arrow it struck as long as the damaged arrow can be identified.

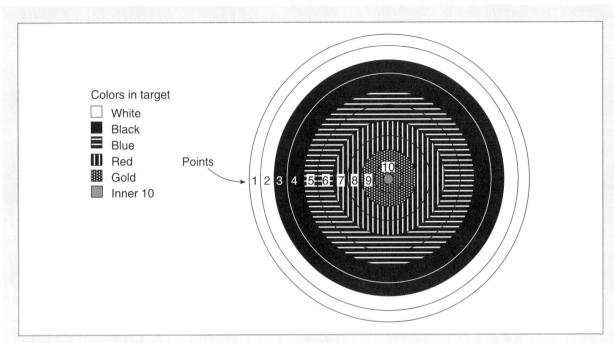

▶ **Figure 3.1** The score in archery is determined by where the shaft lands in the target. Target point values are shown on the target.

■ Hitting another target: An arrow hitting another target scores as a miss.

TERMS

An **end** is a series of either three or six arrows for each archer.

A **gold** is an arrow that lands in the center of the target. The outer portion of the gold is worth 9 points, the inner portion 10.

A **round** is a series of ends—the total number of arrows that each archer shoots in the competition.

OFFICIALS

Officials include a competition director, a director of shooting, and judges.

MODIFICATIONS

Archery can be modified in a number of ways. The following are among the most common.

Field Archery

In field archery, the archer takes on the terrain as well as the target. A course is set up with 24 targets that are marked with the distance to the shooting line. The distances to another 24 targets are unmarked. Three arrows are shot on each target for a total of 144. The targets are placed with such difficulty that the shots do not resemble target archery. Many of the shots are made uphill or downhill and require consideration for obstacles. Field events are held for the recurve (Olympic) bow, compound bow, and barebow divisions.

Flight Archery

The objective of flight archery is shooting for distance. Unlike target or field archery, there is no target. Accuracy is also involved in shooting at a right angle to the shooting line. This is more difficult than it appears, and a distance penalty is incurred if the shot is off this line.

Two types of arrows are used: regular flight and, in the United States only, broadhead flight (arrows with cutting heads, suitable for hunting). These arrows can be combined with many types of bows: standard recurve and compound bows, crossbows, flight bows that have an extended handle and an overdraw, primitive bows, and footbows, though no broadhead footbows are allowed.

In a flight tournament, each archer shoots four ends of six arrows. Each end can be in a different class or division. A different bow can be used for each class, or the archer can shoot the same bow for all four classes.

Clout Archery

Clout archery is a rarely practiced discipline that most archers take part in only for fun. Basically, it is a test of trajectory skill. The target, which is 15 meters in diameter, consists of five concentric circular scoring zones that are outlined on the ground. The innermost circle is worth 5 points, and scores decrease to 1 point for the outermost circle. Each senior recurve archer shoots 36 arrows at the target at a range of 165 meters for men, 125 meters for women; male compound shooters shoot 185 meters, females shoot 165 meters. Junior boys under age 18 shoot at a range of 125 meters, girls at a range of 110 meters; compound shooters in youth rounds shoot 165 meters and 125 meters, respectively.

Crossbow Archery

Crossbow events are held in target (indoor and outdoor) and clout. Outdoor target events are shot at a 60-centimeter, 10-ring multicolored target face. Indoor rounds are shot at a 40-centimeter, 10-ring target face.

Ski-Archery (Ski-Arc)

Recognized in 1991, ski-archery is a relatively new discipline that combines archery with cross-country skiing. It is performed much like the Olympic biathlon, which features rifle shooting instead of archery. Archers carry their bows in a backpack while skiing. The course is 12.5 kilometers long for men and 10 for women. One end of four arrows is shot every 4 kilometers, and, in one of those ends, the archer shoots from a kneeling position. Targets are 16 centimeters in diameter and are positioned 18 meters from the shooter. Each shot is either a hit or a miss. For every target missed, the archer must ski a 150-meter penalty loop before leaving the target site. The first athlete to complete the course is the winner.

Run-Archery

A summer run-archery event is a combination of target archery shooting and cross country running. The athlete is required to run a course and stop at prescribed points to shoot at fixed targets. The typical course is between 5 and 12 kilometers. Athletes make three shooting stops, shooting four arrows at each. The typical event consists of a 1-mile run followed by four arrows shot from a standing position, then another 1-mile run followed by four arrows shot from the kneeling position, and then another 1-mile run followed by four arrows shot from the standing position.

Bows are carried by the competitors. Targets are 16 centimeters in diameter and are positioned 18 meters from the shooter.

3-D Archery

Targets in 3-D events are life-size replicas of a variety of wildlife. These events combine the skills of determining distance to the target, determining what part of the target to hit, and shooting. Most archers who compete in these events use a compound bow. Archers competing in the typical 3-D tournament walk a course and shoot two arrows per animal target in qualifying rounds and one arrow per animal target in elimination rounds.

ORGANIZATIONS

Archery Shooters Association
P.O. Box 399
Kennesaw, GA 30156
770-795-0232
info@asaarchery.com
www.asaarchery.com

World Archery Federation
Maison du Sport International
Avenue de Rhodanie 54
1007 Lausanne
Switzerland
+41 21 614 3050
info@archery.org
www.archery.org

International Bowhunting Organization
P.O. Box 398
Vermilion, OH 44089
440-967-2137
ibo@ibo.net
www.ibo.net

USA Archery
4065 Sinton Rd., Ste. 110
Colorado Springs, CO 80907
719-866-4576
info@usarchery.org
www.usarchery.org

National Field Archery Association
800 Archery Ln.
Yankton, SD 57078
605-260-9279
info@nfaausa.com
www.nfaausa.com

4

Australian Football

Michael Willson/AFL Media/Getty Images Sport

Australian football was originally developed as a game unique to Australia, incorporating elements of rugby with some aspects of Gaelic (Irish) football. The game was initially devised as an off-season training regimen for Australian cricketers. Indigenous Australians played a game called marn grook, which was a kick and catch game with a ball made of possum hide, which is speculated that it also influenced the development of Australian football. It quickly evolved into a fast, rough, and free-flowing sport. The first official match was played in 1858 in Melbourne. Today, Australian football is played by more than 1.5 million players at the senior, junior, amateur, and school levels, including more than 463,364 women. It was a demonstration sport at the Melbourne Olympic Games in 1956.

OVERVIEW

Objective: To score the most points.

Scoring: Goals are worth 6 points; behinds are worth 1 point (see "Scoring").

Number of Players: 18 on each team, plus 4 interchange players each.

Length of Game: Four 20-minute quarters of actual playing time; there are no timeouts. If a game is tied at the end of regulation, it is a draw; there is no overtime.

Play begins with the field umpire bouncing the ball in the center circle; one nominated player from each team contests the ball. The two players contesting the center bounce must be in their team's defensive half of the circle and have both feet within the 10-meter circle. Until the ball has bounced, no other player may enter the center circle, and only four players from each team are allowed in the center square.

Except for when a behind is scored or a ball goes out of bounds, possession of the ball is continually contested. Players advance the ball by kicking it, handballing it, and running with it; throwing it is not allowed. Any player who runs with the ball must dribble it (bounce it or touch it to the ground) every 15 meters. Catching a kicked ball in the air after it has traveled at least 15 meters allows a player to take

a free kick without the risk of being tackled (this is called a mark).

Players are freely interchangeable at any time. A runner conveys messages from the coach to the players in the game. This message bearer must stay away from the ball but can stay on the field as long as necessary.

FIELD

The field is oval shaped, usually between 110 and 135 meters wide and between 135 and 185 meters long (see figure 4.1; the smaller dimensions are common in football played at the junior level). Boundaries are marked with white lines. The center square is at midfield, measuring 50 meters square. The center circle is in the middle of this square; it consists of two concentric circles measuring 3 meters and 10 meters in diameter and is bisected by a lateral line parallel to the goal line.

The goal square is 9 meters long and 6.4 meters wide. It is directly in front of the goal posts, which are set 6.4 meters apart on the boundary line and are at least 6 meters high. Two behind posts, each at least 3 meters high, are set 6.4 meters outside the goal posts. For the players' safety, the posts are padded 2.5 meters.

Many fields have two 50-meter lines drawn in semicircles 50 meters from the center of the goal line to give the umpire a point of reference

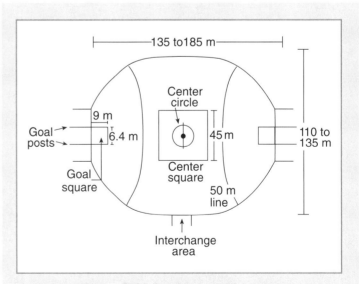

▶ **Figure 4.1** Field dimensions and features for Australian football.

for marking off 50-meter penalties and to give spectators a means of assessing the distance of kicks for goal.

PLAYERS

There are five general lines of play, with three players in each line. The remaining three players are the followers, who roam the whole ground, following the ball. These players are the ruck, rover, and ruck-rover. The rover and ruck-rover, along with center-line players, are part of a group in the modern game referred to as midfielders. The other two groups are forwards and defenders.

The lines of play are shown in figure 4.2. Note, however, that players are free to move anywhere on the ground. There is no offside rule in Australian football.

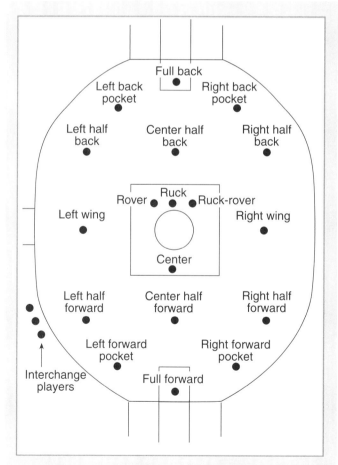

▶ **Figure 4.2** Lines of play for Australian football.

EQUIPMENT

The ball is generally made of leather—red for day games, yellow for night games. It has a symmetrical oval shape and is a standard size of 720 to 730 millimeters in circumference and 545 to 555 millimeters in transverse circumference. It is inflated to a pressure of 62 to 76 kPa.

Uniforms consist of numbered guernseys (jumpers), with or without sleeves; socks; and boots with "sprigs," or stops. No padding is worn, but mouth guards and soft protective headgear are allowed.

RULES

The basic rules of play include those for ball possession, restarting play, ball out of play, and free kicks.

Ball Possession

A player may hold the ball for an unlimited time if they are not held by an opponent. If the player with the ball is held between the shoulders and knees by an opponent, the player must immediately either kick the ball or handball it. The handball requires the player to hold the ball in one hand (must not move excessively) and punch the ball with the other. A player lying on the ball is considered to be in possession of it.

A player running with the ball must bounce the ball or touch it to the ground every 15 meters. When a player catches (marks) a kicked ball that has traveled at least 15 meters in the air without being touched by another player, they have the choice of playing on immediately, kicking, or handballing the ball from where it was received, without being impeded by any opponent.

Within 5 meters of the ball, a player may push an opponent in the chest or side or otherwise block the opponent's path to the ball.

Restarting Play

After a goal is scored, the field umpire restarts play by bouncing the ball (or tossing it up into the air) in the center circle, just as at the start of the game. Play is also restarted in these situations:

▪ When a team scores a behind, a player of the defending team kicks off from the goal (kickoff) square in front of the goal.

▪ When the ball bounces out of bounds, the umpire throws the ball over her head toward the center of the ground; if the ball is kicked out of bounds on the full (without first bouncing in the field of play or being touched), the opposing team receives a free kick from the place where the ball went out.

▪ When no player in a pack can gain clear possession, the umpire bounces the ball where the scrimmage has occurred and play has stopped.

Ball Out of Play

The ball is out of play and the clock is stopped in these situations:

▪ When a team scores a goal; the clock starts when the ball is bounced in the center circle to restart play.

▪ When a team scores a behind; the clock starts when the ball is kicked in by a defender.

▪ When the ball goes out of bounds; the clock starts when the umpire throws the ball back into play or when the team receiving a free kick returns it into play. Note: If any portion of the ball is on or over the boundary line in fair territory, it is still in play. A player can be out of bounds and in possession of the ball, but if the ball is not out of bounds, play is not stopped.

Free Kicks

An umpire may award a free kick against a player either with or without the ball. A player takes the kick (or handballs) where the infringement occurred, unless the player is fouled after disposing of the ball. Then the kick is taken where the ball landed. Infringements against a player with the ball may be called for

▪ not disposing of the ball within a reasonable time when correctly held (tackled) by an opponent,

▪ not disposing of the ball with a kick or a handball,

▪ kicking the ball out of bounds without it bouncing or being touched by another player,

▪ deliberately forcing or carrying the ball over the boundary line, or

▪ running farther than 15 meters without bouncing or touching the ball to the ground.

A free kick is also awarded when any player

▪ grabs or tackles an opponent above the shoulders or below the knees when the opponent has the ball;

▪ pushes an opponent in the back, charges an opponent, or trips or tries to trip an opponent;

▪ bumps or punches an opponent trying to catch a kick in the air;

▪ shepherds an opponent farther than 5 meters from the ball; or

▪ enters the center square before the ball is bounced to restart play.

An infringement is also called if a ball that is kicked back into play after a behind is scored goes out of bounds without any player touching it. In this case, the attacking team receives a free kick.

A 50-meter penalty is called against a player after a free kick if the player refuses to stand on the point indicated by the umpire, deliberately wastes time in returning the ball to the player who is to kick, holds the player who is to take the kick, runs over the mark before or as the ball is kicked, uses abusive or obscene language or behavior toward an umpire, or disputes an umpire's decision.

When a player has been infringed on, the umpire may choose not to award a free kick if the player or a teammate in possession of the ball has an advantageous position. In this case, the umpire immediately calls, "Play on," and play continues. If the player infringed on is injured, a teammate may take the free kick. This call is at the umpire's discretion.

Scoring

A ball kicked between the two larger goal posts is a goal worth 6 points if it does not touch a post or a player. A behind, worth 1 point, is scored when

- a ball passes between a goal post and a behind post;
- a ball hits a goal post, no matter whether it passes between the two larger posts or rebounds back onto the field; or
- a ball is carried over or knocked over the scoring line between the goal posts.

To score, the ball must completely cross the goal line.

TERMS

The **backmen** are the six defenders across the full-back and half-back lines on a team's defensive half of the field.

Ball up describes the moment when the umpire bounces the ball or tosses it up to restart the game after a stalemated scrimmage.

A **behind**, worth 1 point, is scored when the ball passes over the goal line after being touched or kicked by a defender, when it hits a goal post, or when it passes over the behind line without touching the behind post. A behind is sometimes called a *minor score*.

The **behind line** is the line drawn between a goal post and a behind post.

The **behind posts** are the two smaller posts 6.4 meters outside the goal posts.

The **boundary line** marks the boundary of the playing field. The ball must go completely over the line to be out of bounds.

A **bump** occurs when a player uses his hip and shoulder to knock an opponent out of position. A bump is legal if it occurs within 5 meters of the ball and is not in the back or above the opponent's shoulders.

A **center bounce**, made by the field umpire, occurs in the center circle at the beginning of each quarter and after each goal.

The **center circle** has an inner circle 3 meters in diameter and an outer circle 10 meters in diameter; it is where the umpire bounces the ball. No player, other than the players nominated to contest the bounce, can be in the center circle until the umpire has bounced the ball (or tossed it up if conditions are too wet to bounce it).

The **center square** is a 50-meter square in the center of the field. Only four players from each team can be in the center square for a center bounce.

A **drop punt** is the most common kick in Australian football. It travels end over end, spinning backward.

When a player **drops** the ball, a free kick is given to the tackler, provided the tackle is legally executed.

Followers are a team's ruck, ruck-rover, and rover.

A **foot pass** occurs when a player passes to a teammate by kicking.

A **free kick** is awarded for a variety of offenses (see "Free Kicks").

A **goal**, worth 6 points, is scored when the ball is kicked over the goal line by an attacking player without the ball touching any other player or a goal post.

The **goal line** is the line drawn between the goal posts.

The **goal mouth** is the area directly between the goal posts in front of the goal.

The two **goal posts** are 6.4 meters apart. A ball kicked between them scores 6 points.

The **goal square** is the rectangle measuring 6.4 meters by 9 meters in front of the goal posts from which the ball is kicked off after a behind is scored.

Handball is the method of striking the ball with a clenched fist while holding the ball stationary with the other hand. This is also known as a *hand pass*.

When a player **holds** the ball after being tackled, without disposing of it legally in a reasonable amount of time, a free kick is awarded against the player.

Interchange players are a team's substitutes. There are four interchange players.

A **mark** occurs when a player catches a kicked ball in the air if the ball has traveled at least 15 meters and has not been touched by another player.

The **oval** is the playing field, usually between 110 and 135 meters wide and between 135 and 185 meters long.

The **pockets** are the areas on the field close to the behind posts.

A **rocket handball** is a handball that spins end over end backward in flight (similar to a drop punt).

A **runner** is a person who carries messages from the coach to the players during the game.

Shepherding occurs when a player uses her body to block an opponent from the ball or from a teammate in possession of the ball. Shepherding farther than 5 meters from the ball is illegal.

A player **stands the mark** where an opponent has been given a free kick or marks (catches) the ball to ensure that the opponent does not play on and has to kick over the mark.

A player can **tackle** the player with the ball by grabbing the player above the knees and below the shoulders.

A **throw-in** occurs when the ball has gone out of bounds. The umpire throws the ball in over his head toward the center of the ground.

A **torpedo punt**, or *screw punt*, is a kick that spirals the ball through the air.

A **turnover** occurs when a team loses possession of the ball to the opposition.

OFFICIALS

Three field umpires control the game. Each controls about a third of the ground. Two boundary umpires judge when the ball is out of the playing area. Two goal umpires, one at each end of the oval, judge the scoring of goals and behinds and record the progressive scores.

MODIFICATIONS

The national AFL Women's (AFLW) competition has 16 players on the field and 4 interchange players on the bench.

The following modifications are made by many junior leagues to encourage younger players' development:

- The number of interchange players is unlimited.
- Players may bounce a ball only once before disposing of it.
- Players may not soccer the ball off the ground (kick it while it's on the ground).
- After scrimmages, the contest is restarted by throwing a ball up between two players of about equal size.
- Tackling is not permitted.
- The players who may score are limited, and scoring must take place within a certain zone.

Another modified version game is AFL 9's. This version is a less competitive game and is considered fun, social, and recreational in nature. The modifications for this version are significant and are as follows:

- The field is much smaller and is rectangular, rather than the typical oval field discussed above. It is split into three sections and three players must start in each section. The field measures 100 meters in length and 50 meters wide.
- Play begins with an official tossing the ball into the air at the center of the field. A ball up is also used to restart play.
- If a ball goes out of bounds the closest player from the opposite team kicks the ball back into play.
- A player may keep the ball for up to 30 meters, which must include one bounce during the time of procession.
- Turnovers occur when the ball hits the ground.
- Only forwards who are designated as scoring forwards are permitted to score, and they may only score if they are within the scoring zone. Players are not allowed to score from a turnover or an out of bounds play.
- Females competing in a mixed gender match are awarded 9 points for a goal.

ORGANIZATION

Australian Football League
140 Harbour Esplanade
Docklands
Melbourne, Victoria 3001
Australia
61 (03) 9643 1999
www.afl.com.au

5

Badminton

ENGINE OIL

Robertus Pudyanto/Getty Images

Aform of badminton, with players kicking an object similar to a feathered shuttlecock, was first played in the 5th century BC in China. The game derives its name from its introduction in England in 1873 at a country estate called Badminton. By this time players were using rackets, and the shuttlecock was put into play after each point by servants (this is where the term "to serve" comes from). Badminton was introduced in the United States in the 1870s, grew in popularity in the 1920s and 1930s, and became a full-medal Olympic sport in 1992. Today badminton is enjoyed worldwide; international competitions are typically dominated by China, Japan, Indonesia, Malaysia, and Korea as well as Denmark. In the United States, about 7.3 million people play badminton each year.

OVERVIEW

Objective: To score points by hitting a shuttlecock over the net and into the opponent's court so that the opponent cannot return it over the net and in bounds.

Scoring: 1 point for each successful hit that the opponent cannot return over the net and in bounds.

Number of Players: Either two players (singles) or four (doubles).

Game and Match Length: A match consists of the best of three games of 21 points.

Before a match, the winner of a coin or shuttle toss, or of a spin of the racket, chooses either the end of the court on which he will begin or whether he will serve or receive first.

COURT

The court is 17 feet (5.2 meters) by 44 feet (13.4 meters) for singles matches and 20 feet (6.1 meters) by 44 feet for doubles (see figure 5.1). The short service line is 6.5 feet from the net. The long service line for doubles is 12.75 feet behind the short service line. The long service line for singles is 2.4 feet behind the long service line for doubles. This is also the back boundary line. The

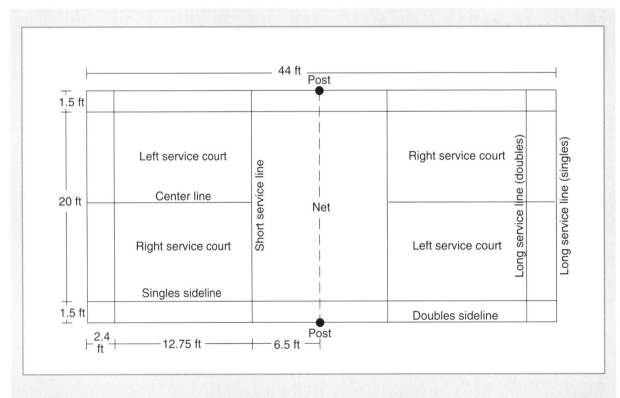

▶ **Figure 5.1** The dimensions and features of a badminton court.

singles sideline is 1.4 feet inside the sideline for doubles play.

The cord net stretches across the center of the court, 5.0 feet high at center court and 5.1 feet high at the extreme ends of the posts. (In doubles play, the extreme ends mean over the sidelines.) The net is 2.5 feet in depth. The net should stretch at least 6.1 meters, ensuring it is long enough to cover a doubles court. The top of the net should be lined with 75-millimeter white tape stretched and doubled over a cord, flush with the tops of the posts on either side of the court.

PLAYERS

A singles match consists of one player on each side; a doubles match is two teams of two players each. Players may not have play suspended to catch their breath or recover from an injury (unless the injury is sustained in the match requiring a medical time out). In international tournaments, coaching is allowed between points (not while a rally is in play) from an assigned chair behind the courts.

Additionally, coaching is allowed during the defined breaks when the coach is allowed onto the court:

▪ 60 seconds when the first player reaches 11 points in each game
▪ 120 seconds between the games

Other tournaments sanctioned by national governing bodies may have their own ruling on breaks and coaching.

EQUIPMENT

The shuttlecock either contains 16 feathers or is made of a synthetic mesh. It has a cork base covered by a thin layer of leather; the base is 1.00 to 1.13 inches in diameter. If feathers are used, they can be from 2.50 to 2.75 inches long (the same length must be used in any one shuttle). The shuttle weighs from 0.17 to 0.19 ounce. The racket frame may not be longer than 27.2 inches (68 cm) or wider than 9.2 inches (23 cm). The stringed portion may not be more than 11.2 inches long and 8.8 inches wide and must be interlaced strings that create a flat surface, which is uniform across the entire face of the racket.

RULES

Under the simplified rally-point scoring system, adopted by the International Badminton Federation (now known as the Badminton World Federation) and USA Badminton in 2006, here are the rules for the scoring system, intervals and end changes, points for singles play, points for doubles play, and faults and lets.

Scoring System

Games are to 21 points; the match goes to the side that wins the best of three games. The side that wins a rally adds a point to its score. If the score is 20-20, the side that gains a 2-point lead first wins the game. However, if the game is still tied at 29-29, the side that wins the next point wins the game. The side that wins a game serves first in the next game.

Intervals and End Changes

When the leading score reaches 11 points, players have a 60-second interval. In between games, players receive a 2-minute interval. In the third game, players change ends when a side scores 11 points.

Points: Singles

At the beginning of the game and when the score is even, the server serves from the right service court. When the score is odd, the server serves from the left service court.

If the server wins a rally, they score a point and serve again from the alternate service court.

If the receiver wins a rally, the receiver scores a point and becomes the new server and serves from the service court accordingly.

Points: Doubles

At the beginning of a game and when the score is even, the server serves from the right service court. When the score is odd, the server serves from the left service court.

If the serving side wins a rally, the serving side scores a point, and the same server serves again from the other service court. If the receiving side wins a rally, the receiving side scores a point and becomes the new serving side. The player on the receiving side who served last stays in the same service court where he served last until his team scores points when they serve. If when the team scores the new point value is odd, the left side of the service court serves. If the new point value is an even number, the person in the right service court must serve.

Faults and Lets

A server commits a fault and loses her serve if she misses the shuttle, if the shuttle becomes stuck in the net on the serve, or if she serves incorrectly. Faults also occur in play, when the shuttle hits outside the court; passes through or under the net; does not pass the net; or touches the roof, ceiling, or any sidewalls.

In addition, a fault occurs when the shuttle touches a player or player's clothing; touches any person or object out of bounds; is caught, held, and slung on the racket; or is hit twice in a row by the same player on the same play. A fault also occurs when both partners hit the shuttle before it is returned to the other side.

A player also commits a fault when the shuttle is in play and

- hits a shuttle when it is on the opponent's side of the net;
- touches the net or posts with their racket, clothing, or any part of their body;
- moves their racket or any part of their body over the net;
- the racket can go under the net as long as there is no contact with the net or the opposing player(s) (exception: a racket can cross the net, without touching it, on a follow-through, as long as the shuttle contact was on the hitter's side of the net); or
- obstructs an opponent's stroke (e.g., obstructing a follow-through as described in the previous situation).

A let is a situation that calls for a halt in play. A let occurs when a shuttle remains suspended on top of the net or passes the net and becomes caught on the other side of the net (except on a serve; this is a fault on a serve). Lets are also called when the server and receiver commit faults at the same time, when the server serves before the receiver is ready, and when the shuttle comes apart.

When a let is called, no score counts for that play, and the server who began the play serves again.

TERMS

A **fault** occurs in a number of situations (see "Faults and Lets"). A fault committed by the serving side gives a point to the opponent; a fault by the receiving side gives a point to the serving side.

A **let** occurs when a point must be replayed. See "Faults and Lets" for such situations.

The **serve** is the hit that begins each play.

The **shuttlecock**, also called the *shuttle* or the *birdie*, is the feathered object the players hit with their rackets.

OFFICIALS

An umpire is in charge of the match. Other officials may include a service judge to call service faults and a line judge to indicate whether a shuttle is in or out of bounds.

ORGANIZATIONS

Badminton World Federation
Unit No. 1, Level 29
Naza Tower Platinum Park
No. 10, Persiaran KLCC
50088 Kuala Lumpur
Malaysia
http://bwfbadminton.com

USA Badminton
1 Olympic Plaza
Colorado Springs, CO 80909
719-866-4808
www.usabadminton.org

6

Baseball

Wayne Bronson/fotolia.com

Alexander Cartwright is credited with formulating the first set of rules, and the first game of record occurred on June 19, 1846, between the New York Knickerbockers and another New York team at the Elysian Field in Hoboken, New Jersey. The game is believed to have evolved from the British games of cricket and rounders, though for decades Abner Doubleday, a Civil War hero, was credited with having invented baseball in 1839 in Cooperstown, New York. That historical fallacy is why the National Baseball Hall of Fame and Museum is located there. Baseball has long been popular in the United States, Latin America, and Japan. It has developed into an international game with the advent of the Little League World Series and more recently the World Baseball Classic. The sport is played at the youth level in more than 80 countries. In the United States, participation has held steady at around 12 million annually; it ranks behind only soccer and basketball in youth participation in the United States.

OVERVIEW

Objective: To score the most runs.

Scoring: A player scores a run when they safely touch first, second, third, and home before their team makes three outs.

Number of Players: Nine per team (ten if a designated hitter is used, though only nine are on the field).

Number of Innings: Nine (six to seven for younger players).

Number of Outs per Inning: Three outs for each team.

The defense fields nine players. Each team has a batting order it must adhere to, although the order can be changed by substitutions. Once a player is removed from the game, they cannot return. The defensive team tries to get batters out after its pitcher delivers to hitters; the offensive team tries to score as many runs as it can before making three outs in an inning, which ends its turn at bat. The defensive team can record

outs when the batter gets three strikes before reaching a base (this is called a strikeout), when a batted ball is caught in the air before it hits the ground, or when a batted ball is fielded on the ground and thrown to a base before runners can advance there safely for a ground out or a force out. Hitters can reach base by taking four pitches out of the strike zone before making an out (this is called a walk), by being hit by a pitch, and by hitting a ball without it being caught in the air and safely advancing to a base without being thrown out. The designated "visiting" team bats first, and the home team gets to bat last. After the team batting first makes three outs, the home team bats until it makes three outs, which ends that inning. The teams alternate batting like that for nine innings.

FIELD

Figure 6.1 shows the dimensions of a major league field. Distances to outfield fences vary, but distances of 320 feet or more down the lines and 400 feet or more to center field are preferable. The figure also shows player positions.

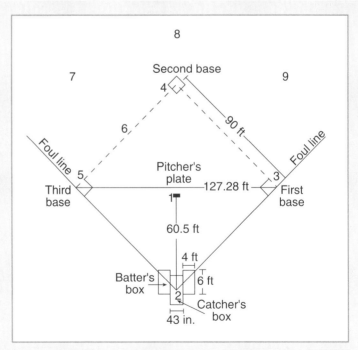

▶ **Figure 6.1**   The dimensions, features, and player positions of a baseball field.

EQUIPMENT

Balls, bats, bases, and batter's helmets are described under "Terms." The catcher's glove must be not more than 38 inches in circumference and not more than 15.5 inches from top to bottom. The first baseman's glove may be a maximum of 13 inches from top to bottom and 8 inches across the palm. In addition to gloves, catchers wear other protective gear: a helmet, face mask, chest and throat protectors, and shin guards. Players may not wear pointed spikes on their shoes.

RULES

The basic play of baseball can be understood through its rules for pitching, batting, and base running.

Pitching

Following are specific pitching rules that have not been previously stated.

1. Once a pitcher begins their motion to home, they must throw home or be called for a balk.

2. Pitchers cannot shift or lift their pivot foot from the pitching rubber during a pitch. If a pitcher does so, a balk is called, and if there are runners on base, they get to advance one base. If there are no runners on base, a ball is added to the pitching count.

3. When the bases are empty, the pitcher has 12 seconds to pitch, or the umpire will automatically call a ball.

4. The pitcher may not bring their pitching hand into contact with their mouth or lips while they are on the pitcher's mound, although exceptions can be made in cold weather if both managers agree. Penalty: Automatic ball called.

    Other reasons for an automatic ball being called include

    ▪ applying a foreign substance to the ball;

    ▪ spitting on the ball, on either hand, or on the glove;

    ▪ rubbing the ball on the glove, body, or clothing;

    ▪ defacing the ball; and

    ▪ pitching a "shine" ball, spitball, mudball, or "emery" ball.

5. The pitcher may rub the ball in his bare hands.

6. The pitcher may not intentionally throw at a batter. If they do, the umpire may expel the pitcher and their manager or may warn the pitchers and the managers of both teams.

7. A manager or coach may make two trips to the mound during an inning to talk to the pitcher. On the second trip, the pitcher must be removed. A recent rule change allows the defensive team to issue an intentional walk to a batter without having to throw a pitch.

Batting

Batting rules that have not been previously stated include the following:

1. Players must hit in the batting order decided by the manager.

2. A batter cannot leave the batter's box once the pitcher becomes set or begins their windup.

3. One of the batter's feet must be in the batter's box (the lines are part of the box). If the batter hits the ball—either fair or foul—with both feet on the ground entirely outside of the box, they are automatically out.

4. A batter may request time, but the umpire does not have to grant this request. If a batter refuses to take their position in the batter's box, the umpire will order the pitcher to pitch and call each pitch a strike, no matter the location.

5. A batter makes an out when

    ▪ their fair or foul fly ball is caught by a fielder;

    ▪ a third strike is caught by the catcher;

    ▪ a third strike is not caught by the catcher when first base is occupied before two are out;

    ▪ they bunt foul on the third strike;

    ▪ an infield fly rule is called (see "Terms");

▓ the fair ball touches the batter before touching a fielder (such as on a bunt);

▓ after hitting a ball in fair territory, the batter hits the ball with their bat a second time (unless the umpire judges that the batter did not intend to interfere with the ball);

▓ after a third strike or a hit into fair territory, either the batter or first base is tagged before they touch first base;

▓ the hitter runs outside the 3-foot line toward first base, interfering with the first baseman taking the throw or with a fielder fielding the ball;

▓ they interfere with the catcher's fielding or throwing;

▓ the hitter uses a bat that has been tampered with (i.e., a bat that has been filled, hollowed, grooved, covered with paraffin or wax, or otherwise altered) to increase hitting distance; or

▓ a runner on first base intentionally interferes with the second baseman or shortstop on a double play opportunity (if the runner leaves the baseline to try to "take out" the pivot person, both the runner and the batter are automatically out).

Base Running

The following are base-running rules that have not been previously covered.

1. A runner is entitled to an unoccupied base when he touches it before he is put out.

2. The baseline belongs to the runner. A fielder not in the act of fielding the ball cannot block the path of a runner between any two bases. In such a case the ball is dead, the runner is awarded the base he would have reached, in the umpire's judgment, had he not been obstructed.

3. A runner is out when

▓ they are tagged by a fielder with the ball while not on a base (however, a runner can run or slide past first base without risking being tagged out if he returns immediately to first base without stepping or turning to second);

▓ the runner fails to reach the next base before a fielder tags him or when they are forced to advance because the batter has become a runner;

▓ the runner runs out of the baseline (more than 3 feet away from a direct line between the bases), unless they are doing so to avoid interfering with a fielder fielding a batted ball;

▓ they intentionally interfere with a thrown ball or hinders a fielder making a play on a batted ball;

▓ two runners occupy the same base, and one runner is tagged with the ball;

▓ a runner is hit by a batted ball in fair territory before it touches a fielder or an umpire (unless they are on a base and an infield fly rule has been called);

▓ they pass a runner on the base paths;

▓ the runner misses a base in advancing to the next base, and a fielder appeals before the next pitch by touching the base with the ball in their possession;

▓ they fail to touch each base in order; or

▓ they intentionally interfere with a fielder or the ball in trying to break up a double play—in this case, both the runner and the batter are out.

Scoring

A win can be recorded in any of the following situations:

▓ When the home team is ahead after the visiting team finishes batting in the top of the ninth inning

▓ When the home team, tied or behind going into the bottom of the ninth inning, scores the winning run in the bottom of the ninth

▓ When the home team, losing in the bottom of the ninth inning, fails to score (the visitors win)

▓ When the teams are tied after nine innings and the game goes into extra innings, where it is played until one team has scored more than the other at the end of a complete inning

- When the game is shortened for bad weather, it has gone at least five innings, and one team is ahead (or 4-1/2 innings if the home team is ahead)
- When the umpire declares a forfeit

TERMS

An **assist** is credited to a fielder when their throw leads to the putout of a runner. Two or more fielders can receive an assist on the same play.

A **balk** is an illegal move (usually toward home plate) by the pitcher with a runner or runners on base. All runners automatically advance one base when a balk is called.

The **ball** is cork or rubber wrapped in yarn and covered by cowhide or horsehide. It weighs 5.00 to 5.25 ounces and is 9.00 to 9.25 inches in circumference. A pitch that the batter doesn't swing at and that is outside of the strike zone is also called a ball.

First, second, and third **base** are made of white canvas, 15 inches square, between 3 inches and 5 inches thick, and secured to the ground. Home plate is five-sided, 17 inches wide, 8.5 inches long on three sides, and 12 inches long on the sides that meet to form the point at the rear of the plate.

A batter is credited with a **base hit** when he reaches base safely on a hit without the aid of an error.

The **baseline** extends 3 feet on either side of a direct line between bases. A runner is out when she runs outside the baseline except to avoid interfering with a fielder fielding a batted ball.

A batter receives a **base on balls** (is awarded first base) when he takes four balls during a time at bat. This is also called a *walk*.

The **bat** is a smooth, round stick no more than 2.75 inches in diameter at its thickest and no longer than 42 inches. The bat handle can be treated with a sticky substance to improve the batter's grip, but this substance may not extend beyond 18 inches from the bottom of the bat.

Batter's boxes are 4 feet by 6 feet on either side of home plate.

Batter's circles, or *on-deck circles*, are in foul territory between home plate and each team's bench.

The **battery** refers to the pitcher and the catcher.

Batters must wear **batting helmets** with at least one ear flap (facing the pitcher as the batter is in their stance).

A batter **bunts** the ball by letting the pitched ball meet the bat to drop a soft ground ball onto the infield. A bunt can be an attempt to achieve a base hit, or it can be a sacrifice to move a runner or runners ahead by a base.

A **catch** means a fielder has secured the ball in their hand or glove. A fly ball is not caught if the fielder simultaneously falls or collides with the fence or another player and the ball is dislodged. A fly ball that is dropped may still be ruled a catch if the fielder had control of the ball long enough before he dropped it.

A **catcher's box**, 43 inches wide and 8 feet long, is directly behind home plate.

Catcher's interference occurs when the catcher hinders the batter from hitting the ball.

Coaches' boxes are set near first and third base, in foul territory, for the offensive team.

A pitcher is credited with a **complete game** when he starts and finishes a regulation game.

A **cutoff throw** is one that is received by a fielder who is not the final target of the throw. For example, a right fielder may throw to the second baseman, who then relays the throw to the third baseman in an attempt to put out a runner.

A **designated hitter** takes the place of the pitcher in the batting order but does not play defense.

A **double** is a hit in which the batter safely reaches second base.

A **double play** is recorded by the defense when two outs are made on the same play.

An **earned run** is charged against a pitcher every time a run scores on a hit, sacrifice, bunt, sacrifice fly, wild pitch, stolen base, putout, fielder's choice, base on balls, batter hit by pitch, or balk. A run is *unearned* if that runner scores by benefit of an error, a passed ball, or defensive interference or obstruction. A relief pitcher who enters a game in progress is not charged with any run, either earned or unearned, scored by any runners who were already on base when the pitcher entered the game.

An **error** is charged to a fielder who misplays a ball (e.g., a dropped fly ball or throw or a fumbled ground ball) and consequently prolongs an at-bat for a batter or the life of a base runner, or permits a runner to advance one or more bases. An error can be charged even if the fielder does not touch the ball (e.g., a ground ball that goes through the legs).

A game goes into **extra innings** when it is tied at the end of nine innings.

Fair territory and foul territory are marked by two foul lines. Each line extends from home plate. One line creates a third baseline and left field line, stopping at the left field fence; the other creates a first baseline and right field line, stopping at the right field fence. Anything on or in between the foul lines is considered fair territory. Foul poles rise above the fence in left field and right field. A ball striking a foul pole is a home run.

A **fielder's choice** occurs when an infielder fields a ground ball and elects to throw to another base rather than to first base to put out the base runner.

A **fly ball** is a ball batted high in the air.

A **fly out** is a fly ball caught before it touches the ground or the fence.

A **force play** occurs when a runner is forced to advance to the next base because the batter becomes a runner. When a batter hits a ground ball with a runner on first base, the runner is forced to run to second. If a fielder touches second base with the ball in his possession before the runner reaches second, the runner is "forced out" at second. If a runner is on second when a ground ball is hit, he is not forced to advance if first base is unoccupied.

A **foul ball** is any ball hit into foul territory.

Foul territory is all territory outside the foul lines. A ball striking a foul line is a fair ball.

A **ground out** occurs when a batter is thrown out at first base after hitting a ground ball.

A **ground rule double** is awarded to a batter when their fair ball bounces into the stands, passes through or under the fence, or is caught in vines or shrubbery in the fence. When a batter is **hit by a pitch** that is not in the strike zone and that they try to elude, they are awarded first base.

A **home run** is recorded when a batter hits a fair ball over the fence or circles the bases on an inside-the-park hit without being thrown out.

The **infield** refers to the portion of the field that contains the four bases. In terms of players, the infield is made up of the first, second, and third basemen and the shortstop. The pitcher and the catcher are also positioned in the infield.

The **infield fly rule** prohibits an infielder from intentionally dropping a fair fly ball that can be caught with normal effort. This rule is in effect with first and second or first, second, and third bases occupied before two are out. When an umpire calls an infield fly rule, the batter is automatically out, and runners may advance at their own risk.

The **losing pitcher** is the pitcher charged with the runs that give the opposing team a lead that is not relinquished.

A **no-hitter** is credited to a pitcher who pitches a complete game and allows no hits.

A fielder can be called for **obstruction** if he impedes the progress of a runner when the fielder does not have the ball or is not fielding the ball.

An **out** can be recorded in a variety of ways, including strikeout, force out, tag out, and fly out.

The **outfield** is that portion of fair territory between the infield and the fence. In terms of players, the outfield consists of the left fielder, the center fielder, and the right fielder.

A **passed ball** is charged to the catcher when they fail to control a catchable pitch and allows a runner or runners to advance.

A **perfect game** occurs when a pitcher throws an entire game without allowing a hit, a walk, a hit batter, a batter reaching on a fielder's error, or any runner to get on base.

A **pinch hitter** is a player who bats for another player. The player replaced cannot return to the game.

A **pinch runner** is a player who runs for another player. The player replaced cannot return to the game.

The **pitcher's mound** is a circular mound of dirt 18 feet in diameter and 59 feet from its center to the back of home plate. The mound has a rectangular rubber plate, called the **pitching rubber**, set perpendicular to home plate. The pitching rubber is set in the ground, and its front edge is 60.5 feet from the back of home plate. The rubber is 6 inches by 24 inches and is set 10 inches higher than home plate.

A **putout** occurs when a batter-runner or base runner is called out (e.g., force out, tag out, caught stealing, and so on).

A **relief pitcher** is any pitcher who replaces the current pitcher after the current pitcher has thrown at least one pitch.

A batter is credited with the appropriate number of **runs batted in (RBIs)** when his hit is responsible for one or more runners scoring. RBIs are not tallied for runs scored as a result of errors or runs scored as the batter grounds into a double play.

A **sacrifice bunt** is placed by a batter to advance a runner or runners. A successful sacrifice bunt does not count as a time at bat; an unsuccessful attempt does.

A **sacrifice fly** is credited to a batter whose caught fly ball results in a runner on third base tagging up and scoring. A sacrifice fly does not count as a time at bat. A run must score for a sacrifice fly to be recorded.

A pitcher may be credited with a **save** when the game ends, their team wins and he is not the winning pitcher—if he meets one of these criteria:

■ The pitcher enters the game with a lead of no more than three runs and pitches for at least one inning.

■ The pitcher enters the game, regardless of the count, with the potential tying run either on base, at bat, or on deck.

■ The pitcher pitch effectively for at least three innings.

The **set position** is one of two positions from which a pitcher can deliver a pitch. In the set position, a pitcher comes set (halts his motion) just before pitching. This is also known as the *stretch position*.

A **shutout** occurs when a team is held scoreless. A pitcher must pitch a complete game to receive credit for a shutout.

A **single** is a one-base hit credited to the batter.

The **starting pitcher** is the pitcher who begins the game for their team.

A runner is credited with a **stolen base** when they advance one base without aid of a hit, putout, error, force out, fielder's choice, passed ball, wild pitch, or balk.

A **strike** is a pitch that the batter takes (doesn't swing at) in the strike zone, that the batter swings at and misses, or that the batter hits into foul territory.

A **strikeout** is recorded after a batter has three strikes. Exceptions to this are if the third strike is a foul ball that is not caught in the air or a strike that the catcher does not catch. In the latter case, if first base is unoccupied, or if it is occupied with two out, the defensive team must put out the batter by either throwing the ball to first base before the batter reaches it or by tagging them with the ball before they reach first. Batters trying to bunt on the third strike are out if the ball is picked up in foul territory. This play is considered a strikeout.

The batter's **strike zone** is over home plate, between the top of the knees and the midpoint between the top of the shoulders and the top of the pants.

Substitutions can be made when play is dead. Once a player leaves the game, they cannot return.

A **suspended game** is one that is halted, to be completed at a later date. The game is resumed at the exact point of suspension with the same lineups intact.

A **tag out** is one way a fielder can record a putout. When a force play is not in order, such as with a runner on second, the runner must be tagged out (touched with the ball, which can be in a fielder's glove or bare hand) when the runner is not touching a base.

On a caught fly ball, a runner must **tag up** (be in contact with their base) after the catch before advancing.

A **3-foot line** to guide the runners is parallel to the first baseline, beginning halfway between home plate and first base and ending beyond first base.

A batter is credited with a **triple** when they reach third base on their hit.

A **triple play** occurs when the defense records three outs on the same play.

The outfield has a dirt **warning track** that alerts outfielders that they are approaching the fence.

A **wild pitch** occurs when a pitch eludes the catcher, allowing one or more runners to advance one base. A wild pitch is judged to be the pitcher's fault, not the catcher's. A ball that bounces in the dirt and allows any base runners to advance is automatically a wild pitch.

The **windup position** is one of two positions from which a pitcher can deliver a pitch. The windup is normally used with no runners on base.

The **winning pitcher** is the starting pitcher if they pitch five or more innings and leaves the game with the lead and the lead is never relinquished. If a pitcher leaves a game with the lead, but the game is later tied or the opponent takes the lead with runs not charged to that pitcher, that pitcher cannot be either the winner or the loser. In most cases, if the winning pitcher is a relief pitcher, they are the pitcher of record when their team has taken a lead that it does not relinquish.

OFFICIALS

The umpire-in-chief (home plate umpire) is in full charge of the game. Any umpire may disqualify any player, coach, or manager for objecting to decisions or for unsporting conduct or language. The umpire's decision on any judgment call is final and may not be appealed. A manager may, however, appeal any call that they believe goes against the rules. For common officials' signals, see figure 6.2.

▶ **Figure 6.2** Common officials' signals in baseball.

MODIFICATIONS

Baseball leagues begin with players as young as 5 years old and go on through the teen years and, of course, beyond. To make the game safe, fun, and appropriate for younger players who are just beginning to develop their talents, various organizations and leagues modify their playing rules. The rules most often modified pertain to the following areas:

- Length of game: Youth leagues typically play between six and seven innings; as the players age, they play more innings. Some leagues have time limits; for example, no inning may start after the game has gone 1.75 hours for age groups under 12 and no more than 2 hours for those between ages 13 and 19.

- Distance between bases and to fences: The distance between bases varies from 50 feet at the youngest levels to 60 to 80 feet in the preteen years to the major league distance of 90 feet by the teen years. Fences down the lines are usually less than 200 feet until the players are 11 or 12 years old; the distance increases as the players get to mid- and late teens, with many leagues having 300-foot fences at that point. In center field, the fences typically begin at 200 feet and increase to 275 feet by age 12 and 350 feet by the mid-teens.

- Pitching: Many leagues make concessions for the abilities of youngsters to pitch. See "Coach-Pitch" and "Tee Ball."
- Base running: Younger divisions of youth leagues typically have "no lead off" and "no stealing" rules. Older divisions may lead off and steal.
- Other modifications: Youth leagues also limit the number of innings young pitchers may pitch in one game and in one week, and many 8-and-under leagues use a safety (softer) ball. Younger divisions often allow up to 12 players on defense and have no infield fly rule.

Coach-pitch and tee ball are two of the major ways in which the game is modified. For specific rule modifications for youth baseball, contact the organizations listed at the end of the chapter.

Coach-Pitch

Coach-pitch is a step between tee ball and regular baseball (player-pitch). A coach or another adult pitches to batters because the pitchers are not able to throw the ball over the plate consistently. With coach-pitch, batters have more of an opportunity to practice their hitting and are less likely to be hit by pitches.

Coach-pitch is usually recommended for ages 8 and under. Some leagues use a pitching machine instead of an adult.

Tee Ball

Many 8-and-under leagues play tee ball instead of baseball. In tee ball, the batter hits the ball off a tee. This results in the ball being put in play more regularly and is appropriate for leagues with young and unskilled players who cannot bat or pitch very consistently. General rules for tee ball include the following, though they are often varied:

- All players on the roster bat.
- An inning is over when nine players have hit or three outs are made, whichever occurs first. The ninth batter must try to score; his scoring or his being put out will end the inning if three outs have not already been made.

- No bunting is allowed. The ball must travel at least 25 feet in fair territory; a 25-foot arc is drawn from foul line to foul line.
- Balls not hit beyond the 25-foot arc are foul balls.
- A "pitcher" on the mound must be in contact with the pitching rubber and make a pitching motion before the batter swings.
- Three misses constitute a strikeout.
- No stealing or leading off is allowed.
- Nine players are on defense (many leagues allow all the players on defense).
- Each player must play at least two innings in the field.
- The coach of the defensive team may stand beyond the infielders and instruct her players.
- A regulation game is by innings or hours—often six innings or 1.5 hours.

ORGANIZATIONS

All-American Amateur Baseball Association
www.aaabajohnstown.org

Amateur Athletic Union's Baseball
P.O. Box 22409
Lake Buena Vista, FL 32830-1000
407-934-7200
www.playaaubaseball.com

American Amateur Baseball Congress
100 W. Broadway
Farmington, NM 87401
505-327-3120
info@aabc.us
www.aabc.us

American Legion Baseball
700 N. Pennsylvania St.
P.O. Box 1055
Indianapolis, IN 46206
317-630-1200
www.legion.org/baseball

Babe Ruth League
1670 Whitehorse-Mercerville Rd.
Hamilton, NJ 08619
800-880-3142
www.baberuthleague.org

Little League Baseball and Softball
539 U.S. Rte. 15
Williamsport, PA 17701-0485
www.LittleLeague.org

National Amateur Baseball Federation
P.O. Box 705
Bowie, MD 20718
301-262-5005
www.nabf.com

National Semi-Professional Baseball Association
4609 Saybrook Dr.
Evansville, IN 47711
812-430-2725
www.eteamz.com/NSPBA

Pony Baseball
1951 Pony Pl.
Washington, PA 15301
724-225-1060
info@pony.org
www.pony.org

USA Baseball
1030 Swabia Ct., Ste. 201
Durham, NC 27702
919-474-8721
www.usabaseball.com

U.S. Amateur Baseball Federation
301 Winters Ct.
San Marcos, CA 92069
760-580-9934
www.usabf.com

7

Basketball

Basketball began with 13 fundamental rules that have been added to and amended greatly over the years since the game's beginnings in 1891. Invented by James Naismith, basketball first featured nine players per team because Naismith had 18 students in his YMCA Training School. After a few years that number was changed to five per side, a metal ring with a net replaced the original peach baskets that players shot at, and running with the ball was eliminated.

Basketball first became an Olympic sport at the 1936 Summer Olympics. It is a widely enjoyed participant sport around the world, with leagues for all ages and abilities. More than 30 million people play the sport, from recreation levels on up, in the United States.

OVERVIEW

Objective: To win by scoring more points than the other team.

Scoring: 1 point per successful free throw; 2 points per 2-point field goal; 3 points per 3-point field goal.

Number of Players: Five per team.

Length of Game: 32 minutes (high school), 40 minutes (college), or 48 minutes (professional).

A team advances the ball by dribbling and passing and tries to score. A shot that does not go into the basket is usually rebounded by a player. If that player is on offense, she can either shoot or set up another scoring opportunity. If the player who rebounds is on defense, she and her team advance the ball downcourt and try to set up their own scoring opportunity. After a made basket, the player who throws the ball in may run the length of the baseline with the ball. On any inbounds play, other than a made basket, the player who throws the ball in must establish, and may not move, a pivot foot before releasing the ball. The player must throw the ball in within 5 seconds or it is turned over to the other team.

COURT

Court sizes vary according to the level of play. In high school, the court is 50 feet by 84 feet; in college and the National Basketball Association (NBA), it is 50 feet by 94 feet. The free-throw line at all three levels is 15 feet from the basket. The free-throw lane, which borders the free-throw line, is 12 feet wide in high school and college and 16 feet wide in the NBA. This lane has a semicircle with a 6-foot radius from the center of the free-throw line.

A 3-point line—an arc at a set radius from the basket—is set at varying distances for high school, college, professional, and international play.

At least 3 feet of unobstructed space should lie beyond the sidelines and end lines (or baselines) that mark the boundaries of the court. The court is split in half by a center line, around which are two center circles.

Two coaching boxes are behind the sidelines, 28 feet long and extending toward center court from each end line. See figure 7.1 for standard court attributes.

PLAYERS

A team consists of five players on the court at a time. Typically, but not always, a team plays two guards (a point guard, considered the team's playmaker, and an off guard or shooting guard), a small forward, a power forward, and a center or post player. These are loosely defined roles; players may be defined differently in different systems. Players are sometimes referred to by position numbers (which have nothing to do with their uniform numbers):

1. Point guard
2. Off guard or shooting guard
3. Small forward
4. Power forward
5. Center or post

Uniforms for a team must include short sleeves or tank tops of the same dominant color. Shirts must be tucked into shorts. Each shirt should include a one- or two-digit number on the front (at least 10 centimeters high and 2 centimeters wide) and back (at least 20 centimeters high and 2 centimeters wide) in a color contrasting with the color of the shirt. In American interscholastic and other formal games, digits over 5 are not used (e.g., 17 and 29 are not allowed but 43 and 55 are) so that referees can easily use hand signals to communicate to the scorer's table which player committed a foul.

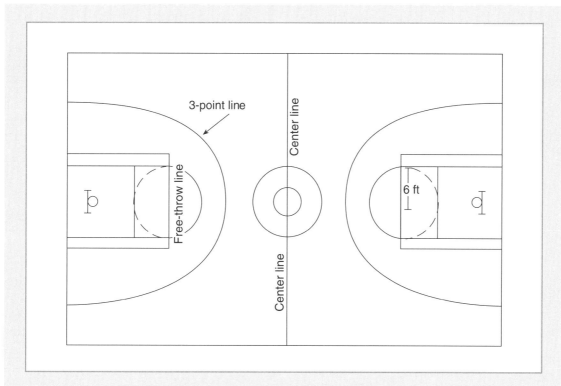

▶ **Figure 7.1**   Dimensions for courts vary according to the level of play, but many of the same features are included on all courts.

EQUIPMENT

The ball has a circumference of 29.25 to 30.00 inches for men and 28.5 to 29.0 inches for women. A men's ball weighs 20 to 22 ounces; a women's ball weighs 18 to 20 ounces. The ball has either a synthetic or a leather cover with eight panels joined by rubber ribs.

The backboard, which supports the basket, can be either 6 by 4 feet or 6 by 3.5 feet for college and high school play; professional basketball uses only the smaller size. In high school play, a fan-shaped backboard may be used. A 24- by 18-inch rectangle is centered on the backboard, behind and above the basket. The bottom and sides of the backboard are padded, as is the backboard support.

The basket is an orange metal ring, 18 inches in inside diameter. A white cord net, 15 to 18 inches in length, hangs from the basket. The upper edge of the basket is 10 feet above and parallel to the floor. The nearest point of the basket is 6 inches from the backboard.

Other equipment includes

- a scoreboard,
- a game clock,
- a shot clock, and
- a possession indicator (which indicates which team will get possession of the ball in the next held-ball or double-foul situation).

RULES

The rules in this chapter are general basketball rules with specific references at times to high school, college, and professional play. How the game is modified at the international level and the youth level is noted toward the end of the chapter.

Game length and other time factors differ according to the level of play; see table 7.1. The shot clock governs the time a team is allowed to be on offense before attempting a shot. If the ball does not leave the shooter's hand before the clock expires, or if the shot does not touch the rim or

TABLE 7.1

Game Length and Time Factors

Level	Length	Overtime	Shot clock	Timeouts
High school	Four 8-min quarters	3 min	None	5 per game
College	Two 20-min halves	5 min	30 sec women; 35 sec men	4 per regulation (3 per televised game); 1 per overtime
Professional	Four 12-min quarters	5 min	24 sec	6 per regulation plus one 20-sec timeout per half; 3 per overtime
International	Two 20-min halves	5 min	30 sec	2 per half

go into the basket, a shot clock violation is called, and the ball is given to the other team. The clock is stopped at the end of each period and when an official blows a whistle for

- a violation,
- a foul,
- a held or jump ball,
- a ball that goes out of bounds,
- suspension of play because of an injury to a player, suspension of play for any other reason,
- when the shot clock sounds (if the shot is in the air when the clock sounds and the shot hits the rim, the clock is ignored and play continues without time stopping), and
- timeouts.

Defense

When a defender is guarding a player who has the ball, the maximum distance between the two players is 6 feet. (No minimum distance is required.) To establish legal position, the defender must have both feet on the floor with the torso facing the opponent. If the opponent is airborne, the defender must have established a legal position before the other player left the floor and must maintain that position.

When a defender is guarding a player who does not have the ball, the defender must give the opponent time and up to two steps to avoid contact. If the opponent is airborne, the defender must have established a legal position before the

other player left the floor and must maintain that position.

Examples of legal use of hands and arms include when a defender vertically extends hands and arms, reaches to block or slap the ball away, or hits the hand of the opponent when the ball is in contact with the opponent's hands. If the extension is not vertical and any contact hinders the offensive player, the movement is not legal. Defenders may use their hands to protect their faces or bodies in absorbing a charge from an opponent, but they can't use their hands to push the offensive player away. Defenders cannot use any part of their bodies to force their way through screens or to hold a screener and then push that player away.

In professional basketball a team cannot play a zone defense, in which each defender is assigned a certain portion of the court rather than an individual player. In college and high school, zone defenses are allowed, as are man-to-man defenses, in which each player defends a specific opponent.

Fouls

A foul occurs when a player or coach breaks a rule in any of a variety of ways. A player is disqualified and removed from a game after being assessed five fouls (high school and college) or six fouls (professional). Specific fouls include these:

- Away from the ball is a foul committed by a player in a play not involving the player with the ball.

- Blocking is illegal contact by a defender, impeding the progress of an offensive player.

- Charging is illegal contact by an offensive player by pushing or moving into the defender's torso.

- Delay of game is called when a player prevents the ball from being promptly put into play. Examples include wasting time after a basket is made or batting the ball away from an opponent before the player can throw the ball in bounds.

- A double personal occurs when two opposing players commit personal fouls at about the same time. No free throws are awarded. In professional ball, the team in possession of the ball at the time of the fouls retains possession; if neither team was in possession, a jump ball is used to put the ball into play. In college, the alternating-possession arrow determines the team that gets possession.

- A double technical foul is called when two opposing players commit technical fouls at about the same time. In college, each team receives two free throws, and the alternating possession arrow determines which team gets possession. In professional ball, this penalty is handled the same way as a double personal foul.

- In professional ball, two free-throw attempts are awarded for an elbow foul. If the contact is made above shoulder level, the player throwing the elbow may be ejected. In college and in high school play, excessive swinging of elbows—even without making contact—may result in a foul.

- A team calling a timeout when it has no timeouts left is assessed a technical foul for excessive timeouts. The timeout is granted, but two free throws and the ball out of bounds are awarded to the opposing team.

- A defender cannot face guard—that is, place a hand in the face or eyes of the opponent he is guarding from the rear if the opponent does not have the ball. Such a play results in a technical foul.

- In the NBA, fighting results in technical fouls assessed against those involved and automatic ejection. No free throws are awarded.

- In both college and the pros, a flagrant foul results in two free throws awarded to the offended team and possession of the ball. Any player committing a flagrant foul is automatically ejected in college; a professional player may be ejected at the discretion of the official.

- Defenders cannot hand check—that is, use their hands to check the progress of offensive players when those players are in front of them.

- If either an offensive or a defensive player hangs on the rim of the basket, a technical foul is assessed. The only exception is if a player hangs onto the rim to protect herself or other players from injury.

- In college, an intentional foul occurs when a player commits a personal foul without trying to directly play the opposing player or the ball. It does not depend on the severity of the foul; it depends on whether the official judges the foul to be intentional. Holding or pushing a player in the full view of an official in order to stop play or shoving a player in the back as she is attempting a layup that cannot be defended are examples of intentional fouls. The penalty for such fouls is two free throws and the ball out of bounds.

- Any player on offense can commit an offensive foul. If a defender has established legal position in a dribbler's path, the dribbler cannot make contact with the opponent. A screener cannot move into an opponent after setting a legal screen. A shooter cannot charge into a defender who has established legal position and who maintains that position.

- The term *personal foul* covers a wide variety of contact fouls that players can commit, including holding, pushing, charging, tripping, and illegally interfering with a player's progress.

- A player-control foul is another term for charging—when the dribbler commits an offensive foul by charging into a defender who has established legal position.

- In professional ball, a punching foul, in which a player tries to punch an opponent, results in one free throw being awarded and the ball out of bounds. The player throwing the punch—whether it connects or not—is automatically ejected. (In college this foul would be handled the same as a flagrant foul.)

▪ A technical foul is a foul committed by anyone—players on the court or bench, coaches, other team officials—that does not involve contact with the opponent while the ball is alive. Examples of technical fouls include the use of profanity, delay of game, excessive timeouts, unsporting conduct, and hanging on the rim (except to prevent injury). Two free throws and possession of the ball are awarded to the offended team when a player commits a technical foul. If a coach, substitute, or other team personnel commit a technical foul, two free throws are awarded (and in college, the offended team would retain possession of the ball). A player who commits two technical fouls is removed from the game. A coach who commits two technical fouls is removed from the competition area.

▪ Throwing the ball or any other object at an official is a technical foul and cause for possible ejection.

▪ Unsportsmanlike conduct is a technical foul resulting from any of numerous unsporting actions, including disrespectfully addressing an official, trying to influence an official's decision, arguing with an official, taunting an opponent, inciting undesirable crowd reactions, and throwing items on the court. The penalty is two free throws and the ball out of bounds to the opposing team.

Scoring

When the ball enters the basket from above and remains in or passes through the net, a goal is scored. If that goal is scored with at least one of the shooter's feet on or inside the 3-point line, a 2-point field goal is scored. If neither of the shooter's feet is on or inside the 3-point line, a 3-point field goal is scored. After releasing the ball, the shooter may touch the 3-point line or land inside the line and still be awarded 3 points on a successful shot. If a goal is mistakenly scored in the opponent's basket by a defender, 2 points are awarded to the nearest offensive player.

A successful free-throw attempt counts as 1 point. If the free throw is not made but the rebound is tapped in, the player who tapped it in is awarded 2 points. Free throws must be attempted within 10 seconds.

Defensive players and offensive players alternate positions along the free-throw lane, with the defensive team getting the positions closest to the basket. The shooter must remain behind the free-throw line until the ball touches the basket. The players in the lane must remain in their positions on the free-throw lane until the ball leaves the shooter's hands.

A player who is fouled while attempting a 2-point field goal gets two free throws; a player gets three free throws if fouled during a 3-point field goal attempt. One free throw is awarded a player who is fouled while making a field goal. After a certain number of fouls are committed in a quarter or a half, a team may be in the bonus situation, where the next player fouled (not in the act of shooting or as the result of taking a charge from an offensive player) receives a chance to make a free throw. If the first free throw is successful, that player receives a bonus of one more free-throw attempt. Bonus free throws are awarded as follows:

▪ High school and college: The one-and-one bonus is awarded on the seventh, eighth, and ninth team fouls of each half. Beginning with the 10th team foul of each half, the team fouled gets two free throws, regardless of the outcome of the first free throw.

▪ Professional: Two free throws are granted for each foul after four fouls in a quarter (or three in overtime).

The penalty for most technical fouls is two free throws and the ball out of bounds to the team attempting the free throws. Any player on the floor may be named by the coach to attempt free throws awarded from a technical foul.

Violations

Violations occur when players break the rules in a way that does not involve contact. Violations include the following:

▪ When a team is in possession of the ball in its frontcourt and the ball goes into the backcourt (last touched by an offensive player), an offensive player cannot touch the ball until a defensive player does. If an offensive player does touch the ball first, a backcourt violation is called, and the ball automatically goes to the defensive team. If, however, the ball was deflected into the backcourt by a defender, then an offensive player may retrieve the ball in the backcourt.

■ Basket interference and goaltending are called when a player touches the ball or the basket when the ball is on or within the basket. A player cannot touch the ball when it is in the cylinder (the basket extended upward) or when it is in flight downward toward the basket and has a possibility of entering the basket. Defensive basket interference and goaltending result in 2 points for the offense; offensive basket interference results in no points and the ball out of bounds to the defense.

■ Double dribble is called when a player stops her dribble and then resumes it. A player can resume a dribble, however, if the ball has been batted out of her hands or if a pass or fumble has been touched by another player. Double dribble also occurs when a player dribbles with both hands at once.

■ A player cannot intentionally kick the ball or strike it with his fist. Doing so results in the ball being given out of bounds to the other team.

■ Any ball that goes out of bounds is awarded to the team opposing the player who last touched the ball.

■ Any shot that does not occur before the shot clock expires results in the ball being turned over to the other team. If the ball is released before the clock expires and hits the rim after it expires, no violation has occurred.

■ Traveling is called when a player advances with the ball without dribbling it.

■ A player making a throw-in (throwing the ball in bounds) may not carry the ball onto the court, hold the ball longer than 5 seconds, touch the ball on the court before another player has touched it, leave the designated throw-in spot (except after a made basket), or step over the boundary line while still touching the ball.

TERMS

These terms are not described elsewhere in this chapter.

To **dribble** is to bounce the ball on the floor, using one hand at a time. (Dribbling with both hands at once is double dribbling, a violation that results in a turnover.) Players may move on the court or be stationary when they dribble. The dribble ends when the ball is caught by the dribbler, who cannot dribble again until another player touches the ball.

A team's **frontcourt** is that half of the court that includes the basket where it scores. The **backcourt** is the half of the court that includes the basket where the opposing team scores. No part of the end line or the center line is considered part of the frontcourt.

A **held ball** occurs when two players from opposing teams each have a firm grasp on the ball or when an opposing player places a hand on the ball to prevent an airborne player from attempting a pass or shot. The team with the possession indicator in its favor is awarded the ball out of bounds.

Incidental contact occurs when opponents are in equally favorable positions to perform normal defensive or offensive movements and contact (even severe contact) is made, such as in going for a loose ball. No foul is called. Similarly, a blind screen may be ruled incidental contact, regardless of the violence of the collision.

A **pass** is the movement of the ball by a player who throws, bats, or rolls the ball to another player.

A **pivot** occurs when a player holding the ball keeps one foot at a point of contact with the floor while stepping in any direction. Picking up the pivot foot before dribbling or getting rid of the ball is a traveling violation.

A **rebound** occurs when a player controls possession of a shot missed by either a teammate (offensive rebound) or an opponent (defensive rebound).

A **screen** occurs when an offensive player reaches a desired position first, causing a defensive player to go around him and delaying the progress of the defender. The offensive player must have feet planted and remain stationary.

Substitutes are alternative players who may enter a game by reporting to the scorer and being beckoned by an official. Substitutes may enter during a dead ball and when time is out (except in college, where a substitute may enter after a successful field goal in the last minute of a game and in overtime). A substitute may not enter a game for a player shooting a free throw unless that player is injured.

Verticality applies to ascertaining who has legal position. A defender who has already established position and who raises her hands and arms within her vertical plane is in legal position and shouldn't be charged with a foul if an offensive player causes contact. The defender can leave her feet within this plane but cannot "belly up," or use the lower part of the body to contact the offensive player outside the vertical plane.

OFFICIALS

A referee and one or two umpires, depending on the level of play, call fouls and violations and make all on-court calls. A scorekeeper operates the scoreboard and records the play; a timekeeper operates the game clock; and a shot clock operator is in charge of the shot clock.

For common officials' signals, see figure 7.2.

MODIFICATIONS

Because basketball is so widely popular and is played by young and old, skilled and unskilled, many organizations adapt the rules to fit their members better. Two major types of groups that modify the rules are youth organizations and international basketball organizations.

Youth Basketball

Variations differ from organization to organization; the following is an overview of the types of adaptations that are made for young players.

- The size of the ball and the court are generally smaller.
- The basket height is lowered to give youths a reasonable chance to score and to help them learn proper shooting technique.
- The free-throw line is closer to the basket. The younger the players, the closer the line (compared with the standard 15-foot free-throw line).
- The duration of the game is shorter, and a shot clock is often not used for the younger levels.
- Officials are not as strict in calling all violations and fouls, and they often help instruct the players in terms of what constitutes violations and fouls. Violations that are typically not called strictly by the book, especially for younger levels, include traveling, double dribble, and backcourt violations.

International Rules

The International Basketball Federation (FIBA) regulates international play for Olympic and other international competitions. Some of the major differences between FIBA rules and the rules presented earlier in this chapter include the following:

- The size of the court is 28 meters long by 15 meters wide. The free-throw lane is 3.6 meters wide at the free-throw line, widening to 6 meters at the baseline. The 3-point arc is a semicircle that is 6.25 meters from the basket at all points.
- Game length is four 10-minute periods with, if necessary, one or more 5-minute overtimes.
- The shot clock is 24 seconds.
- All held balls result in jump balls.
- A player fouls out after committing five fouls.
- A team is in the bonus foul situation when it has committed four team fouls in a period.
- A maximum of five players—three defensive and two offensive—may occupy the free-throw lane places during a free throw.

ORGANIZATIONS

Continental Basketball Association
195 Washington Ave.
Albany, NY 12210
518-694-0100
http://cbaworldhoops.com

National Association of Basketball Coaches
1111 Main St., Ste. 1000
Kansas City, MO 64105-2136
816-878-NABC (6222)
www.nabc.com

National Basketball Association
645 Fifth Ave., 110th Fl.
New York, NY 10022
212-826-7000
www.nba.com

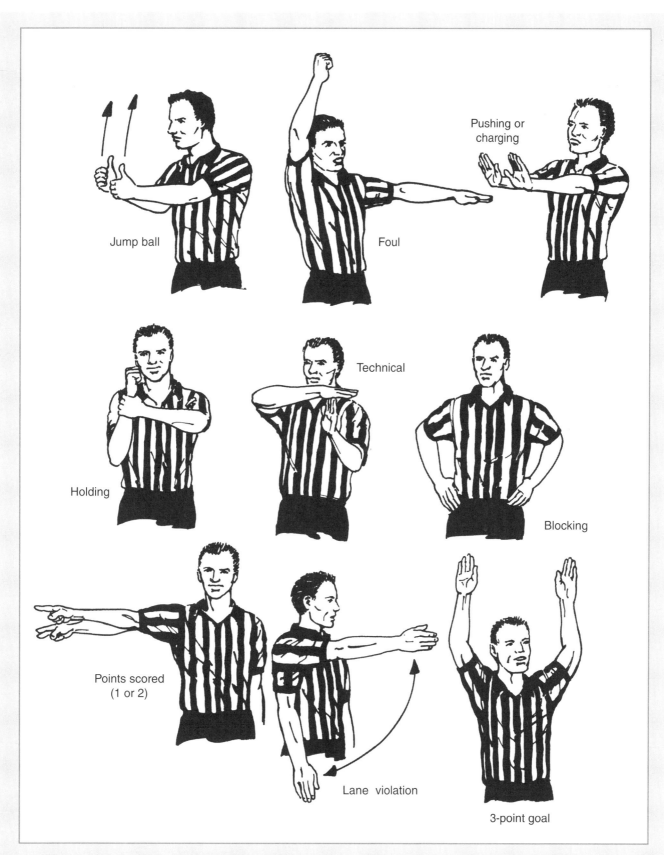

Jump ball

Foul

Pushing or charging

Holding

Technical

Blocking

Points scored (1 or 2)

Lane violation

3-point goal

▶ **Figure 7.2** Common officials' signals in basketball.

National Collegiate Athletic Association
700 W. Washington St.
P.O. Box 6222
Indianapolis, IN 46206-6222
317-917-6138
www.ncaa.org

National Federation of State High
School Associations
P.O. Box 690
Indianapolis, IN 46206
317-972-6900
www.nfhs.org

USA Basketball
5469 Mark Dabling Blvd.
Colorado Springs, CO 80918
719-590-4800
www.usab.com

Women's Basketball Coaches Association
4646 Lawrenceville Hwy.
Lilburn, GA 30047
770-279-8027
www.wbca.org

Youth Basketball of America
5401 S. Kirkman Rd., Ste. 328
Orlando, FL 32819
407-363-9262
www.yboa.org

8

BMX Racing

Carlos Herrera/Icon Sportswire/Corbis via Getty Images

Bicycle motocross racing—better known as BMX racing—got its beginnings in the late 1950s in Europe, with kids racing around tracks in the Netherlands. In 1971, a documentary film called *On Any Sunday*, with an opening scene depicting kids riding bikes off-road, sparked interest in BMX racing in the United States, and in 1973 the National Bicycle Association (NBA) became the first national sanctioning body for the sport in the country. In 1974 the National Bicycle League (NBL) was formed and became the first nonprofit BMX sanctioning body in the world. In 1981, the NBL helped create the International BMX Federation (IBMXF). The first IBMXF World Championships were held in Dayton, Ohio, in 1982. The recognized international governing body for BMX is Union Cycliste Internationale.

The popularity of BMX has grown significantly in the last two decades. There are now an estimated three million BMX riders, and BMX is part of the annual Summer X Games for extreme sports. The sport made its Olympic debut at the 2008 Games in Beijing.

OVERVIEW

BMX racing involves two to eight riders who ride against each other in either two or three separate motos (races) on tracks. The finish places of the riders are determined by their overall performance during these two or three motos. All riders in point classes receive local or national points based on their finishes in the motos they participate in.

TRACK

The length of a BMX track is 800 to 1,500 feet, measured from the center of the track. The width of the start gate is at least 28 feet, and the width of the straight to the first obstacle must remain at least 28 feet. The width of the straight to the second obstacle must be at least 25 feet; after that, the width of other straights must be at least 20 feet (see figure 8.1).

RIDERS

Riders compete in several different classes. In the following sections you'll learn how those classes are broken down and how they transfer to the final race of the competition.

Classes

Riders are categorized based on age, gender, general skill level, status as an amateur or professional, and wheel size. The categories are as follows:

- Novice
- Girl
- Intermediate
- Expert
- Oldest riders of the day: novice
- Oldest riders of the day: girl
- Oldest riders of the day: intermediate
- Oldest riders of the day: expert
- Girls cruiser
- Cruiser
- Opens
- Pro/elite

Local or national points are awarded for all novice, intermediate, expert, cruiser, and girls' classes. Open classes are offered at all events, and they are combined when necessary to meet minimum participation requirements of two riders per race. These open classes combine age and proficiency levels and have no point value except in designated series.

Transfers

Overall winners in every class or combined class are determined by a final race of no more than eight riders, called a main. After the last round of motos, all those riders in motos with five or more participants who are ranked fourth or better (or all but the lowest-ranked rider in motos of four or fewer participants) transfer to the main. If this group numbers more than eight, they transfer to a series

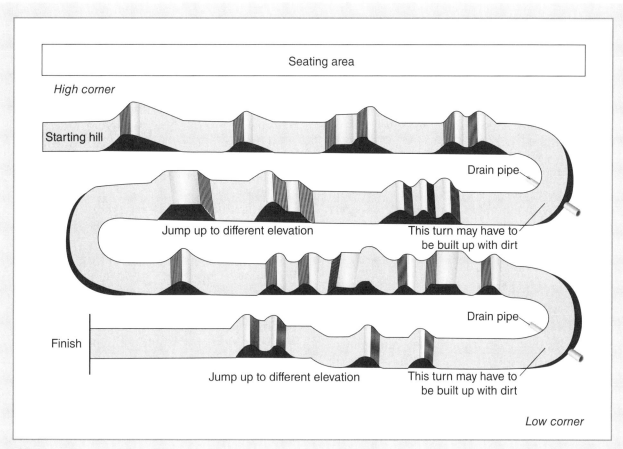

Seating area

High corner

Starting hill

Drain pipe

Jump up to different elevation

This turn may have to be <u>built</u> up with dirt

Drain pipe

Finish

Jump up to different elevation

This turn may have to be built up with dirt

Low corner

▶ **Figure 8.1** An example of a BMX racing course.

Adapted from a track diagram provided courtesy of the National Bicycle League. Special thanks to Erma Miller at NBL.

of qualifying rounds that reduce their number to no more than eight. Mains are also conducted for all point classes having six or fewer riders, with the rider ranked last after the last round of motos being eliminated from the main. However, a track operator can use any qualifying system that fits the track's locale. This change must be submitted to the governing body in a detailed document explaining the alternate system. Therefore, qualifying systems can change from venue to venue.

APPAREL/EQUIPMENT

Riders are required to wear helmets, with a permanent strap, in good condition that meet or exceed recognized bicycle safety standards.

Full-face helmets are recommended. Mouth guards are required and must be used with all open-face helmets. Riders are encouraged to wear long-sleeved shirts, long pants (short loose pant legs can be worn if they are tear resistant and in combination with shin pads approved by the track operator), and shoes that cover the toes. If knee pads and elbow pads are worn, they must be approved prior to racing. Pads on the bicycle's top tube, the handlebar crossbar, and the stem that connects the bars to the fork are recommended.

Bikes must have two wheels of matching size. The wheels on a 20-inch bike must have tires with an inflated diameter not exceeding 22.5 inches in diameter, and the wheels of a cruiser or those in the novice class must have tires with an inflated diameter greater than 22.5 inches. Twelve-, 16-, and 18-inch diameters are all accepted. The wheel diameter for those racing in intermediate, expert, girl, or pro can be 20 inches maximum.

Bikes for those racing in the novice class must be standard flat pedal only. Interlocking-pedal cleat systems, magnetic systems, or toe strap or clip systems are all exclusively for intermediate riders or higher.

Each bike must have an operating braking system. Both hand and foot brake are accepted.

Each bike must be in good condition and equipped with a number plate. Motocross-style handlebars can't exceed 30 inches and must have grips that completely cover the bar ends.

The following equipment is prohibited:

- Drop-style handlebars
- Kick stands, side stands, chain guards, and reflectors
- Axles that extend more than one-quarter inch beyond the hub nuts, unless they are covered to prevent injury to any rider who might come in contact with them
- Bikes with freestyle-type pegs
- Two-way radios facilitating communication between a rider and any other person during a race or practice

All equipment is subject to approval by the governing body or the track operator.

RULES

Only riders who are officially registered can ride or practice on any portion of the course on the day of the event. Racers are expected to check moto sheets to make sure they are in the correct class, race, and lane. Failure to show up or to be in the correct lane can lead to disqualification. Racers must make their way to the staging area 1 minute after hearing their names called. No one except riders and parents of racers ages 6 through 8 are allowed in the staging area. A racer can place the bike's front wheel over the gate before the race to delay the start due to difficulties he may be having.

At the start, each rider's front wheel is placed against the gate and is grounded and stationary during the starter's call. Racers ages 6 through 8 can be assisted in balancing their bikes on the gate, but people assisting them cannot have their hands in contact with either the rider or the bike once the starter's sequence has begun.

A rider who starts a race from a gate position that wasn't assigned to her will be scored in last place, regardless of her actual finish, if another rider in the race protests the offense. Also, a rider whose wheel breaks the gate before it is dropped can be disqualified because this means a gate jump has occurred. If the gate drops and a racer is not ready, a rerun does not occur, and the race continues.

A rider intentionally blocking or impeding another racer during the first 30 feet may be disqualified. A rider cannot come into contact with another rider's body or bike during a race with the intent of impeding that rider. This could lead to disqualification.

Any rider who leaves the track at any point during a race must reenter the track at the first available safe opportunity. Riders cannot leave the track to gain an advantage over other riders when reentering during the race. This means no obstacles can be avoided. (Jumps, chalk lines, hay bales, cones, or any other things that mark turns are obstacles. When the same things are used to mark a straightaway, they are not obstacles.) A racer who reenters ahead of other contestants must wait until he is back in his original position to continue.

If at least three riders fall before the frontmost part of the first jump, the race must be restarted. Any rider who is the victim of a foul will not be returned to the position she had before the foul occurred unless the foul took place between the last obstacle and the finish line.

Riders must finish the race with the same bike they started with. If two bikes become entangled, they must be fully untangled in order to continue. Riders may push or pull their bikes over the finish line, but they must be in contact with the bike as it crosses.

Any rider protesting a particular race or incident must present his case to the head official within 10 motos after the moto it occurred in. Officials can call fouls or disqualify riders without receiving a protest. If officials interfere with a race, only the head official has the power to call a rerun. Poor surface conditions can also prompt a rerun.

A yellow flag displayed by a race official indicates the approximate location of a dangerous condition on the track; a red flag indicates the race has been stopped.

Track operators can modify rules in consideration of track conditions but only to make the race safer. All modifications must be communicated to the racers. The race can also be postponed before or during the race for inclement weather.

Scoring

Each rider's plate number must appear on the moto sheet for the rider to be scored. A rider must participate in at least one moto of competition to receive any points for the event.

Not racing in the main event, starting but not finishing, and being disqualified all lead to a last-place finish. A rider who has been disqualified may still be eligible for other races at the event.

A rider is considered to have finished a race when any part of her person or bicycle breaks the vertical plane of the finish line, providing that she and the bike are in contact at that moment.

For trophy events, riders are assigned point scores equal to the sum of their finishes in the motos that they raced. Riders who either do not start or do not finish a race are given no points for that event. Points used in this system are referred to as transfer points when they are used to determine transfer status and as award points when they are used to determine award status. Transfer or award positions in a qualifying race or in a main are equivalent to the finish positions of the riders (except when classes are combined in a single race).

Each race has a predetermined number of qualifying spots, and the riders finishing in those spots advance. First, second, and third place receive 1, 2, and 3 points respectively. The riders with the fewest points after three motos advance. Ties are resolved in favor of the rider who earns the lower number of points in the third moto. Missing a transfer system race leads to no penalty. Missing a total points race leads to the rider receiving points equal to the total number of riders in that race plus an extra point.

Video assistance can be used but only at national events. Riders have 10 motos to dispute any finishes. The head official can refer to the video at any point for scoring purposes. If any technical difficulties occur, final decisions are made using the scoring sheets.

Point Charts

See tables 8.1 through 8.4 for point charts for district, state/provincial, national, and elite classes.

Conduct

Riders can be penalized or suspended for unsporting conduct, including being disrespectful or abusive to other riders or officials, using radio assistance, betting or soliciting bets, cheating, using drugs, stimulants, or intoxicants, misrepresenting age or proficiency, sandbagging (to avoid being moved up to a higher proficiency level), destruction of private property, and physical violence.

Riders can also be sanctioned for actions of their parents or pit teams (assisting rider physically, verbally or nonverbally, or inappropriate conduct).

Team riding can lead to disqualification. This is when competitors allow team members to pass to affect the end result. Ghost riding is also not allowed and can lead to a 1-year suspension. Ghost riding occurs when competitors have someone else race on their behalf. The race in which the ghost rider participates is also forfeited. Racing out of class can also lead to a suspension.

TERMS

A **berm** is the raised portion of dirt in a turn on the track that allows riders to ride through corners and maintain speed and momentum.

For transfer purposes only, a rider is awarded 2 points of **CR (credit)** plus the number of riders in the moto for his first DNS (did not start). He is not awarded any moto points.

Any rider who starts but fails to finish receives a **DNF (did not finish)**, which is equal to the number of riders in the moto. Last-place moto points are awarded to this rider.

A rider who fails to start a race is scored as a **DNS (did not start)**. No moto points are awarded to this rider.

Similarly, a rider who fails to race in any race at a particular event is scored as a **DNR (did not race)**. No moto points are awarded to this rider.

A **double** is a variably sized jump consisting of two rollers. A double is also the act of jumping and clearing two obstacles.

TABLE 8.1

District Award Point Chart

Amateur points table			
Place	Novice	Intermediate	Expert/girl/cruiser
1st	25 points	50 points	100 points
2nd	20 points	40 points	80 points
3rd	15 points	30 points	60 points
4th	12 points	25 points	50 points
5th	10 points	20 points	40 points
6th	7 points	15 points	30 points
7th	5 points	10 points	20 points
8th	3 points	5 points	10 points

All riders receive 1 point for each rider in their class.

Adapted from a track diagram provided courtesy of the National Bicycle League, 2017, *Official Rules of Competition.* Available: http://s3.amazonaws.com/bmxwebserverprod/attachments/208242/2017_Rulebook.pdf.

TABLE 8.2

State/Provincial Award Point Chart

Gold Cup/state/provincial points table			
Place	Novice	Intermediate	Expert/girl/cruiser
1st	18 points	19 points	20 points
2nd	17 points	18 points	19 points
3rd	16 points	17 points	18 points
4th	15 points	16 points	17 points
5th	14 points	15 points	16 points
6th	13 points	14 points	15 points
7th	12 points	13 points	14 points
8th	11 points	12 points	13 points
DNQ	10 points	10 points	10 points

There are no rider points added to this points table.

Adapted from a track diagram provided courtesy of the National Bicycle League, 2017, *Official Rules of Competition.* Available: http://s3.amazonaws.com/bmxwebserverprod/attachments/208242/2017_Rulebook.pdf.

TABLE 8.3

National Point Chart

National amateur points table			
Place	Novice	Intermediate	Expert/girl/cruiser
1st	60 points	120 points	240 points
2nd	50 points	100 points	200 points
3rd	40 points	80 points	160 points
4th	30 points	60 points	120 points
5th	20 points	40 points	80 points
6th	10 points	20 points	40 points
7th	8 points	15 points	30 points
8th	5 points	10 points	20 points

All riders receive 1 point for each rider in their class.

Adapted from a track diagram provided courtesy of the National Bicycle League, 2017, *Official rules of competition*. Available: http://s3.amazonaws.com/bmxwebserverprod/attachments/208242/2017_Rulebook.pdf.

TABLE 8.4

Pro Point Chart

National pro points table			
Place	AA/Pro/Women Pro/Vet Pro/A Pro	Semi points	Quarter points
1st	240 points		
2nd	200 points		
3rd	160 points		
4th	120 points		
5th	80 points	12 points	4 points
6th	40 points	10 points	3 points
7th	30 points	8 points	2 points
8th	20 points	6 points	1 points

The Pro season begins January 1 of each year and concludes at the Grand National.
All riders receive 1 point for each rider in their class.

Adapted from a track diagram provided courtesy of the National Bicycle League, 2017, *Official rules of competition*. Available: http://s3.amazonaws.com/bmxwebserverprod/attachments/208242/2017_Rulebook.pdf.

The ranking that a rider receives within a class or district at the end of the points season is the rider's **earned number**.

When a rider's wheels leave the ground over a jump or obstacle, she is said to be **getting air**.

The first person to take the lead in the race out of the gate is called a **holeshot**.

The **lip** is the top part of the front of a jump, which generally sends a rider into the air over the obstacle. The lip is also known as the *takeoff*.

The final race of the event in any given class is the **main**. Once riders have qualified through their motos and other quarter- and semifinals, the main determines the riders' final placings for awards and points.

When a rider keeps his back wheel on the surface of the track over a jump to keep traction or improve momentum, this move is called a **manual**.

A **moto** is a single race for one of the many groups and proficiencies held during a BMX event. It is similar to a heat in other sports; the first rider to cross the finish line is the winner of that moto.

A small obstacle (jump) on a BMX course with a smooth, rounded front and top and a long backside is called a **roller**. Rollers are usually no larger than 3 feet tall.

The **starting gate** is a structure at the beginning of the track that holds up to eight riders. When triggered by an electronic voice box, the front portion of the gate falls forward, giving all riders an equal chance to start the race.

A **step-up** is similar to a double but with two different-sized rollers. Typically the first roller is smaller and the second roller is taller, forcing a rider to jump higher (step up) to clear the obstacle.

A **tabletop** is an obstacle with a lip on the front side; a flattened top; and a smooth, rolling backside.

In a **two-moto scoring system**, riders race two times. The score for the first race is placed in the first column on the moto sheet; the score for the second race is placed in the third column. The riders' best finish of the two races is placed in the second column, thus creating three scores and points for three races.

OFFICIALS

Officials for BMX races include

- a director of competition, who governs the sport at the national level;
- a track operator, who overlooks all officials, scorers, and riders at the event;
- a head official, who makes final decisions on disputes at the event;
- a referee, the highest-ranking official at the event, who controls the orderly progress of the event;
- a clerk of course, who is responsible for licensing, registration, and classification of the participants;
- a head scorer, located at the finish line to accurately determine race finishes;
- scorers, who record the finish positions of riders;
- inspectors, who inspect bicycles and safety equipment to ensure compliance with rules;
- stagers, who maintain order in the staging lanes at the starting gates;
- a starter, who conducts the start of the race; and
- corner marshals, who monitor the riders on the track and signal to the referee or other officials anything that warrants their attention.

ORGANIZATIONS

American Bicycle Association
1645 W. Sunrise Blvd.
Gilbert, AZ 85233
480-961-1903
www.ababmx.com

Union Cycliste Internationale
Ch. de la Mêlée 12
1860 Aigle
Switzerland
41 24 468 58 11
www.uci.ch

USA Cycling
210 USA Cycling Pt., Ste. 100
Colorado Springs, CO 80919
719-434-4200
www.usacycling.org

Bocce

Irinmeiff/Dreamstime.com

Bocce is considered the oldest sport known to history; graphic representations of the game have been found that date as far back as 5200 BC. Today, bocce is played all over the world. The exposure of bocce grew after the Romans, having learned the game from the Greeks, began spreading it across their empire. Bocce as we know it today is most closely linked to the bocce that was played by the Romans. Originally, coconuts were used as balls, and later on the Romans started carving balls out of olive wood. Although the material of the equipment has changed over the years, the objective of the games is still the same; rolling a round object on a flat surface toward a fixed target to try and come as close to it as possible. In North America, bocce is mostly played on grass, while in Europe you can find both natural greens and synthetic courts. Since the 1896 Bocce Olympics, the sport has grown on the international stage, and now it is the third most participated-in sport after soccer and golf.

OVERVIEW

Objective: Win the frame by reaching 15 points as a team.

Number of Players: Either one on one or teams of two or three.

Scoring: During their turn of play, each member of the team throws a set number of balls toward a fixed target called a pallino. Players make their shots anywhere between zone A and zone B on a level playing surface 26.5 meters long. The objective is to place the ball as close to the pallino as possible. The team with the closest ball to the pallino counts points for the frame.

Length of Game: Varies, depending on length of frame determined in advance. Fifteen is a common point total.

COURT

The bocce court is 26.5 meters long and 4 to 4.5 meters wide, with wooden or nonmetal planks, 5 centimeters high, that make up the boundaries of the two sides (see figure 9.1). At the end of each court there are swinging headboards; they are hinged to the sideboards but are left unfastened to prevent the ball from bounding back. Each court is marked with transverse colored lines on the court surface and sideboards with the same distance between lines. The vertical reference lines on the sideboards are measured to match the reference lines on the court's surface. The bottom of the court must be made of synthetic material or be natural ground.

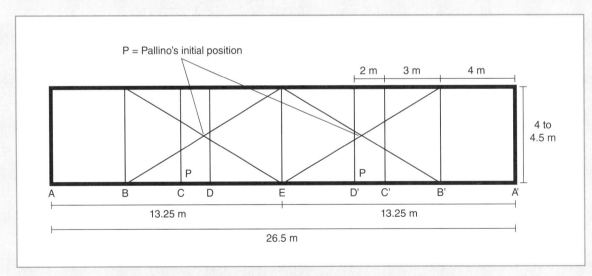

▶ **Figure 9.1** The dimensions and features of a bocce court.

PLAYERS

Games can be played as singles (1 on 1), doubles (2 on 2), or triples (3 on 3). Each player takes the correct number of balls—two per individual for doubles or triples, four each for singles—and a captain from each team is identified. In team play, one substitution can be made during the game, and it must only be done at the end of a frame.

EQUIPMENT

The bocce balls and pallino used must both be round and made of a synthetic material that does not contain any other substance that would throw off their balance. Each team must have a set of bocce balls that are distinct in color from the opposing team. Senior leagues play with bocce balls that are 107 millimeters in diameter and weigh 920 grams. Junior and women's leagues must use bocce balls that measure 106 mm in diameter and weigh 900 grams. The size and weight of the pallino is 4 centimeters in diameter and 60 grams with a 1-millimeter tolerance on the diameter and a 5-gram tolerance on weight.

The scoreboard for bocce looks similar to that of a clock face, with numbers from 1 to 12 positioned around a circle. An arrow hand points to the score for either the red or the green team. To verify points, measuring devices such as measuring tape (12 to 25 feet long), a bocce cup measurer, or a measuring rod can be used. The referee uses signaling devices such as a flag or paddle to identify which team is to be throwing.

RULES

Before the game begins, the court must be prepared; once the court is confirmed as being flat and even to play on, a draw takes place between the teams to determine who has the pallino advantage. The team losing the draw picks its side.

The pallino is tossed underhand from behind the indicated foul line by the team having won the draw. Placement of the pallino must be somewhere across the center line.

While waiting their turn, players must stand behind the area A-B or A'-B' in figure 9.1.

When throwing a bocce ball, players must not pass beyond the indicated foul line. Each team continues to play its turn until it has established a point. A player's turn is over when the ball has come to a rest and has been marked.

Once a point has been made, the turn passes to the opposing team, which then must make a shot until it has successfully rested its ball closer to the pallino or all four balls are thrown. Play switches back to the initial team to attempt to gain the point and get their shot closest to the pallino. The points are tallied at the end of each frame. A total of 15 points are necessary to win a game.

Teams switch sides after each frame, and the pallino is thrown by the team that won in the previous round. If the throw is irregular, then it goes to the opposing team. If the opposing team is unsuccessful in achieving a valid throw, the referee will call the shot void and place the pallino in position P. The first ball of the round is thrown by the team that acquired the pallino at the start of the frame.

Practice Throws

When both teams are present on the court, practice throws can be taken: full frame, one up and one down, starting at the A line. Practice throws are also conducted in the case of a change of court or reschedule of match due to acts of God.

The Pallino

On an initial throw of the pallino, it must rest in the E zone of the court (see figure 9.1). If it falls before this area, is resting on the E line, or is found within 13 centimeters of the sideboards, it is void. If during play, the pallino leaves the court, hits a player or referee, or becomes stuck on the sideboard, the play is void, and the frame is played from the beginning on the same side where it was started. If all balls have left the court and only the pallino stands, the team responsible for the balls going out of the court must play another ball to keep the game moving. If the pallino moves on its own due to outside intervention, it must be returned to the original position where it was marked or to a place that won't jeopardize either team's chances of winning the frame.

Throwing the Ball

A punto, raffa, or volo throw can be used. Raffa and volo throws must be declared before being thrown or the player risks a penalty. While making one of these shots, if the player's foot touches a sideboard, the shot is void. The throwing line cannot be passed with the forward foot. If the ball hits the headboard or sideboard before it hits another object, the ball is also void. Once a ball has been played, it cannot be moved or made to stop intentionally; this action will result in the maximum number of points (total number of balls the team has) being awarded to the other team.

Rules for balls on court are as follows:

▪ A ball in play that hits the sideboards and becomes stuck before hitting anything else is void and will be replayed from the original position. If the ball exits the court and hits an obstacle before reentering the court, it is also considered void.

▪ If while in motion a ball hits another object on the court and keeps moving, it is to be left in position once it stops.

▪ If a foreign object enters the court and interferes with play, the ball or the pallino must be rethrown.

▪ With a punto shot, if two balls end up resting at the same point, the team that was throwing the last ball has a chance to break the tie and score a point. If the teams have thrown all their balls and there is still a tie, the round is void and thus begins again from the same starting side.

Types of Hits

▪ Direct: The ball hits and displaces the pallino or another ball. If the displacement is more than 70 centimeters, the shot is void, and the object that has been moved is placed back in its original spot.

▪ Chain hit: A thrown ball hits another ball or pallino, which then hits a third. If the total distance that both objects are displaced is more than 70 centimeters, a void results, and the objects must be placed in their original locations.

▪ Hit with consequences: A thrown ball travels and displaces one or more objects. If this happens and the displaced objects don't conform to the preceding types of hits, and the thrown object has traveled more than 70 centimeters, the

thrown object will rest in its place while all other displaced objects will be moved back to their original markings.

TERMS

A **frame** is a round of play where all of the bocce balls are thrown and points are assigned based on where they land. When a frame is complete, another is started in the opposite direction.

A **pallino** is a small ball that is used as the fixed target in the game. It is the reference point that players try to come close to.

A **pallino advantage** refers to the team that is able to throw the pallino. The advantage is that this team throws the first ball.

The pallino is placed on the central point of the court where there is a permanent mark, also known as **point P**.

The **punto** throw is one that is thrown with the intention to get as close to the pallino as possible. This throw is only valid with a nod from the official.

A **raffa throw** is one that aims at hitting another ball or the pallino. A valid raffa throw must be done from behind the B-B line and must land within the D-D area (see figure 9.1).

A direct hit to an object would be done with a **volo throw**. A wish to make a volo throw must be declared to the referee, who then draws a 40-centimeter arch around the declared object. If your throw lands in the arch, the shot is void, and all disturbed objects are moved back in place.

OFFICIALS

The referee acts as an official who enforces all rules of the game, starts and stops play, measures shots, and grants points to the teams. All equipment, including the ball and pallino, must be verified by a referee for use in the match, making sure they meet the correct specifications. During the game, the referee calls the points of each frame and reports points earned to the score keepers. It is the job of the referee to handle all disputes and provide the final word on a resolution.

With the referee's approval, a coach can call a 2-minute timeout up to three times during a game. A referee, with valid reason, can call a timeout of up to 10 minutes.

MODIFICATIONS

- Depending on the location where the game is being played, the local officials may add environmental or operational rules to the game in the interest of safety and fair play.
- Court sizes can differ; for example, in the Special Olympics, the bocce court is smaller than a standard court.
- By USBF standards, frames are played to a winning score of 15 points. However, normally a standard frame can be played to 12 unless it is the final.

ORGANIZATIONS

The United States Bocce Federation
http://usbf.us/index.html

Confederazione Boccistica International
Via Bossi, 23, P.O. Box 2739
6830 Chiasso
Switzerland
www.cbi-prv.org/index.cfm

Bocce Standards Association
Online reference only
www.boccestandardsassociation.org

World Bocce Association (WBA)
Elmhurst, IL
https://uia.org/s/or/en/1100019750

10

Bowling

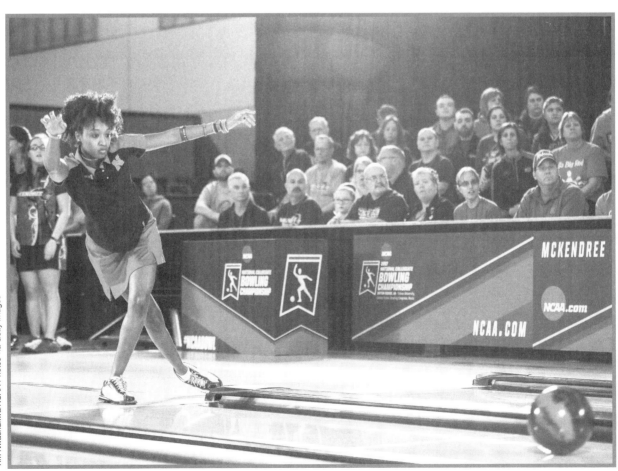

Tim Nwachukwu/NCAA Photos via Getty Images

Bowling was introduced in North America in the 1600s. Tenpin bowling, which is currently played, is believed to have sprung up when nine-pin bowling was declared illegal in Connecticut in the 1840s.

The American Bowling Congress formed in 1895 and adopted rules that were distributed by mail to nearly 1,000 bowling groups in the United States. The Women's International Bowling Congress was established in 1916. One of bowling's attractions is that it can be played by young and old, large and small, male and female. Bowling is one of the most popular recreational activities in the United States, with more than 46 million participants age 6 and older bowling each year. Its greatest growth is at the youth levels, especially in high schools, where bowling is the fastest-growing sport in this decade. The rules described in this chapter are for tenpin bowling.

OVERVIEW

Objective: To score the most points by knocking down pins with a ball rolled down a lane.

Scoring: Depends on the number of pins knocked down; scoring is increased by spares and strikes (see "Terms").

Number of Players: Played either between individuals or between teams, with up to five players on a team.

Length of Game: 10 frames.

Players take turns, rolling one frame at a time. In team play, players must bowl in the order they have designated and switch lanes after every frame, bowling five frames on their own lane and five on their opponent's. A player delivers two balls in each of the first nine frames, unless she scores a strike on the first ball by knocking down all the pins (in that case, only one ball is delivered). In the 10th frame, the player delivers either two or three balls. If she scores a strike, she rolls two more balls. If she scores a spare (by knocking down all the pins in two attempts), she rolls one more ball.

LANE

The lane, or alley, measures 60 feet from the foul line to the center of the head (first) pin (see figure 10.1). The total length of the lane to the back of the pin deck, where the pins stand, is 62.85 feet. A lane's width is 41 to 42 inches.

The pins are wood, plastic-coated wood, or synthetic material. Each pin is 15 inches tall and weighs between 3 pounds 6 ounces and 3 pounds 10 ounces. Pins are set 12 inches apart from each other in a triangular pattern on the pin deck.

The approach, or runway, which ends at the foul line, is a minimum of 15 feet. Grooved gutters (channels) on either side of the lane catch errant balls.

BOWLERS

Team captains enter lineups before the start of each scheduled series, sign the scorebooks, and have scores verified by the opposing team captain.

A lineup consists of three or more eligible players in five-player team leagues, unless rules

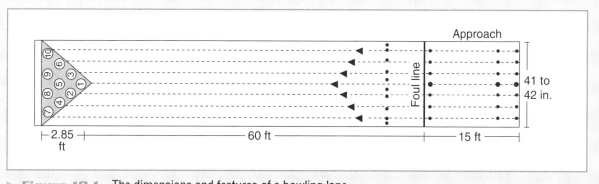

▶ **Figure 10.1** The dimensions and features of a bowling lane.

state two or more. Two or more eligible players make up a lineup in three- or four-player team leagues, and one eligible player is required for two-player team leagues.

Pacers are bowlers who fill in to balance the rotation of the teams. Scores bowled by pacers do not count toward team totals.

EQUIPMENT

The ball is made of a nonmetallic composition material (usually a plastic, urethane, resin, or particle compound) with a circumference no greater than 27 inches and a weight of no more than 16 pounds. It can have up to five holes for finger grips.

RULES

Following are rules that pertain to scoring, fouls, pinfalls, dead balls, and provisional balls.

Scoring

Except when a strike is scored, the number of pins knocked down by the player's first delivery is marked next to the small square in the upper right corner of that frame (see figure 10.2). The number of pins the player knocks down on the second delivery is marked inside the small square. If none of the pins is knocked down after two deliveries, the player marks the score sheet with a minus sign.

When a player scores a strike, he marks an X in the small square in the upper right corner of that frame. His final score for that frame is 10 (for the strike) plus however many pins he knocks

down in his next two deliveries. For example, if he rolls three consecutive strikes, his score for that first frame is 30 points. The score for a perfect game—12 strikes—is 300.

Fouls

A foul occurs when any part of the player's body encroaches on or goes beyond the foul line and touches any part of the lane or the foul line during or after a delivery. On a foul, the delivery counts, but any pins knocked down are not recorded. Except in the case of a deliberate foul, the player who fouls on her first delivery is still allowed her second delivery, but any pins knocked down on the first delivery are first respotted.

Pinfalls

Pinfalls are legal when pins are knocked down by the ball or by another pin, including a pin that rebounds from a side panel, rear cushion, or sweep bar when the bar is at rest on the pin deck. A pin that leans and touches the kickback or side partition is also considered to have legally fallen. These pins are called dead wood and must be removed before the next delivery.

Pinfalls are not legal when

- a ball leaves the lane before reaching the pins,
- a ball rebounds from the rear cushion and knocks down any pins,
- a pin is touched by the mechanical pin-setting equipment,
- a pin is knocked down while dead wood is being removed,

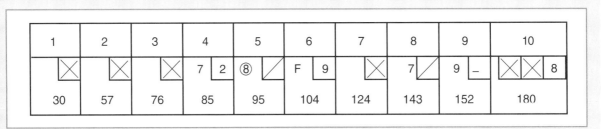

▶ **Figure 10.2** This scorecard shows strikes were bowled in frames 1 to 3. The bowler knocked down seven pins on the first ball in frame 4 and two pins on the second ball. Frame 10 shows two strikes and two pins left standing.

Adapted from American Bowling Congress/Women's International Bowling Congress/Young American Bowling Congress, *1995-96 Playing Rules Book* (Greendale, WI: American Bowling Congress, 1995), 6.

- a pin is knocked down by a human pinsetter, or
- the bowler fouls.

Any pins that have illegally fallen on a player's first delivery must be respotted before the second delivery. A pin that rebounds onto the lane and remains standing is not considered to have been knocked down.

If the pins are improperly set and the player delivers a ball, the delivery and pinfall count. Once a delivery has been made, the pin position cannot be changed unless the pinsetter moved or misplaced a pin.

Dead Ball

When a dead ball is called, the delivery does not count. Any pins knocked down with a dead ball must be respotted, and the player receives a new delivery. A dead ball occurs in the following cases:

- After a delivery, a player immediately reports that one or more pins were missing from the setup.
- A human pinsetter interferes with any standing pin before the ball reaches the pins.
- A human pinsetter interferes with a downed pin before it stops rolling.
- A player bowls out of turn or on the wrong lane.
- A player is interfered with during delivery. (The player may choose to accept the resulting pinfall.)
- Any pin is knocked down as a player delivers the ball but before the ball reaches the pins.
- The ball contacts a foreign obstacle on the playing surface.

Provisional Ball

When a protest involving a foul, legal pinfall, or dead ball is made and is not immediately resolved, a provisional ball could be rolled. A record of both scores (with and without the provisional ball) for the frame is kept, and the protest is referred to the league board or tournament director for a decision.

The procedures for rolling a provisional ball vary according to the situation. For the first ball of a frame, or the second ball in the 10th frame, if the first ball was a strike, these rules apply:

- For a protested foul, the player completes the frame and then bowls one provisional ball at a full setup of pins.
- For a protested pinfall, the player completes the frame and then bowls one provisional ball at the same setup that would have occurred had the disputed pin or pins not fallen.
- For a protested dead ball, the player completes the frame and then bowls a complete provisional frame.

For a spare attempt or third ball of the 10th frame, these rules apply:

- For a protested foul or illegal pinfall, no provisional ball is necessary.
- For a protested dead ball, the player bowls a provisional ball at the same setup that was standing when the disputed ball was bowled.

TERMS

A **double** occurs when a player rolls two consecutive strikes.

An **error** is made by a player who leaves any pins standing in a frame, unless the pins left standing after the first delivery constitute a split.

A **frame** consists of two deliveries by a player (unless the first delivery is a strike, in which case the frame is over).

A **spare** is scored by a player who knocks down any remaining pins on the second delivery of the frame. The player scores 10 points plus the number of pins he knocks down on his next delivery.

A **split** refers to a setup of pins left standing after the first delivery, when the head pin is down and the remaining pins are far apart.

A **strike** is recorded by a player who knocks down all the pins on her first delivery. A strike cannot occur on the second delivery, even if no pins were knocked down on the first delivery. A strike counts 10 pins plus the number of pins the player knocks down on her next two deliveries.

A **triple**, or **turkey**, refers to three successive strikes by one player.

OFFICIALS

Officials can be used for both scoring and judging fouls, but automatic scoring and foul-detection devices are typically used.

MODIFICATIONS

The following modifications are taken from the United States Bowling Congress.

In individual match play format, the scores for the corresponding players in each team's lineups are compared, with the higher score being awarded the specified number of points. Teams with less than a full lineup receive a score of zero for each open position for the purposes of determining the winner of the individual point(s).

In the Baker system, each player in the lineup completes one frame in successive order until she has completed 10 frames. The player who begins the 10th frame of the game executes all deliveries for that frame. The scores of the opposing teams are then compared, with the higher score being awarded the specified number of points. Teams with less than a full lineup receive a score of zero for each open position in the rotation for the purposes of determining the team total score.

In team match play format, the individual scores of the players in the lineup are added together and compared with the score of the opposing team. The team with the higher score for each game is awarded the specified number of points. Teams with less than a full lineup receive a score of zero for each open position for the purposes of determining the team total score.

ORGANIZATIONS

European Bowling Proprietors Association
P.O. Box 13044
600 13 Norrkoping
Sweden
www.ebpabowl.com

The National Bowling Association
9944 Reading Rd.
Evendale, OH 45241-3106
513-769-3596
www.tnbainc.org

Professional Bowlers Association
55 E. Jackson Blvd., Ste. 401
Chicago, IL 60604
206-332-9688
www.pba.com

United States Bowling Congress
621 Six Flags Dr.
Arlington, TX 76011
800-514-2695
www.bowl.com

11

Boxing

Boxing dates back more than 5,000 years. It became a more formally organized sport in 18th-century England; bare-knuckle contests were the norm until the 1870s, when padded gloves were introduced.

The sport is contested at both amateur and professional levels; boxers who become professionals cannot return to amateur status. Amateur boxing begins at age 8 and continues through several age divisions (up through age 40) and weight categories. The length and number of rounds depend on the division. Boxing grew in popularity in the 1900s in the United States, but because of its violent nature, it has had a controversial history and has declined in popularity in recent years.

OVERVIEW

Objective: To score points by landing scoring blows on the opponent.

Scoring: Determined by the number of scoring blows a boxer lands each round (see "Scoring").

Number of Boxers: Two.

Length of Match: Three or four rounds, depending on the age and classification of the boxers.

Boxers 17 and 18 years old (youth) box three 3-minute rounds. Boxers 15 and 16 years old (junior) box three 2-minute rounds; 13 and 14-year olds (intermediate) box three 1.5-minute rounds; 8 to 12 year olds box (peewee and bantam) three 1-minute rounds.

The boxers try to land legal blows and score points. If a boxer is knocked down, the referee begins to count to 10 (see "Count"). For the ways in which a boxer can earn a decision (win), see "Decisions." In Olympic-style boxing, safety comes first.

RING

The ring is a square, 16 to 20 feet long on each side, measured from inside the ropes (see figure 11.1). The ring is bordered by at least four ropes, made of manila, a synthetic, or plastic and not less than 1 inch in diameter. All rings have two spacer ties on each side of the ring to secure the ropes. The apron of the ring extends at least 2 feet

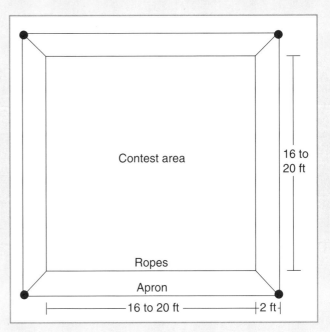

▶ **Figure 11.1** The dimensions and features of a boxing ring.

Data from USA Boxing, 2006, *Technical Rules*. Available: http://www.usaboxingofficials .org/RULEBOOK/USABoxingTechnicalRules2006.pdf.

beyond the ropes. The floor of the ring is not more than 4 feet above ground.

BOXERS

Boxers weigh in on the day of competition. A boxer must weigh more than the minimum for the weight classes shown in tables 11.1 and 11.2 and no more than the maximum for the weight class they want to box in. The ringside physician must deem the boxer fit before weigh-in. Women may compete against other women. Facial hair is not allowed, although beards may be allowed in some masters competitions or for religious purposes. Boxers may be required to seek exemption prior to competition. No type of body accessory is permitted during a bout.

EQUIPMENT

Approved headgear and custom-made or individually fitted mouthpieces must be worn. Gloves are 10 ounces for weight classes up to 141 pounds and 12 ounces for heavier weight

TABLE 11.1
Elite Male Weight Classes

Class	Pounds
Light flyweight	108
Flyweight	114
Bantamweight	123
Lightweight	132
Light welterweight	141
Welterweight	152
Middleweight	165
Light heavyweight	178
Heavyweight	201
Super heavyweight	>201

Adapted from United States Amateur Boxing, Inc., USA Boxing: Official Rules 1995-1997 (Colorado Springs: USAB, 1995r), 57, 59.

TABLE 11.2
Elite Female Weight Classes

Class	Pounds
Flyweight	106
Bantamweight	112
Featherweight	119
Lightweight	125
Light welterweight	132
Welterweight	141
Middleweight	152
Light heavyweight	165
Heavyweight	178
Super heavyweight	>178

0Adapted from United States Amateur Boxing, Inc., USA Boxing: Official Rules 1995-1997 (Colorado Springs: USAB, 1995r), 57, 59.

classes, except for masters competitors, who wear 12-ounce gloves regardless of their weight class.

RULES

During each bout, referees must be prepared to count and to watch for fouls.

Count

If a boxer is knocked down during a round, the referee commands the action to stop and begins to count to 10, with 1 second between numbers, indicating each second with their hand. The count begins 1 second after the boxer is down. The referee motions the boxer who caused the knockdown to a neutral corner; the referee will not start or continue the count until the opponent goes to the neutral corner.

At the count of 8, the referee decides to continue the bout, terminate it, or continue the count.

The bout never continues before the count of 8, even if the downed boxer rises and is ready to continue before then. If the boxer cannot continue at the end of the count, the bout is over, and the opponent wins.

If a boxer is down at the end of a round, the referee will count as usual. If both boxers are down at the same time, counting continues as long as one remains down. If both remain down

past the count of 10, the bout is stopped, and the boxer who has the most points wins. If a boxer has three counts in one round or four counts in a bout, the bout is stopped and the opponent wins.

Fouls

A referee may caution, warn, or disqualify a boxer who commits a foul. A referee may not caution a boxer without stopping the bout; they must stop the bout to issue a warning. If a referee warns a boxer about a particular foul, they may not later issue a caution for the same foul. Three cautions for the same foul require a warning. A boxer is disqualified if they receive three warnings in one bout.

Examples of fouls include

- hitting below the belt, holding, tripping, kicking, or butting;
- using head butts or blows;
- hitting with the shoulder, forearm, or elbow;
- pushing or shoving;
- pressing an arm or elbow into the opponent's face;
- pressing the opponent's head back over the ropes;
- hitting the opponent's back, neck, kidneys, or back of head;

- hitting with an open glove (called slapping);
- hitting while holding the ropes;
- hitting an opponent who is down or who is rising;
- holding and hitting;
- locking the opponent's arm or head;
- not stepping back when ordered to break;
- using aggressive or offensive language;
- spitting out the mouthpiece;
- lying on, wrestling, and throwing in the clinch;
- pivot blows, that is, backhand;
- speaking;
- behaving aggressively toward a referee;
- keeping the advanced hand straight in order to obstruct the opponent's vision;
- biting; and
- faking an injury.

Scoring

A scoring blow is one that lands directly with the knuckle part of the closed glove on any part of the front or sides of the head or body above the belt.

Each time a boxer scores a scoring blow, they are awarded a point. Scoring is also based on the domination of the competitor based on technical and tactical superiority and competitiveness. However, the number of scoring blows is the most important criteria. Points are totaled at the end of each round and placed on a scorecard. At the end of the bout, the judge adds the points for each boxer and circles the winner.

Decisions

Types of decisions are as follows:

- Win by points: The boxer with the most points wins.
- Win by abandon: If a boxer quits a bout voluntarily, the opponent wins. This also applies when a coach throws a towel into the ring or appears on the apron.
- Win by retirement: If a boxer quits a bout because of injury or fails to resume after a round break, the opponent wins.

- Win by RSC or by RSC-I: A referee may stop a bout if a boxer is being outclassed or injured.
- Win by disqualification: If a boxer is disqualified, the opponent wins.
- Win by knockout: If a boxer cannot resume fighting before the 10 count, the opponent wins.
- Win by walkover: If a boxer fails to appear within 1 minutes of the bell, the opponent wins.

Injury

If the referee believes a boxer cannot continue because of injury, the referee may stop the bout and declare the opponent the winner. This decision is the referee's, although he may consult with a doctor. The ringside physician also has the right to terminate a bout for medical reasons. If the referee consults a doctor, they must abide by the doctor's recommendation.

TERMS

A referee may **caution** a boxer for a foul. The action stops for a caution.

A referee begins a **count** 1 second after a boxer is down. If the boxer is not ready to resume the bout by the count of 10, the bout is over.

A boxer is **disqualified** for fouls that have resulted in three warnings.

A boxer is **down** when any part of their body other than the feet touch the floor, when a boxer is hanging on the ropes, or when the boxer is standing but semiconscious and not fit to continue.

A **low blow** is a hit delivered below the beltline. This is a foul.

A boxer receives a **mandatory 8 count** if they go down. If the boxer is ready to go after a count of 8, the bout resumes. Even if the boxer is ready to go before 8, the referee will count to 8 before allowing the bout to resume.

A **round** is a determined length of time, depending on the division, in which the boxers compete before breaking. The number of rounds varies depending on the competition.

RSC (referee stopped the contest) refers to body or head injuries to one boxer that are severe or excessive enough to cause the referee to stop the bout and declare the opponent the winner.

A referee may issue a **warning** to a boxer for a foul. A warning gives 2 points to the boxer who did not commit the foul.

OFFICIALS

The referee controls the bout. There are three basic commands: "Stop," "Box," and "Break" (the latter in breaking a clinch). The referee may terminate a match at any time if it is too one-sided or if a boxer is endangered. The referee also issues cautions and warnings and may disqualify a boxer for fouls.

The judges independently judge the merits of the boxers and determine the winner. Either five or three judges are present. A timekeeper keeps time for each round and between rounds. During championship events, a three- or five-panel jury checks the scorecards of the judges to make sure that points and penalties are correctly recorded.

MODIFICATIONS

Amateur boxing uses the same set of rules worldwide. There are, of course, differences between amateur boxing rules and professional boxing rules. Here are some of the primary differences:

In amateur boxing, the main objective is to score points. The force of a blow or its effect on the opponent does not matter; a blow that knocks a boxer to the mat receives no more points than a regular blow. In professional boxing, more credit is given for knocking down an opponent.

In amateur boxing, head guards are mandatory; in professional boxing, head guards are prohibited. In amateur boxing, the referee has more control and cautions boxers if they are violating fundamentals or rules; in pro boxing, boxers are warned only for a harm foul, not for technique. Referees in amateur boxing stop a bout if a boxer is outclassed, which rarely happens in pro boxing.

ORGANIZATIONS

International Boxing Federation
899 Mountain Ave., Ste. 2C
Springfield, NJ 07081
973-564-8046
www.ibf-usba-boxing.com

USA Boxing
1 Olympic Plaza
Colorado Springs, CO 80909-5778
719-866-2323
www.teamusa.org

12

Canoeing and Kayaking

Comstock

Canoeing and kayaking offer several forms of competition, including sprint, slalom, freestyle, and wildwater racing. This chapter focuses on those four types of competitions.

Sprint's beginnings are traced to the early 1900s; the first sporting association for kayakers was founded in Copenhagen in 1924, and the first European championships were contested on flatwater in 1933. Slalom got its beginnings in Switzerland in 1932, coming from the idea of ski slalom. It began on flatwater and soon moved to whitewater. It is popular in North America and Europe and is also growing in popularity elsewhere. The freestyle worlds competition (then called rodeo) started in 1991 in England. Wildwater canoeing began in 1959, with most courses between 4 and 6 kilometers in length; sprint courses between 500 and 1,000 meters were added in 1988.

OVERVIEW

Sprint competitions take place on unobstructed flatwater courses of varying lengths; the fastest time wins. In slalom racing, competitors negotiate a rapid river course defined by gates. The objective is to record the fastest time while avoiding penalties in negotiating the course. The time of the run in seconds plus the penalty points determine a competitor's final score; the lowest score wins. In freestyle competitions, contestants demonstrate aerial stunts, evaluated by judges. In wildwater competitions, the start is directly upstream or downstream; no angled starts are allowed. Boats are held in the starting position until the start; competitors may use only standing starts. Individual starts are separated by at least 30 seconds; team starts have intervals of at least 1 minute.

COURSE

Following are basic descriptions of course requirements for flatwater, slalom, wildwater, and freestyle courses.

Flatwater Course

The course consists of nine straight lines which are each 9 meters wide. The lanes are made up of buoys placed every 10 meters along the three races distances of 200, 500, and 1000 meters. For long distance and marathon races held in flatwater, turning points are permitted and the courses typically vary between 5, 20, and 30 kilometers.

Slalom Course

The course must be at least 200 meters long, with 18 to 25 gates, where the gates are 1.2 to 3.5 meters in width. Six of those gates are required to be upstream and can be distinguish by red and green rings on the poles. Gates that are to be completed moving downstream are painted with green and white rings. All gates are required to be completed in numerical order beginning with one and must be completed in the correct direction as indicated by a diagonal red line on the opposite side of which the individual must pass.

Freestyle Course

Interpretive freestyle canoeing is similar to long program figure skating. The competition area is 25 by 50 meters; competitors must stay within the competition area. Paddlers must use a single-bladed paddle and paddle an open canoe to music of their choice. Music used must be no more than 5 minutes long. They must choreograph a routine that includes four compulsory maneuvers—axle, Christie, post, and either cross axle or cross post, with maneuvers for the rest of the routine being their choice. The scoring is 60 percent technical merit and 40 percent artistic merit.

Wildwater Course

The course for classic races can be approximately 5 to 10 kilometers long, whereas sprint races range from 200 to 600 meters. Whitewater difficulty can range from Class II to Class IV difficulty. Although there are some participants who specialize in distances most competitors race in both the classic and sprint events.

EQUIPMENT

The athlete's name must be placed on each side of the boat under the cockpit. Athletes should wear the appropriate official clothing with easy identification.

Trademarks and advertising on boats, accessories, and clothing may carry trademarks, advertising symbols, and written text. At the Olympics, however, stickers, logos, and symbols are extremely limited. The advertising of tobacco smoking and strong spirit drinks is not permitted. Images, symbols, and slogans unrelated to sport funding or political messages are not permitted.

Following are basic equipment requirements for flatwater, slalom, freestyle, and wildwater competitions.

Flatwater Equipment

Canoes and kayaks may be constructed of any material; electric or electronic devices, such as pumps, are not allowed. Kayaks may have one steering rudder and may be propelled only with double-blade paddles. Canoes may not have a steering rudder or any guiding apparatus; Canadian canoes may be propelled only with single-blade paddles. The paddles may not be fixed to the boat.

Slalom Equipment

Each boat must have handles attached no more than 30 centimeters from the bow and the stern. Handles may be an integral part of the boat construction or may be loops of rope. A competitor cannot tape the handles. If a competitor breaks or loses a paddle, she may use an extra paddle that she carries in the boat.

Freestyle Equipment

Paddles are a single blade with no ridge where the blade intersects with the shaft. Most freestyle paddles tend to have a blade that is wider than a typical touring paddle. They may be straight shaft or bent shaft. Typically solos use straights, while tandem paddlers use straights or bents. Paddlers may use a kneeling pad that runs the entire seating area. The pad can be larger if the paddler moves around in the boat. Boats are typically lighter weight, often wood ribs with Dacron skin, or of a lightweight composite, designed to be responsive to turning and heeling.

Wildwater Equipment

Wildwater boats must be rudderless. As with flatwater boats, kayaks are propelled only with a double-blade paddle and Canadian canoes only with a single-blade paddle.

RULES

In this section, you'll learn how competitions in flatwater, slalom, freestyle, and wildwater take place.

Flatwater Rules

Men's flatwater events include the 200, 500, 1,000, and 5,000 meter; women's races include the 200 meter, 500 meter, and 5,000 meter. A race involves at least three kayaks or canoes; if heats are necessary, lots are drawn to place competitors into the heats. Heats are not used, however, for 5,000-meter races. Lots are also used to determine the starting position.

At the start of a race, the bows of the boats must be on the starting line and stationary. An official uses a starter's pistol to begin the race. The starter may recall the race to realign the boats. If a racer makes a false start, they will be given a warning. Any racer who makes two false starts is disqualified. If a racer breaks a paddle within the first 25 meters, the starter will recall the race.

A competitor may not take pace or receive assistance from boats not in the race. Such boats may not proceed on the course, even outside the boundary buoys. In races up to 1,000 meters, competitors must stay in the middle of their marked lanes. In 5,000-meter races, they may go outside their lanes as long as they do not obstruct other competitors.

In races with turns, competitors must make the turns counterclockwise. If two competitors are approaching a turn together, the competitor on the outside must leave room for the competitor on the inside if the inside competitor's bow is even with the front edge of the cockpit of the outside boat. A competitor may touch a turning buoy as long as he doesn't gain an advantage from the touch.

A craft that is being passed cannot obstruct the craft overtaking it. The boat that is passing must, however, keep clear of the boat it is overtaking. A competitor who causes a collision may be disqualified.

A competitor finishes a race when the craft's bow crosses the finish line with all of the crew members in the boat. In case of a tie for a position that determines which boat will advance to the next level of competition, if not enough lanes are available to accommodate both boats at the next level, the two boats race again. This race takes place one hour after the last race of the day. If the two tie again, lots are drawn to determine who advances.

Slalom Rules

In individual slalom competitions, each craft is allowed two runs, the better of which counts. In team competitions, either one or two runs may be allowed. Team members may be substituted between runs.

Starts may be directly upstream or downstream; starts angled into or against the current are not allowed. Boats are held in position by the starter's assistant until the start. Slalom competitions are guided by rules covering gate and course negotiation, penalties, finish line and point calculation, and equipment.

Negotiating Gates   Competitors negotiate gates according to the established direction. A gate consists of two suspended poles painted with five green and five white rings for downstream gates and five red and five white rings for upstream gates. The poles are between 1.2 and 3.5 meters apart and are 3.5 to 5.0 centimeters in diameter. The lower end of each pole should be about 15 centimeters above the water.

The gates are numbered, and competitors must negotiate them in numerical order. Negotiation begins when a competitor crosses the line between the two poles or when a competitor's boat, body, or paddle touches a pole. Negotiation of a gate ends when a competitor begins to negotiate the next gate or when she finishes the race.

To correctly negotiate a gate, a competitor must

- maneuver his boat and body between the poles on the correct side of the gate;

- cross his boat between the poles at the same time as his body crosses between them;

- pass at least his entire head between the poles in the proper direction; and

- not touch a pole with his body, paddle, or boat for a faultless negotiation.

Penalties   Competitors are penalized for incorrect gate negotiations and other acts as follows:

- 2 points—touching one or both poles while correctly negotiating the gate. Repeated touching of the same pole or poles is penalized only once.

- 50 points—touching one or both poles while incorrectly negotiating the gate. Intentionally pushing a gate to facilitate negotiation, crossing a gate line while the body is upside down, and negotiating the gate in the wrong direction are 50-point penalties. Missing a gate and failing to cross the finish line within 15 seconds of teammates are also 50-point penalties.

A competitor is not penalized for undercutting a gate or for making repeated attempts at a gate, as long as she does not touch the poles or pass her body across the line between the poles. A competitor cannot be penalized more than 50 points at any one gate.

On the Course   A competitor who is being overtaken must give way if the section judge whistles for him to do so. The competitor who is passing, however, must be trying to negotiate the course properly. If he is passing because the competitor ahead has missed a gate, he cannot hinder the competitor as he approaches. Any competitor who is hindered may repeat the run if authorized to do so by the chief judge.

A craft is considered capsized when it has turned upside down and the competitor has left the boat. After a capsize, a competitor may not negotiate any further gates. An Eskimo roll is not a capsize.

Finish and Point Calculations   A competitor finishes when her body crosses the finish line (in team competition, when the first body in the boat crosses the line). In team events, all three craft must finish within 15 seconds of each other. The time for team events begins when the first boat starts and ends when the last boat finishes.

A competitor's or team's point total is figured by adding the time of the run, in seconds, plus penalty points. For example, a running time of 135.8 seconds plus 55 penalty points equals a final score of 190.8. If two competitors are tied, the one with the better noncounting run is placed ahead of the other competitor. A competitor who accepts outside assistance or leaves his boat is disqualified.

Freestyle Rules

In freestyle kayaking, each squirt boating competitor has three 60-second runs in the preliminary round. The best two rides count, and the top 10 competitors advance to the semifinals. In the semifinals, each competitor has two rides, and the best ride counts. In men's competitions, the top five advance to the finals; in women's competitions, the top four advance. In the finals, all competitors do one ride, and the lowest-scoring competitor is eliminated. This continues until only one competitor remains; this person is the winner.

As each ride is performed, three technical judges and three variety judges score the competitors. A competitor's technical score and style score are combined for a base score. A mystery score of 1 to 10 is transposed to a decimal system (1.1, 1.2, and so on, up to 2.0), and the base score is multiplied by the mystery score to determine the final score. The mystery score is based on a rider's ability to demonstrate a controlled and intentional "charc" (charging arc) going into the move, obvious control while down, and control on exit.

Wildwater Rules

In wildwater competitions, a craft being overtaken by another craft must allow passage if the competitor on the overtaking craft shouts, "Free!" If a competitor sees another in real danger, he must help him or risk disqualification for life. A competitor may resume competition after capsizing. If two or more competitors record the same score, the tie stands.

TERMS

A **brace** is a defensive maneuver in which a kayaker uses a paddle blade and hip action to keep upright.

Classes I to VI is the whitewater river rating system, from easiest to most difficult.

The **deck** is the top of the boat, which keeps the water out.

An **eddy** is a calm spot in whitewater, just downstream of a rock.

Flotation bags, filled with air, are fitted on either side of a kayak's walls to provide buoyancy in case of a capsize.

Kayak paddle blades are usually **offset**, which means the blades face different directions. The difference in blade direction is usually about 45 degrees.

A **spray skirt** fits around the rim of the boat and around the competitor's waist to keep water out.

A **sweep** is the primary stroke used to turn a boat.

OFFICIALS

Officials who supervise competitions include chief officials, starters, aligners, turning and course point judges, finishing line judges, timekeepers, and boat controllers.

ORGANIZATIONS

American Canoe Association
503 Sophia St., Ste. 100
Fredericksburg, VA 22401
540-907-4460
www.americancanoe.org

International Canoe Federation
Av. de Rhodanie 54
CH-1007 Lausanne
Switzerland
41 21 612 02 90
www.canoeicf.com

13

Cheerleading

In 1898, University of Minnesota student Johnny Campbell directed a crowd in a cheer at a football game, and soon after, the University of Minnesota formed a "yell leader" squad of six males. Cheerleading began as an all-male endeavor, but females began participating in 1923, incorporating gymnastics, tumbling, and megaphones into cheerleading.

Today, cheerleaders use organized routines that incorporate tumbling, dance, and stunting to lead cheers at sporting events and to compete in cheerleading competitions. Cheerleading organizations such as the American Association of Cheerleading Coaches and Administrators sprang up to create safety guidelines to lessen the chances of injury. The United States All Star Federation for Cheer and Dance Teams (USASF) was formed in 2003 to be the national governing body for all-star cheerleading and to create rules and standards for competitions.

OVERVIEW

Cheerleaders can compete at varying age and skill levels beginning at a level for ages 5 and younger. Teams consist usually of either all female or a mix of male and female cheerleaders, with each team having anywhere from 5 to 36 members. Teams have choreographed routines, performing tumbling, stunting, jumping, and dancing to their chosen music. Judges watch for illegal moves and score teams based on their synchronization, creativity, sharpness, showmanship, difficulty, and overall execution.

CHEERLEADERS

Under USASF rules, cheerleaders compete in these divisions:

- Tiny Novice Cheer—3 to 6 years
- Tiny Cheer—6 years and younger
- Mini Cheer—8 years and younger
- Youth Cheer—11 years and younger
- Junior Cheer—14 years and younger
- Senior Cheer—18 years and younger
- International Open Cheer—14 years and older
- Special Needs Cheer—any age
- Open Cheer—17 years and older

EQUIPMENT

Cheerleaders must wear soft-soled shoes while competing. No dance shoes, boots, or gymnastics slippers (or similar types of slippers) are allowed. Shoes must have a solid sole.

Jewelry of any kind is prohibited; this includes ear, nose, tongue, belly button, and facial rings, clear plastic jewelry, bracelets, necklaces, and pins on uniforms, among other types.

Any height-increasing apparatus used to propel a competitor is prohibited.

Flags, banners, signs, pom-poms, megaphones, and pieces of cloth are the only props allowed. Cheerleaders may not use props with poles or similar support apparatus in conjunction with any kind of stunt or tumbling. All props must be safely discarded out of harm's way (e.g., throwing a hard sign across the mat from a stunt would be illegal). Any uniform piece purposefully removed from the body and used for visual effect is considered a prop.

RULES

The guidelines and rules in this chapter come primarily from the USASF, which has guidelines for six levels of competition. These guidelines are geared toward Level 5 teams, which have age categories for 11 and younger, 14 and younger, and 10 through 18. Guidelines and rules are adjusted for various levels. Please note that some of these rules are illegal for high school sideline cheerleading or at those competitions that choose to use the National Federation of State High School Associations rule book. We will point out some of those differences along the way.

Tumbling

All tumbling must originate from and land on the performing surface, with one exception: A tumbler may, without hip-over-head rotation, rebound from her feet into a stunt transition. Rebounding to a prone position is allowed.

Tumbling over, under, or through a stunt, person, or prop is prohibited. However, forward and backward rolls over a prop are legal, as well as when doing airborne tumbling skills in which the hands are not being used for support.

Tumbling while holding or while in contact with any prop is prohibited, as is spotted, assisted, or connected tumbling. Dive rolls performed in a swan or layout position are also prohibited.

Standing and running tumbling skills can have up to one flipping and one complete twist rotation.

Stunts

A spotter is required for most extended stunts and for all extensions. Single-based split catches are prohibited.

When catching a transitional stunt that is above prep level (see "Terms"), at least three catchers are required. If the weight of the top person does not remain within the vertical axis of the stunt, three stationary catchers that are not original bases are required. Physical contact must be maintained with at least one original base or with another person at prep level or below.

Single-based double awesomes/cupies require a separate spotter for each top person. Twisting mounts and twisting transitions are permitted, with up to one-and-one-quarter twisting rotations by the top person; double twists are illegal.

Dismounts

Cradles from single-based stunts at prep level or above must have a spotter, with at least one hand or arm supporting the head and shoulder area through the cradle.

Cradles from multibased stunts at prep level or above must have two catchers and a separate spotter positioned at the head and shoulder area through the cradle.

When cradling single-based double awesomes/cupies, there must be a separate catcher for each top person. Catchers and bases must be stationary before the initiation of the dismount.

Dismounts to the performing surface from stunts and pyramids must have an assisted landing by an original base or spotter.

No free-flipping dismounts are allowed.

Up to one-and-one-quarter twisting rotations are allowed for all stunts.

Tension drops or rolls of any kind are prohibited.

Release Moves

Release moves do not refer to pyramid transitions; they refer only to freestanding stunts.

Release moves must not exceed more than 18 inches above extended arm level. If the base

releases the stunt, then it must come back to its original base.

Release moves may not land in a prone position.

Helicopters are allowed up to a 180-degree rotation with no more than a half twist and must be caught by at least four catchers, one of whom is positioned at the head and shoulder area of the top person.

Inversions

Extended inverted stunts are allowed. Downward inversions are allowed from an extended position if the primary weight of the top person is assisted by at least three bases, at least one of whom is acting as a head-and-shoulders spotter. Contact must be initiated at the shoulder level (or above) of the bases. The exception to this rule: A controlled power-pressing of an extended inverted stunt to shoulder level is allowed.

Downward inversions must maintain contact with an original base.

Inversions may release to a stunt at prep level or below, or a loading position or dismount with no more than a half turn.

Pyramids

Braced inversions in a pyramid that do not flip or roll are permitted under the following conditions:

- Two bases, or a base and a spotter, are provided for the inverted top person.

- If the inverted top person is released, each bracer must be at prep level or below; the bracers must not provide primary support, and the top person must be caught by the original base(s) and not land in an inverted position. No more than a quarter turn is allowed by the top person or the base(s).

- A braced roll is permitted if two bases, or a base and a spotter, are provided for the inverted top person and the bracer(s).

- A braced flip in a pyramid requires 12 people including the flipper. The bases must remain stationary except for safety adjustments. The top person must

  have three people who were the original bases or spotters,

  maintain continuous hand-to-hand and or hand-to-arm contact with two bracers,

- not end in an introverted position,
- not perform more than one and a half flipping rotations and no more than a half twist.

Tosses

Tosses must be performed from ground level and must land in a cradle position. The top person must be caught in a cradle position by the original bases and the head-and-shoulders spotter. Bases must remain stationary during the toss unless they have to move to safely catch the flyer.

Tosses are allowed up to a total of four tossers. One of these tossers must be the head-and-shoulders spotter.

No stunt, pyramid, person, or prop may move over or under a toss, and a toss may not be thrown over, under, or through stunts, pyramids, persons, or props.

Up to two-and-one-half twisting rotations are allowed. No flipping rotations are allowed. (National Federation rules allow only one-and-one-quarter rotations.)

Basket tosses and other similar multibased tosses are permitted only on appropriate mats, grass, and rubberized or other soft, yielding surfaces.

Scoring

Judges score teams in various categories, depending on the association involved. Each team earns points in these categories, leading to the total score. A subjective score sheet for judging, taken from the Indiana Cheerleading Association, includes categories for the following:

- Formation/spacing/use of floor/transitions
- Motion technique and fundamentals
- Showmanship/spirit/voice/expression
- Partner stunts
- Pyramids
- Use of jumps, technique of jumps
- Use of tumbling, technique of tumbling
- Cheer and dance choreography/creativity/effectiveness/incorporation
- Degree of difficulty for routine
- Overall execution/precision/timing/technique

TERMS

An **airborne tumbling skill** is a skill performed in which there is no contact with a person or the performing service.

An **awesome** is an extended stunt in which a top person has both feet together in the hands of the base(s). This is also referred to as a *cupie*.

A **base** is a person in direct weight-bearing contact with the performance surface who provides primary support for another person.

A **basket toss** is a toss bye multiple bases in which a person loads into the bases' interlocked hands and wrists.

A **braced flip** is when a braced top person performs a hip-over-head rotation while being released from all persons on the performing surface, while a **braced roll** is the same rotation while the braced top person remains in contact with a person on the performing surface. A **braced inversion** refers to a braced top person being in an inverted position.

A **bracer** is a top person who is connected to another top person but does not provide primary support. The stunt should remain stable without the bracer.

A **dismount** is the movement from a stunt or pyramid to a cradle or the performing surface. It is considered the end of the stunt.

A **dive roll** is an aerial forward roll where the hands and feet are off of the performing surface simultaneously.

A **hanging pyramid** is a pyramid in which one or more people are suspended off the performing surface by one or more top persons.

A **layout** is a stretched body position, straight, hollow, or slightly arched.

A **Liberty** is a one-leg stunt, usually extended that may include variations. A **Switch Liberty** starts with one foot of the top person in a load. The top person is then tossed and lands in a Liberty on the other foot.

A **log roll** is a release move whereby the top person's body rotates at least 360 degrees while remaining parallel to the performing surface before being caught by the original base in a horizontal position or a cradle. This is also known as a *barrel roll*.

Prep level is when the height of the bases' hands and at least one foot of the top person is at shoulder level (also known as shoulder height).

A **pyramid** is a grouping of multiple-partner stunts that may or may not be connected to create a visual effect.

A **roll** is a tumbling skill where the person does a hip-over-head rotation. It is done either on the performing surface or in a stunt where the top person is in contact with the person on the ground.

The **second level** refers to any person being supported away from the performing surface by one or more bases.

A **spotter** is a person whose primary responsibility is the protection of the head and shoulder area of a top person during the performance of a stunt or toss. Spotters must be in direct weight-bearing contact with the performing surface. They must be attentive (i.e., they have to stay visually focused on the flyer at all times).

Standing tumbling is a tumbling skill (or series of skills) performed from a standing position without any previous forward momentum. Any number of steps backward before the execution of tumbling skills is defined as *standing tumbling*.

A **stunt** is any skill in which a top person is supported above the performance surface by one or more people. This is also referred to as a *lift* or *partner stunt*.

A **suspended flip or roll** is a stunt in which a top person performs a hip-over-head rotation while the upright base holds the top person's hand(s) or arm(s).

A **swing roll down** is a stunt in which the hands or arms and feet or legs of the top person are held while swinging forward and face down into a roll.

A **tension roll or drop** is a pyramid or stunt in which the bases and tops lean in formation until the top persons leave the bases without assistance.

A **toss** is an airborne stunt in which the bases execute a throwing motion from below shoulder level to significantly increase the height of the top person. The top person becomes free from all bases.

The **top person** is the person on top of a stunt or toss. The top person is also referred to as the *flyer* or *partner*.

In **tuck position**, the knees and hips are bent and drawn into the chest; the body is bent at the waist.

Tumbling is any gymnastics or acrobatic skill executed on the performing surface.

A **two-high pyramid** occurs when all top persons are primarily supported by bases that are in direct weight-bearing contact with the performing surface.

OFFICIALS

Judges at cheerleading competitions pay attention to the following:

- The placement, execution, and poise of movement during jumps
- The timing and rhythm of moves, jumps, transitions, and routines
- The choreography and originality of a routine
- The voices of the cheerleaders
- The overall appearance of the performers
- The gymnastics aspect of the performance
- The timing and ease of spins, jumps, tosses, and any movement between two or more cheerleaders

ORGANIZATIONS

American Association of Cheerleading Coaches
 and Administrators
6745 Lenox Center Ct., Ste. 318
Memphis, TN 38115
800-533-6583
www.aacca.org

International Cheer Union
P.O. Box 752830
Memphis, TN 38175-1210
901-251-5979
www.cheerunion.org

International Federation of Cheerleading
Aoyama Success Building, 7th Floor
2-11-13 Minami-Aoyama Minato-ku
Tokyo 107-0062
Japan
81 3-5770-5747
www.ifc-hdqrs.org

U.S. All Star Federation
8275 Tournament Dr., Ste. 325
Memphis TN 38125
(888) 315-9437
www.usasf.net

14

Climbing (Sport)

Alysta/fotolia.com

Sport climbing uses permanent protection fixed to the rock, which is in contrast to traditional climbing that requires climbers to place removable anchors as they climb. Sport climbing has many disciplines, including lead, speed, bouldering, deep water soloing, and duel. Though rock climbing has long been an outdoor pursuit worldwide, sport climbing has blossomed in popularity through indoor gyms and climbing walls that are more convenient, require less equipment, and are less intimidating to beginners than traditional climbing.

The first international rock climbing competition was called Sportroccia, held in Bardonecchia, Italy, in 1985, and by the fourth event there, in 1988, an artificial wall was used. The first indoor climbing gym in North America, Vertical World, was established in Seattle in 1987. In 1989, the International Climbing and Mountaineering Federation (UIAA) held the first World Cup in speed and lead. The International Federation of Sport Climbing (IFSC) was founded in 2007. Sport climbing is popular in the Americas, most of the Western Europe, Asia, and many other developing countries.

The popularity of sport climbing led to its inclusion at the 2020 Olympic Games. The event will award medals based on the combined results of three disciplines: lead, bouldering, and speed.

OVERVIEW

Objective: In all types of competition, the climber has to start from the base and finish at the top, but the difficulty levels and types of routes are different for lead, speed, and bouldering, the three disciplines covered in this chapter. In lead climbing, the climber is not protected by a rope from above, and she is belayed from below with each piece of protection clipped sequentially. The climber has a set time frame in which to climb a progressively tougher route. Speed climbing uses a fixed mechanical device placed at the top of the wall which functions as a belayer to the climber, quickly retracting the slack as the climber progresses through the route. Whoever finishes first is the winner. Bouldering requires climbers to reach the top without any ropes, and the emphasis is on the number of problems completed. Landing mats provide protection for ground falls.

Length of Competition: Each climber is given an allotted time to complete routes. The length of a competition can vary from 1 to 12 days depending on the type of event. Events may be local or can range up to national and world caliber events.

Climbers: Governing bodies such as USA Climbing hold local, regional, and national competitions in lead, speed, and bouldering in youth from ages 5 to 19 as well as professional, adaptive, and collegiate levels.

Scoring: Climbers receive points based on varying factors. In bouldering rounds, the scoring system gives points based on controlling holds assigned with points and also for completing problems in the fewest amount of tries. In lead climbing, the number holds controlled on each route along with the number of quickdraws clipped will give the climber their ranking.

COURSE

Each discipline of competitive climbing has different rules, styles of movement, and complexity to challenge the athletes.

Lead

Lead climbing competitions, the most common type, are organized on a long routes designed by expert routesetters. The climber clips the rope into quickdraws attached to the wall as they progress up the route. Lead routes typically feature slow and precise movement that requires complete body control the entire time. Due to the length of routes, the climbers build a "pump" in their forearms and need to have built up a good amount of endurance to complete the routes. They receive points for the highest hold they have controlled and the last quickdraw they have clipped their rope into. There are normally two qualifying rounds followed by a semifinal and final. In the semifinals and final rounds, the climber is given only 6 minutes of "observation" to visualize the route and talk about the skills required to complete the route. Climbers compete in order of their placement in the previous round, starting with the lowest qualifier and ending with the highest qualifier.

Speed

In speed climbing, speed and reaction time are the only factors considered as participants race up a 15 meter standardized route that has been created by the IFSC. An electric timing system is used in a way that climbers cannot start the round until the correct command has sounded. If the climber reacts poorly to the commands, they are considered to have "false started," and they are eliminated from the competition. Once the timing system has started, their time will not be stopped until they have slapped the timing pad at the top of the wall. There is one qualifier round, based on the fastest of two times, which will rank the climbers progression moving onto the next round. Followed by a semi-final, quarter final, 1/8th final, and final round (broken into "big race" and "small race" for podium), you must win the race against your opponent in hopes to continue through to the final race.

Bouldering

These competitions are held without belay ropes, and usually the route is comprised of short walls with more powerful and gymnasticlike movement. Each category is given a specific set of routes that test different styles and skills. Points are awarded for different designated holds that the climber has controlled on each route. The climber has never seen the routes prior and only has 4 minutes to figure out how to complete the route. To prevent injuries, gymnastic mats are placed on the ground below the climbers.

EQUIPMENT

The technical equipment used in the International Climbing Competitions must adhere to the European (EN) Standard. This equipment includes:

- Belay devices (locking)
- Belay devices (manual)
- Climbing holds
- Climbing harness
- Climbing rope
- Climbing structures
- Karabiners (screwgate)
- Karabiners (self-locking)
- Quickdraw/tape slings
- Quickdraw/connector (karabiner)
- Quickdraw/connector (quick link)

Other than this, a climber is free to use any type of chalk or climbing helmet.

RULES

The basic rules are broken into the following sections: isolation, routesetting, termination, timing, scoring, and safety.

Isolation Area

Because of the obvious advantage for later climbers to see a route attempted repeatedly by other climbers, competitors check in to an isolation area before the event and are brought out one at a time to climb. There may be an authorized period for observation of the route or problem prior to a competitor's attempt. Competitors can discuss a route with others in the isolation area who have not yet attempted the route or problem, but receiving information about a route before or during an attempt results in disqualification.

Routesetting

The host facility is expected to set up new routes or problems for competition. If they are not new, the chief judge eliminates them from competition and either disqualifies all competitors who had prior knowledge of them or adjusts scores accordingly. Routesetters may only discuss the routes or problems with other members of the routesetting team, judges, or event organizers, and they should not provide an advantage to a competitor. To protect the integrity of competition, routesetters should avoid the appearance of impropriety. Coaches may take part in routesetting for local, regional, and divisional competitions, but they may not communicate with competitors about their routesetting work. No competitors may routeset in an event they are competing in.

Route Termination

An attempt at a route is considered terminated when the competitor falls, exceeds the allotted time, or returns to the ground with any part of the body after having started the attempt. In addition, a competitor can be charged with an infraction for using any artificial aid, marking the wall with a tick mark, or using any of the following to climb any part of the wall (including the edge unless the edge is specifically marked as part of the route or problem): handholds, bolt holes, bolt hangers, or any other features that have been marked as not allowed for climbing. When an infraction is called, the judge instructs the competitor to stop. The competitor or coach can immediately appeal the decision, in which case the competitor is taken to a separate isolation zone. If the appeal is upheld, the competitor is given a new attempt with a rest period similar to those granted to competitors after a technical incident and is allowed to use the best of the attempts on the route for scoring.

Timing

A predetermined time for attempting a route or problem is set in advance. For a lead route, a 1-minute tie-in period may be added. The chief judge may also grant a maximum of one additional minute to allow competitors to make their way to the next route or problem. Lead competitions can range anywhere from 5 minutes to 8 minutes or even no time limit. Bouldering competitions typically range from 4 to 5 minutes.

The route time is started when the competitor is instructed to turn around and climb when ready. The predetermined allotted time must include a 40-second final preparation period at championship events; this is optional at local competitions. During this period, the competitor can stay on the ground. If the competitor has not started climbing after 40 seconds, any further delay results in disqualification on that route or problem.

Scoring

Competitors are scored based on the highest hold reached as defined by the path of the route or problem in the route map. The routesetters have created the route map based on the intended sequence of moves along the route they have set. Only handholds "controlled" are scored. This requires holding a handhold for at least 2 seconds and being in a stable position, controlling the momentum of the climbing movement.

In lead competition, competitors are only allotted one attempt for each of your round's climbs.

For bouldering, there is no limit on the number of attempts a competitor may make on a route, as long as it is within the allotted time limit. Each attempt is recorded. After the attempts are completed, the judge tells the competitor at which point she was scored on the route or problem. If she disagrees, the competitor can file an appeal.

Each route or problem is worth a specific number of points based on that route's anticipated rating or difficulty.

In competition rounds, a competitor's score is based on four factors.

1. Number of the highest handhold controlled: There is no point advantage for skipping a handhold.
2. Positive movement: A decimal score of 0.3 is awarded if the competitor makes a "positive movement," which is classified as a significant change in the person's center of mass and if at least one hand moves toward the higher handhold.
3. Usable surface: A score of 0.5 is given if the competitor moves from a controlled handhold and touches the "usable surface" of a higher-numbered handhold.
4. Number of quickdraws clipped: In lead climbing, 0.01 is given for a successfully clipped quickdraw.

An easy way to understand the scoring is to think of the highest handhold (factor 1) as a whole number and the next three (factors 2–4) as decimals added to that number. For example, a competitor who has controlled the handhold scored as 27 receives 27 points. If she has made positive movement toward a handhold scored 28 (but has not touched the usable surface of a handhold scored 28 or higher), she adds 0.3, putting her at 27.3. If she has clipped six quickdraws, she adds another 0.06, giving her a total of 27.36 points.

In bouldering, the score is determined by the number of routes "sent" (completed). If two competitors are tied, the climber requiring fewer attempts places higher. A total of 20 climbers reach the semifinals, with six (bouldering) or eight (lead) climbers advancing to the final round.

Safety

Floor padding must be used. Each route should be designed to decrease the likelihood of a competitor's fall injuring bystanders or obstructing another climber. Competitors tie in with a figure-eight knot with a follow-through. A harness is required for sport and speed competitions.

OFFICIALS

Officials are responsible for safety. The three main jobs are an event organizer, a chief judge, and a chief routesetter. The event organizer is responsible for maintaining overall safety, including the public areas. The chief judge makes safety decisions within the competition area, including ensuring that all officials, belayers, spotters, judges, and others are following safety procedures. The chief judge consults with the event organizer or chief routesetter as needed. Either the chief judge or the chief routesetter must inspect each route before the first round for the maintenance of technical standards.

TERMS

An **anchor** is an arrangement of gear set up to facilitate the rope used to belay the climber.

The **approach** is the hike to get to the base of the climb.

To **ascend** is to climb a rope using an aid device.

Belaying is a technique used to manage the climbing rope to ensure that the climber does not fall far.

Beta is advice on how to successfully complete a particular climbing route.

A **bolt hanger** is a metal point of protection permanently installed in a hole drilled into the rock. Carabiners are placed in bolt hangers and then the climber clips the rope into the carabiner.

Grade is a rating given to the climbing route that describes the difficulty of the route.

A **project** can be either a new route that has not been attempted yet or an established route that a climber has not achieved.

A **quickdraw** is used to attach a rope to bolt hangers or anchor points.

Redpointing a route means completing a route after having practiced or fallen on the route beforehand.

To **send** a route means to complete a route.

Spotting protects the competitor during bouldering or before the leader has placed a piece of protection. The spotter stands below the climber, ready to direct him away from hazards.

Static climbing is a style of movement where the climber is very slow and precise and has complete control of their body.

Static rope is a nonelastic style of rope that is not meant for falling on.

Top-rope climbing (or top roping) is a style of climbing in which a rope runs from a belayer at the base of a route through one or more carabiners connected to an anchor system at the top of the route and back down to the climber, usually attaching to the climber by means of a harness.

ORGANIZATIONS

USA Climbing
4665 Nautilus Ct., Ste. 502A
Boulder, CO 80301
303-499-0715
www.usaclimbing.org

IFSC Office:
Via Carlo Matteucci 4
10143, Torino, Italy
IFSC Legal Seat:
Effingerstrasse 1
3001 Bern, Switzerland
www.ifsc-climbing.org

15

Cornhole

U.S. Navy photo by Mass Communication Specialist 3rd Class Huey D. Younger Jr.

The origin of cornhole harkens back to 1883, when Heyliger Adams De Windt, a Harvard graduate and the great-grandson of President John Adams' youngest daughter, filed a patent for "Parlor Quoits." De Windt's variation was the first to use beanbags and a slanted board with a hole as the target. Within months, newspapers across the United States reported the sport's growing popularity. Advertisements for "Faba Baga," a version of the game with two holes of different point values on the board, circulated in 1888 from the first large-scale toy manufacturer in America, Converse E Marketing & Company, of Massachusetts.

The sport's popularity faded as time went on, but cornhole, also known as beanbags or bags in Chicago, experienced a resurgence with an article in *Popular Mechanics* magazine in September 1974. The story showed readers how to make their own boards, and soon the sport's popularity soared throughout the Midwest, particularly in Chicago and northwest Indiana, throughout the 1970s and 1980s. The modern-day game as we know it is closely associated with football tailgating parties. Many manufacturers even make cornhole boards with designs featuring NFL and NCAA football team logos or mascots.

OVERVIEW

Objective: Be the first team to score 21 or more points.

Scoring: A "cornhole," the name for when a bag is tossed into the target hole, is worth 3 points. A bag landing on the board is worth 1 point. A beanbag toss has no scoring value unless it goes through the hole in the board or comes to rest on top of the board. Groups play until one side totals 21 or more points at the end of an inning. Innings are complete when players have tossed all four beanbags down and back.

Number of Players: Either one on one (singles) or two on two (doubles).

Length of Game: The time it takes for one team to reach 21 points. A game can end in the middle of the inning with the first team to score 21 or more points, and a team does not need to out-score an opponent by 2 or more points to win.

In a singles match, players compete head-to-head while tossing beanbags at the same cornhole board. In a doubles match, teams of two players compete against each other and toss beanbags at opposing cornhole boards.

COURT

A cornhole court is designed in a rectangular layout, 8 feet wide and 40 feet long, per American Cornhole Organization (ACO) guidelines. The court contains two cornhole boards, preferably set up in a north-south pattern for outdoor games to minimize the effects of the sun and should be 27 feet apart measuring from the front edge of each board. Players toss their beanbags from a designated pitcher's box area, a 4- by 3-foot rectangle parallel and on both sides of the cornhole board (see figure 15.1). Players must remain in the pitcher's box while throwing their bags. There are two sets of foul lines, one for adults and one for children. Adult foul lines are the front edge of the board. Junior foul lines are imaginary lines 21 feet from the hole of the target cornhole board.

PLAYERS

Contests can be played as singles or doubles. Tournaments feature women's, men's, coed, and junior divisions.

EQUIPMENT

Per American Cornhole Organization guidelines, each cornhole board is a 47.5- to 48.0-inch by 23.5- to 24.0-inch rectangle made of plywood at least a half-inch thick. There is a significant difference between wooden and plastic cornhole boards, so ACO-sanctioned tournaments are only allowed to use wooden boards. The hole in the cornhole board should be 6 inches in diameter, and they should be centered 9 inches from the top and 12 inches from the sides of the cornhole board. The front of the cornhole board should be 4 inches from bottom to top and at a near 90-degree angle to the deck face (top of the board). The back of the cornhole board should be 12 inches from the ground to the highest point of the deck at a 90-degree angle to the deck face.

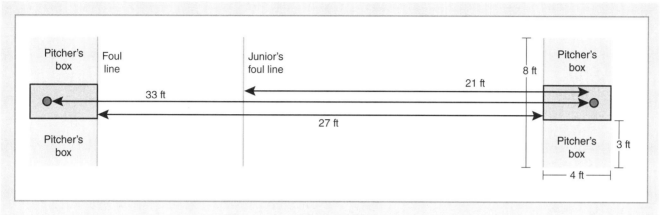

▶ **Figure 15.1** The dimensions and features of a cornhole court.

The ACO also requires cornhole boards to be sanded to a smooth finish so that there are no blemishes on the surface to affect the game and painted with a high gloss latex paint that will provide a smooth surface for beanbags to slide but one that isn't so slippery that the bags slide back down the board.

Cornhole beanbags should be made from two 6-1/4-inch fabric squares. Canvas, twill or synthetic suede are acceptable fabrics and are sewn together, with a quarter-inch, double-stitched seam on all four sides. The bags can be any color that is easy to see during the game. Finished bags should be a minimum of 6 inches by 6 inches square and should weigh between 15 and 16 ounces.

RULES

Most cornhole rules are the same for both doubles and singles play. However, in doubles play, teammates pitch at opposite cornhole boards. In singles play, both competitors pitch at the same board.

A cornhole match is broken down into innings, during which all four bags for each team are tossed. In singles play, the top of the inning is complete when the first competitor throws all four bags. The bottom of the inning is complete when the other competitor throws all four bags. In doubles play, the top of the inning is complete when both competitors pitching from the same cornhole board each pitch their respective four bags. The bottom of the inning is complete when both competitors pitching from the other board each pitch their respective four bags.

In both singles and doubles play, the pitcher must remain in contact with the pitcher's box while pitching the bag and remains in their lane for the entire game. The only exception is for junior and physically challenged contestants, who must simply remain completely behind the 21-foot foul line when the bag is released. Competitors have 15 seconds to pitch the bag once the opponent's bag comes to a rest.

The player or team that scored in the previous inning begins the next inning. If neither pitcher or team scores, the team or player who pitched first in the preceding inning pitches first in the subsequent inning.

Scoring Values

■ A cornhole (also called a hole-in): Worth 3 points, a hole-in occurs when the bag is thrown through the hole or is knocked in by another bag.

■ A woody or cornhole bag in the count (also called on the board): Worth 1 point, this occurs when the bag is not in the hole but comes to rest on the board. The bag cannot touch the court or the surrounding ground before coming to a complete stop on the board. If the bag touches the ground, it is called a foul, and play will not continue until the bag is removed.

▪ Foul or cornhole bag out of the count: A bag that is not in the count or in the hole is a foul and has no scoring value.

Foul Bags

A foul cornhole bag is one thrown in violation of the rules. It scores as a bag out of the ones counting toward the team score and should be removed before any additional bags are pitched. Beanbags that were knocked out of scoring areas on the court by a foul bag should be put back where they were. Also, beanbags that were knocked into the target hole by a foul bag should be put back where they were.

Beanbags are considered foul bags if any of the following occur:

1. The bag is tossed by a competitor who has either contacted or crossed over the foul line or started or stepped outside of the pitcher's box before releasing the bag.

2. The bag is pitched from a different pitcher's box than the first bag.

3. The bag contacts the ground before landing on the cornhole board.

4. The bag strikes a previously defined, out-of-bounds object such as a tree limb, wire, or ceiling.

5. Any bag that leaves a competitor's hand once the final forward swing of the delivery process has started counts as a pitched bag. If the bag is dropped before the final forward swing has started, it is not considered foul, and it can be picked up and pitched.

6. Any bag removed by a competitor before scoring of the bag has been agreed upon by both teams is considered a foul bag. In official tournament play, a judge can be called if teams cannot agree on scoring, and the judge shall rule.

7. In official tournament play, any bag not delivered within the 15-second time limit is considered a foul bag.

SCORING

A cornhole match is played until a team reaches or surpasses 21 points. An inning does not have to be completed after 21 points is scored. Unlike some other games, the winning team is not required to beat its opponent by more than 1 point. If the match is tied at 21 or higher at the end of an inning, it continues until one of the teams ends a subsequent inning by a higher point value.

There are two scoring systems that can be used in cornhole, simple and cancellation. Simple scoring may be used in recreational games and some forms of competition, but it is not recognized as an approved scoring system by the ACO. With simple scoring, the points are totaled at the end of each half inning (i.e., top and bottom). The smaller score is subtracted from the higher score and the difference in points is awarded to the team scoring the higher number of points in that half inning. In simple scoring, only one team scores per half inning.

Cancellation scoring refers to like shots being cancelled out at the end of an inning in singles play and at the end of each half inning in doubles play. As mentioned above cancellation scoring is the approved method by the ACO. This means that bags in the hole and bags in the count delivered by opposing teams cancel each other out to determine the score. Specifically, a bag in the hole of one player cancels a bag in the hole of another, and therefore neither scores a point. If there are no bags to cancel, a bag in the hole scores 3 points. Similarly, a bag in the count cancels another bag in the count of the opposite team, and therefore neither scores points. Bags in the count score 1 point each if there are no bags to cancel them. Unlike in simple scoring, either team can record a score in an inning.

If a team scores 7 or more points at the end of an inning before the opponent scores any points, the game is considered a skunk and the team that scores 7 or more points wins the match.

TERMS

An **ace** or **cow pie** occurs when a bag comes to rest on the cornhole board, scoring 1 point.

A **back door** or **dirty rollup** occurs when a bag goes over the top of a blocker bag and into the target cornhole.

A **backstop** occurs when a bag lands past the hole but rests on the board. This creates a wall to help a slider to go into the hole without falling off the end of the board.

A **blocker** is an ace bag that lands in front of the hole, blocking sliders from going in.

A **cornhole** or **drano** is a bag that falls into the hole, scoring 3 points.

A **dirty bag** is one that lands on the ground or hangs off the side of the board and touches the ground.

A **flop** is a type of toss that has no rotation or spin on the bag.

A **frame** is players throwing all four bags from each team or player down the court.

An **inning** is players throwing all four bags from each team or player down and then throwing them back. A Cornhole inning is stitching two frames together.

A **hanger/shook** occurs when a bag hangs partially in the hole, ready to drop.

A team is granted **honors** of throwing bags first because that team scored last previously.

A **hooker** occurs when a bag hooks around a blocker and goes in the hole.

A **jumper** is a bag on the board that jumps up into the hole after being struck by a thrown bag.

The **police** are the cornhole referees.

A **Sally/Alvord** is a weak toss that hits the ground before reaching the board.

A **screaming eagle** is a bag toss that completely clears the back of the board without touching it.

A **shortbag** is a bag that lands on the ground right in front of the board.

A **slippery granny** occurs when a player scores three bags in a row on the board only.

A player is called a **shucker** when he tosses a bag that knocks an opposing player's bag off the board.

A **skunk/whitewash/shutout** is a game abbreviated to an 11-0 decision for the winning team.

A **slider** is a bag that slides up the board into the hole.

A **swish/airmail** occurs when a toss goes straight through the hole without touching any part of the board.

A **shotgun** occurs when a player tosses all four bags at once.

A **trip dip** occurs when a player cornholes three of her four bags in one turn.

A **wash** occurs when teams score identical points in an inning, washing out all the points factored into the final score.

OFFICIALS

Cornhole referees or judges make sure that players don't foul by violating the rules of pitching bags, and they can make official rulings on scoring when teams cannot agree on scoring in an inning. A judge can also rule on any protests raised by competitors during the game.

MODIFICATIONS

As mentioned previously, junior foul lines for kids and physically challenged competitors can be shortened to 21 feet from the beginning of the hole in the target cornhole board.

ORGANIZATIONS

American Cornhole Organization
208 Locust St.
Milford, OH 45150
888-563-2002
play@americancornhole.com
http://americancornhole.com

American Cornhole Association
www.playcornhole.org

16

Cricket

EcoView/fotolia.com

Cricket has been played for hundreds of years and is one of the most popular sports in the world, with more than 100 countries affiliated with the International Cricket Council, the sport's governing body. The first recorded instance of cricket in the English language refers to a game of kreckett being played at the Royal Grammar School in Guildford, England.

The Marylebone Cricket Club (MCC), formed in 1787 in London, drew up the code by which the game is played and has continued as the guardian of the sport's laws ever since. The first official cricket club in America was formed at Haverford College, near Philadelphia, in 1833, but the sport has never caught on in the United States the way it has in other countries.

OVERVIEW

Objective: To score the most runs.

Number of Players: 11 per side.

Length of Game: Determined by which of the three formats is being played.

1. Test Cricket: Maximum two innings by each team in a maximum of five days. An innings, which is a singular term, is usually finished when all 11 batsmen have batted and 10 are out (because a team always has two batsmen "in" at a time, the last batsman is left "not out"; more on that later). The team in the field then bats in the same way until either four total innings are complete, the team batting last has scored more runs than its opponents, or five days of the game are complete.

2. One-Day Cricket: This format is finished in one day. Each team gets the chance to bat one innings limited to 50 overs maximum (one *over* is six deliveries; see a more detailed explanation in "Rules"). The first innings is finished either after 50 overs or when the batting team has lost 10 wickets. The second innings ends after either 50 overs, 10 wickets, or the team batting second passes the number of runs scored by the team that batted first.

3. Twenty-20 Cricket: Similar to one-day cricket but the maximum number of overs is limited to 20 instead of 50.

FIELD

The field is an open oval expanse of closely cropped turf divided into two equal halves by an imaginary line running down the middle of the pitch (see figure 16.1). From the point of view of a right-handed batsman as he faces the bowler, the right side of the ground is the offside; the left side is the on (or leg) side. The field is encircled by a roped or chalked boundary line. There is no official size for the field, but most high-level contests are played on fields with diameters of 150 to 200 yards.

Wickets are placed opposite each other, 22 yards apart. Each wicket is made of three poles, or stumps. The stump closest to the batsman is the leg stump; the stump in the middle is the middle stump; and the stump farthest from the batsman is the off stump. The wickets are 28 inches high and 9 inches wide. Set in grooves on the tops of the stumps are two bails—cylindrical pieces of wood that measure 4.38 inches in length.

Running 4 feet in front of and parallel to each wicket is a 12-foot popping crease. Any time a batsman is away from her wicket and beyond her popping crease, she may be dismissed (stumped or run out) by dislodging the bails with the ball. If any part of her body or her bat is touching the ground behind the line, she may not be put out. Intersecting the popping crease are two lines, 8.6 feet apart, running back toward the wicket. These are the return creases, which serve as guidelines for the bowler, who must not overstep the second line before releasing the ball. If the bowler does, a no ball is called.

The bowling crease runs parallel to and 4 feet behind the popping crease. The wickets are set on this crease. The pitch is the stretch of turf between the two wickets. It is 10 feet wide—5 feet on either side of the imaginary line running between the middle stumps at either end. The grass on the pitch is very short and smooth; in some instances, the pitch is artificial turf.

PLAYERS

Officially, there are 11 players per side. The lineup is set before each game, and the lineup may not be changed without the consent of the opposing captain. In a practice match, if both sides agree, more or fewer than 11 may play, but no more than 11 may field. The traditional cricket uniform is

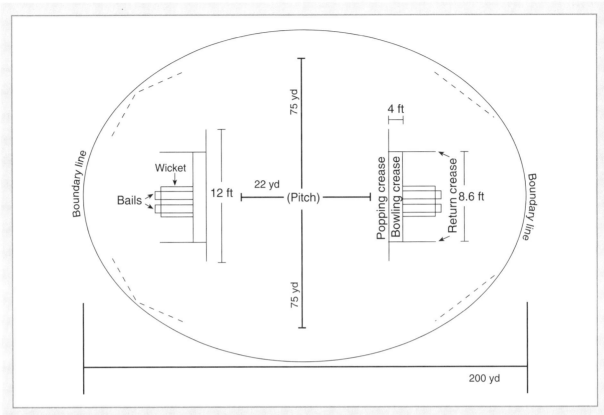

▶ **Figure 16.1** The dimensions and features of a cricket field.

pants, shirts, sweaters, and shoes. The color of the uniform depends on the format of the game. In Test cricket, the color is white, and for limited overs cricket, the uniform is colorful. Club insignias are on players' caps and shirts.

A substitute may field for a teammate only if the teammate is injured or ill. If a fielder has to leave for another legitimate reason, and the umpire consents, a team may use a substitute for the fielder or the wicketkeeper. However, no substitute is allowed to bat, bowl, or act as captain.

A player who was substituted for may return to bat, bowl, or field. However, he may not always be allowed to bat or bowl immediately. Rules for when he is allowed to bat or bowl again are complex, but the basic principle is that players must be back on the field for the length of time they were off it before they can bat or bowl again.

Bowlers

The bowler may take a run-up before delivering, but she must have at least part of her front foot behind the popping crease when she releases the ball. Failure to do so results in the umpire calling no ball, which gives the opponents a one-run penalty. "No ball" will also be called if the bowler throws the ball. A no ball does not count as part of the over, and the batsman is protected from most, but not all, ways of being dismissed (for example, he can still be run out). In some forms of cricket, the batting team receives a free hit offer for one ball as a result of a no ball. This means the batsman gets the same protection from being out as he did for the no ball.

The bowler must deliver the ball within reach of the batsman. Failure to do so results in the umpire calling a wide, which also results in a one-run penalty for the opponents. A wide does not count as part of the over.

The bowler most often tries to "attack the off stump" (aiming at that stump or just outside) and bounce the ball at the wicket, not too close to the batsman. Most bowlers don't want to bowl short; when the ball bounces far from the batsman, a high, easily-hit long hop results. Bowlers also usually stay away from full tosses, which are deliveries that reach the batsman without bouncing; these are easiest of all to hit. Bowlers often try to vary the angle of their deliveries, sometimes bowling over the wicket (on the left side of the wicket if the bowler is right-handed) and sometimes around the wicket (on the right side of the wicket if the bowler is right-handed).

Batsmen

A skilled batsman doesn't just swing indiscriminately for the boundary. Rather, she may start out trying to hit the ball with a high-percentage vertical stroke, deflecting or spoiling a bowler's good deliveries, and using various strokes for various deliveries, including baseball-like cross-bat strokes and sweep or reverse-sweep strokes to divert the ball to her left or right; she may even run down the pitch to meet the ball and drive it straight over the bowler's head.

Regardless of the stroke or situation, the batsman doesn't want to give the fielders a chance to catch a ball in the air. The skilled batsman may score a century (100 runs) during an innings.

Fielders

The wicketkeeper is the only player who is allowed to wear gloves; he wears one on each hand and acts much like a baseball catcher. He positions himself opposite the bowler and behind the batsman who is batting. The other nine fielders vary their positions, according to the skills of the bowler and the batsman, but in loose terms they fit into these positions:

- One or more slips play alongside the wicketkeeper, to the off side of the field. The faster the bowler is, the more slips might be employed, expecting the batsmen to hit, in baseball terminology, "foul balls," or in cricket terminology, "an edge."
- A gully stands wider than the slips and a little deeper.
- A point, a cover, and a mid-off fielder stand on the offside, beginning with the point about 15 yards from the batsman; these fielders are 5 to 10 yards apart from each other. They try to stop balls from getting past their side of the field.
- Mid-on, mid-wicket, square leg, and fine leg are on the on side, or leg side, of the field. Depending on the situation, fielders might be closer or farther from the batsman, so for example, you might have a "short cover" or a "deep fine leg."
- A team may shift a fielder finer (closer to parallel to the line of the pitch), or squarer (at more of a right angle to the line of the pitch).

Other rules regarding fielders include the following:

- No more than two fielders may be behind the popping crease on the on side when the bowler delivers the ball. The umpire will call no ball if this is the case.
- In some forms of one-day cricket, there is a limit on the number of fielders who may be outside the 30-yard circle at certain times. This overs limit for fielding is called a *powerplay*.
- Until the batsman makes contact with the ball or the ball strikes the batsman or goes past her, no fielder may be on the pitch except the bowler, or no ball will be called.
- When fielders' protective helmets are not in use, they are placed behind the wicketkeeper. If a ball in play strikes a helmet, the batting team is awarded five penalty runs.

EQUIPMENT

The ball is hard, weighing, when new not, less than 155.9 grams and not greater than 163 grams. The ball when new must measure not less than 8.8 inches and not more than 9 inches in circumference. It is red (for Test cricket) or white (for one-day or Twenty-20 cricket), with a double-stitched seam down the middle. The ball is made of cork and wool and bound in leather. The bat is paddle shaped. It is made of willow and may be of any weight. Its maximum length is 38 inches and its maximum width is 4.25 inches. The batsman wears protective gear: padded leg guards, padded gloves, and a helmet with a face guard. A batsman may also wear an arm guard, chest guard, and any other desired protection under clothing. The wicketkeeper wears two flat, long-cuffed leather gloves and padded leg guards.

RULES

A batsman stands at each wicket. The bowler for the team in the field, much like a baseball pitcher, delivers a ball to the batsman standing near the opposite wicket. In simple terms, the ball must not be thrown, and a throw involves straightening the arm during delivery. A straight arm is common, but an arm that remains bent throughout the delivery is also allowed, so long as it does not straighten.

The batsman may swing and miss any number of times; she cannot strike out, as in baseball. She also cannot hit a foul ball because all territory is fair—even if she hits the ball to the side or behind her. Batsmen do not have to run after hitting the ball, but if they choose to, they score a run each time they cross the opposite popping creases (see figure 16.1). Each time they make it safely from one wicket to the other while the ball is in play, their team scores a run.

The batsmen carry their bats with them when they run. This can be an advantage because the bat is considered an extension of the batsman's arm, and he can reach over with his bat to touch down beyond the popping crease to score a run. Each time a batsman hits the ball over the boundary line without bouncing (similar to a home run in baseball), his team gets six runs; each time a ball goes over the boundary line having bounced, his team scores four runs. This is true whether or not a fielder has touched the ball or is in possession of it when it crosses the boundary line.

A batsman continues to bat until the fielding team can get her out or the maximum over limit is achieved. One way to dismiss a batsman is "out, bowled," referring to the bowler getting the ball past the batsman so that it hits the wicket and knocks off at least one bail. Other ways to get a batsman out are detailed in "Scoring."

Because a batsman is at each wicket, the direction of bowling is reversed every six deliveries. A bowler bowls a sequence of six fair deliveries toward one wicket, and then another fielder becomes the bowler and bowls a sequence of six fair deliveries toward the opposite wicket. The six fair deliveries is called an over, and this pattern continues throughout the match. The fielding team may change bowlers for every over, and a bowler may bowl multiple overs, but the bowler may not bowl two overs in a row.

The wicketkeeper acts similar to a baseball catcher; he is the only player with gloves (he has, in fact, one on each hand). He shuttles from wicket to wicket after every over; he is always behind the wicket opposite the bowler.

Batsmen always bat in pairs, one at each wicket; therefore, a team never has all 11 batsmen out because the last remaining batsman cannot bat alone. Once the 10th is out, the innings is over. Even so, a normal two-innings match can go on for days. At the end of the match, the team with the most runs wins. If the team batting second needs 200 runs to win and scores 200 when, say, seven of its batsmen are out, then the contest is over and the result is described as a win "by three wickets"—the number of batsmen they didn't need. The teams draw, regardless of the score, if it is not possible to finish the match. If the match is finished with the score even, it is a tie.

"Limited overs" cricket, typically played in one day, is becoming more popular. The length of the game is controlled by the number of overs each team is allowed. A 50-over match is one in which each team bats for 50 overs (i.e., each team gets 300 legal deliveries). Often, not all batsmen get to bat in limited overs.

Twenty-20 cricket is the newest version of the game and is played over 40 overs, with each team batting for 20 overs. The game is played with greater speed and excitement because of the fewer overs, while the batting depth remains the same at 11 per team. That means more attacking shots, more fours, and more sixes.

Scoring

A team scores one or more runs in these situations:

▪ When a batsman hits a the ball over the boundary line without bouncing, that's worth six runs.

▪ When a batsman hits a ball that goes over the boundary line after bouncing, that's worth four runs.

▪ When both batsmen cross the opposite popping crease, one run is scored.

When the opposing bowler delivers a wide ball (one that's out of reach of the batsman) or a no ball (an illegal delivery), the batting team adds one run to what it had already scored on the play. The batting team gets five extra runs when a fielder illegally stops the ball.

A bye is called when the batsman hasn't hit the ball but still runs. Any number of runs may be scored.

A leg-bye is called if the ball hits the batsman but not his bat and the batsman runs. Any number of runs may be scored.

A batsman is out when she

allows a delivery to knock a bail off her wicket (in which case she is "out, bowled");

hits a ball caught in the air by a fielder ("out, caught");

uses her body to block a delivery from hitting her wicket, even if unintentional ("out, leg before wicket" [lbw]). This is a complex rule in which the umpire must take into consideration several points if the fielding team asks for an lbw decision. The batsman is not out if the pitched ball is "outside leg stump," outside the line of the leg stump, the ball hits the bat, or a no ball is bowled;

is not over the popping crease when a fielder throws a ball or uses the ball held in her hand to knock the bail off the wicket that the batsman is nearest ("run out");

crosses the popping crease while trying to hit the ball, and the wicketkeeper grabs the ball and knocks the bail off her wicket before the batsman can return ("out, stumped");

deliberately hits a ball twice ("out, hit the ball twice");

intentionally interferes with a fielder ("out, obstructing the field"); or

breaks her wicket while receiving, or preparing to receive, a delivery ("out, hit wicket").

Violations

The following rules fall under the category of maintaining fair play:

No player may rub the ball on the ground, rub an artificial substance on the ball, or take any other action to alter the condition of the ball, except to dry a wet ball or to remove mud from a ball.

If a fielder intentionally obstructs a batsman in running, the umpire will signal "dead ball" and allow any completed runs, plus the run in progress, to score, as well as giving the batting team five penalty runs.

Bowling short-pitched balls are dangerous because they might injure the batsman are not allowed. In international cricket, two short balls ("bouncers") that pass between the batsman's shoulder and head are allowed every over.

Bowling fast, high, full pitches—deliveries that pass, on the fly, above the batsman's waist height—will result in the umpire calling "no ball" and cautioning the bowler.

Wasting time is unfair and results in a caution.

Any player damaging the pitch to assist a bowler will be cautioned by the umpire.

The nonstriker may not attempt to steal a run during the bowler's run-up.

A ball is ruled dead when

it settles in the hands of the wicketkeeper or the bowler,

it goes over the boundary,

a batsman is out,

it lodges in the equipment or clothing of a batsman or umpire,

it is lost, or

a player has, or is suspected to have, a serious injury.

TERMS

Backing-up is the nonstriker's, or nonbatsman's, "leadoff" of her popping crease when she expects to run. As the bowler releases her delivery, the nonstriker goes over her popping crease, taking a few steps toward the opposite wicket. This is risky, however. The bowler can run them out instead of bowling the ball.

A **beamer** is a fast, above waist-high delivery.

A **bouncer** is a ball delivered short and fast so that it bounces up over the batsman's shoulder.

A **boundary** is a "four" (a ball hit over the boundary line after bouncing) or a "six" (a ball hit onto or over the boundary line without bouncing).

A batsman is **bowled** when the delivery gets by him and knocks a bail off his wicket. This is similar to a baseball strikeout.

Any number of runs may be scored when a fair delivery does not touch the batsman or her bat and gets by the wicketkeeper; this is called a **bye**. (This is similar to a passed ball in baseball.)

The **middle stump** is the center pole of the wicket.

A batsman makes a **century** when he scores 100 runs in a single at bat (roughly equivalent to rushing for 100 yards in American football). In Test cricket, it is extremely difficult but not unheard of to score a double-century, triple century, or even, on one occasion in history, a quadruple century.

A **cutter** is a medium-paced delivery that spins or bounces into or away from the batsman.

A **declaration** is a strategy in which the team batting may stop before all of its batsmen are out (Test cricket); this is usually done to allow enough time to get the opponents out.

A **duck** signifies a batsman who gets out without scoring any runs.

Fall of wicket refers to an out; "the sixth wicket fell" means six members of the batting team have been dismissed.

Follow-on is a strategy in a two-innings (Test cricket) match that allows the team that bats first, if ahead by a certain number of runs, to reverse the second-innings batting sequence.

A **four** is a ball that goes into or beyond the boundary line having bounced; this automatically scores four runs.

A **hat trick** occurs when a bowler takes three wickets on three successive deliveries.

A **leg-bye** is a run scored from a delivery that hits the batsman's body.

The **leg stump** is the pole of the wicket closest to the batsman.

A **maiden** is an over in which no runs are scored off the bat.

No ball signifies an illegal delivery; the batting team gets an automatic run.

Offside is the half of the playing area that the batsman is facing.

The **off stump** is the pole of the wicket farthest from the batsman.

On side is the half of the playing area behind the batsman.

An **over** is a set of six fairly delivered balls to one wicket. The direction of the deliveries switches to the opposite wicket at the end of each over.

The **pitch** is the area between the two wickets.

A **quick single** is a run scored on a shallow hit, similar to a baseball bunt.

A **short run**, which does not count as a run, occurs when a batsman fails to touch part of his body or his bat behind the popping crease when running.

A **six** is six runs automatically scored when a ball goes onto or beyond a boundary line without bouncing.

A **strike rate** is the average number of runs a batsman makes per 100 deliveries.

A **stump** is the name for a wicket's three individual poles. A wicket is often referred to as "the stumps."

A **wide** is called by the umpire when the bowler doesn't deliver the ball within reach of the batsman. This results in a run for the opponents.

OFFICIALS

Two umpires officiate a cricket match, although international cricket also has a "third umpire," or television umpire, to help with some decisions. One umpire stands at the bowlers' end, several meters behind the stumps, to have a clear view of the ball being bowled from behind the crease. The other umpire stands at square leg, which is in a position to see that the batsmen make their ground by being behind the crease line when the fielders retrieve the ball.

MODIFICATIONS

Teams may agree to alter some of the rules for particular games. Other rules supplement the main laws and change them to deal with different circumstances. For example, the playing structure and fielding position rules can be modified to apply to one-innings games that are restricted to a set number of fair deliveries.

Kwik Cricket is not played under the Laws of Cricket. It is a high-speed modification of cricket that has been designed for children, often for those under 11 years of age. Both ball and bat are made of plastic. It is a 16 overs game; each team can bat for 8 overs maximum. The boundary is a maximum of 38.28 yards wide, but it can be reduced to accommodate more matches. The two sets of wickets are 16 yards apart. Each player on the fielding side must bowl one over, and bowling takes place from one end only.

Generally, eight players (both boys and girls) can play on each team. Squads are limited to 10 players. In the event of injury to a player, a substitute is allowed to field but not bowl. Should such an injury prevent the player from batting, a substitute is allowed to bat only with the permission of the opposing captain.

The following are the main rules in Kwik Cricket that are different from other forms of the game:

- The batting side is divided into pairs, each pair batting for two overs, with a new pair starting at the end of the second, fourth, and sixth overs.
- Each team starts batting with a score of 200 runs.
- Each time a batsman is out, five runs are deducted, and the other batsman of the pair faces the next ball.
- A batsman may be out by being bowled out, caught, run out, or stumped or by a hit wicket.
- There is no "leg before wicket" rule to record an out unless the batsman deliberately blocks the ball with a leg or foot.
- Runs are scored in the normal way, as are byes.
- Two runs are awarded to the batting team for each wide ball and no ball bowled, but no extra ball is allocated except in the final over of each innings when, in addition to the two runs, an extra ball is bowled.

- At the end of the first two overs, the first pair of batsmen retires and is replaced by the second pair until all four pairs have batted for two overs each.
- The second team then bats for its eight overs.

ORGANIZATIONS

ECB Association of Cricket Officials
The England and Wales Cricket Board
Lord's Cricket Ground
London NW8 8QZ
England
44 020 7432 1200
www.ecb.co.uk/ecb/ecb-association-of-cricket-officials

International Cricket Council
Street 69
Dubai Sports City
Sheikh Mohammed Bin Zayed Rd.
Dubai
P.O. Box 500 070
United Arab Emirates
971 4 382 8800
www.icc-cricket.com

Marylebone Cricket Club
Lord's Cricket Ground
St. John's Wood
London NW8 8QN
England
44 020 7616 8500
www.lords.org

17

Croquet

Jupiterimages/The Image Bank/Getty Images

Though similar ball-and-mallet games date back to the Middle Ages, croquet is a modern sport with origins in the British Isles in the mid-19th century. Croquet spread overseas in the 1860s and 1870s, but it was soon eclipsed in popularity by lawn tennis in England. Croquet was an event at the 1900 Summer Olympics, and roque, an American variation, was played at the 1904 Games. Croquet has become one of the most popular activities in the United States to be played at parties, family gatherings, and social events, but it also has competitive versions in the United States. It also remains popular for competition and recreation in the United Kingdom and other countries formerly in the British Commonwealth, such as Canada, New Zealand, South Africa, Australia, and Ireland. The United States follows a different set of rules than the Commonwealth countries. Traditionally croquet is a nine-wicket game, but six-wicket games and other variations, such as gateball in Asia, were later developed. There are more than 200 croquet clubs affiliated with the U.S. Croquet Association in the United States and Canada.

OVERVIEW

Objective: The object of the game is for a side to score 26 points before the opposing side, which is done by passing through all wickets and hitting the stake. In timed versions, the object is to score more points (pass through more wickets) than the opponent before time expires.

Number of Players: In six-wicket croquet, two to four players (singles or doubles); in nine-wicket, two to six players can play.

Scoring: A point is scored for each wicket passed through and for hitting the stake.

Length of Game: Though the length of a croquet match is based on scoring, it may be played with time limits (normally 1 hour, 10 minutes to 2 hours); a game clock is used to measure this. When time is called, each of the balls may play a final turn, beginning with the ball in play. A shot clock may be used to limit a player's time to shoot to 45 seconds.

The distinctive feature of croquet is that when the striker ball hits another ball, it is said to have made a "roquet" on that ball. What happens as a result of the roquet differs according to the variation of the game being played.

TYPES OF CROQUET

The most common forms of croquet are American, international, golf, nine-wicket, and gateball.

American Croquet

Six-wicket croquet is also called American croquet because it is widely played in the United States and has a complete set of rules called American rules. It is played with six wickets, one stake, and four balls.

International Croquet

As the name suggests, this is the internationally played version of croquet, and it follows a different set of rules than the American rules. It is increasingly gaining popularity in America as well. Officially this game is called Association Croquet. It is played with six wickets, one stake, and four balls.

Nine-Wicket Croquet

Nine-wicket croquet is the traditional game, and it goes back the farthest in time. Nine-wicket croquet is less formal than six-wicket croquet. It is also called extreme croquet when played with six players or on long grass. It is played with nine wickets, two stakes, and four to six balls.

COURT

The playing area of croquet is called a court. American croquet, international croquet, and golf croquet all follow the same standard court practices. The standard court measurement is 105 by 84 feet. Unless short grass is available (one-quarter inch or less), these proportions should be followed. On ordinary areas such as playgrounds, sports fields, or lawns, 50 by 40 feet is acceptable. American croquet can be played on an ordinary lawn with inexpensive equipment, although it is advisable to play it on a very smooth lawn for a better experience. A gateball court consists of a rectangular inner field, which is 15 meters by 20 meters, and an outer field, which surrounds the inner field 50 to 100 centimeters out. Most of the play is on the inner field, and it is often called the court. The surface can be lawn, artificial lawn, or clay.

EQUIPMENT

Wickets

The wickets are to be made of iron with a 5/8-inch diameter and uniform thickness. Their height must be 12 inches measured from the ground to the top of the crown of the wicket. All wickets must have the same dimensions regardless of the court surface being used. The wickets are painted white, the crown of the first wicket is painted blue, and that of the last wicket, called a rover wicket, is painted red.

Stake

The stake can be made of any material and must have a diameter of 1-1/2 inches and a height of 18 inches above the ground. It is vertical, solid, and firmly fixed to the ground. The stake is white with bands of blue, red, black, and yellow descending from the top. The first 6 inches above the ground are white, and the rest consists of the bands. A detachable extension one-half inch in diameter and 6 inches in length is designed to hold the clips.

Balls

Croquet balls come in blue, red, black, and yellow. Only balls approved by the World Croquet Federation are used in official games. The size of the balls is 3-5/8 inches in diameter with a milled surface and even weight (neither less than 15-3/4 ounces nor more than 16-1/4 ounces). In U.S. Croquet Association–titled events, the rebound range of the balls when dropped from a height of 60 inches onto a 2-inch steel plate embedded in concrete should be between 30 and 45 inches. The rebound of balls in a set should not vary more than 3 inches.

Mallet

The head of the mallet is made of wood. No mallet should give the player an unfair advantage. Metal may be used for weighting or strengthening. The two end faces are parallel, perpendicular at the bottom, and must have identical playing characteristics. Mallets are generally 3 feet long.

Accessories

The following accessories are used for guidance and convenience but are not required:

1. Clips
2. Deadness board (especially for American rules)
3. Clocks
4. Corner flags
5. Check fences

RULES

The rules for six-wicket and nine-wicket croquet are provided here, but first it is useful to review the principles of deadness and aliveness as a fundamental aspect of both versions of the game.

Deadness and Aliveness

Once a striker ball does a roquet and takes the two bonus shots, it is considered dead on that ball. That striker's ball may not hit it again until the striker scores the next wicket, thereby "clearing" the deadness. When a ball scores a wicket, it is "alive" on all the other balls that have scored that wicket—that is, it is again eligible to hit them to earn bonus strokes. A player may roquet each of the other balls only once in a turn, unless the player scores a wicket, thereby earning the right to roquet each of the balls once again.

Deadness may be cleared on either ball on a side when the opponent scores wicket 7 (also called *one-back*) with each of the opponent's balls. You must announce to the opponent the clearing of one your balls *before* your side plays the next turn by saying, "We are clearing blue." (Note: American six-wicket croquet is the only game in which deadness carries over to the next turn.) This is why at U.S. Croquet Association clubs, deadness boards are an essential part of the equipment. Combinations of deadness are constantly changing.

A ball that has run through all 12 wickets is called a rover. It can roquet any other ball in the game but only once per turn. A rover may clear itself of deadness only after it has roqueted at least two balls (but not the same ball twice in succession). If a rover ball is dead on two or three balls, it may run any wicket in any direction to clear deadness and earn a continuation shot, but it will maintain last deadness on the last ball it hit. A rover leaves the game by hitting itself into the center stake or by being driven into the stake by another rover. In both cases, the rover exiting the game scores the stake point.

Six-Wicket (American and International) Croquet

The objective is to be the first to reach 26 points—each of the six wickets is run through twice, and the center stake counts for a point, for a total of 13 points maximum for one ball or 26 points maximum for a side.

The order and direction in which the wickets must be scored are shown in figure 17.1.

The players take turns in the following order: blue, red, black, and yellow. Blue and black always play as a team against red and yellow. In singles, one person plays both balls. In three-player games, one side has only one player who plays both balls on that side. A coin toss determines the playing order, with the side winning the toss given the choice of playing first and third (with blue and black) or second and fourth (with red and yellow).

Each ball is played from anywhere in the starting area (3 feet behind the number 1 wicket, 16-1/4 inches wide, and equally divided by a line that passes through the center of the wicket). If other balls are already crowding the starting area, the ball may be placed up to 9 inches on either side of the starting area.

Each player gets one shot at the beginning of a turn. It is possible for the striker ball to earn an additional shot or shots by doing the following:

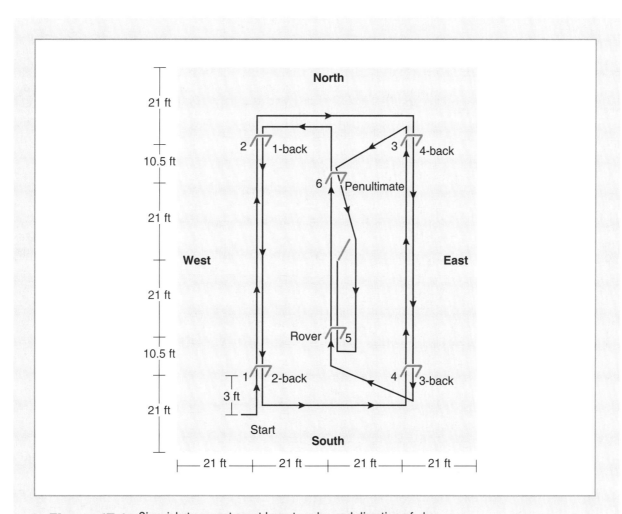

▶ **Figure 17.1** Six-wicket croquet court layout, order, and direction of play.

■ Scoring a wicket. One bonus stroke is awarded for passing through a wicket in the proper order and direction.

■ Roqueting (hitting) another ball. Two consecutive bonus strokes are earned when hitting another ball. The first is called the croquet stroke. The striker's ball is placed in contact with the opponent's ball that was hit. The striker's ball is hit so that both balls move, either a little or a lot. The hand or foot are not allowed to be placed on the ball during the stroke. The second is called the continuation stroke, and it is played from wherever the striker's ball lies after the croquet stroke. If in the croquet shot either the croqueted ball or the striker ball is sent off the court, then the turn ends.

Bonus strokes may not be accumulated; only the last-earned bonus stroke(s) may be played. For example, if a ball scores a wicket and in the same stroke hits another ball beyond the wicket scored, this does not count as a roquet; the balls remain in their new positions, and the striker continues play with the earned wicket bonus stroke, which may be used to roquet the other ball.

A player's turn ends when the shot clock expires, a shot is completed without a croquet or continuation shot, a fault occurs, or the player misses the ball when attempting to strike it.

A player is permitted to pass a turn or shot. To pass, a player must make it clear to the opponent the color of the ball that should be played and his intention to give up his turn. Once the announcement has been made, the turn is considered finished.

A player must not interfere with any ball while a shot is in progress. All balls are in play until the shot is over, and they must be allowed to completely cross the boundary or come to a complete stop before being touched by any player or equipment. The only exception is when a roquet is made. (Note: A ball passing through a wicket in the wrong direction shall not receive credit for that wicket or receive a continuation shot.) A rover ball that has 2 or 3 ball deadness can earn a continuation shot by going through any wicket in any direction.

A player must not interfere with the boundary string during a shot. A player may move, stand on, or have a partner stand on the string so that the striking of the striker ball is not interfered with.

1. The four corner flags should be at least 4 inches outside the boundary string and may be temporarily removed so as not to interfere with the striker's stance or swing.

2. No player is entitled to advice from anyone other than one's partner when playing doubles.

3. The rules provide that a fault or misplay shall be called by any player as soon as it is observed.

4. The winner of a game is responsible for removing the balls and clips (but not before the final score is agreed upon) from the court at the end of the game.

Nine-Wicket Croquet

The basics of six- and nine-wicket croquet are the same. The following discussion indicates where nine-wicket differs from six-wicket. Like six-wicket, the object of nine-wicket croquet is to score points for each wicket and stake in the correct order and direction, but the courses are set up differently. The nine wickets and two stakes are arranged in a double-diamond pattern (see figure 17.2).

The winning side is the first side to score 14 wicket points and 2 stake points for each of its balls. In a timed game, the team with the most points when time expires wins.

For a two- or four-player, two-sided game, use four balls (blue, red, black, and yellow, in that order). One side (with one or two players) plays with blue and black, and the other with red and yellow. For a six-player team game, use six balls (blue, red, black, yellow, green, orange, in that order). In team play, one side plays blue, black, and green, and the other side plays red, yellow, and orange. In "one-ball" games, each player chooses one ball.

All balls are played into the game from a spot halfway between the finishing stake and wicket number 1. The order of play is determined by flipping a coin or striking the ball to get closest to the middle wicket. The side winning the coin toss has the choice of playing first or second. In one-ball games, colors may be drawn by lot. After all balls have started the game, play continues in

Each ball can score points for its side by being shot through a wicket or hitting a stake in the proper order and direction. A ball that scores a wicket or stake during another person's turn receives the point, but the player does not receive a bonus shot. A ball scores a wicket point only if it clears the playing side of the wicket (see figure 17.2). If a ball does not pass all the way through a wicket or rolls back, it has not scored.

The striker ball earns one bonus shot if it scores a wicket or hits the turning stake. The striker ball earns two bonus shots if it roquets another ball, and it becomes dead until it clears the next wicket or at the start of the next turn, whichever comes first. The maximum number of bonus shots earned by a striker is two. The first of these two shots may be taken in any of four ways:

1. Taking a mallet-head. The striker ball is placed a mallet-head distance or less away from the ball that was hit.

2. Foot shot or hand shot. The striker ball is placed in contact with the ball that was hit and is held in place by the striker's foot or hand.

3. Croquet shot. The striker ball is placed in contact with the ball that was hit but is not held in place by the striker's foot or hand.

4. Playing the lie. The striker ball is played from where it stopped after the roquet. (If the striker's ball went out of bounds, it shall be placed one mallet length from where it left the boundary.)

The second bonus shot after a roquet, called a *continuation shot*, is played from where the striker ball came to rest. Bonus shots are not accumulated, and therefore any bonus shot previously awarded is forfeited. The exception is that two extra shots are earned if two wickets are scored in the same shot. No extra shots are awarded if the striker ball roquets another ball and hits it again within the same turn before scoring the next wicket in order. However, there is no penalty for hitting the ball again. When the striker ball scores a wicket and then in the same shot hits another ball, only the wicket counts, and the striker has earned only the one extra shot for scoring the wicket. The striker may then roquet any ball to earn two extra shots. When the striker ball roquets

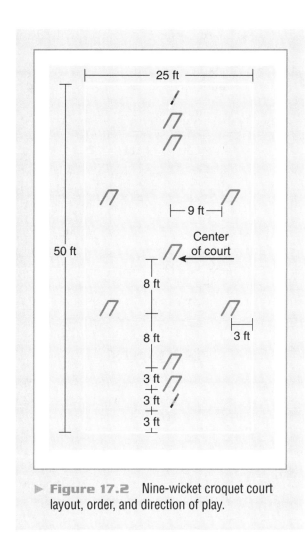

▶ **Figure 17.2** Nine-wicket croquet court layout, order, and direction of play.

the same order until a ball is staked out. When a ball is out of the game, the remaining balls continue in the same order, skipping the ball that has finished the course.

If a player goes out of turn, there is no penalty. Any ball that is moved during the out-of-turn play gets put back to the position it was in before the error occurred and play proceeds. If an out-of-turn play is discovered after one or more balls have been played, only the last ball played out of turn is replaced.

If the striker takes a swing and misses the ball entirely, the miss counts as a shot, and the turn ends unless the striker had a second "bonus" shot.

If the striker's mallet accidentally hits another ball, the shot must be redone, but the turn is not lost.

another ball and then goes through a wicket, the wicket has not been scored, but the striker earns two extra shots for the roquet.

After a ball scores all of the wickets, it can be a rover used for strategic reasons to advance the remaining ball(s) for that side and to inhibit the advancement of the opposing team. During this rover's turn, it may hit any ball once per turn. The rover may not earn wicket points, but it can earn a point for hitting the stake. Once the rover hits the stake, it is taken out of the game.

If boundaries are used, whenever more than half a ball crosses outside the boundary, it should be placed one mallet length into the court. If more than one ball crosses the boundary on the same spot, the striker measures any ball in bounds first and then place the other(s) up to a mallet-head's length away from it on either side.

If a time limit is set beforehand, a "sudden stop" occurs when time expires. If the score is tied in the sudden stop format, the ball closest to its contested wicket gets an extra point for the win.

Violations

A striker shall strike the ball with either striking face of the mallet. If the striker strikes the ball with the adjacent edge, beveled edge, or corner of the striking face, it shall not be deemed a fault unless the striker's swing is hampered. If a fault does occur, the penalty is end of turn and replace balls.

The "striking period" begins when a striker starts the backswing with an intent to strike the ball and ends at the conclusion of the follow-through. When the striker repeatedly swings or casts the mallet over the ball, the backswing starts when the mallet head has passed the ball on the final backswing the striker intends to make before striking the ball. If the striker deliberately interrupts the swing after the striking period has begun, and before the mallet reaches the ball or a fault is committed, the striker has not made a shot and may begin the striking period again.

TERMS

An **agari** (finishing) is hitting the center pole in gateball to score an additional 2 points. A **continuation stroke** occurs when a wicket is scored and the player is entitled to play one more shot.

A **deadness board** is used to keep track of the dead or alive status of all the balls in six-wicket croquet.

Making a break is a series of shots, roquets, croquets, and continuation shots to make points in a single turn.

A **roquet** occurs when another ball (opponent's or partner's) is hit by the striker ball. The striker is said to have made a roquet on that ball.

A **rover ball** has passed through all wickets and is eligible to hit the stake to complete the round.

At the start, the player may choose either of the two balls in her turn. Whichever ball she chooses must be played throughout the turn. This is called the **striker ball**. The first shot is known as a **croquet shot** and is made by placing the striker ball in contact with the roqueted ball.

To **send** an opponent's ball is to strike it on a bonus shot.

OFFICIALS

The game is governed by referees. Any issues during the game are to be reported or discussed with the referee. The referees are certified by the USCA. A referee is called by raising the mallet above the head or, if necessary, by calling out "referee." In certain conditions, the referee can also be summoned to watch a shot if the opponent believes the striker is making repeated faults.

VARIATIONS

Golf croquet and gateball are two variations of the original sport of croquet. Golf croquet is considered the fastest growing version of the game due to the fact that it is a simpler version. Gateball is a similar game, inspired by croquet, but invented in Japan. It is gaining in popularity, as well. Rules specific to these variations are outlined below.

Golf Croquet

Golf croquet is fast paced and suitable for beginners as well as professionals. It is played with six wickets, one stake, and four balls. Golf croquet is played as a doubles or a singles game. In doubles, one side plays with the blue and black balls (or green and brown) and the other side with red and yellow (or pink and white). Each player plays the same color ball for the entire game. The balls are played in the sequence blue, red, black, and yellow. A match is the best of one, three, or five games that are played to either 7, 13, or 19 points.

In a 7-point game, following the first six wickets, the seventh point is scored by playing the first wicket for a second time. In a 13-point game, the first 12 wickets are played, and the 13th point is scored by playing the third wicket for another time. In a 19-point game, the first 12 wickets are played, then wickets 3, 4, 1, 2, 11, and 12 are played again as wickets 13 through 18 respectively. The 19th point is scored by contesting the third wicket for a third time.

Each turn consists of a single stroke. If a striker accidentally touches the ball, it counts as a stroke, but if the striker misses the ball completely on the swing, it is not counted as a stroke and the striker may continue. A ball scores a point by "running a wicket"—passing through the correct wicket.

A nonstriking fault is committed if a moving ball touches any part of a player or mallet or if a player touches or moves a stationary ball.

Gateball

In Asia, this five-on-five team version of croquet is popular. It is complicated but precise in rules, and the pace of the game is fast since playing time is just 30 minutes. Each player receives a number between 1 and 10 to determine order of play. Passing a gate successfully results in 1 point, and a 2-point bonus is given after a player passes all three gates. Team totals are added up at the conclusion. This section provides a general overview of the game. A 2-centimeter-wide goal-pole sits in the center of the court. If the ball hits the goal-pole after passing all three gates, the ball makes an agari (finishes). The arrows show the direction for passing the gates.

In official games, gateball includes a chief referee, an assistant referee, and a recorder. One side has five red balls and the other side has five white balls. Each player has a number from 1 to 10 and plays the fixed ball with that number throughout the game. Every time a player successfully passes the gate, 1 point is earned. After a player passes all three gates and hits a goal-pole, 2 additional points are earned. Points are added at the end of 30 minutes, and the team with more points wins.

After the chief referee calls "play ball," Red 1 plays first. After his turn ends, White 2 plays, and the order continues until White 10's turn (which concludes the first round), at which time Red 1 plays again to start the second round. Five or six rounds in a 30-minute game is typical. The player who is up is called a stroker.

The game ends when the chief referee calls "game set." If the white team is playing, the game will end when its stroker's turn is over. If the red team is playing, in order to give an equal number of turns to both teams, the game will end when the following white team stroker's turn is over.

There are only two scoring plays in gateball: tsuka (passing the gate) and agari (finishing). If a stroker's ball makes a successful pass through the gate, the stroker gains a continuous stroke.

From the start area, each player must pass the first gate to get to play "in the court." If the ball completely crosses over the gate line, it is a successful pass, a point is scored, and the player gets the right to a continuous stroke from the spot where the ball stopped. (If the ball goes out of bounds, the point for passing the gate is earned, but a continuous stroke is not given).

If the player cannot make a successful pass for the first gate, her ball is immediately removed from the court, and she has to try for the first gate again when her turn comes in the second round.

Two important plays are "touching" the ball and "sparking" because they enable you to move opponents' balls to help your teammates. Touching occurs when the stroker's struck ball makes contact with another ball. This requires the stroker to spark—the stroker moves his ball and places it against the touched ball, then strikes his own ball underneath his foot to send the opponent's ball. After a successful sparking, a continuous stroke is gained.

Although gateball is a team sport, during play points are given to the ball, not the team. Each ball begins as a zero-point ball. Every time it passes a gate, it becomes a 1-point ball, a 2-point ball, or a 3-point ball. Each ball can score by passing a specific gate only once. The ball can still pass through the same gate twice or from the back side without receiving a foul. A 3-point ball gets agari by hitting the goal-pole and receives 2 bonus points if successful. An agari ball is known as a 5-point ball and is removed from the court. Each ball has 5 possible points: 0, 1, 2, 3, and 5. A perfect game is 25 points, meaning all five balls on one side make agari.

ORGANIZATIONS

United States Croquet Association
700 Florida Mango Rd.
West Palm Beach, FL 33406
561-478-0760
USCA@msn.com
www.croquetamerica.com

The Croquet Association
Old Bath Rd.
Cheltenham GL53 7DF
United Kingdom
01242 242318
www.croquet.org.uk

18

Cross Country

The sport of cross country running began in England's public schools in the early 1800s. From 1868 through the early 1880s, many clubs were formed in England. The English Cross Country Union was created in 1883, and it staged the first national championship in that year. The English clubs were typically named "Harriers" or "Hare and Hounds" because in early races, a few runners (the hares) would take off first, laying a "scent" by scattering a paper trail for the "hounds" to follow.

Cross country got its beginnings in the United States in 1878. Today, the International Association of Athletics Federations holds annual world cross country championships.

OVERVIEW

Cross country features teams of runners who run the same course. Courses vary in terrain and length. The objective is to have the lowest team score; the first five runners on a team to finish the course score points for that team. Points are awarded according to the place a runner finishes. The first five finishers for a team score points for their team. (Finishers six and seven do not score points for their team but can push scoring runners from other teams into higher-scoring positions. This is explained in "Rules").

COURSES

Cross country races are run over a variety of terrains and settings, including fields, woods, grasslands, parks, and golf courses. Because of the varying terrains and hills, it's difficult to compare times from one course to another. Distances vary as well; in high school, courses range from about 1.6 to 3.1 miles (2,500 to 5,000 meters); in college, courses range from 3.1 to 5.0 miles (5,000 to 8,000 meters) depending on the nature of the meet (championship or non-championship). See figure 18.1 for a sample cross country course.

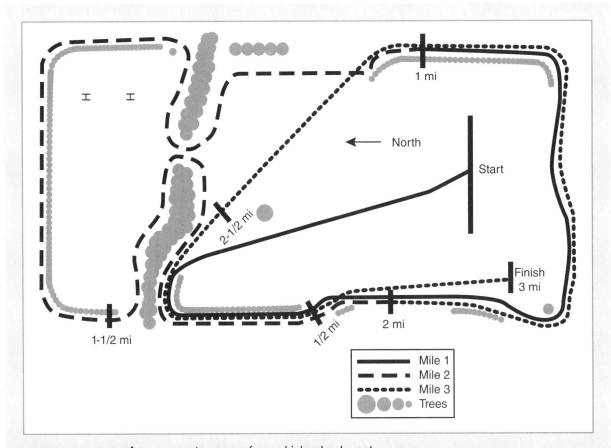

▶ **Figure 18.1** A cross-country course from a high school event.

Adapted by permission from Illinois High School Association, *State Final Course*. (Detweiller Park, Peoria, 2008). Available: http://www.ihsa.org/activity/ ccb/2008-09/ cc%20sf%20course.pdf.

College courses can become narrow (between 2 and 5 meters wide for nonchampionship races and not less than 10 meters wide for championship races), but narrowing should not occur before the first 600 to 800 meters. In high school, the recommendation is to have the course at least 3 feet wide at its narrowest.

The course must be clearly marked for runners, and should follow the natural terrain. Courses are marked by white or colored lines on the ground (particularly at turns) and by the use of directional flags.

Flags and course markings are placed on the edge of the measured line that marks the course.

RUNNERS

Many meets are open to unlimited numbers of runners; in others, the field is restricted to a certain number. Regardless, the first five finishers for a team finish in scoring positions, and finishers six and seven are displacers and can affect the scoring position for other runners from other teams. Finishers 8 through 12 for a team do not count in the scoring and do not affect the scores of runners from other teams.

EQUIPMENT

The uniform tops of team members must be identical. Pants can be of any length but must be of identical color. Either shoes or spikes may be worn. In high school, jewelry is not allowed, although religious medals (worn under the uniform and taped to the body) and medical alerts (taped to the body) are not considered jewelry. Runners may wear watches.

RULES

Points are awarded according to the scoring place each runner finishes in (1 point for first place, 2 points for second place, and so on for each scoring place). The lowest score wins.

Take this example, where the seven scoring positions for each team (among its 12 runners) are in bold:

- Team A's runners place: **4, 5, 7, 12, 13,** 24, 26, 27, 32, 33, 35, 36.
- Team B's runners place: **3, 8, 10, 14, 20, 22, 23,** 28, 29, 30, 31, 34.

- Team C's runners place: **1, 2, 6, 9, 11,** 15, 16, 17, 18, 19, 21, 25.

As demonstrated in table 18.1, Team A would score 41 points (4 + 5 + 7 + 12 + 13). Team B would score 52 points (3 + 8 + 10 + 14 + 17; the runner who placed 20th is awarded 17th-place points because team C had nonscoring runners in 17th, 18th, and 19th places). Team C would score 29 points (1 + 2 + 6 + 9 + 11) and would win the race.

In the event of a tie, the score is determined by dividing the total of the finish places by the number of runners who tied.

Teams that have fewer than five finishers do not factor into the scoring at all.

The lowest score possible for a team is 15 points (1 + 2 + 3 + 4 + 5).

Start and Finish

Runners are called to the starting line for final instructions. Each team starts in its assigned lane; the lanes are assigned by lot. The start should begin with a long straightaway, with the first turn preferably between 200 and 400 meters from the start (and farther away for championship races).

The finish is usually close to the start and should include a straightaway of 200 to 300 meters (college) or 150 yards (high school). For races with finish chutes, the finish line should be at the mouth of the chute area. Fifteen to twenty-five feet from the finish line, the chute narrows to a rope chute about thirty inches wide and one hundred feet long.

When the runner's torso breaks the plane of the finish line, the runner has finished the race.

Some races use computerized chips to record the finish of each runner. A chip is attached to both shoes of each runner. When a runner's chip passes the finish line, the runner has completed the race; the torso doesn't matter in this case.

TERMS

Blind spots are locations on a course where trailing runners cannot see those ahead. Trees, bushes, or hills often create blind spots.

A **caller** calls the number of each runner in the order of their proper place in the chute.

A **checker** keeps a record of the runners and their order of finish as announced by the caller.

The **chute director** supervises the finish chute. This includes directing gate controllers when more

TABLE 18.1

Sample Team Scoring

Place	Score	Team	Runner Name
1	1	C	
2	2	C	
3	3	B	
4	4	A	
5	5	A	
6	6	C	
7	7	A	
8	8	B	
9	9	C	
10	10	B	
11	11	C	
12	12	A	
13	13	A	
14	14	B	
15	15	C	
16	16	C	
17		C	
18		C	
19		C	
20	17	B	
21		C	
22	18	B	
23	19	B	
24	20	A	
25		C	
26	21	A	

than one chute is used, directing marshals to keep the chute area free of unauthorized persons, and assigning positions for chute umpires and for any other needed personnel.

The **chute umpire** supervises the runners after they enter the chute and sees that they are properly checked to prevent any irregularity in the order of finish. They see that all runners who cross the finish line are given their proper order as they go through the chute.

The **clerk of course** places the teams in proper position on the starting line.

The **course umpire** observes the runners during the race. If any runner fails to run the proper course or otherwise violates the rules, the umpires report the infraction to the referee.

A **false start** occurs when a runner leaves the starting line before the race is started.

Fartlek is taken from the Swedish words for "speed play." A fartlek is a workout consisting of easy running with the addition of hills or short, fast bursts, followed by a return to easy running.

The **finish judge** stands outside the chute and on the finish line to determine the proper order in which competitors enter the chute.

Marshals keep the competitive area free from all persons except officials, runners, and other people authorized by the games committee.

The **meet director/referee** is the person ultimately responsible for the meet scheduling and preparation. This role also requires the individual to oversee the meet and is responsible for holding athletes accountable for their conduct or for any rule violations.

Racing flats are lightweight shoes designed for racing.

Splits indicate a runner's time as they pass a predetermined mark on the course. For example, splits might be taken at the half-mile, mile, and mile-and-a-half marks in a 2-mile race.

The **starting box** is the area a team is assigned on the starting line.

A **surge** is a tactical increase in the pace during competition.

Timers record the called-out times of all competitors who finish the race. Timers can also be assigned to designated positions along the course to call out elapsed time or splits to runners during the race.

Training flats are running shoes designed for wear in daily training.

OFFICIALS

Officials can include callers, checkers, chute directors, chute umpires, clerks of course, course umpires, finish judges, marshals, meet directors/referees, and timers. Many of these positions are held by volunteers. Any course violations would be reports by the volunteers to the meet director/referee. The duties for these various roles are described in "Terms."

ORGANIZATIONS

Amateur Athletic Union
P.O. Box 22409
Lake Buena Vista, FL 32830
407-934-7200
www.aauathletics.org

International Association of Athletics Federations
17 rue Princesse Florestine
BP 359
MC98007
Monaco
377 93 10 8888
www.iaaf.org

National Collegiate Athletic Association
700 W. Washington St.
P.O. Box 6222
Indianapolis, IN 46206
317-917-6222
www.ncaa.org

National Federation of State High School
    Associations
P.O. Box 690
Indianapolis, IN 46206
317-972-6900
www.nfhs.org

USA Track & Field
132 E. Washington St., Ste. 800
Indianapolis, IN 46204
317-261-0500
www.usatf.org/groups/CrossCountry

19

Cross-Country Skiing

FABRICE COFFRINI/AFP/Getty Images

A petroglyph on a rock wall in Norway depicts a skier on long skis. Dating from 2000 BC, this petroglyph attests to the longevity of Nordic, or cross-country, skiing. Scandinavian immigrants sparked interest in cross-country skiing in the United States in the 19th century. Advances in equipment helped create two distinct forms of skiing: downhill (Alpine) and cross-country. The latter experienced a boom in the United States in the 1970s, and in the 1980s two forms of cross-country skiing evolved: classical (traditional) skiing in tracks and freestyle (skating) out of tracks, on groomed trails. Nordic downhill, which combines both Alpine and Nordic elements, has also emerged as a type of skiing. Cross-country skiing is popular both as recreation and as competitive sport.

OVERVIEW

Objective: To record the fastest time.

Number of Competitors: There are individual and team events; see "Skiers."

Length of Course: From 1 to 50 kilometers. Competitions include sprint, team sprint, individual, relay, and pursuit events, as well as combination events, which take place over 2 days and include both classical and freestyle forms of skiing.

COURSE

Cross-country courses range from 1 to 50 kilometers; they are marked with various colored boards, arrows, and ribbons, depending on the competition. A course must be at least 3 meters wide and prepared so that skiers can safely compete. Two ski tracks are set 17 to 30 centimeters apart, measured from the middle of each track. The tracks are 2 to 5 centimeters deep. A typical course consists of

- one-third uphills, with climbs between 9 and 18 percent, plus some steeper, short climbs;
- one-third rolling terrain, with short climbs and downhills and height differences of 1 to 9 meters; and
- one-third varied downhills, demanding versatile downhill techniques.

Table 19.1 shows rules for height differences, maximum climbs, and total climbs.

SKIERS

Cross-country skiing offers competition for all levels of interest. Men, women, persons with special needs, seniors, and youth can all enjoy the sport at various distances and tracks of difficulty. Those categories are broken down as follows:

TABLE 19.1

Height and Climb Regulations

Distance (km)	Maximum height differential (m)	Maximum single climb (m)	Maximum total climb (m)
Sprint	50	0-30	0-60
5	100	30-80	150-210
10	125	30-80	250-420
15	150	30-80	400-630
Longer than 15	150	30-80	400-630

Adapted by permission from International Ski Federation (FIS), *The International Ski Competition Rules* (Oberhofen/Thunersee, Switzerland: FIS, 2013), 40. Available: http://www.fis-ski.com/mm/Document/documentlibrary/Cross-Country/02/95/69/ICRCross-Country2013_clean_English.pdf.

- Men: 1-kilometer sprint; 10-kilometer, 15-kilometer, 30-kilometer, 50-kilometer, and 70-kilometer races; team sprint; 4 × 10-kilometer relay; pursuit races; and overall

- Women: 1-kilometer sprint; 5-kilometer, 10-kilometer, 15-kilometer, 20-kilometer, and 50-kilometer races; team sprint; 4 × 5-kilometer relay; pursuit races; and overall

- Disabled men: 1-kilometer sprint; 5-kilometer, 10-kilometer, 20-kilometer, and 30-kilometer races; 3 × 5-kilometer relay; 10-kilometer pursuit; and overall

- Disabled women: 1-kilometer sprint; 5-kilometer, 10-kilometer, and 20-kilometer races; 3 × 5-kilometer relay; 7.5-kilometer pursuit; and overall

Competition is categorized as follows:.

- Seniors: between 20 to 29 years old
- Masters: at least 30 years old
- U20: 18 to 19 years old
- U18: 16 to 17 years old
- U16: 14 to 15 years old
- U14: 12 to 13 years old
- U12: 10 to 11 years old
- U10: 8 to 9 years old
- U8: 6 to 7 years old
- U6: 5 years old and younger

EQUIPMENT

Skis may be made of any material. They must be at least as long as the height of the skier, minus 10 centimeters; they cannot be longer than 230 centimeters. The middle of the ski must be between 43 and 47 millimeters wide. The tips must be curved at least 5 centimeters for classical skis or 3 centimeters for freestyle skis. The tail must not rise more than 3 centimeters. Skis must weigh at least 750 grams per pair. Both skis must be constructed in the same way and be of the same length. Edges may not face upward. The running surface can be smooth or slightly grooved. Scale patterns, to aid climbing,

are allowed. There are no limitations for boots and bindings.

A skier's poles must be of equal length; they may not be longer than the competitor's height or shorter than the distance from hip to ski. The poles' length must be constant; they may not have telescopic qualities. They also may not have any springs or mechanical devices to assist in pushing off. Poles have no weight restrictions. Poles may be constructed with differences between them. A grip must attach to the shaft, but there are neither limits on the grip's material or design nor on the shaft's material.

RULES

Competitors use one of two skiing techniques: classical or freestyle. Classical skiing is what most people associate with traditional cross-country skiing: using a diagonal stride, double-poling and using a herringbone technique without a gliding phase. Skiers cannot skate in a classical race. For individual competitions, skiers follow a single track. Freestyle skiing employs skating methods, including marathon and no-pole skating. This is normally a faster method than classical skiing.

Competitors must follow the marked course from start to finish, using their marked skis and their own means of propulsion. They cannot be paced or pushed. In individual competitions, a competitor may exchange poles but not skis. During relays and combined competitions, a competitor may exchange one ski if it is broken or damaged.

A competitor may not wax, scrape, or clean their skis during competition, with one exception: In classical skiing, a competitor may scrape their skis to remove snow and ice and add wax if necessary. They must do this on their own, outside the track.

A competitor who is being overtaken must give way on the first demand, unless they are in the final 200 meters of the course. This is true in classical competitions even if two tracks are in use.

Start

The starter calls "Attention" 10 seconds before the start, then counts down beginning at 5. The competitor's feet must be behind the start line; the poles should be over the start line. If electric timing is used, the competitor may take off anywhere from 3 seconds before to 3 seconds after the command to go. If they start more than 3 seconds before, they must go behind an extension of the start line outside the start gate.

The following starts are used in competitions.

∎ Single or double start: One or two skiers begin, and after a specified interval—10, 15, 20, or 30 seconds—another skier or pair of skiers starts.

∎ Group or mass start: Competitors are divided into groups. The start line is in the form of an arrow, where the first place ranked person receives the most favorable position. For the classical technique, the first 100 to 200 meters is marked with parallel tracks that the competitors must follow. The number of tracks is reduced by half over the next 100 meters, and the course converges into two or three tracks shortly after that. For the freestyle technique, competitors ski in 100 to 200 meters of parallel tracks; they cannot use skating techniques in the tracks. The course then opens up into at least 100 meters without tracks.

∎ Pursuit start: The winner of the first combined competition starts first, the second-place finisher starts second, and so on. The start intervals are the same as the differences between the competitors' times from the first day's results. The first 200 meters must be prepared at least 6 meters wide. A modified pursuit start may be used when time differences are substantial. The bottom half of the field may use a mass start 1 minute after the last person from the top half of the field has started.

Finish

The final 200 meters should be as straight as possible. For classical competitions, the final 200 meters is set with three to four tracks; for freestyle competitions, the final 200 meters is prepared at least 9 to 12 meters wide, depending on whether the start was interval or mass, respectively. A competitor finishes when he contacts the electric beam in electric timing, or, in hand timing, when their first foot crosses the finish line. Times are recorded to one-tenth of a second.

TERMS

A **christie** is a skidded turn in which both skis skid on the same edges.

Cross-country downhill skiing is a combination of Alpine and Nordic skiing also known as *telemarking*.

A **diagonal stride** is the most common cross-country maneuver for gliding across flat terrain and up hills. It employs arm and leg actions similar to walking.

A **diagonal V** is a skating maneuver in which the skier glides aggressively uphill with the skis in a V-shaped position.

Double poling is a maneuver in which a competitor uses both arms to push simultaneously on the poles to provide momentum.

A **gliding herringbone** is a maneuver used to slide uphill with skis in a V shape.

A **herringbone** is a maneuver used to step uphill with skis in a V shape.

A **kick double pole** refers to pushing off with both poles while also pushing off from the leg to provide more power. This is also known as a *single-step double pole*.

A **marathon skate** is a technique that combines double poling with an extra push from an angled or skating ski. Skiers use this to gain extra power in tracks.

Poling refers to skiers planting their poles to increase momentum or to guide themselves through a turn.

The **power side** is the side on which poling occurs during skating moves.

Sideslipping refers to skidding on the skis to the side and forward down a hill.

Sidestepping refers to lifting one ski at a time across the snow to move sideways.

A **skate turn** is a technique used to accelerate around turns, using the skis in a V shape. The competitor shifts their weight from one ski onto the other, bringing the first ski parallel.

Skating with no poles occurs when the skier steps off one ski, glides onto the other, and then glides back to the first ski.

A **snowplow** is a downhill maneuver a skier uses to control speed by angling the skis in an A shape and pressing them into the snow.

A **telemark turn** occurs when the skier sinks into a curtsy and the skis form one long curve.

V1 is a skating maneuver that combines skating with double poling. The skier poles once for every two steps. This maneuver is done on groomed snow with no tracks and is mostly used on uphills.

V2 is a fast skating technique that combines double poling with skating. The skier poles twice for every two steps. As with V1, this maneuver is done on groomed, trackless snow and is mostly used on flats and gentle uphills.

V2 alternate (open field skate) is the fastest technique; it combines double poling once for every two skating steps. This is mostly used on flats and gentle downhills.

A **wedge turn** is a turn made with the skis in an A shape.

OFFICIALS

A competition committee is responsible for conducting the technical aspects of the competition. The committee includes a chief of competition; a competition secretary; and chiefs of course, timekeeping, stadium, and, at large competitions, security.

ORGANIZATIONS

International Ski Federation
Marc Hodler House
Blochstrasse 2
CH-3653 Oberhofen
Switzerland
www.fis-ski.com

Snowsport GB
Hillend, Biggar Rd.
Midlothian EH10 7EF
Scotland
www.snowsportgb.com

U.S. Ski and Snowboard Association
P.O. Box 100
1 Victory Ln.
Park City, UT 84060
435-649-9090
www.ussa.org

Curling

Curling dates back to 16th-century Scotland and was originally played on frozen ponds. Players used stones of varying shapes, which often curved, or "curled," as they slid down the ice; some believe this is how the name curling originated. Players used brooms to clear the snow in the stone's path.

The game was introduced to North America in the late 18th century by immigrants. By the 1850s, curling clubs had sprung up in various Canadian and northern U.S. cities. In the 20th century the game moved indoors and equipment was standardized. Today there are more than 1.2 million curlers and 1,200 curling clubs in Canada and about 22,500 in the United States. Curling has spread around the globe, with 60 nations having member associations in the World Curling Federation, and it has become a recognized Olympic medal sport.

OVERVIEW

Objective: To score the most points by placing stones within the 12-foot circle called the "house" and closer to the tee than those of the opposing team.

Scoring: Determined after each end of 16 stones is completed; a stone that is within a 6-foot radius of the tee and is closer than any opponent's stone to the tee scores a point.

Number of Players: Two teams of four players. Recently, a mixed doubles competition has been added as a sanctioned world championship event by the World Curling Federation and an Olympic discipline. See "Variations."

Game Length: Eight or ten ends; ten for championship play and eight for wheelchair curling.

Player 1 from team A delivers a stone, followed by player 1 from team B. Each player shoots two stones per end. While one player shoots, two teammates sweep the ice, if necessary, to help the stone travel farther. Some rocks may be placed to block or guard other rocks that are in scoring position and are not intended to be scoring rocks themselves. The team that scores in an end throws the first rock in the next end. There is no sweeping in wheelchair curling.

PLAYERS

Each of the four players on a team delivers two stones during each end, delivering alternately with his opponent. The established rotation must be maintained throughout the game. A team may not substitute for more than one of the original players in a competition (or one male and one female in mixed competition), but any number of substitutions is allowed for that one player (or couple, in mixed competition). In championship play, substitutes must be eligible team members.

EQUIPMENT

Stones are circular and weigh no more than 44 pounds, with a circumference no greater than 36 inches. Stones must be at least 4.5 inches in height. Brooms or brushes are used for sweeping. Players may not wear shoes that damage or mark the ice; shoes should be flat-soled and should grip the ice well for walking. For consistency, teams that throw stones with the lighter-colored handles wear lighter-colored shirts, and conversely those throwing the darker stones wear darker shirts. Measuring tools can be used for the purpose of determining points.

RULES

Players from each team alternate delivering stones; each player shoots two stones per end. Teammates sweep the ice for their team's shots, helping to guide the stone. The stone that is closest to the tee, and other stones of that team within a 6-foot radius of the tee and closer to the tee than any opponent's stones, scores a point. Other stones, while not scoring points, can aid a team's efforts by blocking the path of stones delivered later. Once an end of 16 stones is completed, the team that scores goes first in the next end. In championship games, teams are subject to a time limit for their game, similar to the chess clock concept.

Stones

A stone (or rock) is removed from play when it

- rolls over or comes to rest on its side or top,
- does not clear the far hog line (see figure 20.1) and has not struck another stone in play,

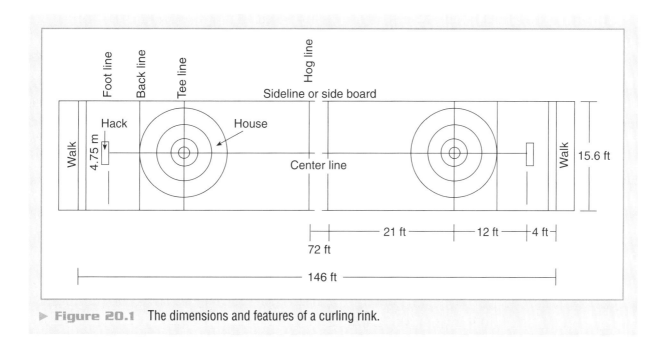

▶ **Figure 20.1** The dimensions and features of a curling rink.

- comes to rest beyond the back line,
- hits a side board or touches a sideline, or
- is touched while in motion by the playing team.

A stone's position is not measured until the last stone of the end is delivered, unless a skip requests that a stone be measured to determine whether it is in play. All 16 stones are delivered in an end unless the players in charge of the house agree on a score for that end or one of the teams concedes the game.

The opposing skip may choose, however, to place a stone where she thinks it would have ended up if not touched, if she believes it is to her opponents' advantage to have the stone removed. The player may also reposition any stone inside the hog line at the playing end that would have been displaced had the running stone not been touched.

If a running stone is touched by an opponent or opponent's equipment, the skip of the playing team may place the stone where he believes it would have come to rest had it not been touched.

Delivery

Many times the order of play is predetermined by the last stone draw. If it is not, a coin toss determines which team delivers the first stone of the game.

Right-handed players deliver stones from the hack (a rubber foothold) on the left side of the center line; left-handers play from the hack on the right side of the center line. A stone is removed from play if this rule is violated.

The player must release the stone before it reaches the hog line. Otherwise, the stone is removed from play. Any displaced stone hit by a stone released in violation of this rule is replaced in its original position to the satisfaction of the opposing skip. In nonchampionship play, a stone may be delivered by a push-stick, often used by players with injured hips or knees. The approval to use a stick has extended the playing careers of many curlers.

Sweeping

Sweeping may not begin until a stone is in motion. Players may sweep between the tee lines for their teammates' delivered or struck stones. They may not sweep for their opponents' stones between the tee lines. Neither the sweepers nor their equipment may touch the stone at any time.

Behind the tee line, only one player from each team—the skip or acting skip—may sweep at any one time. A player may not begin sweeping an opponents' stone until it reaches the tee line. If the delivering team's choice is not to sweep behind the tee line, that team cannot prevent the opposing team from sweeping the stone.

VARIATIONS—MIXED DOUBLES

A team consists of one male and one female player. Ends are scored in the same way the four-player game is scored. Each game consists of eight ends in which five stones per team are delivered and one stone per team gets preplaced. This allows 6 points to be awarded per end. Due to the uneven number of stones thrown per end, the player delivering the first stone of the end also delivers the last stone. Following a throw, either one or both players have the opportunity to sweep the stone in play. It is important to note that a takeout is not allowed before the fourth rock is thrown.

A power play may be used once per game when the team has the last stone advantage. This option is only available during regulation play and not when the game goes into extra ends. A power play means that the preplaced stones are moved from the center of the sheet to one side or the other with one stone placed as a guard and the other directly behind it touching the tee line.

TERMS

A **bonspiel** is a recreational tournament.

A **cashspiel** is a tournament with cash prizes.

A **championship** is a tournament leading to national or international play.

An **end**, with some similarities to an inning in baseball, is a portion of the game in which all eight players (four per team) deliver two stones each. Scoring is determined at the completion of each end; a game lasts 8 or 10 ends.

The **house** is the scoring area of the rink, with a 12-foot diameter and a tee at the center.

A **match** is a contest between two or more teams on each side; the winner is determined by the total number of points or by games won.

A **skip** is the team captain and strategist. Only the skip or the acting skip can be in the house when the opposition is throwing. The skip of the delivering team is in charge of the house.

OFFICIALS

Recreational games are self-officiated. In championship play, an umpire supervises the game and settles any disputes between opposing skips. A chief umpire is overhead of the umpire and has an extensive list of roles and responsibilities starting before the competition begins.

ORGANIZATIONS

Curling Canada
1660 Vimont Ct.
Orleans, ON K4A 4J4
613-834-2076
www.curling.ca

USA Curling
5525 Clem's Way
Stevens Point, WI 54482
715-344-1199
www.usacurl.org

World Curling Federation
3 Atholl Crescent
Perth PH1 5NG
Scotland
44 1738 451 630
www.worldcurling.org

Cycling

Today's bicycles, whether for the road, for off-road, for the track, or simply for recreation, bear little resemblance to the early models, which were made entirely of wood and were essentially two wheels attached to a hobby horse. These wooden models, first created in 1817, gave way in the 1870s to metal bikes with solid rubber tires. Pneumatic tires came on the scene in 1888, and 3-speeds and 10-speeds first appeared in the 1960s.

The invention of the bicycle was followed almost immediately by the start of bicycle racing, which developed gradually over the years. By the 1890s, racing as we know it today had begun, and the first Tour de France was held in 1903. Bicycle racing was initially seen as an endurance sport, with distances that often exceeded 500 kilometers per day, but developments in bicycle manufacturing and the expansion of paved roads slowly changed the emphasis to speed.

OVERVIEW

Bicycle races today take many shapes and forms within the three main types of racing: track racing, road racing, and off-road racing. Road racing is the most popular brand of cycling, with the annual Tour de France, covering approximately 3,500 kilometers in 21 stages over 23 days, well known to even the most casual of fans. Off-road racing has evolved from recreational off-road bicycling and is a fast-growing sport in itself. There are many types of races contested on the track (see "Track Racing").

Races are held for individuals and for teams over one or more events. Depending on the event, the objective of cycling is to finish first, to finish with the overall best time, or to score the most performance points.

RIDERS

Riders compete in both individual and team competitions, which may be further classified according to gender and age. Age groups normally are in 5-year groupings (30 to 34, 35 to 39, and so on). Junior age groups are 10 to 12, 13 to 14, 15 to 16, and 17 to 18.

All riders are classified according to age as shown in table 21.1.

TABLE 21.1

Rider Class Age Ranges

Rider classification	Age range (yr)
Youth	Less than 9
Juniors	9-18
U23	19-22
Master	30 and above

Master riders may hold an elite status. Professional riders are always considered elite regardless of their age.

COURSES

As noted, riders take part in races on a track, on the road, or on off-road courses. Following are a few particulars about different types of courses.

Tracks (or Velodromes)

The track surface is made of asphalt, cement, or wood, and it has curves and straightaways. There are 333-meter, 400-meter, and 500-meter tracks, but the world standard is 250 meters. The corners of a velodrome are banked so that the riders can maintain maximum speed through them. The degree of inclination varies. Some tracks have very shallow banking (10 degrees or less), while others have very steep banking (over 45 degrees). Two pursuit finish lines are in the middle of the two straightaways, perpendicular to the direction of travel and even with each other. These lines are usually red. There is a start/finish line on one side of the track, called the home straight. This is a black line in the middle of a white background. There are also lines that parallel the track. There is a black line, called the measurement line, 20 centimeters from the bottom of the track. The official track distance is measured on this line. There is a red line parallel to the track 90 centimeters from the bottom of the track. This is called the sprinters line, and in some of the track events there are rules about when a rider can and cannot enter or leave the space below this line, called the sprinter's lane. About a third of the way up the track is a blue line, called the stayers line, that is also parallel to the track. The stayers line is officially used in a type of event where riders are paced by motorcycles, although this type of track race is rarely seen anymore. Typically, the stayers line is now used in training to separate riders who are riding slowly around the track from those who are trying to go fast.

Road Courses

Road courses can be around a circuit or from point to point. Ideally, these courses are closed to public traffic and do not use roads that have traffic lights or railroad crossings.

Off-Road Courses

Off-road courses can vary greatly. Mountain bike downhill courses start at a higher elevation and finish at a lower elevation, traversing rough paths and rocks and going through forests and plains. Cross-country courses are closed courses that traverse various landscapes, including forests, rocks, mud, grasslands, and whatever the terrain has for the riders. A very popular event these days is cyclo-cross, which uses short circuits similar to mountain bike cross country, but riders use modified road bikes instead of mountain bikes. Cyclo-cross is currently the most popular type of event in the United States and is a blend of road cycling and mountain bike cycling.

EQUIPMENT

Bicycles may be no more than 2 meters long and 75 centimeters wide. Tandem bicycles may be up to 3 meters long. Bicycles may be propelled only by the riders' legs. They may have no protective shield to reduce wind resistance. Wheels may be either spoked or of solid construction. Handlebars should be solidly plugged; ends that point up or forward or provide support for the rider's forearms are allowed only in time trials and pursuits.

For track races, only a bicycle with a single-cog fixed wheel (one gear on the rear wheel) and without derailleurs may be used. For road races, only a bicycle with a freewheel (multiple gears on the rear wheel) and one working brake on each wheel shall be used. Riders must wear a protective helmet that has met standard laboratory testing procedures and a jersey that covers the shoulders. Footgear must be fully enclosed. Eye protection is recommended, as is additional helmet padding for downhill and dual slalom events. For races that follow international rules, the bicycle regulations are much more extensive. Dimensions, weights, and wheel characteristics are all regulated.

RULES

Cyclists begin a race in one of three ways: all with holders; all with one foot on the ground; or all with a rolling start. Holders cannot step over the starting line. When a rolling start is used on a track, at least one neutral lap is taken to ensure a fair start. A race is begun with a signal—usually a gun or a whistle.

Any rider who appears to present a danger to the other competitors may be disqualified. Pushing or pulling among riders is prohibited in all races except the Madison; no rider may hold back or pull an opponent. A cyclist may not progress unaccompanied by a bicycle. A cyclist who crashes may run with his bike.

The last lap is indicated by the ringing of a bell. A cyclist finishes a race when her front tire first penetrates an imaginary vertical plane perpendicular to the leading edge of the finish line. Should two or more track riders tie for first place in which there is a prize, they may ride either the full distance or a shorter distance, as determined by the race officials, to determine the winner.

Track Racing

Track races are held on an oval track, usually 200 to 400 meters in length (see figure 21.1). The track is usually banked slightly on the straightaways and more so on the turns. Marked lines include the starting line (if it doesn't coincide with another line), the 200-meter line (placed 200 meters before the finish line), two pursuit finish lines (in the middle of the two straightaways), and a finish line. The finish line is black and is placed in the middle of a 72-centimeter-wide white strip for contrast.

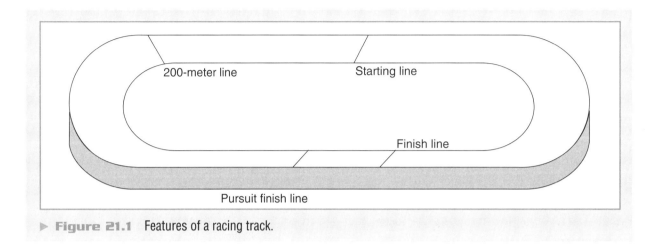

▶ **Figure 21.1** Features of a racing track.

Track races include the following:

▤ Handicap: Faster riders must travel farther or must start later than the other cyclists.

▤ Individual pursuit: Racers start on opposite sides of the track on the pursuit line. The race is run until one rider catches the other rider or until the distance is completed. Pursuits are 2, 3, or 4 kilometers, depending on the age and gender of the riders. In championship events, pursuits are run in two rounds, a qualifying round and then a final. In the final, the riders who qualified first and second compete for the gold medal. The riders who qualified third and fourth compete in the final for the bronze medal.

▤ Keirin: Up to nine riders compete in a paced event for five laps on tracks of 333 meters or less, or for four laps on longer tracks. A pacer rides a motorized bike. Sprint rules apply; during the first lap, the speed is about 40 to 45 kilometers per hour. The pacer gradually accelerates to 45 to 50 kilometers per hour and then moves off the track with two laps to go. No rider may pass the pacer while it is still on the track.

▤ Madison: Teams of two riders each compete in a relay points race. No more than one member of a team may race at one time; while one rider is racing, his teammate is riding around slowly at the top of the track waiting for his turn. The rider racing makes an exchange with the rider on relief and pushes him up to speed, usually with a hand sling. Sprints for points are conducted the same as in a points race. In case of a mishap, one teammate must take over until the injured rider returns. If both riders suffer a mishap, they are entitled to a number of free laps that is closest to 1,000 meters, after which at least one of them must resume racing.

▤ Mass start: All riders start from the same point at the same time. The race is run over a specified number of laps; lapped riders are normally removed from the race.

▤ Miss and out: In this mass-start race, the last rider over the line on designated laps is eliminated. This may occur on every lap, every other lap, or on some other announced schedule. Either the winner is the last rider left or the race is run until a specified number of riders remains, at which point a free lap may be followed by a sprint lap to determine the finish.

▤ Omnium: Riders compete for points in a set of races; final places are determined by total points for all the events, with points being awarded in each event on a 7-5-3-2-1 basis for first place through fifth. A tie is broken by the rider who has the most first-place finishes; if the score is still tied, the rider who has the most second-place finishes wins, and so on. If it is still tied, the rider who placed highest in the final event wins.

▤ Points race: Riders begin in a mass rolling start; sprints for points are held on designated laps. On these laps, the first four riders are awarded points (5, 3, 2, and 1). A rider who laps the field gets 20 points. A rider who is lapped by the field loses 20 points.

Sprint: A sprint is a series of short races with a small number of competitors, usually two to four. Sprint races are two laps on tracks of 333 meters and larger and three laps on shorter tracks. The rounds may be preceded by a flying-start 200-meter time trial to seed or select riders. Round-robin sprints, held with a small number of riders, pit each competitor in an individual race against every other competitor. In championship formats, riders are advanced through qualifying sprints to the finals.

Team pursuit: Similar to individual pursuit, except the event is contested by teams. Usually there are three to four riders on a team. Team pursuits are usually 4 kilometers for men and 3 to 4 kilometers for women.

Time trial: Riders compete one at a time over a fixed distance. In a kilometer time trial, two riders start at the same time on opposite sides of the track. In the kilometer time trial, the event is a final. Each rider only rides once, with the fastest time being the winner.

Road Racing

A road course may be out and back, around a circuit, from place to place, or any combination of these, but the course may not cross itself, forcing riders to cut through other riders. A marker denotes the final 1,000 meters. A white flag or a sign indicates the final 200 meters, which should be a straightaway.

If the road is open to traffic, riders must keep to the right of the center line. A rider may pass on either side of another rider. If the lead riders are stopped by a temporary road closure (such as at a train crossing), the race is neutralized, and all riders begin at the same time intervals as their arrival at the closure. If the lead rider or riders make it through and others are stopped, this is an unforeseeable incident, and no compensation is allowed.

Riders may exchange food and drink among themselves. A rider who suffers a mishap may be helped back on his bike and may be pushed for 10 meters.

Road races fall into the following categories:

- Criterium
- Individual road races
- Individual time trial

- Stage race
- Team time trial
- Time trial

Off-Road Racing

Following is a very truncated version of the regulations for off-road racing in general and for specific types of races. Races are discussed within their subdisciplines, mountain biking and cyclo-cross.

For all off-road races, participants must begin and complete the event on the same bicycle. Any repairs must be made by the racer; no outside support is permitted. Spare parts and tools must be carried by the racer. Riders who take shortcuts or cut trail switchbacks are disqualified.

The most common mountain bike races are as follows:

- Cross country: Water and food are available only in designated zones. Riders have the right-of-way over racers pushing bicycles. Lapped riders must yield to other riders. A rider cannot bodily interfere with another rider's progress.

- Short track: This is a shorter version of a typical cross-country race. The race takes a maximum of 30 minutes to complete and consists of multiple laps. These laps should not take the faster riders any more than 2 minutes to complete.

- Downhill: Riders race against a clock one at a time. Whichever rider reaches the bottom of the course with the fastest time wins. Courses must be marked with signs to ensure that riders proceed in the correct direction and follow the route.

- Dual slalom: Each rider gets at least one qualifying run. The fastest qualifier is seeded against the slowest, and so on. The winner of each head-to-head competition moves on to the next heat. A rider who gets a jump start is penalized 1.5 seconds. Riders must ride around gates; a missed gate costs 1.5 seconds. Other 1.5-second penalties include changing from one course to another, not passing both wheels around a gate, interfering with the other rider, and not finishing in possession of the bike. Ties are broken by comparing the overall times on the course that both riders completed.

Another form of off-road racing is cyclo-cross. These races take place on multiple terrains that vary in difficulty to allow racers to make up time lost on difficult portions of the course. The course for the race is between 2.5 and 3.5 kilometers and includes a maximum of six obstacles.

TERMS

A **criterium** is a circuit road race held on a short course (800 meters to 5 kilometers) closed off to traffic. Primes (sprints) may be held within the race.

A **cyclo-cross** is a race held on rough terrain, only about 75 percent of which is traversable by bike, forcing riders to dismount and carry their bikes periodically.

A **handicap start** is one in which the faster riders either ride longer or start later.

A **keirin** is a paced sprint, held on a velodrome, in which a motorized bike leads a pack of riders, accelerating until there are two laps to go, at which point the motorized pacer drops out and the riders sprint for the finish.

A **mass start** is a race in which all riders begin on the same line.

In a **miss-and-out** race, the last rider on designated laps is forced to withdraw from the race.

In a **pursuit race**, riders begin at equal intervals around the track. The race is run until one rider catches the others or until a certain distance is covered, as specified in advance.

A **stage race** is a series of road races for individuals and teams in which the overall winner is the rider with the lowest accumulated time for all of the stages.

In a **time trial**, riders compete one at a time over a fixed distance.

OFFICIALS

Races are officiated by a chief referee, a chief judge, assistant referees, assistant judges, and a starter.

ORGANIZATIONS

Union Cycliste Internationale
Ch. de la Mêlée 12
1860 Aigle
Switzerland
41 24 468 58 11
www.uci.ch

USA Cycling
210 USA Cycling Pt.
Colorado Springs, CO 80919
719-434-4200
www.usacycling.org

Equestrian

Comstock

The Olympic history of events involving horses dates back to 682 BC, when chariot races were contested at Greece's 25th Olympiad. In the modern Olympic era, the full program of dressage, show jumping, and three-day eventing was introduced in 1912. Equestrian is the only Olympic sport in which humans and animals are teamed up and in which men and women are pitted against each other on absolutely equal terms.

The United States Equestrian Federation, the national governing body for the sport, annually sanctions more than 2,500 competitions across the United States. In addition, there are many nonsanctioned equestrian events with competitors at all levels.

OVERVIEW

Objective: To score the most points.

Disciplines: Dressage, show jumping, three-day eventing.

- In dressage, horses are trained to high levels of impulsion, collection, and obedience. The goal is for horses to perform naturally as they are requested to perform while running loose.

- Show jumping is a timed event in which competitors are judged as the horses jump over a series of obstacles in a given order. Higher scores are given to horses with the fewest refusals or knockdowns of portions of the obstacles.

- Three-day eventing, which is sometimes called combined training, horse trials, or the complete test, combines the obedience requested in dressage with the athletic ability of show jumpers. It also requires fitness to complete the event, particularly the cross-country jumping portion. In this portion, horses leap over fixed obstacles (e.g., stone walls, banks, ditches, and water) as they try to finish in optimum time.

Scoring: In dressage, competitors are judged and score points based on their performance in many criteria. In show jumping, the team of horse and rider that covers the course in the shortest time with the fewest jumping faults wins. In three-day eventing, the team of horse and rider with the fewest penalties wins.

ARENA

The standard arena is 20 meters by 60 meters and is used for tests in both dressage and three-day eventing. A small arena is 20 meters by 40 meters. The standard dressage arena letters are A-K-V-E-S-H-C-M-R-B-P-F (see figure 22.1).

The letters on the long sides of the arena nearest the corners are 6 meters in from the corners and 12 meters apart from each other. The letters in the middle of the arena are D-L-X-I-G, with X marking the center.

At the start of the test for dressage and three-day eventing, the horse enters at A. One judge sits at C, although for upper-level competition, there are up to five judges at different places around the arena (at C, E, B, M, and H), which allows the horse to be seen in each movement from all angles. This helps prevent certain faults from going unnoticed, which may be difficult for a judge to see from only one area of the arena.

RULES

In dressage, a horse and rider perform prescribed tests that include walking, trotting, and cantering. In show jumping, a horse and rider go through at least one change of direction and over at least eight obstacles. In three-day eventing, a horse and rider compete in dressage, cross country, and stadium jumping. The following sections describe the rules applying to each event.

Dressage

The discipline of dressage displays and tests the complete training of the horse as demonstrated through the walk, trot, and canter. A horse and rider perform a prescribed test in an enclosed, flat arena. The requisite movements, such as transitions between gaits, circles, or lead changes, must come at markers designated by letters placed along the outside of the arena. Each test reviews the basics of training, as demonstrated through the collection or extension of stride and lateral movements. The horse and rider are judged according to numerous criteria; the highest score wins.

The intent of dressage is "the development of the horse into a happy athlete through harmonious education" (*USEF Rule Book*, 2018, p. 493, www.usef.org/forms-pubs/F3p8pgrWgAo/dr-dressage-division). Each element of dressage

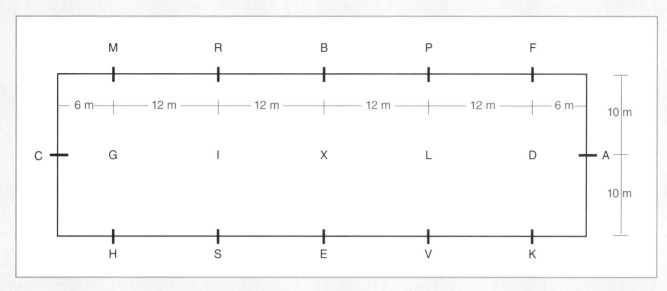

▶ **Figure 22.1** A sample equestrian arena.

plays a role in reaching this objective. The walk is to be regular, free, and unconstrained. The trot is free, supple, regular, and active. The canter is united, light, and balanced. Following are brief descriptions of the main elements of dressage (the word is French for *training*):

■ Walk: The horse's walk is a marching gait in which the footfalls of the horse's feet follow one another in "four time." There are four types of walks—collected, medium, extended, and free—that should demonstrate the proper training of the horse.

■ Trot: The horse's trot is a gait of "two time" on alternate diagonal legs (left front, right hind, and vice versa) separated by a moment of suspension. The trot is judged by its general impression, the elasticity and regularity of the steps, and the rhythm and balance. The collected, working, medium, and extended trots should demonstrate the training of the horse.

■ Canter: The horse's canter should be light and cadenced with a regular stride. The gait is "three time;" there is a moment of suspension when all four feet are in the air before each stride begins. The canter is judged on general impression, the regularity and lightness of the gait, and the rhythm. The proper training of the horse is demonstrated through four canters: the collected, working, medium, and extended.

■ Rein back: The rein back is an equilateral, retrograde movement in which the feet are raised and set down by diagonal pairs moving backward.

Performance During a test, the horse and rider may perform the following figures and movements:

■ Volte—a circle with a diameter of 6, 8, or 10 meters

■ Serpentine—S-pattern movements demonstrating changes of direction

■ Figure eight—two voltes of equal size, joined at the center

Judging The following factors are judged: collection and balance, correct outline of the horse, and impulsion. A judge may warn a competitor of an error in the test, such as a wrong turn or an incorrect movement, by ringing a bell. Subsequent errors are penalized by 2 points, then by 4, and then by elimination. Riders perform some of the tests from memory, although at the lower levels, the tests may be read to them.

Judges rate performances of movements and transitions on a scale of 0 to 10, with 0 being "not executed," 1 being "very bad," and 10 being "excellent." Judges award collective marks for gaits, impulsion, submission, and rider's position and seat.

Show Jumping

In show jumping, the horse and rider jump a course of a minimum of eight obstacles, attempting to make jumps that are "clean" (i.e., that do not knock down the obstacle) within the time allowed. The team of horse and rider that covers the course in the shortest time with the fewest jumping faults wins.

Jumpers are scored on faults incurred while on the course, including disobediences, falls, knockdowns, touches, and time penalties. In combinations, each obstacle is scored separately. If a horse refuses to jump or runs out at one element, it must repeat the entire combination. Ties involving championships must remain tied; classes with a tie for first place only are decided by a jump-off.

Course   The course must include at least one change of direction, one combination, and at least 10 jumping efforts. At least three of the first eight jumping efforts must be spread obstacles. Obstacles can consist of combinations (two or more separate jumping efforts), spreads, water jumps, single rails, gates, and brush. (Note: Certain categories of competitions have variances to the types of obstacles used.) The height of obstacle rails ranges from 2.75 feet to 6.00 feet.

Water obstacles must be at least 16 feet wide at the face and have at least an 8-foot spread of water; they may be up to 15 feet long. For every foot in length, they may have 2 inches in depth of water. There may be an obstacle no higher than 2.6 feet on the takeoff side. Knocking down or displacing such an obstacle is not a penalty.

Penalties   Horse and rider may be penalized for disobediences, knockdowns and touches, falls, and time penalties. Following are examples of disobediences:

- Refusal to jump (stopping in front of the obstacle and then backing up or circling to make the jump)
- Running out (evading or passing the obstacle)

- Loss of forward movement (halting or stepping backward after crossing the starting line); a disobedience is not called when the horse comes to a standstill before attempting the obstacle, provided the horse immediately completes the jump; however, if the halt continues or if the horse backs up even one step, a disobedience is called
- Circling

Three-Day Eventing

The three-day event, previously known as combined training, is an all-around test of the horse. The event consists of dressage, cross country, and show jumping. Each test takes place on a separate day. Cross country should be the most influential test in scoring, and dressage should be slightly more influential than the jumping test.

Dressage must be held first; cross country and show jumping may follow in either order. The dressage test is similar to a dressage competition. The cross-country test is a test of endurance, speed, and jumping ability and consists of four phases; these follow one another without interruption. Phase A begins at a trot or a slow canter; this is called "roads and tracks." Phase B is the steeplechase; this phase is normally carried out at the gallop over obstacles. Phase C is again roads and tracks, reverting back to a trot or a slow canter. The final phase, D, is cross country, normally carried out at the gallop over obstacles where horse and rider negotiate solid jumps, ditches, banks, and streams. Cross country is considered the heart of the sport. The final test, show jumping, requires the horse and rider to compete on a show jumping course within an arena. The team of horse and rider that completes the three days of competition with the fewest penalties is the winner.

TERMS

A **canter** is a three-beat gait, similar to a gallop.

A **clean round** signifies that a jumper has completed a course within the allotted time and without incurring any jumping faults.

A **combination** is two or three jumps taken in quick succession, separated by only a stride or two. If a horse stops or runs out at any part of the combination, it must rejump the entire series.

A **curb** is a bit with leverage action that works on the top of the horse's head, the chin, and the bars of the mouth.

A **gait** is a pace: a walk, trot, canter, or gallop, or varying speeds of each, as well as the slow gait and rack of the American Saddlebred horse.

A **hand** is a unit of measurement equaling 4 inches. A horse is measured from the ground to the top of its shoulder, which is called the withers.

A **knockdown** occurs when a horse or rider lowers an element of a jump that establishes the height of an obstacle.

A **snaffle** is a bit that works directly on the corners of the horse's mouth.

A **trot** is a diagonal two-beat gait, faster than a walk and slower than a canter.

A **walk** is a marching gait in "four time."

OFFICIALS

A ground jury is responsible for adjudicating and judging the events, although additional judges may be appointed for dressage and jumping events. An appeals committee addresses any protests or charges.

ORGANIZATIONS

Fédération Equestre Internationale
HM King Hussein I Building
Chemin de la Joliette 8
1006 Lausanne
Switzerland
41 21 310 4747
www.fei.org

International Equestrian Organization
16780 Cumberland Hwy.
Newburg, PA 17240
www.ieodressage.org

United States Equestrian Federation
4047 Iron Works Parkway
Lexington, KY 40511
859-258-2472
www.usef.org

23

Fencing

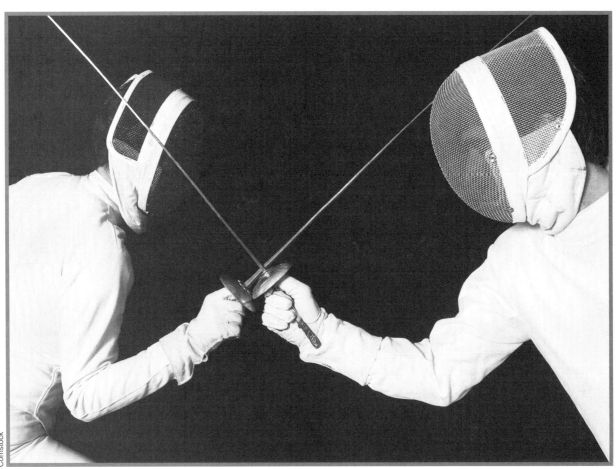

Comstock

Fencing originated from a form of combat and began as a sport in either Italy or Germany—both claim to have originated the sport—in the 14th or 15th century. Three innovations in the 17th century led to fencing's popularity: the development of the foil (with a padded tip to reduce the risk of injury), the development of a set of rules that limited the target to certain areas of the body, and the creation of the wire-mesh mask.

Fencing is one of the few sports that have been contested at every Olympic Games. There are about 450 dedicated fencing clubs in the United States with about 500 additional organizations that offer fencing classes. Nearly 17,000 people in the United States belong to the U.S. Fencing Association, the national governing body for the sport.

OVERVIEW

Objective: To touch and not be touched; the winner is the fencer who accumulates the appointed number of touches first.

Number of Fencers: Two.

Scoring: A fencer scores by touching the opponent's target area with the point of the weapon (for foil and epee) or with its edges and point (saber).

Length of Bout: 3 minutes or until one fencer scores five touches.

Winning: If no fencer has reached the appointed number of touches within 3 minutes, various rules apply to determine the winner.

When the command "Fence" is given, the bout begins. The weapon must be held and used with one hand only; a fencer may not change hands during a bout unless permitted to do so because of injury. After each valid touch, the fencers return to the on-guard lines.

When two fencers are in contact, the bout is stopped. In foil and saber, all contact is prohibited. Contact in foil and saber results in a yellow card warning. In epee, no intentional contact is allowed. No warnings are given for contact in epee unless it is deemed to be "jostling." When a bout is temporarily halted, it is resumed at the spot where it was halted until a touch is made. When a fencer leaves the strip, the bout is halted. A fencer is not penalized for accidentally leaving the strip (e.g., in being jostled).

FIELD

The field of play is a strip of even surface of wood, linoleum, cork, rubber, or other material (see figure 23.1). The strip is 1.5 to 2 meters wide and 14 meters long. Five line markings are used on the strip to clearly mark different sections of the strip. There is one center line clearly marked

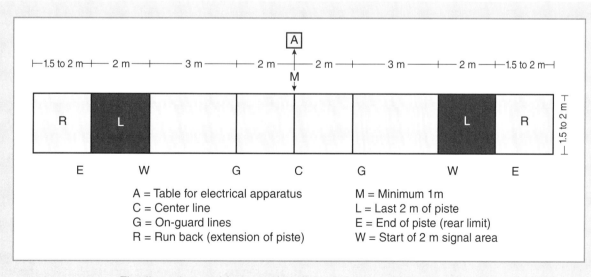

▶ **Figure 23.1**   The dimensions and features of the field of play, or fencing strip.

across the entirety of the width of the strip. In addition, there are two lines called on guard lines 2 meters away from the center line and two lines at the end of the strip to indicate the end of the playing zone. The last two meters should be a different color. This allows the competitors to be aware of their positioning and determine if they are close to the outer limited of the playing area.

Fencers compete in individual or team competitions and in various age divisions and classifications, including the following:

▫ Veterans

▫ Senior

▫ Junior

▫ Cadet

▫ Youth 14

▫ Youth 12

▫ Youth 10

▫ Wheelchair

DURATION OF THE BOUT

The duration of the bout is the effective duration, that is, the total of the intervals of time between the orders "Play" and "Halt."

The effective duration of a bout is:

▫ For pools, 5 touches, maximum 3 minutes.

▫ For direct elimination bouts, 15 touches, maximum 9 minutes, divided into three periods of 3 minutes, with 1 minute's pause between any two periods.

▫ For team matches, 3 minutes for each bout.

EQUIPMENT

All weapons have a flexible steel blade that comes to a point; a grip, which may include a handle and a pommel (which locks the handle onto the tang of the blade); and a metal guard between the blade and the grip, to protect the hand.

For foil and epee the guard must be padded to minimize the effect of a blow, it should also contain the connector to which the body cord is attached. A fencer's outfit must be white or a light color on the torso. The rest of the clothing may be of a different, singular color. The glove's cuff must cover about half of the forearm of the sword arm. The mask must include a rear safety strap,

and the space between the wires (mesh) must be no more than 2.1 millimeters apart. The mesh must have a minimum gauge of 1 millimeter in diameter. Transparent masks are not allowed in USA Fencing competitions.

RULES

Fencers try to touch their opponents while keeping from being touched themselves. Following are rules that pertain to positioning in foil, epee, and saber competitions.

Positioning of Fencers

The fencer whose number is called first stands to the right of the referee. (In a bout between a right- and left-hander, when the left-hander is called first, the left-hander stands to the left of the referee.)

In foil and epee, the referee places each of the competitors in such a way that the front foot of each is 2 meters from the center line of the strip (behind the on-guard lines). In sabre, each competitor's back foot is placed 2 meters from the center line of the strip.

Competitors are always put on guard, whether at the beginning of the bout or subsequently in the center of the width of the strip. When the competitors are placed on guard during the bout, the distance between the them must be such that when they are in the point-in-line position, the points of the two blades cannot make contact.

After the scoring of a valid touch, the competitors are put on guard in the middle of the strip. If no touch is awarded, they are replaced in the position that they occupied when the bout was interrupted.

Foil

To score a touch, the point must touch the target—the opponent's trunk, which is covered with a metallic cloth vest called a lame. When an opponent's tip hits the vest, it sets off a light and a buzzer on the scoring machine on the side of the fencer who hit. A valid hit is signified by a colored light; an invalid (off target) hit is signified by a white light. The limits of the target are the collar (6 centimeters above the collarbone), the seams of the sleeves, and the tops of the hip bones (see figure 23.2).

five touches. The fencer who hits first gets a point; if both fencers hit within 1/25th of a second, each scores a point.

For epee fencers, double touches still count. If double touches arrive when the score is 4-4, nothing is written on the score sheet. The score remains 4-4, and the fencers do not return to the center. If the score is tied when time runs out, 1 minute is added, a coin is tossed, and the bout continues until a single touch is scored or time runs out. The coin toss determines who has priority if the score remains tied.

Sabre

The referee places each of the two sabre competitors so that the back foot of each is 2 meters in front of the on-guard lines. Touches made with the point, the cutting edge, the side edge, or the back edge of the blade is valid. Hitting with the guard of the weapon is not valid and is penalized. Touches with the point that graze the target or cuts that slip along the opponent's body are not valid. The target is the entire body above a horizontal line between the top of the folds formed by the thighs and the trunk when in the on-guard position.

If the score is tied when time runs out, 1 minute is added, a coin is tossed, and the bout continues until a single touch is scored or time runs out. The coin toss determines who has priority if the score remains tied.

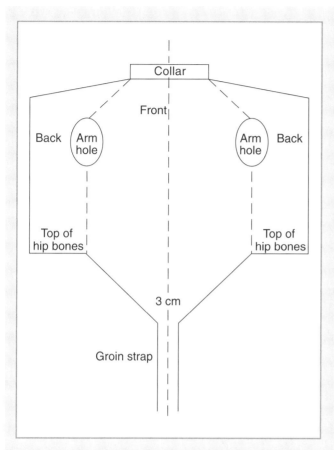

▶ **Figure 23.2**   A point is scored when the foil point touches the target. The boundaries of the target are the collar, the seams of the sleeves, and the tops of the hip bones.

TERMS

The **attack** is the initial offensive action executed with the weapon arm extending and the point or blade threatening the valid surface with a progressive forward motion.

A **bout** is a contest between two fencers.

A **competition** is the aggregate of bouts or matches that determine a winner. Competitions are distinguished by weapon. They can also be categorized by gender, age, or other classification and by individual or team events.

A **compound attack** is offensive action preceded by one or more feints, or actions, on the blade.

A **counterattack** is an offensive action executed after the start of the opponent's offensive action.

If the score is tied when time runs out, 1 minute is added, a coin is tossed, and the bout continues until a single touch is scored or time runs out. The coin toss determines who has priority if the score remains tied. If the score of the bout was 0-0 after 3 minutes of fencing and no touch was scored after the extra minute, then the score is recorded as V0-D0 in favor of the fencer with the priority. If a touch is scored in the additional minute, the score is V1-D0 in favor of the person scoring the touch.

Epee

The touch must be made on the target, with the point. The target is the whole of the fencer's body, including clothing and equipment. Bouts are for

A **counter-riposte** is an offensive action executed after parrying the riposte. It may be either simple or compound.

A **direct attack** is a simple offensive action executed in a straight line.

An **indirect attack** is offensive action executed in a line other than the one in which it originated.

"On guard" is a pronouncement by the referee for competitors to get into stance for combat.

A **parry** is a defensive blade movement that blocks the opponent's offensive action.

The **point-in-line position** is when the fencer's sword arm is kept straight and the point of the weapon continually threatens the opponent's valid target.

Redoublement is a forward conformation with new footwork (e.g., lunge, fleche) after an initial offensive action is short or parried.

A **remise** is a simple direct offensive or counteroffensive action made after the initial offensive or counteroffensive is parried, when the riposte is delayed or absent.

A **reprise** is a simple indirect, compound offensive or counteroffensive action made after the initial offensive or counteroffensive is parried, when the riposte is delayed or absent.

A **riposte** is an offensive action executed after a parry. It may be either simple or compound.

OFFICIALS

Fencing bouts are directed by a referee, who may be assisted by judges. Judges are required when there is no metallic strip and in the final bout of a competition. Scorers and timekeepers are also used. When a judge sees a touch arrive, she raises her hand to advise the referee. The judges and the referee vote on the "materiality of the touch" to decide whether to award a touch to the fencer. Each judge's opinion counts as one vote; the referee's opinion counts as a vote and a half.

In bouts judged with a scoring machine, the referee places himself in view of the machine, and the materiality of the touch is indicated by the machine. Only touches that are registered by the machine are counted as such.

ORGANIZATIONS

British Fencing
1 Baron's Gate
33-35 Rothschild Rd.
London W4 5HT
England
www.britishfencing.com

International Fencing Federation
Maison du Sport International
Av. de Rhodanie 54
CH-1007 Lausanne
Switzerland
www.fie.ch

U.S. Fencing Association
4065 Sinton Rd., Ste. 140
Colorado Springs, CO 80907
719-866-4511
www.usfencing.org

24

Field Hockey

One of the world's most popular games, field hockey is also one of the world's oldest competitive team sports. Evidence of games played with a ball and stick date back more than 4,000 years to the Nile Valley in Egypt, and similar games were played by civilizations ranging from the Greeks and Romans to the Ethiopians and Aztecs.

The sport was introduced in the United States at Harvard in 1901 and soon caught on at many women's colleges in the eastern United States. The game is played by both women and men at club and international levels. At the high school and college levels, it is primarily a girls' and women's sport. In Olympic competition, the Netherlands, Australia, and Germany tend to dominate among the men and the Netherlands, Argentina, and Australia among the women.

OVERVIEW

Objective: To score more goals than the opponents.

Scoring: A goal is scored when an attacking team member plays the ball within the shooting circle and it completely passes the goal line between the goal posts. The ball may be deflected by a defender and still count as a goal, but it may not go outside the shooting circle.

Players: 11 players per side, including a goalkeeper for each side.

Length of Game: Two 35-minute halves with a 10-minute break between the halves.

A game begins with a center pass, in which a member of the attacking team hits the ball from the center line to a teammate. Players on a team pass the ball to each other and attack the opponent's goal. A game is also restarted with a center pass after a goal is scored; the opponents scored on put the ball into play.

FIELD

The field is 100 yards long and 60 yards wide (see figure 24.1). It has a center line marking and two 25-yard-line markings. The shooting circles are 16-yard semicircles in front of the goal. Penalty spots for penalty strokes are marked 7 yards in front of each goal. The goal is placed in the center of the back line, and the front of the goal touches the back line. No equipment, towels, or water bottles are allowed in or on the goal. The goals are 4 yards wide, 7 feet high, and 4 feet deep. Each goal has a backboard 18 inches high spanning the width and sides of the goal. Goals are netted loosely to prevent the ball from rebounding onto the field.

PLAYERS

A team has a maximum of 18 players in international matches, 11 of whom may be on the field at one time. Players wear uniforms and may wear guards for shins, ankles, and mouths. Goalkeepers may wear upper-body protectors and must wear different-colored shirts from those of either team. Goalkeepers also wear protective helmets and may wear protective padding on their legs and elbows.

A team captain wears a distinctive armband. Captains ensure that player substitutions are made correctly, and they are responsible for the proper behavior of their team members. Time is not stopped for a substitution except when a goalkeeper is replaced; the substitute may enter the field only after the player coming out is off the field. Substitutions are only permitted at the center line or an otherwise designated area. Players who have been suspended are ineligible to substitute for any player while serving their suspension.

EQUIPMENT

The ball is spherical, weighing 5.50 to 5.75 ounces, with a circumference of 8.80 to 9.25 inches. Its surface is smooth. The stick has a flat side and a rounded side. The maximum length of the curved head, measured from the lowest part of the flat face, is 4 inches. The stick must weigh between 12 ounces and 28 ounces. The diameter of the shaft must not exceed 2 inches.

RULES

The field hockey rules of conduct state that players may not

- intentionally play the ball with the rounded side of the stick;
- participate in a play without a stick in hand;

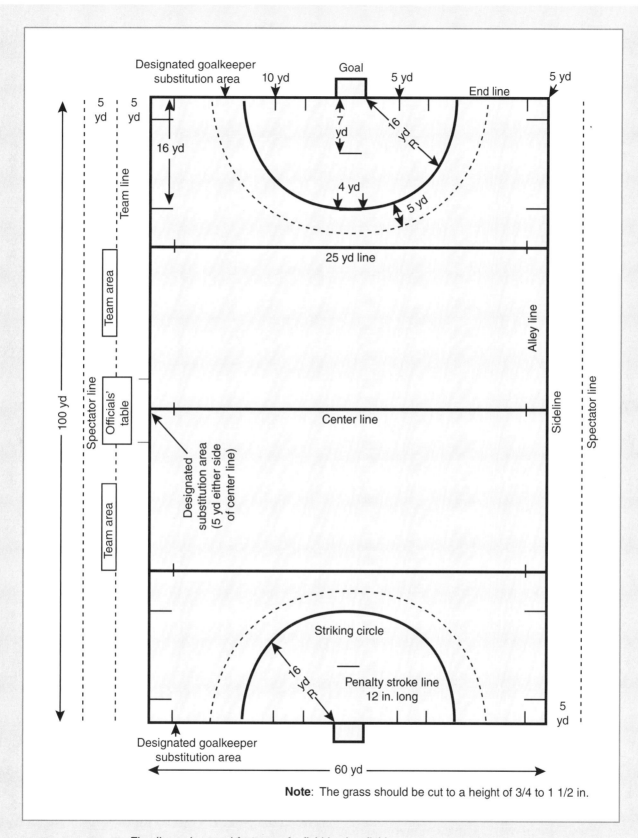

Designated goalkeeper substitution area

10 yd

Goal

5 yd

End line

5 yd

5 yd

5 yd

Team line

16 yd

7 yd

16 yd R

4 yd

5 yd

Team area

25 yd line

Alley line

100 yd

Spectator line

Officials' table

Designated substitution area (5 yd either side of center line)

Center line

Sideline

Spectator line

Team area

Striking circle

16 yd R

Penalty stroke line 12 in. long

5 yd

Designated goalkeeper substitution area

60 yd

Note: The grass should be cut to a height of 3/4 to 1 1/2 in.

▶ **Figure 24.1** The dimensions and features of a field hockey field.

▪ lift their sticks over the heads of players;

▪ use their sticks dangerously or play the ball in a way that is likely to lead to dangerous play;

▪ hit, hook, hold, or strike another player's stick or uniform;

▪ catch or stop the ball with the hands (except in protection);

▪ use their bodies to propel the ball;

▪ use their feet or legs to support the stick in a tackle;

▪ intentionally raise the ball from a hit, except for a shot at goal;

▪ approach within 5 yards of a player receiving a pass in the air (the ball must be played and on the ground); or

▪ use their bodies or sticks to shield the ball from an opponent (obstruction).

Scoring the most goals during the allotted game time is the purpose of field hockey. In doing so, players must follow specific guidelines.

▪ During a center pass, opponents must be at least 5 yards from the ball. A field player may play the ball with the flat side of the stick only. A goalkeeper may use any part of her body to stop the ball within the shooting circle as long as she has a stick in her hands.

▪ A bully is a play used to restart a game when the ball lodges in the goalkeeper's pads, or when time is stopped for an injury or for any other reason in which no penalty has been awarded. Two opposing players face each other where the stoppage happened, with the ball between them and all other players at least 5 yards away. (If the occurrence happened inside the shooting circle, the ball is placed 16 yards from the goal line, even with the edge of the circle.) Each of the two players taps his stick on the ground, on his side of the ball, and then taps the flat face of the opponent's stick one time, over the ball. At this point the players may try to put the ball into play.

▪ When a ball goes out of bounds, it is put back into play according to where and how it went out.

▪ When the ball goes out over a sideline, play is restarted by a member of the opposing team. The restart occurs where the ball went out, but the player does not have to be wholly in or out of bounds.

▪ When the ball goes out over a back line, play restarts in one of three ways:

1. When the attack knocks the ball out of play, a defender puts the ball back into play up to 16 yards from, and opposite, where it crossed the back line, parallel with the sideline.

2. When the defense unintentionally knocks the ball out of play over a back line, an attacker restarts play on the 25 yard line, in line of where the ball went out.

3. When the defense intentionally knocks the ball out of play over a back line, the attacking team is awarded a penalty corner on the back line, 10 yards from the closer goal post.

Penalties are awarded for fouls that clearly disadvantage the player or team fouled. An umpire may award a free hit, a penalty corner, or a penalty stroke.

Free Hit

A free hit is awarded for a foul by an attacker or for an unintentional foul by a defender outside the shooting circle. The hit takes place at or near where the foul occurred.

Penalty Corner

A penalty corner is awarded when the defense commits an intentional foul inside the 25 yard line, when the defense intentionally plays the ball out of bounds over the back line, or when the defense unintentionally fouls an attacker within the circle who does not have the ball. An attacker takes a penalty corner from a spot on the back line 10 yards from a goal post. At least one of the attacker's feet must be out of bounds; no other player may be within 5 yards. The other attackers must be outside the circle. Not more than five defenders, including the goalkeeper, may be behind the back line; the remaining defenders must be beyond the center line.

An attacker may not attempt a shot at goal until the ball has come completely outside the circle. If the first shot at goal is a drive, the ball must cross the goal line no higher than the height of the backboard for a goal to be scored, unless it touches a defender or a defender's stick while in flight. The attacker putting the ball into play may not score directly.

Penalty Stroke

A penalty stroke is awarded when the defense commits an intentional foul in the circle to prevent a goal from being scored or when the defense unintentionally fouls in the circle, thereby preventing a probable score.

Time stops when a penalty stroke is taken. The player taking the stroke stands behind the ball, which is placed 7 yards from the goal. All other players, other than the goalkeeper, must stand beyond the 25-yard line. The goalkeeper may not move until the attacker plays the ball. The attacker may push, scoop, or flick the ball from the penalty spot, raising the ball to any height. She may touch the ball only once, and she may not feint before she touches it. If the player scores a goal, the game restarts with a pass back. If the player doesn't score, the game restarts with a defender playing the ball 16 yards in front of the center of the goal line.

TERMS

A **bully** is a play that restarts action by employing a face-off between two opponents who tap each other's sticks one time and then attempt to play the ball.

A **center pass** is used to begin play and to resume play after a goal has been scored. It takes place at the center line and involves a member of the attacking team passing the ball in any direction to a teammate.

Dangerous play is any action that endangers any player, including raising the ball, tackling from the wrong position.

A **flick** occurs when a player pushes the ball and raises it off the ground.

A **free hit** is given for a foul committed outside the shooting circle.

A **penalty corner** results from a foul committed inside the circle; an attacker hits the ball from a point on the goal line at least 10 yards away from a goal post.

A **penalty stroke** is awarded when a foul is committed inside the circle if the defenders have intentionally fouled. An attacker shoots at goal from 7 yards away in a one-on-one confrontation with the goalkeeper.

OFFICIALS

Two umpires control the game. Each umpire is primarily responsible for play on his half of the field, diagonally from the near left corner to the far right corner as he faces the field. This broad latitude means they each make decisions in one half of the field pertaining to free hits in the circle, penalty corners, penalty strokes, and goals. Umpires must keep track of goals scored and warning or suspension cards used throughout the game.

ORGANIZATIONS

International Hockey Federation
Residence du Parc
Rue du Valentin 61
CH-1004 Lausanne
Switzerland
41 21 641 0606
www.fihockey.org

National Field Hockey Coaches Association
3352 E. Virgil Dr.
Gilbert, AZ 85298
480-789-1136
www.nfhca.org

U.S. Field Hockey Association
5540 N Academy Blvd.
Colorado Springs, CO 80918
719-866-4567
www.usfieldhockey.com

Figure Skating

Ulrik Pedersen/NurPhoto via Getty Images

In the early 20th century, figure skating competitions and tests became established in the United States and Canada; figure skating was an Olympic sport in 1908 and was reintroduced to the Games in the first Winter Olympics in 1924. In 1976, ice dancing was added as an Olympic sport. Competitions are held in various events, including singles skating, pairs skating, ice dancing, and synchronized team skating. The grace, strength, and athleticism of figure skating have made the sport popular among athletes and spectators. Although skaters at all levels and ages compete in figure skating, the rules in this chapter pertain to senior-level events.

OVERVIEW

Objective: For individuals, pairs, and teams to score points based on program components, skating skills, transitions, performance, interpretation, and choreography.

Start: The order of skating is based on an officials' draw; competitors must take their starting positions within 30 seconds of being called to perform.

Length of Program: Ranges from 2 minutes 40 seconds for the short program up to 4 minutes for free skating.

Music: Competitors choose their own music, and vocals are allowed.

RINK

The rink consists of a smooth ice surface, typically 100 by 200 feet (minimum size is 85 by 185 feet). It has rounded corners and a low wall.

SKATERS

Skaters compete in singles skating, pairs skating, ice dancing, and synchronized skating. In singles skating, the age limits are under 13 for juvenile girls, under 14 for juvenile boys, and under 18 for intermediate women and men. In pairs skating and ice dancing, the age limits are under 16 for juveniles and under 18 for intermediates. In all three types of competition (singles, pairs, and ice dancing), there are no age restrictions in the United States for novices, juniors, and seniors. In contrast, age restrictions apply for these types of competition when participants compete in international events governed by the International Skating Union (ISU).

EQUIPMENT

The skates are the most important piece of equipment for a figure skater. They must fit properly and provide adequate support for the skater's body type and ability. Boots and blades are sold separately and must be custom mounted for each skater's preference. There are also different blade types for free skating, ice dancing, and synchronized skating.

Skaters must wear clothing that is modest and dignified, not garish or theatrical; clothing considered inappropriate results in a deduction. Skaters may choose clothing that reflects the character of the music. Men must wear full-length trousers. Women must wear skirts, trousers, or tights (including unitards). Clothing must not give the effect of excessive nudity inappropriate for the discipline.

RULES

Each discipline in figure skating (singles, pairs, ice dance, and synchronized) has specific rules and objectives.

Singles Skating

In singles skating, the short program consists of up to seven required elements with connecting steps to be completed in 2 minutes 40 seconds, plus or minus 10 seconds. Jumps, spins, and step sequences are common to short programs. Scores are given based on the following:

- Jumps—height, length, technique, and clean starting and landing of required jumps
- Spins—strong, controlled rotation of spins; number of revolutions and speed of rotation; height (for flying spins)
- Step sequences—difficulty of steps; swing, carriage, flow, and musicality

The free skate includes jumps, spins, steps, and other linking movements executed with a minimum of two-footed skating in harmony with the music. The program lasts 4 minutes. The skater may choose the elements of the program.

Special attention is given to choreography, expression, interpretation of the music, and intricacy of footwork. The skater must use the full ice surface. A well-balanced senior singles program must contain jumps, jump combinations, spins, and step sequences.

Pairs Skating

Pairs skating is performed by two skaters (a woman and a man) skating in unison and in harmony with the music. Skaters perform the moves of singles skating either symmetrically (mirror skating) or in parallel fashion (shadow skating), executing spins, lifts, partner-assisted jumps, and similar moves, linking their moves with harmonious steps.

In a short program for pairs, skaters must perform seven required elements with connecting steps within 2 minutes 40 seconds, plus or minus 10 seconds. These elements include

- one overhead lift (minimum of one revolution by the man),
- one twist lift (double or triple),
- one throw jump (double or triple),
- one solo jump (double or triple),
- one solo spin (with one change of foot and minimum of two positions),
- one death spiral, and
- one step sequence (must be visible and identifiable and should be performed using almost the full ice surface).

A senior pairs free skate must contain three different overhead lifts and one twist lift, two different throw jumps, one solo jump, one jump combination or jump sequence, one pairs spin combination; one death spiral, and a choreographic sequence that must be clearly visible.

Ice Dancing

For competition, a dance couple is composed of a woman and a man. For the senior level, ice dancing includes a rhythm dance and a free dance. Skaters skate closely together, performing difficult footwork sequences in a variety of dance holds. Ice dancing often looks like ballroom dancing on ice, but couples may perform any variety of dance styles.

Couples are scored on accuracy of positions, steps, and movements; placement of steps and use of the ice surface; upright body carriage and flowing motion; close and effortless unison; timing to the music; and expression of the character of the music. The length of the dance varies.

In the rhythm dance, couples dance to music with a prescribed rhythm and tempo, which changes each year, and they perform elements such as sections of pattern dances (dances with prescribed steps), lifts, step sequences, and twizzles.

The free dance is relatively unrestricted, and skaters select the mood and tempo as long as it is danceable. Skaters are allowed 4 minutes to display their full range of technical skills, interpretation, and inventiveness. Dancers perform elements selected from lifts, spins, step sequences, twizzles, and choreographic elements.

Synchronized Skating

Synchronized skating is an emerging discipline in figure skating. It is a highly technical form of team skating characterized by speed, accuracy, intricate formations, and transitions. In the senior division, teams of 16 members perform one short program and one free skate. Both the short program and the free skate must include required elements such as lines, circles, wheels, blocks, intersections, step sequences, moves in the field, and additional elements choreographed to music of the team's choice. The points earned for each segment of the competition are added together for the team's final result and placement.

Scoring

All senior-level competitions are scored under the international judging system (IJS). The IJS is based on cumulative points rather than the former 6.0 standard of marks and placement.

Under the IJS, points are awarded for a technical score combined with points for five components—skating skills, transitions, performance, composition, and interpretation of the music/timing. If a skater performs more than the defined elements of a well-balanced program, points are not deducted, but the values of additional elements are not calculated into the skater's score. (The exception to this is ice dancing, which takes a 1.0 deduction for each extra element.) If a skater does not perform all the required elements, he receives fewer points, not deductions.

The system focuses on the skaters and not on the judges. Judges no longer have to use their memories to compare all aspects of every skater and decide where to place them; judges simply evaluate the qualities of each performance. Starting order does not influence a skater's score; in the old system, starting early typically kept skaters' scores lower than if they had performed later in the competition. Also, a skater can now win coming from a much lower position—she no longer needs to count on another skater's mistakes to climb in the standings.

TERMS

A **crossover** is the most efficient way to gain speed on a curve; it can be done skating either forward or backward.

A **death spiral** is a pairs move in which the man rotates in a pivot position while holding one hand of his partner, who is rotating in a horizontal position with her body low and parallel to the ice.

A **double jump** is a jump with two complete revolutions and allowable further rotation of less than 360 degrees.

Edges are sustained one-foot glides on a curve, with the skater's body leaning into the center of the curve.

A **flying spin** is a spin that begins with a jump in which the position of the spin is evident during the jump. Sit spins and camel spins are the two most common flying spins. There are also death drops, butterflies, and flying-change sit spins.

Footwork includes steps, turns, edges, and directional changes that are performed by the skater in a deliberate way and in time to the music to connect other moves.

A **half-revolution jump** is a jump of one-half revolution (180 degrees) in the air.

A **lift** is when one partner (usually the man) assists the lifted partner into a sustained position. In pairs, the lifted partner is usually held over the head of the lifting partner. In ice dancing, the man may not lift his arms over his shoulders to assist the woman.

A **Mohawk** is a transition from forward to backward, or vice versa, from one foot to the other; the curve of the exit edge continues the curve of the entry edge. There are many variations of Mohawks.

The **pattern** of a dance is the dance's design. A pattern can be *set*, in which the steps are prescribed; *optional*, which allows for more than a set pattern; and *border*, in which the pattern is laid out progressively around the rink, never repeating at the same place in the rink.

A **single jump** is a jump of one complete revolution and allowable further rotation of less than 360 degrees.

A **spin** is a move in which the skater continuously rotates in small circles. Spins can be rotated forward and backward in a variety of positions.

A **spiral** is a move in which the upper body bends forward at the hip, with the body almost parallel to the ice, and the head and the free leg are up, with the free leg past the horizontal level.

A **throw** is a combination of a lift and a jump in which the man assists the woman on the takeoff by lifting and "throwing" her. The woman continues the rotation and lands the jump without assistance on a back outside edge.

A **twist** is a pairs move in which the man lifts and throws the woman in the air before catching her at her waist and lowering her to the ice. Unlike a traditional throw, where the throwing action carries the woman horizontally across the ice, in a twist the woman is thrown vertically into the air. The man has to exit on one foot from this lift.

OFFICIALS

There are two panels of officials in the competition scoring process—the technical panel and the judging panel.

The technical panel is generally made up of five persons: technical specialist, assistant technical specialist, technical controller, video replay operator, and data operator. This panel works in direct communication with each other as each skater performs a program. In real time, the technical specialist identifies the elements the skater performs. For example, for spins, he identifies the type of spin and the level of difficulty of that element based on published preset criteria. The work of the technical specialist allows the judges to concentrate on marking the quality of each element. When an element is identified by the technical specialist, it is referred to as the "call."

The assistant technical specialist and the technical controller support the technical specialist to ensure that any potential mistakes are corrected immediately. The technical controller is the leader of the technical panel, just as the referee is the leader of the judges' panel. Any element can be reviewed by the technical controller, the technical specialist, or the assistant technical specialist. The judges can ask for a review of an element by notifying the technical panel.

The video replay operator videotapes all of the elements that are scored. The video is available to the technical panel for their review of any element to ensure that the correct assessment of the element was made. If video replay is available to the judges, the judges can view the videotape for their analysis of the quality of or errors made on any given element.

The data operator enters all the coding for the elements onto either paper or the computer as they are performed and as the levels of difficulty are assigned.

The judges focus totally on scoring the quality of each element and the five program components. Their marks are based on specific criteria for each element and provide a comprehensive assessment of each skater's skills and performance. The referee judges the competition along with the judging panel and is assigned specific tasks in the running of the event.

ORGANIZATIONS

International Skating Union
Avenue Juste-Olivier 17
1006 Lausanne
Switzerland
41-21-612-6666
www.isu.org

Professional Skaters Association
3006 Allegro Park Ln. SW
Rochester, MN 55902
507-281-5122
www.skatepsa.com

U.S. Figure Skating
20 First St.
Colorado Springs, CO 80906
719-635-5200
www.usfigureskating.org

26

Football

Photodisc/Getty Images

American football evolved from rugby, which is a spin-off of soccer. Early roots of the modern game can be traced to a college game played in 1869 between Princeton and Rutgers universities. Each team had 25 players on the field; the game more closely resembled soccer than modern football. Running with the ball, passing, and tackling were not allowed. Harvard and McGill universities played a game in 1874 that combined elements of rugby and soccer; this game caught on in eastern U.S. schools and developed into the beginnings of modern football.

Early rules included playing with a round ball and needing to make 5 yards in three downs. Rules have continually evolved to make the game fair, exciting, and less violent. From its beginnings in the United States on college campuses, football has grown into a widely popular sport in the United States, where it is played in youth leagues, in high schools, and professionally. American football is played all over the world, although it is not a great spectator sport outside the United States.

OVERVIEW

Objective: To score the most points via touchdowns, extra points, field goals, and safeties.

Number of Players: 11 per team on the field.

Scoring: A touchdown is worth 6 points; teams can try for 1-point (kicking) or 2-point (running a play from scrimmage) conversions after a touchdown; a field goal is worth 3 points; a safety is worth 2.

Length of Game: Four 15-minute quarters in the National Football League (NFL) and college and four 12-minute quarters in high school.

The team on offense tries to advance the ball down the field and score a touchdown by crossing the goal line with the ball or, alternatively, tries to kick a field goal through the goal posts. The team on defense tries to regain possession of the ball by intercepting a pass in the air, recovering a fumble, stopping the offense from making 10 yards in four downs (plays), or forcing the offense to punt (kick) the ball to them.

FIELD

The playing field is 53.33 yards wide by 120 yards long (see figure 26.1). The length of the field is marked by boundary lines called sidelines. The end zones, located at both ends of the field, are 10 yards deep, bordered by a goal line in front and an end line in back. The two goal lines are 100 yards apart. Any part of the goal line is considered part of the end zone; any part of the end line and the

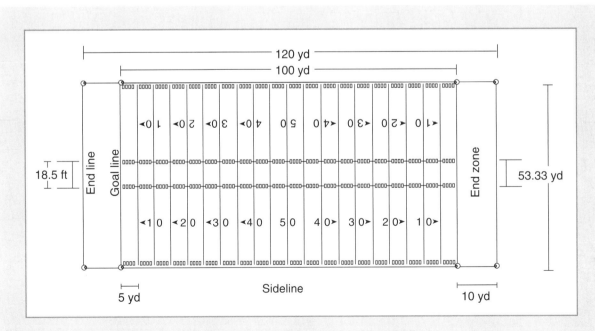

▶ **Figure 26.1** The dimensions and features of a professional football field.

sideline that borders the end zone is considered out of bounds.

The front and back corners of the end zones are marked with pylons. These pylons are out of bounds. The field is lined, widthwise, at intervals of 5 yards; along the sidelines each yard is marked. Yard lines are numbered every 10 yards in multiples of 10; these numbers are 2 yards long. Inbounds lines, or hash marks, run parallel to the yard lines. Hash marks are set 70.75 feet from each sideline in professional football and 53.25 feet from each sideline in college football.

Goal posts are at the back of each end zone, with a horizontal crossbar 18.6 feet in length (23.4 feet for high school) and 10 feet above the ground. The crossbar is directly above the end line. Two vertical posts extend 30 feet above the crossbar and are topped by ribbons measuring 4 inches by 42 inches.

PLAYERS

Offensive and defensive units have 11 players each. Player positions are designated depending on the system and terminology employed by the coach. Generally speaking, on offense, players are the quarterback, running backs, wide receivers, tight end, and offensive linemen (center, tackles, and guards).

On defense, players are generally identified as defensive linemen (ends and tackles), linebackers, and defensive backs (cornerbacks and safeties). Special teams are the units on the field when kicking takes place—during a kickoff, a field goal attempt, a point-after conversion attempt, or a punt. Primary among these players are the holder (who receives the snap and holds the ball for the placekicker), the placekicker (who kicks field goals and extra points), the punter, and the kick returners (who return kickoffs and punts).

Substitutes may enter a game during a dead ball (when play is stopped). A player is not limited to a certain number of times he may enter a game, but neither team may have more than 11 players on the field at the snap of the ball.

EQUIPMENT

The ball is oval shaped, leather bound, and inflated to a pressure of 12.5 to 13.5 pounds per square inch; it weighs 14 to 15 ounces and is 11 to 11.5 inches long and 28 to 28.5 inches at its largest circumference. (Youth league footballs are smaller.)

Players wear helmets, face masks, pads, and other protective equipment. This gear includes shoulder, chest, rib, hip, thigh, knee, shin, elbow, wrist, and forearm pads. Jerseys must cover all pads on the torso and upper body. Pants must cover the knee, and stockings must cover the lower legs from the feet to the bottom of the pants. Metal and aluminum cleats are prohibited. Conical cleats with tips measuring less than 0.375 inch in diameter are also prohibited. Nylon cleats with flat steel tips are permitted.

A crew of three operates yardage chains on the sidelines. The chains are 10 yards long and are attached to two sticks 5 feet tall. Traditionally, down markers have four flip-over numbers (1, 2, 3, and 4) on a stick 4 feet tall. In some leagues, a digital number has replaced the flip-over indicators. These numbers denote the down that is coming up, and the marker is placed at the nose of the ball.

A play clock is used between plays. Various levels have rules denoting how much time can run off a play clock (which begins at the end of one play and ends with the snap of the ball beginning the next play) before a team is penalized for delay of game. In the NFL and college, it's 40 seconds between plays.

RULES

The rules in this chapter are general football rules, with specific references to both National Collegiate Athletic Association (NCAA) rules and NFL rules. Important modifications for other levels and variations of the sport are addressed near the end of the chapter. It is important to note that different rules apply for high school, college, and pro levels.

Before the game, the winner of a coin toss either opts to receive the kickoff or chooses which goal his team will defend. At the end of the first and third periods, the teams switch goals. To start the second half, the team that lost the pregame coin toss chooses between the same two privileges.

The game begins with a kickoff from the kicking team's 35-yard line in the NFL and in college and from the 40-yard line in high school play. All players on the kicking team must be behind the yard line from which the ball is kicked, and all players on the receiving team must be no closer than 10 yards away from the kickoff line.

If the kickoff goes out of bounds without being touched by a receiver, the receiving team may elect to take the ball either where it went out of bounds or 35 yards beyond the kickoff line. If the kick touches a receiver and then goes out of bounds, the receiving team puts the ball into play at the yard line where the ball went out of bounds.

Each team normally huddles before a play to call the play and the coverage. (Sometimes an offensive team will go directly to the line of scrimmage without a huddle; in that case, the quarterback will call the play through coded signals.) The players line up on the line of scrimmage before the snap of the ball. The offensive team must have at least seven players on its line at the snap. Offensive players not on the line must be at least 1 yard behind it.

After the ball is snapped, the offensive team may advance the ball by running with or passing it. Although a team may attempt only one forward pass during a down, it may attempt multiple backward passes or laterals. Backward passes may be advanced by both teams even if the ball touches the ground before a receiver secures possession.

An airborne NFL receiver must come down with both feet in bounds (on the ground in the playing field) while in possession of the ball in order to record a legal reception. At other levels, only one foot needs to be in bounds. In high school, if a receiver is pushed out of bounds but would have landed in bounds otherwise, the catch is allowed.

In the NFL, a ball carrier may fall and get back up and continue running if he is not tackled or touched by a defender while on the ground. In amateur play, once a runner touches any part of their body to the ground, except for their hands and feet, they are considered down.

During each play, offensive players try to block defenders to protect the passer and ball carrier. The defense tries to tackle the ball carrier or knock him out of bounds or to intercept or knock down a pass. A defender records a sack when they tackle the quarterback for a loss of yardage during a pass attempt.

The offensive team has four downs, or plays, to advance 10 yards from the line of scrimmage at the first down. A team may, in certain instances, be awarded a first down (a new set of four downs)

on a defensive penalty, even if the necessary 10 yards are not made.

In many cases, if a team has not made a first down in three plays, it will punt (kick) the ball to the opponents on the fourth down. The player receiving the punt may try to catch and advance the ball, let it roll dead (it may not be recovered by the kicking team if it does not touch a player on the receiving team), or call for a fair catch by waving a hand above his helmet. The kicking team may not touch a player who has signaled for a fair catch unless the player fumbles the ball.

From high school on up, teams get three time-outs per half. The clock starts when

- the ball is snapped after a timeout;
- the ball is placed ready to play after a penalty; or
- an official spots the ball at the inbounds mark after an out-of-bounds play, and the referee gives the ready signal (except in the last 2 minutes of the first half and the last 5 minutes of the game, when the clock doesn't start again until the next snap). Note: In NCAA play, the clock doesn't start on any kickoff until a player on the receiving team touches the ball.

The clock stops when the ball is out of bounds; when a pass drops incomplete; when a play is completed during which a foul occurs; when 2 minutes remain in a half (NFL only); when a first down occurs (college only); when a period expires; when a field goal, safety, or touchdown is scored; when an official signals a timeout; or when a down involving a change of possession is completed.

If time expires as a play is in progress, time is not called until the play is completed. If either team commits a foul on the last play of a period, the offense may run another play. If the offense commits a foul on the last play of a half, the half is over.

For games in which the score is tied at the end of regulation time, overtime is played. In the NFL, overtime is begun with a coin toss and a kickoff; each team has a chance to score unless the first team to receive the ball scores a touchdown. If the receiving team only scores a field goal, the other team has the opportunity to score. In college and high school, each team has a chance to score in the overtime.

Scoring

A player scores a touchdown (6 points) when they possess the ball and the ball touches the plane of, or crosses over, the opponents' goal line. A touchdown can be made by running with the ball, by catching a pass, or by recovering a fumble on or over the opponents' goal line. The defense may intercept a pass, return a kick, or recover a fumble or blocked punt and return it for a touchdown.

After a touchdown is scored, a team has the choice of attempting a 1-point or a 2-point try, or conversion. In the NFL, the ball is placed at the 2-yard line for a 2-point conversion attempt or at the 15-yard line for a 1-point attempt; in amateur football, the ball is placed at the 3-yard line. A 1-point conversion is scored by kicking the ball through the uprights. A 2-point conversion is scored by an offensive player possessing the ball on or over the goal line (in what normally would be considered a touchdown).

A field goal (3 points) is scored by placekicking or dropkicking the ball through the opponents' goal post uprights (though dropkicking is rare in modern football). If the kick is no good and the ball is beyond the opponents' 20-yard line, the ball is given to the opponents at the spot of the kick. If the unsuccessful kick was attempted from on or inside the 20-yard line, the ball is given to the opponents at the 20-yard line. If, however, the kick is blocked and recovered by the opponents, the ball goes to the opponents at the spot where the ball is downed, regardless of the yard line.

A safety (2 points) is scored when the defense tackles a ball carrier behind the opponents' own goal line. A safety is also scored if the offense maintains possession of the ball out of bounds on or behind its own goal line. Examples of safeties are a runner or quarterback being tackled in their own end zone or a punt being blocked and going out of bounds beyond the goal line. After a safety, the team that was just scored on kicks off from its own 20-yard line. The kick can be a punt or drop kick, but no tee can be used.

Fouls and Penalties

Many rules in football are geared for safety. The following list contains brief explanations of common violations, listed in alphabetical order, that result in penalties. The length of the penalty appears at the end of each listing. Unless otherwise noted, information is based on NFL rules.

- Batting or kicking the ball: A player may not bat a ball toward the opponents' end zone or bat a ball in any direction in the end zone. Although stripping the ball (raking the ball from the player's grasp) is legal, trying to bat the ball in a player's possession is not legal. Neither is kicking any loose ball or ball in a player's possession. *10 yards*

- Defensive holding: No defensive player can tackle or hold an opponent other than the ball carrier. *5 yards and automatic first down*

- Delay of game: A team must put the ball into play in the allotted time (40 seconds from the end of the previous play, or 25 seconds after a timeout, measurement, injury, or other delay). *5 yards*

- Double (offsetting) foul: When live-ball fouls are committed by both teams, the penalties offset each other, and the down is replayed at the previous spot.

- Encroachment: No part of a player's body may be in the neutral zone, and no contact may occur before the ball is snapped. The neutral zone is a space the length of the ball between the offense's and defense's scrimmage lines. *5 yards*

- Fair catch interference: A player signaling for a fair catch of a punt must be given the opportunity to make the catch before the ball hits the ground. No contact may be made by a defender unless the ball has touched the receiver or touched the ground. *15 yards*

- False start: A false start occurs when an offensive player, once in the set position, moves in such a way as to signify the snap of the ball. *5 yards*

- Helping a runner: No offensive player can pull a runner or use interlocking interference to aid a runner. *10 yards in NFL play; 5 yards in NCAA play*

- Illegal contact: A defender may make contact with an offensive receiver who is in front of them and within 5 yards of the line of scrimmage. Beyond 5 yards, or if the receiver has moved beyond the defender, the defender may not make contact that impedes or restricts the receiver. Incidental contact is legal, as long as it does not significantly impede the progress of the receiver or create a distinct advantage for the defender. *Loss of 5 yards and automatic first down*

- Illegal forward pass: A team may make one forward pass from behind the line of scrimmage (a player with the ball may not cross the line of scrimmage and then retreat behind it and throw a pass). Any other forward pass is illegal, with penalties as follows: for passing from a point beyond the line of scrimmage. *5 yards from the spot of the pass and loss of down*; for a second forward pass thrown, or for a pass thrown after the ball was returned behind the line of scrimmage. *Loss of 5 yards from the previous spot*; for a forward pass not from scrimmage—*loss of 5 yards from the spot of the pass*

▦ Illegal motion: Only one offensive player—a backfield player—may be in motion before the snap. The motion can be parallel to, or backward from, the line of scrimmage. Any other motion by other players, prior to the snap—including movement of the head, arms, or feet and swaying of the body—is illegal. *5 yards*

▦ Ineligible player downfield: Before a pass is thrown, an offensive lineman (unless they are designated as an eligible receiver) may not lose contact with an opponent and advance beyond 1 yard of the line of scrimmage. *5 yards*

▦ Intentional grounding: A passer may not throw an incomplete pass without a realistic chance of completing it in order to avoid being tackled. A quarterback may stop the game clock, however, by receiving a snap and, in a continuous motion, immediately throwing the ball to the ground in front of him. (Note that in college, as long as the quarterback is outside the "tackle box"—the area that extends vertically through the outside foot of each tackle—they can throw the ball away, as long as the ball is thrown past the line of scrimmage.) *Loss of down 15 yards from previous spot*

▦ Offensive holding: No offensive player, in attempting to block, may use their hands to grab or obstruct a defender, except to initially contact the defender. The hands cannot be used to hang onto or encircle the opponent or to restrict her movement. *10 yards*

▦ Offside: A player is offside when any part of him is beyond the line of scrimmage when the ball is put into play. *5 yards*

▦ Encroachment A defensive player enters the neutral zone or contacts and offensive play prior to the snap. *5 yards*

▦ Pass interference: Once a ball is thrown, no player may hinder the progress of an opponent who has a chance to catch the pass. Incidental contact that does not impede a player or affect his chance to catch the ball is legal. Restrictions on pass interference end once the pass is touched. *First down for offensive team at the spot of the foul if penalty is on the defensive player; loss of 10 yards if the penalty is on the offensive player.*

The following personal fouls result in penalties.

▦ Blocking below the waist: Players on the receiving team on a kickoff or punt cannot block below the waist. After a change of possession, neither team may block below the waist. *15 yards*

▦ Chop block: No offensive player may block a defensive player at thigh level or below while the defender is being blocked by another offensive player. *15 yards*

▦ Clip: Except for close-in line blocking, no player may clip an opponent below the waist from behind. *15 yards*

▦ Crack-back block: An offensive player aligned 2 yards or more from a middle lineman may not clip or contact a defender below the waist while they are within 5 yards either way of the line of scrimmage. *15 yards*

▦ Grabbing the face mask: No player may grasp the face mask of an opponent. *5 yards for incidental grasping; 15 yards for twisting, turning, or pulling the mask*

▦ Head slap: A defensive player may not contact an opponent's head with their palms except toward them off the line. This exception may not be a repeated act during a single play. *15 yards*

▦ Piling on: Players may not pile on a runner after the ball is dead or intentionally fall upon any prostrate player. *15 yards*

▦ Roughing or running into the kicker: No defensive player may run into or rough a kicker unless the defender has touched the ball or the kicker initiates the contact. There is no penalty if a defender is blocked into the kicker. *5 yards for running into the kicker; 15 yards and an automatic first down for roughing the kicker*

▦ Roughing the passer: After the passer has released the ball, the rusher may make direct contact only up through the rusher's first step. Even if the timing of the contact is legal, a rusher may not be unnecessarily rough, club the passer's arm, or hit the knee or below if the rusher has a direct route to the passer. *15 yards and automatic first down*

■ Striking, kicking, or clubbing: No player may strike with the fists, club, kick, or knee another player in the head, neck, or face. *15 yards*

■ Too many players on the field: A team may not have more than 11 players on the field at the snap of the ball. (There is no penalty for having fewer than 11.) *5 yards*

■ Tripping: No player may intentionally trip an opponent. *10 yards*

■ Unnecessary roughness: This call covers a variety of illegal actions, including spearing with the helmet, tackling out of bounds, throwing the runner to the ground after the ball is dead, running or diving into a player who is obviously out of the play, and kicking an opponent above the knee. *15 yards if penalty on offensive player; 15 yards and automatic first down if on defensive player*

■ Unsportsmanlike conduct: This call is used for any unsporting act, including baiting, taunting, or using abusive or threatening language; unnecessary physical contact with an official; and jumping or standing on another player in an attempt to block a kick. *15 yards*

TERMS

Following are brief explanations for terms that are not described elsewhere in this chapter.

A **dead ball** occurs when a ball carrier is downed or out of bounds, when a quarterback drops to his knee, when a ball carrier slides feet first, when a ball carrier is held or otherwise restrained so that their forward progress is stopped, when a pass drops incomplete, when a kick receiver does not try to run out a kick from the end zone, when a fair catch is made, when a field goal attempt passes the crossbar, or when an official sounds their whistle. When the ball is dead, the play is over.

A **free kick** happens when a kick is "free" (undefended) during a kickoff and after a safety. A team may also choose to free kick immediately after a fair catch of a punt. A free kick may be a dropkick, placekick, or punt. This is true for high school and pro football but not college.

A **fumble** occurs when a player loses possession of the ball while the play is still in progress.

During a kickoff, the kicking team may put on a play—an **onside kick**—to retain possession of the ball. The kick must travel 10 yards or first touch a player on the receiving team before the kicking team can recover the ball.

A player or a ball is **out of bounds** when either has touched a boundary line (or touched ground beyond the boundary line).

Special teams is a term used for the units on the field during kickoffs, placekicks, and punts.

A **touchback** occurs when a ball is dead on or behind a team's own goal line, provided the ball's impetus came from an opponent and it is not a touchdown.

OFFICIALS

Any official may rule on any foul; there is no territorial division in this regard. Although each official has many duties, the main duties for each include the following.

■ The referee has general control; they have the final say in any disagreement, including score and number of downs. They start and stop play, spot the ball after each play, signal coaches for the 2-minute warning (in NFL play) and when they have used their timeouts, and announces penalties.

■ The umpire watches for scrimmage line violations. They record timeouts, watch for line violations on short passes, and assist the referee in ball possession decisions close to the line; they are also in charge of legality of equipment.

■ The linesman watches primarily for offsides, encroachment, illegal motion, and other violations occurring on the line before or at the snap. They are in charge of the chain crew.

■ The line judge operates on the opposite side of the field from the linesman. They are responsible for timing the game and for spotting violations, including illegal motion and illegal shift, on their side of the field. They assist on calls of holding, encroaching, offside, forward laterals, and false starts, and they mark the out-of-bounds spot of all plays on their side.

■ The back judge operates on the middle of the field as the line judge, 20 yards deep. They count the number of defensive players and watch the eligible receivers on their side of the field, concentrating on action in the area between the field judge and the umpire. They signal when time is out and when the ball is dead, and they assist in calls regarding legal catches. They also judge whether field goals are good.

◼ The side judge operates on the same side as the head linesman, 20 yards deep. They count the number of defenders and watch the eligible receivers on their side. They watch the action between the umpire and the field judge and assists on calls regarding legal catches, fumble recoveries, and out-of-bounds plays.

◼ The field judge is primarily responsible for covering kicks and forward passes that cross the goal line. They time the halftime and timeouts and the time between plays. They also assist on calls regarding legal catches, fumble recoveries, and out-of-bounds plays. They are positioned on the line judge's side of the field.

For common officials' signals, see figure 26.2.

▶ **Figure 26.2** Common officials' signals in football.

MODIFICATIONS

Football can be played in various forms, including flag, touch, Canadian, and arena football, which is played indoors on smaller fields. Youth leagues also have rule variations to enhance players' safety and make the sport more appropriate for kids. Following are some of the basic differences in the rules for flag and touch football, Canadian football, and youth football.

Flag and Touch Football

For the purpose of this chapter, NIRSA flag and touch rules will be used to describe the game.

The defining feature for both flag and touch football is the absence of tackling. In flag football, players wear a belt with detachable flags. When the flag is detached, a player is down. In touch football, a player is down when legally touched with one hand between the shoulders and knees by an opponent.

Flag and touch football have several variations. These include number of players, size of the field, duration of play, and rules for positional players. A primary distinction for leagues in this sport is the permissible level of contact, notably for offensive and defensive lineman.

Contact blocking allows contact between the opponent's waist and shoulders. Blockers must be on their feet throughout the block, and no cross-body or rolling blocks are allowed. Screen blocking is contact free. A player can impede progress by positioning him/herself in the opponent's way, but no intentional contact is allowed. Incidental contact, as determined by the referee, is not penalized.

A game lasts 48 minutes (four 12-minute periods). The clock runs continuously for the first 22 minutes of a half with the following exceptions, a team or referee timeout or the end of the first or third period. The referee will also stop the clock with 2 minutes remaining in the second and third periods to announce the time remaining to the team captains. The clock stops, as with regular football rules, during the last 2 minutes of a half. Teams get three timeouts per half, lasting 1 minute each. In flag football, when a flag is removed from the ball carrier, the play is over. In touch football, the play is dead when the ball carrier is legally touched. A new set of downs is awarded each time a team advances to the next zone (a regulation field is divided into five zones of 20 yards each).

To begin play a snap must occur. All offensive players are required to be at least 5 yards in bounds, even only momentarily, before the snap occurs. The player who receives the snap is required to be a minimum of 2 yards behind the offensive scrimmage line.

When running, a player is permitted to pass the ball backward but cannot be caught by themselves. Fumbling is acceptable to lose possession of the ball, but may not be thrown out of bounds intentionally, in order to delay the game. If the ball is caught at the same time by both teams in a backward pass or fumble, the play is considered dead, and it is given to the offensive team.

A forward pass is only illegal if the passing player's foot crosses the scrimmage line as the pass occurs, if the ball is thrown after possession has changed, if the ball gets thrown to the ground intentionally, or if the player catches their own pass and it has been untouched by any other player or there is more than one forward pass in a down. Similar to the backward pass, if a forward pass is caught by two opposing players at the same time, the play is considered dead.

Punts are allowed in adult games, with the exception of quick punts, whereas no punts are permissible in youth flag football games governed by NIRSA.

Points are awarded as follows:

- Touchdown: 6 points
- Touchdown made by a female player (in coed play and is league dependent): 9 points
- Extra point (from the 3-yard line): 1 point
- Extra point (from the 10-yard line): 2 points or 3 points from the 20-yard line
- Return of extra point by defense: 2 points

When a player scores, the player is required to raise their arms and an official pulls their flag loose. If the flag does not detach from the flag belt, the score is not counted, the team is penalized, and the player is disqualified from the game.

Canadian Football

Canadian football is similar to American football. The following list includes some of the significant differences:

- The playing field is 65 yards by 150 yards; goal lines are 110 yards apart.

- The goal posts are on the goal line.

- The end zone is 20 yards deep.

- Teams play with 12 players each.

- Teams have three downs to gain 10 yards.

- Once the referee whistles in the play, the offensive team has 20 seconds to put the ball into play.

- In the last three minutes of each half, the clock is stopped more than during the rest of the halves. This means many plays can be run in the final three minutes of the half.

- Fair catches on punts are not permitted. Players on the punting team must give at least 5 yards to the player attempting to catch or field the punt.

- Any players on the punting team who are on-side (the punter and any player behind the punter when the ball is punted) do not have to give 5 yards and are eligible to recover the ball for the offense. A punt, a kickoff, or a missed field goal that is not returned from the end zone results in 1 point awarded to the kicking team (this is called a rouge). After a rouge, the ball is placed on the 35-yard line for the offense.

- In amateur Canadian football, if a punt or missed field goal is brought out of the end zone and the ball carrier is tackled between the goal line and the 20-yard line, the team receiving the ball automatically gets the ball on the 20-yard line. Each team gets two timeouts per half.

- There is no sudden death overtime; teams do matching series where each team starts from the opponent's 35-yard line.

- The ball is placed on the 5-yard line for extra point conversions; 1 point is awarded for kicking an extra point; 2 are awarded for running or passing the ball over the goal line.

Youth Football

Many leagues have both age and weight classifications. Some have a mandatory play rule, with players required to play a minimum number of plays per game, depending on the number of players on the team. Leagues for younger players (11 and under) often choose to use an 80-yard field. The smaller field is also used for six-man and eight-man leagues. As there are many leagues, with various modifications to length of game, size of the playing field, amount of contact, and rules for specific youth level and age categories should be reviewed through the player's organization.

ORGANIZATIONS

National Football League
345 Park Ave.
New York, NY 10154
www.nfl.com

Pop Warner Football
586 Middletown Blvd., Ste. C-100
Langhorne, PA 19047
215-752-2691
www.popwarner.com

U.S. Flag and Touch Football League
6946 Spinach Dr.
Mentor, OH 44060
440-974-8735
www.usftl.com

Football Canada
825 Exhibition Way, Ste. 205
Ottawa, Ontario
Canada
613-564-0003
http://footballcanada.com

27

Golf

Golf is believed to have had its beginnings in 15th-century Scotland, where players first used wooden balls and then leather balls stuffed with feathers. Golf was introduced in the United States in the late 1700s and has grown in popularity with the advent of improved equipment, professional tours, and television coverage.

Today golf is popular worldwide; in the United States nearly 26 million golfers play at least once a year. More than half are age 45 or older.

OVERVIEW

Objective: To use as few strokes as possible to hit the ball into a series of holes arranged on a course.

Scoring: In stroke play, the player that has the lowest total score wins; in match play, the winner is the side that leads by a number of holes that is greater than the number of holes remaining to be played.

The order of play is determined by a draw. Partners can decide their own playing order. The side that wins the hole in match play or scores the lowest in stroke play "takes the honor" by going first at the next tee. If each side scores the same on a hole, the side that teed first at that hole retains the honor.

In match play, if the sides are tied at the end of regulation, play continues until one side wins a hole, which ends the match. In stroke play, if sides are tied at the end of the round, they may play until one side has a lower score on a hole. This is a sudden-death playoff. In tournaments, ties are sometimes broken by an 18-hole playoff, after which sudden death applies, or however a committee decides to break the tie.

COURSE

Although courses vary in hole lengths, design, and playing characteristics, they share common components (see figure 27.1). A standard course contains 18 holes, usually between 100 and 600 yards long; each hole is on a putting green and is 4.25 inches in diameter and at least 4 inches deep. Each hole has a teeing ground from which play for that hole begins. The most forward point from which the ball may be played is designated by tee markers; the farthest point back from which

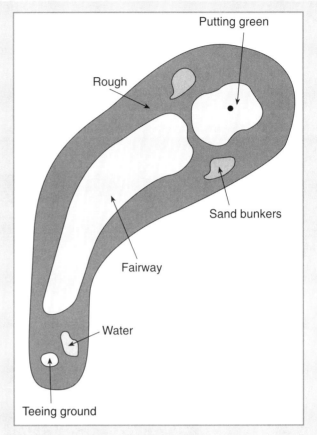

▶ **Figure 27.1** Common features of a golf course.

a ball may be teed is two club lengths behind these markers.

The fairway lies between the teeing ground and the putting green, which is the short-cropped surface around the hole. The apron (short collar) around the green is not considered part of the green. Penalty areas and bunkers lie between and around the teeing ground and the green. The rough is the longer grass and rough terrain bordering the fairway and green.

The flagstick is a movable pole about 8 feet long that is placed in the hole to show the position of the hole on the putting green.

PLAYERS

The players and their caddies are responsible for knowing the rules. For any breach of a rule by a caddie, the player incurs the applicable penalty. In match play, players determine from one another their respective handicaps (see "Scoring"). If a player declares a handicap higher than that to which the player is entitled, and this affects the number of strokes given or received, that player is disqualified; otherwise, the player must play off the declared handicap.

In stroke play, the player must make sure that her handicap is recorded on her scorecard before returning it to the committee. If the player doesn't record a handicap on her scorecard, or if the recorded handicap is higher than that to which they are entitled and this affects the number of strokes received, the player gets disqualified from the handicap competition; otherwise, the score stands.

It is the player's responsibility to know the holes at which handicap strokes are to be given or received.

A player is entitled to ascertain from an opponent during the play of a hole the number of strokes the opponent has taken and, after the play of a hole, the number of strokes taken on the hole just completed. A player must not give wrong information to his opponent. If a player gives wrong information, they lose the hole.

EQUIPMENT

A maximum of 14 clubs is allowed. The clubs are carried in a golf bag; players may carry the bag or transport it in a hand or motorized cart. The three types of clubs include the following:

- Woods: The clubhead is wood (modern woods can also have aluminum, steel, carbon, or titanium heads); these clubs are used for longer shots. Woods are numbered 1 through 10; the most commonly used are 1, 3, and 5.
- Irons: The clubhead is usually steel, and the club has a shorter shaft than a wood. Irons are used for shorter shots and are numbered 1 through 10, plus the wedges.
- Putters: There are many styles of clubheads; putters are usually all metal and are used on the putting green.

The ball is dimpled and has a synthetic shell. It weighs not more than 1.62 ounces and is not less than 1.68 inches in diameter. On a teeing ground, the ball is placed on a tee, which is a peg about 2 inches long. A tee is used when a player drives the ball.

RULES

Golf is a unique sport in that there are rules governing play and etiquette both on and off the actual area of play, along with general standards of etiquette no matter where you are on the course.

General Area

The following rules apply to play in the "general area," which is the entire course except for the teeing ground, the putting green of the hole being played, bunkers, and penalty areas.

- No player may give advice to anyone other than her partner. A player may receive advice from her partner, from her caddie, or from her partner's caddie.
- A player is penalized for discontinuing play unless the committee has discontinued play or is ruling on a disputed play, or the player believes there is danger from lightning.
- In stroke play, when there is doubt as to the correct procedure, the player may complete the hole with two balls after announcing this to his fellow competitor. The player reports the facts to the committee before signing his card; if the rules allow for play of the second ball, the player's score for the hole is what it was with the second ball.
- A player dropping a ball must hold the ball at knee height and drop it. The ball must not be impeded as it falls by the player's equipment or body. The ball must come to rest in the relief area. If it does not, a re-drop is required, and if it does not remain in the relief area on the second drop, it will be placed where it first touched the ground on the second drop.
- A ball embedded anywhere area, with the exception of a bunker, may be lifted, cleaned, and dropped within one club length behind where the ball was located but not closer to the hole.
- When a ball is in a penalty area or bunker, a player may not test the condition of the penalty area or bunker. The player may, however, touch or move loose impediments in the penalty area or bunker, in order to clear outside obstacles such as leaves and rocks. If the ball is in a penalty area, a player

may take a one-stroke penalty and either (a) play a ball from the spot it was last played or (b) drop a ball any distance behind the hazard but along an imaginary line from the hole through the point at which the original ball last crossed the penalty area margin. Because there is a lateral penalty area, there is another option. A player can drop a ball within two club lengths of the point where the ball last crossed the margin, no nearer the hole.

▪ To identify a ball, a player may lift a ball they believe to be their own and clean it as necessary for identification. They must then return it to the same spot.

▪ A ball in motion touched by an outside influence is played where it lies. In stroke play and match play, if it is touched by the player, their partner, caddie, or any of their own equipment, the player incurs no penalty.

▪ A player may mark and lift her ball if it is interfering with or assisting play. A player must play the ball as it lies. They may not improve the position of their ball, the area of her swing, or her line of play. This includes moving or bending anything growing, tamping down grass, replacing old divots before the shot, and so on. Loose impediments may be removed, however.

▪ When lifting a ball, a player must first mark the position of the ball. If the position is not marked, the player incurs a one-stroke penalty.

▪ If there is reason to believe a ball is lost out of bounds or outside a water hazard, a player may take a one-stroke penalty and play a provisional ball as close as possible to the spot where the original ball was played. A ball is defined as "lost" if the player has searched for 3 minutes; if the player has put another ball into play (a provisional ball) and it is hit after it goes past the original ball; or it is declared lost. If the ball is moved accidently while the search is being conducted, there is no penalty. The ball needs to be replaced in an estimated original spot or if the spot is known, the exact original sport.

▪ If a ball is moved by the player, partner, caddie, or equipment, the ball is replaced and a one-stroke penalty is incurred. In stroke play, no penalty is assessed against a fellow competitor for moving a ball. A ball moved by another ball is set back in place.

▪ If a ball is played from outside the teeing ground in match play, the opponent may ask for the shot to be replayed (no penalty) or let the stroke played stand. In stroke play, there is a two-stroke penalty, and the ball must be replayed.

▪ A player may not play a practice stroke except when between two holes. Then they may practice putting or chipping on or near the teeing ground of the next hole, provided the practice does not unduly delay play. Note that a practice swing is not a practice stroke.

▪ In striking the ball, the player must fairly strike at the ball and not push or scoop it. If a player unintentionally strikes a ball twice there is no penalty, however, if the double hit is intentional, the player receives one penalty strike and a general penalty for deliberately deflecting a ball in motion.

▪ If a ball falls off a tee while a player is addressing it, he may replace it with no penalty. But if the player swings at the ball, whether the ball is moving or not, the stroke counts.

▪ A player may declare her ball unplayable anywhere, unless it lies in or is touching a penalty area. The player may take a one-stroke penalty and play a ball as near as possible to the spot where the last shot was played. Or they may drop a ball within two club lengths of where the unplayable ball lies (but not nearer to the hole) and add a penalty stroke. A third option is to take a penalty stroke and drop a ball behind the unplayable lie, keeping that spot between the hole and the drop area. There is no limit to how far back a player may drop the ball.

▪ When a player plays a wrong ball (any ball other than the ball in play or a provisional ball) while in match play, they lose the hole. In stroke play, playing a wrong ball brings a two-stroke penalty.

▪ The line of play may be indicated by anyone, but no one may stand on or close to the line while the stroke is played. (See also line of play in "On the Green.")

On the Green

The following rules apply to play "on the green."

- A player or caddie may clean a ball when they lift it. They must mark and replace the ball where they lifted it. The individual who lifts the ball is the only authorized person to replace the ball.

- The flagstick may remain in place, be attended, be removed, or be held up to indicate position. If a ball rests against a flagstick and falls in the hole when the flagstick is picked up, the ball is considered holed on the previous stroke. If the flagstick is left in a hole and the ball strikes it, there is no penalty stroke given to the player.

- A line of play for putting may be pointed out before the stroke, but the player is not allowed to improve on it.

- If a ball from off the green strikes and moves a ball on the green, there is no penalty, and the ball moved is returned to its original position. If a player on the green strikes a ball that hits another player's ball, there is a two-stroke penalty in stroke play and no penalty in match play. A player cannot take a practice stroke on the green before completing play of the hole.

General Etiquette

The following rules are matters of courtesy and safety:

- Before swinging, the player should make sure that no one is in a position to be hit with the club or ball.

- The player who has the honor should be allowed to play before the next player tees off.

- While a player is addressing or stroking the ball, no one should talk, move, or stand directly behind the ball or the hole.

- Players should play without delay. Players should make their strokes in no more than 40 seconds.

- Players searching for a ball should signal the players behind them to pass when it becomes apparent that the ball will not be found quickly. In most cases they should not complete the 3-minute search time before letting players behind them play through.

- When players complete a hole, they should immediately leave the green and record their scores elsewhere.

- Priority on the course is determined by the pace of play. Any group playing faster than the group in front of them is entitled to play through regardless of the number of players in the group.

- A player should smooth over any holes and footprints they make before leaving a bunker.

- A player should replace any turf they cut through the green and repair any damage on the green made by the ball. Damage to the green made by golf spikes should be repaired after the hole is completed. All divots should be replaced and tamped down.

- Players should not damage the green by leaning on their putters.

- A player should call "fore" if they think their ball may hit another person.

- A player should not take his golf bag, cart, extra clubs, or any other equipment onto the green or tee.

- A player attending the flagstick should take care that their shadow does not fall across the line of the putt.

- Players should place an identification mark on their golf balls.

Scoring

Players are responsible for keeping their own scores. In stroke play, players add each stroke and penalty stroke to arrive at their total scores. At the end of a round, each player should review and sign his scorecard before turning it in. If a player signs for a lower score for a hole than they shot, they are disqualified. If he records a higher score for a hole, that score stands. No changes on the scorecard may be made once it is turned in to the committee.

Handicaps allow players of varying abilities to compete fairly against each other. Handicaps are determined by a player's recent play. A player with a 10 handicap who shoots an actual 100 would finish with a net score of 90.

TERMS

A player is said to **address the ball** when they take their stance and grounds the club in preparing to strike the ball.

An **approach shot** is a shot that is made to hit the ball onto the green.

A **birdie** is one stroke under par.

A **bogey** is one stroke over par; a **double bogey** is two strokes over.

A **bunker** is an area of the course usually filled with sand. It is considered a hazard.

A **caddie** carries a player's clubs and offers advice on how to play holes.

Temporary water is a temporary accumulation of water.

A **chip shot** is a low approach shot from a position close to the green.

A **divot** is a piece of turf dug from the ground by the clubhead.

A **draw** is a controlled right-to-left shot for a right-handed player (as opposed to a *hook*, which curves sharply to the left).

A player **drives** the ball when she hits the ball off a tee with a driver.

An **eagle** is two strokes under par.

A **fade** is a controlled left-to-right shot for a right-handed player (as opposed to a *slice*, which curves sharply to the right).

A **halved hole** occurs when each side scores the same on a hole.

A **hazard** is any bunker or water hazard.

A **hook** is a shot that curves sharply to the left (or to the right, for a left-handed player).

Loose impediments are natural objects on the course, such as pebbles or leaves, that are not embedded in the ground.

Obstructions are any artificial objects except for out-of-bounds markers or objects that are an integral part of the course.

Out describes the first nine holes; **in** signifies the second, or back, nine holes.

Boundary markers denote all areas that are **out of bounds**; play is not allowed out of bounds.

Par is the number of strokes that an expert player is expected to take to hole out. The yardage guidance for par is shown in table 27.1.

A **pitch** is a high shot near the green that is intended to roll minimally after landing.

A group may **play through** when the group ahead of them is slowing them down.

TABLE 27.1

Yardage Guidance for Par

Par	Men (yd)	Women (yd)
3	Up to 250	Up to 210
4	251-470	211-400
5	471-690	401-590
6	691 and over	591 and over

Reprinted by permission from United States Golf Association, *The USGA Handicap System Manual 2016-17.* Available: http://www.usga.org/content/usga/home-page/Handicapping/handicap-manual.html#!rule-14401.

"Rub of the green" is the term used when a ball is deflected or stopped by something or someone other than anyone part of a match or competitor's side in stroke play.

A **shank** is a shot that goes off the heel of the club, causing it to veer in the wrong direction.

A player's **short game** refers to his pitching, chipping, and putting.

A **slice** is a shot that curves sharply to the right (or to the left, for a left-handed player).

Winter rules allow for improving the lie of the ball on the fairway (but not closer to the hole); check local rules.

OFFICIALS

Officials are involved in a committee that establishes the conditions under which a competition is to be played. The committee has no power to waive any rules. Certain rules governing stroke play are so different from those governing match play that combining the two forms of play is not permitted. In stroke play, the committee may limit a referee's duties.

ORGANIZATIONS

United States Golf Association
P.O. Box 708
Far Hills, NJ 07931
908-234-2300, ext. 1346
www.usga.org

Ladies Professional Golf Association
100 International Golf Dr.
Daytona Beach, FL 32124-1092
386-274-6200
www.lpga.com

Gymnastics

Photodisc/Getty Images

The roots of gymnastics can be found in ancient Greece, but the modern development of the sport began in 19th-century Germany, where many of the sport's apparatuses—the rings, the horse, and the bars—were developed. Immigrants brought the sport to the United States. Men competed in gymnastics in the first modern Olympics in 1896; women began Olympic competition in 1936.

Historically, Germany, Russia, Bulgaria, Romania, and Japan have dominated the world championships and Olympic Games. Recently, the United States, China, Ukraine, and Romania have enjoyed greater successes. Gymnastics is a highly popular Olympic sport; for the past three to four Olympic Games, artistic gymnastics has had the highest viewer ratings of all the Olympic coverage.

OVERVIEW

Events: Women compete in four artistic events (vault, uneven bars, balance beam, and floor exercise). Men compete in six artistic events (floor exercise, pommel horse, rings, vault, parallel bars, and horizontal bar). Gymnasts may also compete in trampoline and tumbling, acrobatic gymnastics, group gymnastics, and rhythmic gymnastics. The International Gymnastics Federation also includes aerobic gymnastics and parkour events.

Starting an Event: Gymnasts begin their exercise when a green light is lit or when the judge signals for them to begin.

Continuing an Event: If gymnasts fall during an exercise, they have 30 seconds to remount and continue.

Scoring: Scoring is based on judges' evaluations; see "Scoring and Evaluation" and the sections on individual events for more information.

Gymnastics is most popular among the youngest age groups, with children being introduced to the sport as early as 2 years of age. USA Gymnastics has more than 200,000 registered members (athletes, coaches, judges, and administrators). Male and female gymnasts compete in various events, attempting to score the highest number of points possible through their performances. High score wins.

GYMNASTS

Gymnasts must wear proper attire, including leotards for women and a tank and shorts or pants for men. Gymnasts must begin their exercise within 30 seconds once they are given the signal. On the horizontal bar and rings, a coach or another gymnast may assist a gymnast into a hanging position.

RULES

Women's artistic events consist of the vault, the uneven bars, the balance beam, and the floor exercise. Women also compete in rhythmic gymnastics. Men's artistic events include the floor exercise, the pommel horse, the rings, the vault, the parallel bars, and the horizontal bar. The following sections cover the basic rules for each of these events.

Women's Artistic Events

Women compete in the following events: vault, uneven bars, balance beam, and floor exercise (see figure 28.1).

Vault The vault table is made of wood on a metal frame and has a thin layer of padding covered with leather or vinyl. In compulsories, women get one attempt; in optionals, they get two. During event finals for international competition, both optional vaults are scored and averaged. The two vaults must be from different vault groups and show a different second flight phase. The vaulter runs down a runway, springs off a springboard, and vaults over the table. She is judged on four portions of the vault, including

- the first flight phase (from the springboard to the table),
- the repulsion (pushing off the table),
- the second flight phase (from the table to the dismount), and
- the landing.

Uneven Bars The bars are made of wood or fiberglass, with a metal support. The evaluation begins with the gymnast's takeoff from the board or floor. The exercise must contain one flight element from the high bar to the low bar and one flight element on the same bar. The exercise

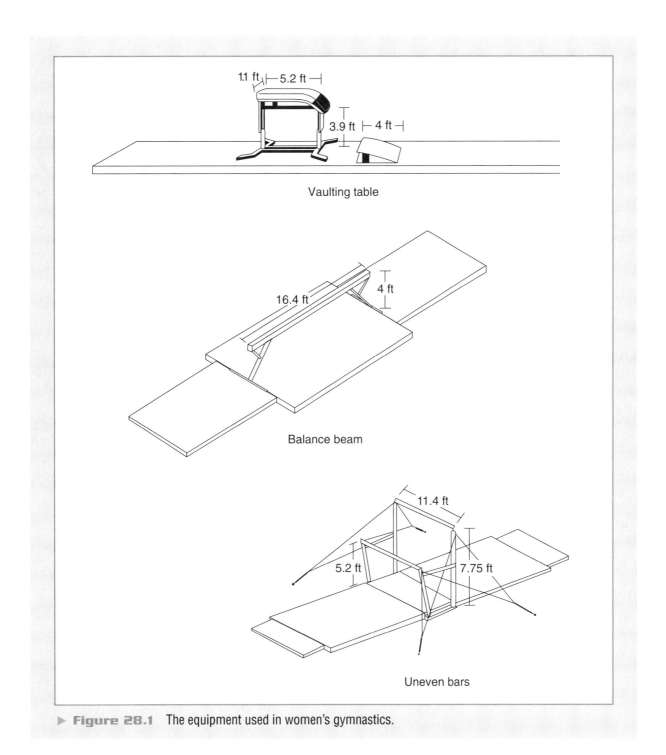

Vaulting table

Balance beam

Uneven bars

▶ **Figure 28.1** The equipment used in women's gymnastics.

must include different grips and there must be a nonflight element with a directional change of at least a 360-degree turn. Elements must be performed without pause and without an intermediate swing.

Balance Beam The beam is made of wood padded with foam rubber and covered with synthetic or real suede. The evaluation begins with the takeoff from the board or floor. The exercise must not exceed 90 seconds. The routine must include three acrobatic, three dance, and two optional elements.

Acrobatic elements include forward, backward, or sideways flight; dance elements include leaps, turns, hops, step combinations, and balance elements. The gymnast will execute some or all of these items:

- one 360-degree turn,
- one acrobatic series of two or more flight elements (one must be a salto),
- one dance series of two elements (one being a leap or a jump with a 180-degree turn split, or straddle position),
- and acrobatic elements in different directions.

Floor Exercise   The floor exercise must not exceed 90 seconds. The exercise is done to music and begins with the first gymnastics or acrobatic movement. Stepping outside of the floor area (a square measuring 12 meters on each side) results in a deduction of one-tenth of a point. The exercise should consist of both acrobatic elements and dance elements (turns, leaps, jumps, and balance elements in various positions). It should include elements from different structure groups, level changes, directional changes and creative movements, and connections and transitions into acrobatic lines and elements. There should be dynamic changes between slow and fast movements and must be done in harmony with the music.

Rhythmic Events

Rhythmic gymnastics involves body difficulties executed while using hand apparatuses, including rope, hoop, ball, clubs, and ribbon. An individual exercise is set to music and lasts 75 to 90 seconds; a group exercise lasts from 2 minutes 15 seconds to 2 minutes 30 seconds. Gymnasts may perform preacrobatic elements such as rolls, cartwheels, and walkovers, but no handsprings or aerials are allowed. Each individual exercise is scored based on four difficulty components. These are body difficulty, dance step combinations, dynamic elements with rotation, and apparatus difficulty.

During an exercise, the gymnast performs the following technical elements with the apparatus: The ball may be thrown, caught, rolled, and bounced. The rope may be thrown, caught, swung, and spun. The hoop may be thrown, caught, rolled, and passed through. The clubs

may be thrown, caught, flipped, and circled in small movements called mills. The ribbon may be thrown and caught while remaining above the floor with spirals and snakelike patterns.

The maximum score is 20.00: 10.00 is the maximum execution score; the difficulty score and artistry score are added together and divided in half for the remaining 10.00 points. A routine composition may contain a maximum of 18 difficulties; difficulties are valued from A to M (an A = 0.1 and upward). The difficulty total for each composition establishes the difficulty start value, and the complexity of manipulations, throws, and catches with the equipment establishes the artistry bonuses. The artistry score is also calculated by evaluating the coordination between the music and the performance of the composition.

Men's Artistic Events

Men compete in the following events: floor exercise, pommel horse, rings, vault, parallel bars, and horizontal bar (see figure 28.2).

Floor Exercise   The floor exercise lasts up to 70 seconds. The gymnast must use the entire floor area—a square measuring 12 meters on each side. He may step on, but not over, any boundary line. He also may not pause for more than 2 seconds before an element or acrobatic sequence.

The exercise should consist of acrobatic jumps and gymnastics elements of flexibility, strength and balance. Examples of errors, for which points are deducted, include attaining a low height during a tumbling pass, not having the knees and shoulders in a straight line during a standing scale, and stepping outside the floor area.

Pommel Horse   The gymnast performs circular and pendulum swings on the horse, using various positions of support and using all three parts of the horse. The gymnast must execute leg circles with the legs together. The element groups on pommel horse are (I) single-leg swings and scissors; (II) circles, spindles, and handstands, Kehrswings and Wendeswings, flops and combined elements; (III) travel elements; and (IV) dismounts. The gymnast may not pause during the routine. Errors, for which points are deducted, include not using all three parts of the horse equally, skewed body position in longitudinal travels, and general form errors.

Rings   The gymnast must perform swing, strength, and hold parts in about equal propor-

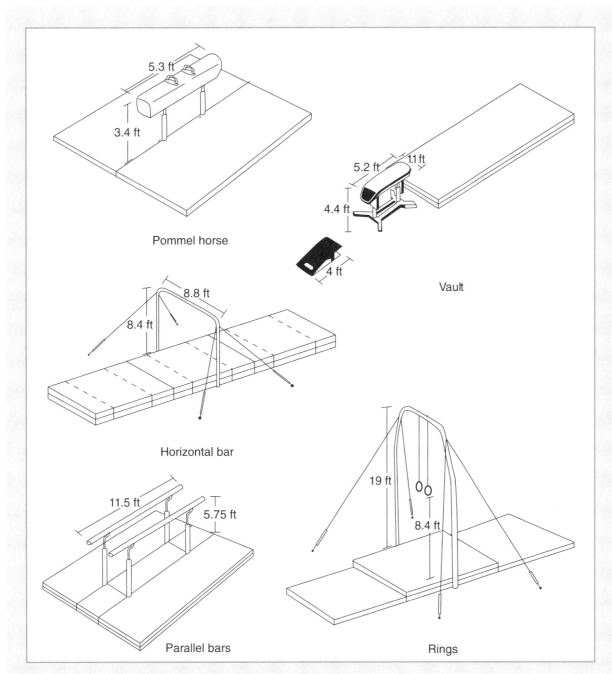

5.3 ft

3.4 ft

Pommel horse

5.2 ft   1.1 ft

4.4 ft

4 ft

Vault

8.8 ft

8.4 ft

Horizontal bar

19 ft

8.4 ft

11.5 ft

5.75 ft

Parallel bars

Rings

▶ **Figure 28.2**   The equipment used in men's artistic events.

tions. The gymnast executes these parts in a hang position, to or through a support position, and into a handstand position with straight arms. The gymnast should not let the cables swing; points are deducted for this.

Types of errors for which a gymnast is penalized include body position errors, touching the cables with his feet or any part of his body, and not holding strength elements level or for 2 seconds.

Vault   Male gymnasts use the same vault table as the women. A gymnast runs up, jumps onto a springboard, and executes single or multiple rotations around the body's transverse and longitudinal axes before and after touching the vault table. The vault is judged on its start value, on the flight from the springboard to the table, on the body position during execution, on the push-off from the table, and on the flight from the table to a landing position.

Male gymnasts perform only one vault except during apparatus finals, when they complete two different vaults and have their scores averaged.

Errors resulting in penalties include opening or straddling the legs while going from the board to the table or while on the table, insufficient height off the table, deviation from the axis of the table during the vault or during the landing, and form errors during the flight from the table to the landing.

Parallel Bars   The gymnast performs elements of swing and flight both above and below the bars. He can execute elements in a side position as well. The exercise should include elements in support or through support on two bars, elements which start in an upper arm position, long swings in hang on one or two bars and underswings and the dismount. He may not perform more than three hold parts or unnecessarily straddle his legs. Other errors that may result in penalties include walking during a handstand, touching the bars or floor with any part of his body other than his hands, and general form errors.

Horizontal Bar   The gymnast performs elements of uninterrupted swing, including giant swings (360-degree rotations), turns, and flight elements. He may perform a one-arm swing. The routine must include at least one release and regrasp of the bar showing flight. The gymnast is penalized for errors, including stopping in a handstand or any other position, executing swing elements with strength, deviating from the direction of the movement, bending his arms during a circular swing, and failing to regrasp the bar after a flight element.

Scoring and Evaluation

The men's and women's scoring system incorporates credit for a routine's artistic content, difficulty, and execution.

The difficulty score is determined by a two-person panel that totals values for the 10 most difficult skills, including the dismount. The difficulty value of a skill or element is not recognized if the gymnast fails to meet its technical requirements. A connection value is awarded when specific skills or skill types are executed successfully in succession. The two judges independently record their difficulty scores and then compare their scores and reach a consensus. Coaches may inquire verbally and in writing about difficulty scores, and an inquiry using video may be used to resolve the issue.

The execution score is determined by a six-person panel. This score begins at 10, and deductions are made for errors and faults in technique, execution, and artistry or composition. Judges independently determine their scores; the highest and lowest scores are dropped, and the execution score is the average of the remaining four judges' scores.

The total score is the total of the difficulty and execution scores less any deductions for neutral errors.

TERMS

An example of an **acrobatic element** is a salto (somersault) or handspring executed from a stand or a run.

In international competition, the **difficulty** of an element is categorized into one of seven value groups (A, B, C, D, E, F, or G) for the women and six for the men, based on the strength and physical requirements of the movement.

An **element** is the smallest independently executed movement in gymnastics, with definite starting and ending points.

An **element of flexibility** shows an extreme range of motion in one or more joints (e.g., shoulders, hips, or spine).

An **element of flight** is a movement in which the gymnast releases a grip, executes a distinct flight phase, and regrips the apparatus.

An **element of strength** is a movement in which gravity is conquered slowly or a gymnast achieves balance through static force.

An **element of swing** is a dynamic movement executed with great amplitude and without stopping or visibly showing strength.

An **exercise** is the complete presentation of all the elements; *optional exercises* have specific requirements but also allow for the gymnast's preferences.

A **gymnastics element** is a nonacrobatic move, such as performing a body wave, separating the legs, rolling, or jumping.

A **hold part** refers to the gymnast's holding his body for 2 seconds in a prescribed position.

OFFICIALS

Up to eight judges evaluate each routine.

MODIFICATIONS

To make the sport safer and more appropriate for younger athletes, various organizations have modified events (for instructional classes, not for competition) in the following ways:

- For the balance beam, gymnasts may use a lower or wider beam.
- For the floor exercise, gymnasts may be allowed to use "cheese-wedge" mats to assist them with their rolls, and larger mats may be used to assist their rotational movements.

ORGANIZATIONS

International Gymnastics Federation
Av. de la Gare 12
1003 Lausanne
Switzerland
41-21-321-5510
www.fig-gymnastics.com

USA Gymnastics
130 E. Washington St., Ste. 700
Indianapolis, IN 46204
317-237-5050
http://usagym.org

Handball

Chad Springe/Image Source/Getty Images

Handball's origins date back to ancient Rome. The game was played on dirt floors in Ireland in the Middle Ages and was brought to the United States by 19th-century Irish immigrants. Little about the sport has changed since its introduction in the United States, except that it now uses a smaller, softer ball and a smaller court. Handball is most popular in the United States, Canada, Mexico, Ireland, and Australia.

Handball can be played on a four-walled, three-walled, or one-walled court. The rules for the main body of this chapter are for four-wall handball. "Modifications" addresses three-wall and one-wall rule differences.

OVERVIEW

Objective: To win rallies and score points by serving or returning the ball so that the opponent cannot keep the ball in play.

Scoring: A rally is won when one player cannot return the ball before it hits the floor twice or when a player returns a ball that hits the floor before it hits the front wall; only the serving player or team can score.

Number of Players: Two players (singles) or four players (doubles).

Game Length: First team to 21 points.

Match Length: Best two of three games; the third game (the tiebreaker) is played to 11 points.

The winner of a coin toss serves to begin the game. The other player or side serves to begin the second game. To begin a tiebreaker, the player or team with the most points in the first two games serves. If both sides have scored the same number of points, another coin toss is used to begin the tiebreaker.

COURT

A standard four-walled court is 20 feet wide, 20 feet high, and 40 feet long (see figure 29.1). The recommended minimum height for the back wall is 14 feet. The short line is parallel to the front and back walls; its outside edge is 20 feet from the front wall. The service line is parallel to the short line, and its outside edge is 5 feet in front of the short line.

The service zone is the area between the outer edges of the short line and the service line. The service boxes are located at each side of the ser-

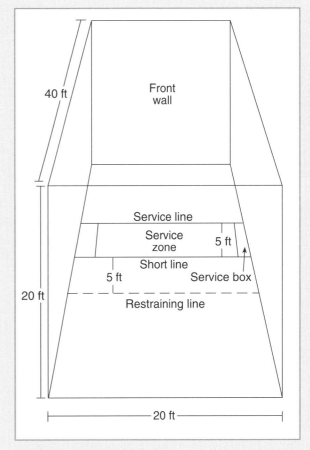

▶ **Figure 29.1** The dimensions and features of a handball court.

vice zone. Each service box is marked by a line parallel to the side wall, 18 inches from the wall. The receiver's restraining lines are 5 feet behind the short line. They are parallel to the short line and extend 6 inches from each side wall.

PLAYERS

Two, three, or four players can play handball. Games played by three players are called cutthroat. The player serving plays against the other two; the serve rotates. The rules for singles apply to the server; the rules for doubles apply to the two other players.

EQUIPMENT

The ball is rubber or synthetic and has a 1.90-inch diameter, with a variation of 0.03 inch. It weighs 2.3 ounces, with a variation of 0.2 ounce. Players must wear gloves that are light in color and made of soft material or leather. The fingers may not be webbed, connected, or removed, and the gloves may not have holes that expose skin. Players may not use any foreign substance, tape, or rubber bands on the fingers or palms outside the gloves. They may wear metal or hard substances underneath if, in the referee's opinion, this does not create an advantage for the player wearing them. Players must change gloves when they become wet enough to dampen the ball.

Customary handball attire includes full-length shirts; players may not wear shirts cut off at the torso. Their shoes must have soles that do not mark or damage the floor. Players must wear protective eyewear at all times during play.

RULES

The fundamental rules of play are found in the rules for serving, returning serve, and rallies.

Serving

The server serves from anywhere in the service zone (see figure 29.1). A foot fault is called if any part of either foot is beyond the outer edge of either service zone line. The server must remain in the service zone until the ball passes the short line.

The server must come to a complete stop before beginning a serve by bouncing the ball. She may bounce and catch the ball several times before beginning her serve, but when she begins the serve she must bounce the ball once and hit it. More than one bounce is a fault; bouncing the ball outside the service zone is also a fault.

The serve must strike the front wall first, and it must hit beyond the short line. It may touch one of the side walls. As soon as a rally ends, the referee calls either "point" or "sideout," and the receiver has 10 seconds to get into position. When the receiver is in position, or when 10 seconds elapse, whichever comes first, the referee announces the score and the server has 10 seconds to serve.

A server may commit one service fault. If he commits two faults on the same serve, he loses his serve. In doubles, the first serving team gets only one serving turn—when the receiving team wins the rally, it wins the serve. After that, both players on a team get a serving turn each time they gain the serve. The serving order of the partners is kept throughout the game. Each player continues his serve until the opponents score a sideout.

It is not necessary for partners on the receiving team to alternate receiving the serve. The server's partner must stand within the service box until the ball passes the short line. A violation is a foot fault. Other faults include the following:

- short serve—a serve whose first bounce hits before or on the short line
- three-wall serve—a serve that hits the front wall and two other walls before hitting the floor
- ceiling serve—a serve that hits the ceiling after the front wall but before hitting the floor
- long serve—a serve that hits the back wall before hitting the floor
- out-of-court serve—a serve that hits the front wall and then goes out of the court without touching the floor
- two consecutive screen serves—serves that pass too close to the server or the server's partner, obstructing the receiver's view

The first screen serve is called a defective serve and is not penalized; the server serves again. Other defective serves that are replayed with no penalty include serves that hit the server's partner in the air (on the bounce results in a fault), straddle balls (serves that travel between the server's legs), court hinder (a serve that bounces erratically because of a court obstruction or wetness), and a ball that breaks on the serve. The server loses her turn when she

- misses the ball while attempting to serve,
- serves so that the ball strikes anything other than the front wall first,
- serves so that the ball strikes the server in the air,
- strikes her partner with the serve when her partner's foot is outside the service box,
- commits two consecutive service faults,
- hits a crotch serve—a serve that hits the crotch in the front wall (if the serve hits a crotch in the back wall or side wall, after legally hitting the front wall first and going beyond the short line, it is legal),
- serves out of order, or
- goes beyond the allotted 10 seconds in serving.

Returning Serve

The receiver must stand at least 5 feet behind the short line until the serve is struck. Not doing so results in a point for the server. No part of the receiver may extend on or over the plane of the short line when contacting the ball. A violation results in a point for the server. The receiver may go beyond the short line, however, after hitting the ball.

The receiver must return the ball before it strikes the floor twice. A serve can be returned before it strikes the floor. A return of serve can hit the back wall, one or both side walls, and the ceiling before it touches the front wall, but it must touch the front wall before it strikes the floor.

Rallies

A rally is played out until one side cannot legally return the ball. Teams alternate hits—team A is obligated to return team B's hit, and vice versa—but partners on a team do not have to alternate hits. In doubles play, both partners may swing at a ball but only one player can touch it.

The front or back of the hand may be used to hit a ball; the wrist or any other part of the body may not be used. If a rally needs to be replayed for any reason, any previous fault against the server is voided. A player loses a rally if she intentionally hinders her opponent from returning the ball. A rally is replayed for dead-ball hinders, such as unavoidable interference or contact.

Scoring and Penalties

Scoring and penalties are affected by avoidable hinders and technicals.

Avoidable Hinders

An avoidable hinder results in a sideout if the offending player was serving and a point if the player was receiving. A player commits an avoidable hinder when he

- doesn't move out of the way to allow his opponent a shot;
- moves into a position that blocks his opponent as he is about to return the ball;
- moves into the path of the ball just struck by his opponent;
- pushes his opponent;

- obstructs his opponent's view just before his opponent is about to strike the ball; or
- interferes in any way with the opponent's stroke, including restricting the opponent's follow-through.

Technicals

An offender loses 1 point for a technical, which may be assessed for frequent complaints, profanity, arguing, threats made to the opponent or the referee, excessive kicking or throwing of the ball between rallies, failure to wear proper eye protection, or for any unsporting behavior. A technical does not result in a sideout or affect the serve order.

If a technical occurs between games, the offending player begins the next game with a negative score. Three technicals in a match result in a forfeit. A warning, with no point deduction, may be given instead of a technical. This is at the discretion of the referee. A player may be assessed a technical without first receiving a warning.

TERMS

An **ace** is a legal serve that eludes the receiver.

An **avoidable hinder** is interference that the offending player could have avoided; the penalty is loss of serve or a point for the opponent.

A **back wall shot** is one that is made from a rebound off the back wall.

A **ceiling shot** is one that is hit directly to the ceiling.

A **court hinder** occurs when an erratic bounce is caused by an obstacle, construction abnormality, or wetness on the court.

A **crotch ball** is one that hits the juncture of any two walls, any wall with the floor, or any wall with the ceiling.

A **defensive shot** is one that is made to get the opponent out of an offensive position but is not made with the intent of winning the rally.

A **dig** is made by a player who retrieves a low shot.

A **fault** is an illegally served ball.

A **fly shot** is one that is played before it bounces.

A **foot fault** occurs when a portion of the server's foot is outside the service zone before the served ball passes the short line.

A **hinder** occurs when a player accidentally hinders an opponent from making a shot or hinders the flight of the ball. A hinder is not penalized but is replayed.

A **hop serve** is a serve that has spin on it, causing it to hop to the right or the left.

A **kill shot** is one that hits the front wall so low that the opponent has no chance to return it.

A **lob** is a soft shot high on the front wall.

An **offensive shot** is one intended to win a rally.

A **passing shot** is one that is driven past an opponent's reach on either side.

A **point** can be scored only by the server or serving team.

The **service line** is the line parallel to and 5 feet in front of the short line.

The **service zone** is the area of the court between, and including, the short line and the service line.

The **short line** is the line halfway between, and parallel to, the front and back walls.

A **sideout** occurs when the receiving player or team wins a rally and gains the serve.

OFFICIALS

The referee is in charge of the match and makes all decisions regarding points, equipment, protests, and hinders. A linesman and a scorer are used for larger events.

MODIFICATIONS

Three-wall handball is played on a court that is 20 feet wide and 40 feet long. The three-wall game abides by four-wall rules, except for the following:

▪ The recommended length for side walls is 44 feet, extending 4 feet beyond the long line, which runs parallel to the front wall and whose outer edge is 40 feet from the front wall.

▪ Shirts are not required for outdoor play unless requested by an opponent.

▪ A long serve is one that hits the front wall and rebounds past the long line before touching the floor.

▪ During tournament play, a referee awards the server a point when the receiver catches a serve the receiver assumes to be long.

▪ A long ball is one that hits the front wall and doesn't bounce until it is past the long line.

One-wall handball is played on a court measuring 20 feet wide and 34 feet long. One-wall play abides by four-wall rules, except for the following:

▪ The wall is 16 feet high.

▪ A long line, parallel to the wall, is marked 34 feet from the wall.

▪ A minimum of 6 feet of floor, and ideally 20 feet, should extend beyond each side line; 16 feet should extend beyond the long line.

▪ The short line runs parallel to the wall, 16 feet from the wall.

▪ Two service markers, at least 6 inches long, extend from the sidelines, parallel with the short and long lines and halfway between them. The imaginary extension of these lines indicates the service line.

▪ The serving zone is the floor between the short line, the sidelines, and the service line.

▪ The receiving zone is the floor beyond the short line, inside and including the sidelines and long line.

▪ Shirts are not required in outdoor play unless requested by an opponent.

▪ The server's partner must stand outside the sidelines, straddling the extended service line until the served ball passes him.

▪ If a player attempting to play a ball is blocked by an opponent who has stood still after hitting her shot, no hinder is called.

▪ If a ball hits an opponent on the way to the wall, this is always a hinder, regardless of whether the referee believes the ball had a chance to hit the wall on the fly.

▪ During a rally, if a player on the serving side hinders an opponent, the serving side begins the next serve with a fault.

ORGANIZATION

United States Handball Association
2333 N. Tucson Blvd.
Tucson, AZ 85716
520-795-0434
handball@ushandball.org
www.ushandball.org

Horseshoe Pitching

United States Marine Corps

Horseshoe pitching probably evolved from a sport known as quoits, in which a large ring is tossed a certain distance in an attempt to land it on an upright stake or pin. (The children's game called ring toss is a scaled-down, indoor version of quoits.) Quoits must have been fairly popular in the 14th century, when it was banned, along with most other sports, so that men would practice archery instead of wasting their leisure time on unimportant pursuits. A very plausible theory is that peasant farmers, unable to afford quoits, bent horseshoes into rings to play quoits and then created their own version of the sport that used unaltered horseshoes. It is known that the new sport had been brought to North America by the late 18th century, since soldiers pitched horseshoes in their Revolutionary War camps.

Horseshoe pitching is a popular recreation for families and outdoor gatherings, usually played on a nonofficial court in a backyard or a park setting. The National Horseshoe Pitchers Association (NHPA) estimates that about 15 million people take part in the sport annually, but only about 15,000 belong to the NHPA. More than 6,000 of those members participate in league play. While horseshoe pitching is basically an outdoor sport, indoor courts are being built in many northern areas so the sport can be played all year.

OVERVIEW

Objective: To score the most points, whether after a specified number of innings or reaching a specified point total first.

Scoring: Players can score by a "ringer" (3 points) or by tossing the horseshoe within 6 inches of the stake, including a "leaner" that is leaning against the stake (1 point).

Number of Players: Singles or doubles can be played.

Length of Game: There are three ways of determining the length of a game. Most common is an inning or shoe limit—for example, 25 innings, which amounts to 50 shoes. In case of a tie, extra innings are played until the tie is broken. Another option is a point limit—for example, 40 points. The third method is a combination of the first two—for example, 25 innings or 40 points, whichever comes first.

A match is made up of an odd number of games. The 11-game match is more or less standard in major tournaments.

COURT

The horseshoe court is 46 feet long by 6 feet wide, as shown in figure 30.1. For safety, a buffer zone 2 feet wide is recommended all the way around the court, making the total area 50 feet long and 10 feet wide. Another safety factor is a backboard or backstop at least 3 feet high at each end of the court.

Also at each end of the court is a pitcher's box, 6 by 6 feet. A pitcher's box contains a pit 3 feet wide and 4 feet long, which is filled with clay, dirt, sand, or a synthetic compound so that a horseshoe will not bounce or roll after landing. In the center of the pit is a metal stake, 14 to 15 inches high, tilted forward at an angle of 12 degrees (thus the angle of the stake with the ground is 78 degrees).

There are pitching platforms, 6 feet long and 18 inches wide, at each side of the pit. Each pitching platform is extended 10 feet forward to create a short-distance pitching platform. It is recommended that the pitching platform be extended the full length of the court to form a walkway from end to end.

Imaginary stakes are marked at distances of 23 and 30 feet from the opposite stake. They serve as reference points showing short-distance pitchers where to stand.

EQUIPMENT

Horseshoes are made especially for the sport. A horseshoe can measure no more than 7-1/4 inches wide and 7-5/8 inches long; the maximum weight is 2 pounds, 10 ounces. The maximum opening is 3-1/2 inches.

RULES

The winner of a coin toss decides which competitor pitches first. If more than one game is played, the choice of starter alternates. Both players pitch from the same end. In singles, the players pitch from one end of the court, walk down to the other end of the court for scoring, and then pitch back. In doubles play, partners are separated, with one at each end. Two players pitch from one end and,

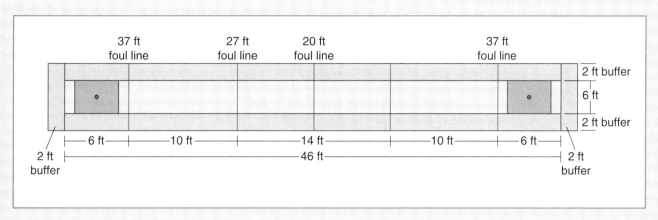

▶ **Figure 30.1** The dimensions and features of a horseshoe pit.

after the score is tallied, the other two players pitch back toward the first stake.

Shoes have to be pitched underhanded. The first player pitches two shoes, one at a time, and the second then does the same. There is a time limit of 30 seconds between a player's pitches.

If a player takes more than 30 seconds, it is a foul shoe. A foul shoe also results if the player steps over the foul line that marks the front of the pitching platform or if the shoe touches anything outside the pit before coming to rest. Foul shoes are removed from the court before any other shoe is pitched. If the last shoe in an inning is a foul shoe, it's removed before scoring.

SCORING

There are two methods of scoring, cancellation and count-all. In cancellation scoring, only one contestant can score in an inning. In count-all scoring, all scoring shoes are counted.

A ringer is scored if a shoe encircles the stake. A straightedge placed between the two points of the shoe must clear the stake entirely for a ringer to be scored. It's worth 3 points. If a shoe comes to rest within 6 inches of the stake, it is worth 1 point. This includes a shoe that is leaning against the stake (a "leaner").

In cancellation scoring, if each player has a ringer, they cancel each other out. However, another shoe can still be scored. For example, if Player A has two ringers and Player B has only

one ringer, Player B's second ringer counts. If Player A has a ringer and her second shoe is 3 inches from the stake, while Player B has a ringer and his second shoe is 5 inches from the stake, the ringers cancel one another but Player A gets 1 point. In count-all scoring, however, Player A would get 4 points and Player B would get 3 points. Whether count-all or cancellation, the winner is determined by mutual agreement at the beginning, either number of points or a certain number of innings.

MODIFICATIONS

The full pitching distance of 37 feet from the foul line to the stake is standard for most men's competition. The distance is shorter for other competitors.

Women, elder men (age 70 and over), juniors (boys and girls age 18 years and under), and physically challenged men of any age pitch from the extended platform, using a pitching distance of 27 feet.

Junior cadets (boys and girls age 12 years and under) observe the 20-foot foul line.

TERMS

A **backboard** or **backstop** is one of the barriers placed at each end of the court.

A **caliper** is a tool used to measure the distance of a shoe from the stake.

Cancellation scoring is a method in which opponents' ringers cancel each other out.

Count-all scoring is a method in which all live shoes are scored.

A **dead shoe** is a foul shoe or a ringer that has been canceled by an opponent's ringer.

Doubles is an event in which two teams of two players each compete against one another.

A **feeler gauge** is a measuring tool that contains strips of metal of various thicknesses. It's used to measure the distance of a shoe from the stake and occasionally to determine if a shoe is a ringer.

A **foot foul** occurs when a player steps over the foul line when delivering a shoe. The result is a foul shoe.

A **foul shoe** is a shoe that was delivered in violation of the rules. Foul shoes are removed from the pit before scoring.

An **inning** consists of four pitched shoes, two by each player.

A **leaner** is a shoe that comes to a stop leaning against the stake.

A **live shoe** is a legally delivered shoe that lands in the pit.

The **pit** is the rectangular area around a stake. It is filled with clay, dirt, sand, or an approved synthetic compound.

A **pitcher's box** is a 6-foot-square area at the end of the court.

A **pitcher's platform** is the area from which a player pitches the shoe. There's one on each side of the pitcher's box.

A **ringer** is a live shoe that encircles the stake. It's worth 3 points.

The **scoring area** is a circular area, 6 inches in diameter, which surrounds the stake.

ORGANIZATION

National Horseshoe Pitchers Association of America
3085 76th St.
Franksville, WI 53126
www.horseshoepitching.com

31

Ice Hockey

Dmytro Aksonov/Getty Images

The history of ice hockey is a bit murky: Some claim that it originated from play by British soldiers on frozen Lake Ontario in 1855, while residents of Halifax, Nova Scotia, Canada, say the sport had already begun there. Hockey is likely a descendant of a sport called bandy, developed in England in the late 18th century. The first set of rules was developed at McGill University in Montreal in 1879. Hockey was first played in the United States in the 1890s, and today the sport is most popular in North America and northern Europe. The National Hockey League was formed in 1917.

Women's ice hockey began in the 1890s. More than 100 years later, in 1998, women's hockey became an Olympic medal sport. The only rule difference between men's hockey and women's is that there is no body checking in the women's game.

OVERVIEW

Objective: To score a goal by shooting a puck into the opponents' goal; the team that scores the most goals wins.

Number of Players: Six per team.

Length of Game: Three 20-minute periods; each team gets one timeout.

Overtime: If the score is tied at the end of regulation, an overtime is played. The first team to score wins. If the score is still tied at the end of overtime, a shootout is used to determine the winner.

A game begins with a face-off (see "Face-Offs"). Face-offs are also used to begin each period and to resume play after a penalty or other stop in the action. Players advance the puck toward the opponents' goal by skating with the puck or passing it. The puck must be in motion at all times.

RINK

The rink has an ice surface; its components are shown in figure 31.1. The rink is divided into thirds by two blue lines, each of which is 64 feet from the nearest goal. The blue lines separate the rink into three zones: the defending zone, where the goal is defended; the neutral zone, or central portion; and the attacking zone, where the goal is attacked.

The center face-off spot, 12 inches in diameter, is inside the center circle, which has a 15-foot radius. Two face-off spots are 5 feet from each blue line, and 44 feet apart, in the neutral zone. The end zone face-off spots are 20 feet from each

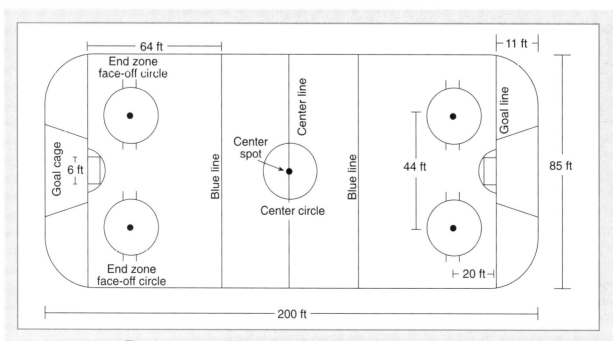

▶ **Figure 31.1** The components and dimensions of an ice hockey rink.

goal line and 44 feet apart. These spots are in end zone face-off circles with a 15-foot radius.

The goal cages are 6 feet long by 4 feet high, centered on the goal lines, which run the width of the rink, 11 to 13 feet from each end. The goal crease is 4 by 8 feet, centered on each goal line and marked with a red semicircle 71 inches in radius and 2 inches in width. A red L-shaped marking is located at each front corner 48 inches from the goal line to the edge of the semicircle. Goal creases are measured from the outside edges of the lines in order to ensure consistency in size across venues.

The referee's crease is a semicircle with a 10-foot radius at the center of one side. The boards around the rink are white wood or fiberglass, 40 to 48 inches high. Safety glass, 40 to 48 inches high, rises above the boards. Players' benches are on one side of the rink, opposite the penalty box.

PLAYERS

Each team has six players on the ice: a goalkeeper, two defensemen, and three forwards (although all six players play defense when the other team has possession of the puck). In most leagues, a team can dress 20 players, including two goalies. The team captain is the only player who can discuss calls with the referee.

Players may be changed at any time, but the player or players leaving the ice must be within 5 feet of the bench and out of play before the change is made. For minor injuries, play is not stopped. For injuries in which the player cannot leave the ice, play is continued until the injured player's team has possession of the puck and is not in scoring position. At the officials' discretion, play may be stopped immediately for any severe injury, no matter who has possession of the puck.

EQUIPMENT

The puck is hard rubber, 1 inch thick and 3 inches in diameter. It weighs between 5.5 and 6.0 ounces. The stick is wood or another approved material; its maximum length is 63 inches from the heel to the top of the shaft. Its blade can be no longer than 12.5 inches and must be between 2 and 3 inches wide. Tape can be used to reinforce the stick.

The blade of the goalkeeper's stick may be up to 15.5 inches long. Its maximum width is 3.5 inches, except at the heel, where it may be 4.5 inches. The shaft extending up from the heel, for up to 26 inches, is 3.5 inches wide. Goalkeepers wear leg pads, chest protectors, gloves (one to block shots, the other to catch shots), helmets, and full face masks.

All protective equipment—padded pants and pads for shins, hips, shoulders, and elbows—must be worn under the uniform. All players must wear a helmet with a chin strap.

RULES

Following are rules pertaining to face-offs, passes, offside, and the puck.

Face-Offs

A referee or linesman drops the puck between two opposing players whose stick blades are on the ice. Each player faces the opponents' end of the rink and tries to hit the puck to a teammate. No other players may be in the face-off circle or within 15 feet of the players facing off. Players must stand on the side during the face-off, and no substitutes may enter the game until the face-off is complete.

All face-offs shall take place at one of the nine designated face-off spots.

If a defender in her team's defensive zone causes play to stop, the face-off occurs at the nearest end zone face-off spot. Any stoppage of play in the neutral zone results in a face-off at the nearest neutral zone face-off spot. If play is stopped between the end of the rink and the end face-off spots, the face-off occurs at the nearest end face-off spot.

Icing

Icing occurs when a player shoots the puck across both the center line and the opposing team's goal line without the puck going into the net. When icing occurs, a linesman stops play if a defending player (other than the goaltender) would be the first player to touch the puck before an attacking player is able to. Play is resumed with a face-off in the defending zone of the team that committed the infraction. Icing is not enforced for a team that is short-handed. If the goaltender makes a move from his net to play the puck, the icing is immediately waved off (in contrast to minor league where the goaltender must play the puck for it to be waved off).

Icing can also be waved off if, in the officials' opinion, the defending team had a viable opportunity to play the puck before it crossed the goal line.

Offside

An attacking player is offside if she is in the attacking zone before the puck completely crosses the blue line. Both skates must be past the line when the puck enters the zone for a player to be offside. An offside call results in a face-off.

If a defender reaches the puck and passes or skates with it into the neutral zone, an attacking player is not offside. Similarly, if a player moves across the line before the puck but is in control and moving the puck forward, she is not offside.

Puck

Specific rules for handling the puck include the following:

- Out of bounds: If the puck goes out of bounds, it is faced off at the nearest face-off spot in the same zone from where it was shot or deflected.
- Lodged or frozen: If the puck becomes lodged in the netting outside the goal or becomes "frozen" between opposing players, the puck is faced off at the nearest face-off spot—unless the referee believes an attacking player caused the stoppage, in which case the face-off takes place in the neutral zone.
- Player on puck: If a scramble takes place and a player accidentally falls on the puck, play is stopped and a face-off occurs.
- Striking an official: Play is not stopped when a puck strikes an official. If a puck strikes an official and deflects into the goal, however, the goal does not count.

Also, players may kick the puck in any zone, but a goal may not be scored by kicking the puck, whether or not the kick was intentional. If a player on a team who is not short-handed shoots a puck across the center line and past the opponents' goal line (icing the puck), play is stopped, and a face-off occurs at the end face-off spot of the offending team. If, however, a goal is scored on the shot, the goal counts. Finally, players on the

attacking team may not enter the attacking zone before the puck does. Such a violation results in a face-off in the neutral zone.

Penalties

When a player whose team is in possession of the puck violates a rule, the referee immediately blows her whistle and imposes the appropriate penalty. The game is resumed with a face-off. If the player who commits the penalty is on the team that is not in possession of the puck, the referee blows her whistle and imposes the penalty after the play is completed. The kinds of penalties are discussed next.

Minor Penalty Any player who is charged with a minor penalty, other than the goalkeeper, sits in the penalty box for 2 minutes; no substitutes are allowed. The goalkeeper's penalty may be taken by a teammate. A sampling of minor penalties includes delay of game, dislodging the net from its moorings, closing the hand on the puck, holding an opponent, hooking, interfering with an opponent who is not in possession of the puck, interfering with the goalkeeper, playing with a broken stick, and tripping.

Depending on the severity of the offense, minor penalties may be assessed for

- board checking or checking from behind (minor or major),
- charging (minor or major),
- cross-checking (minor or major),
- elbowing, kneeing, or head-butting (minor or major),
- high sticking (minor, double minor, or major),
- slashing (minor or major), or
- roughing (minor or double minor).

Bench Minor Penalty A coach may remove any one of his players from the ice, except the goalkeeper, to serve this 2-minute penalty. If a team is short-handed by one or more minor or bench minor penalties, and the opposing team scores, the first penalty assessed is terminated.

Major Penalty Any player, except for the goalkeeper, who commits a major offense serves a 5-minute penalty. No substitution is allowed. A player who commits two major penalties in a game is ejected from the game. Major penalties may be assessed for

- elbowing or kneeing an opponent and causing injury,
- fighting,
- grabbing or holding an opponent's face mask,
- hooking or cross-checking and causing injury,
- slashing and injuring an opponent, or
- spearing or butt-ending with the stick.

Misconduct Penalties   Players may incur misconduct penalties, game misconduct penalties, and gross misconduct penalties. Team personnel may also incur gross misconduct penalties.

Any player, except the goalkeeper, who commits a misconduct penalty must sit for 10 minutes. This player may be replaced immediately. A player whose misconduct penalty has expired must remain in the penalty box until a stoppage in play. When a player commits a misconduct penalty and either a major or a minor penalty at the same time, her team must put a substitute player in the penalty box to serve the major or minor penalty.

For a game misconduct penalty, a player is suspended for the duration of the game, but a substitute is allowed. Depending on the league, a player or coach receiving a game misconduct penalty may also face additional suspension.

Acts resulting in misconduct or game misconduct penalties, depending on the severity of the violation, include

- disputing a call after receiving a penalty;
- continuing to fight after being ordered to stop;
- entering the referee's crease while officials are in it consulting;
- being the first player to intervene in an altercation;
- leaving the players' bench or penalty box to enter an altercation;
- using obscene, profane, or abusive language or gestures;
- physically abusing officials;
- shooting a puck out of reach of an official who is retrieving it;

- spearing an opponent;
- throwing the puck or any equipment out of the playing area;
- touching or holding an official in any way; and
- using threatening or abusive language to incite an opponent.

Match Penalty   The player is replaced for the rest of the game and ordered to the locker room. A substitute may replace this player after 5 minutes of playing time have elapsed. Match penalties are assessed for

- deliberately injuring an opponent,
- trying to injure an opponent, or
- kicking or trying to kick an opponent.

Goalkeeper's Penalty   A teammate must serve a goalkeeper's minor or major penalty. If a goalkeeper incurs two major penalties in one game, he is ruled off the ice, and a substitute goalkeeper may take his place.

Delayed Penalty   If a third player of a team is penalized while two teammates are serving penalties, the penalty time of the third player doesn't begin until the first teammate's penalty time elapses. Nonetheless, the third player must go to the bench immediately and be replaced by a substitute, who may play until the third player's penalty time officially begins.

Penalty Shot   Penalty shots may be awarded for many reasons. The following list includes some of the common violations that result in a penalty shot:

- Falling on the puck, holding the puck, or gathering the puck into the body when the puck is within the goal crease (goalkeeper exempted)
- Interfering with an opponent in possession of the puck and with no defender between her and the goalkeeper
- Throwing a stick or any object at the puck in the offending player's defending zone (if a goal is scored on the play, no penalty shot is given)

The referee places the puck on the center face-off spot, and the player taking the penalty shot tries to score on the goalkeeper. The player may take the puck anywhere in the neutral zone or in his own defending zone, but once the puck crosses the blue line into the attacking zone, it must be kept in forward motion, and once it is shot, the play is complete. No goal may be scored on a rebound. While the penalty shot is being taken, all other players except the two involved withdraw to the sides of the rink on the attacker's side of the center line.

If a goal is scored on a penalty shot, play resumes with a face-off at center ice. If a goal is not scored, play resumes with a face-off at one of the end face-off spots in the zone in which the penalty shot was attempted.

Goalkeeper Interference

A goal can be waved off and revoked if an attacking player did not allow the goalie to move freely within the crease or defend the goal when the goal was scored. This can be caused by direct contact with the goaltender or by the player's position. Goals are also disallowed if an attacking player makes contact with a goalie. This contact must be intentional in order for the goal to be called off. Incidental contact with a goaltender is permitted when contact is initiated outside of the crease, and the goal is counted for the opposing team. It must be evident that the player made an effort to avoid goalie contact in order to avoid the interference call.

TERMS

A player receives an **assist** when her pass leads to a teammate's scoring a goal. No more than two assists are allowed on any one goal. An assist counts for 1 point in the player's record.

A **body check** is the use of the body to block a player's progress.

A **breakaway** occurs when a player in control of the puck has no defenders between him and the opponents' goal.

Butt-ending is using the end of the stick in a jabbing motion.

Charging is called when a player jumps into or uses more than two steps to skate into another player.

A team **clears a puck** when it gets the puck away from the front of its goal.

Control of the puck is determined by the last player to propel the puck in a desired direction.

Cross-checking occurs when a player delivers a check to an opponent with two hands on the stick while extending the arms.

Delayed offside is called when an attacking player precedes the puck across the attacking blue line but the defending team possesses the puck and is in position to bring it out of its defending zone without any delay or contact with an attacking player. If the defending team advances the puck out of its defending zone, no offside is called.

A **drop pass** is one that is left behind for a teammate.

A **flat pass** is one that doesn't leave the surface of the ice.

A **flip pass** is one that travels through the air.

A player **freezes** the puck in an attempt to stop play.

A **goal** (1 point) is scored when the puck crosses the goal line between the goal posts and under the crossbar. If a defender accidentally knocks the puck into her own goal, the opponents are awarded a goal. If a puck deflects off an official and across the goal line, the goal does not count. A goal does not count if an attacking player is in the **goal crease** (a marked area in front of the goal) when the puck crosses the goal line or if an attacking player bats or kicks the puck across the goal line.

A **hat trick** is accomplished by a player who scores three goals in one game.

High sticking means carrying or using the stick above shoulder height.

A **hip check** occurs when a player uses his hip to knock an opponent in possession of the puck off balance.

Hooking is called when a player uses her blade to interfere with an opponent's progress.

When a player goes **intentionally offside** to try to gain a stoppage in play, the puck is faced off at the end zone face-off spot in the defending zone of the offending team.

Possession of the puck is determined by the last player touching it (including deflections).

A team is in a **power play** when it has more players on the ice than its opponent.

A **rebound** is a puck that bounces off the goalkeeper or the goal post.

A **save** is recorded by a goalkeeper who prevents a goal from being scored.

A team is **short-handed** when it has fewer players on the ice than its opponent. This occurs because of penalties. When a goal is scored against a short-handed team, the minor or bench minor penalty that caused the team to be short-handed is ended, and the penalized player returns to action.

A **slap shot** is a shot taken by a player who lifts her stick in a backswing before hitting the puck.

Slashing is called when a player hits, or tries to hit, an opponent with his stick.

A **slow whistle** refers to a play in which an official raises his arm in preparation for blowing his whistle for an infraction, depending on how the play turns out. For example, a delayed offside situation results in a slow whistle. The whistle will be blown in this case if the defending team does not advance the puck out of its defending zone and an attacker is offside.

Spearing occurs when a player uses her stick blade to stab an opponent.

A **wrist shot** is taken by a player who does not lift his stick off the ice before hitting the puck.

OFFICIALS

The referee is in charge of the game and of the other officials: two linesmen, who watch for rules violations; a penalty timekeeper, who records all the penalties and keeps the time for the players in the penalty box; an official scorer, who records all game data; and a game timekeeper, who runs the game clock. See figure 31.2 for officials' signals.

MODIFICATIONS

Various youth and other leagues modify the rules to best suit their purposes. Following are some examples of modifications:

- No body checking is permitted.
- Time is shortened (e.g., three 14-minute periods of playing time).
- Ties are broken by alternating penalty shots taken by different members of each team, with the first team that scores winning.

ORGANIZATIONS

Hockey Canada
151 Canada Olympic Road SW, Ste. 201
Calgary, AB T3B 6B7
403-777-3636
www.hockeycanada.ca

International Ice Hockey Federation
Brandschenkestrasse 50
Postfach
8027 Zurich
Switzerland
41-44-562-2200
www.iihf.com

USA Hockey
1775 Bob Johnson Dr.
Colorado Springs, CO 80906-4090
719-576-8724
www.usahockey.com

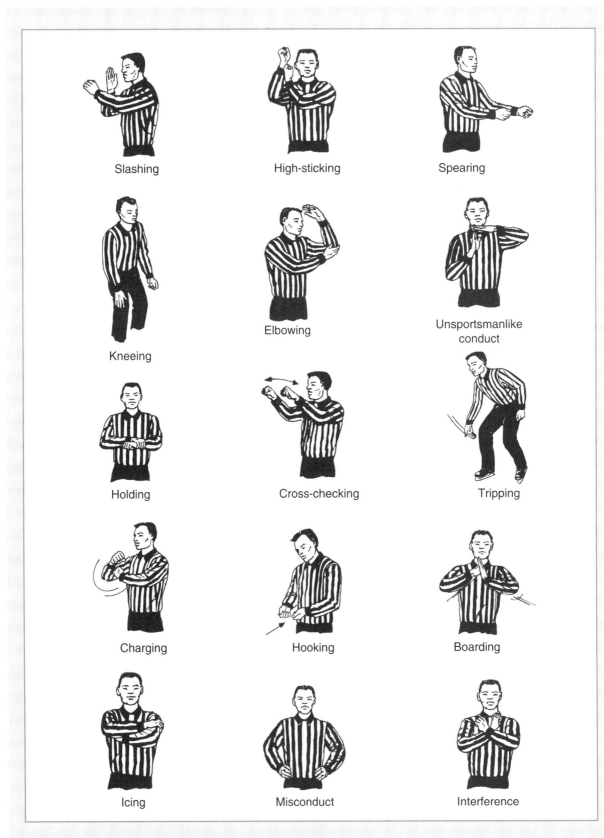

▶ Figure 31.2 Common officials' signals in ice hockey.

32

Judo

Bob Elsdale/The Image Bank/Getty Images

Judo is a martial art that was developed from ju-jitsu by Professor Jigoro Kano in Japan in 1882. *Ju* means "gentle" or "supple"; *do* means "the way of" or "art of."

Although judo is a full-contact combative sport similar to wrestling, which is concerned with attacks and defenses against an opponent, it also develops physical conditioning, self-discipline, and total health. More than 4 million people in 150 countries participate in judo, which has been an Olympic sport since 1964; about 40,000 people in the United States take part.

OVERVIEW

Objective: To defeat the opponent by using throws (hands, hips, legs, and sacrifice techniques) and groundwork techniques (hold-downs, chokes, and armlocks).

Scoring: Points are scored for various throws and hold-downs. The competitor with the most points wins.

Contest Length: 4 minutes for men and women (senior, junior, and cadet competitions); 3 minutes for youth competitions for 13 and 14 year olds and 2 minutes for 11 and 12 year olds (real contest times).

Contest Ends: The contest ends when a competitor scores an ippon (1 point). A competitor can also win because of default (opponent not showing up), disqualification (hansoku-make), withdrawal (generally injury), or when contest time expires.

If the contest goes the full duration, the competitor with the highest score wins. If the score is tied, the contestants compete in a "golden score" (sudden death) contest in which the first called score or penalty wins the contest.

Judo is a form of wrestling while wearing a durable jacket, pants, and belt (judogi). It emphasizes throws using the jacket, hold-downs (pins), chokes (13 years old and over), and armlocks (seniors only). There are no punching or kicking techniques in sport judo; however, in the martial art of judo at the higher levels, striking and kicking techniques are learned in the kata (prearranged forms).

Judo is a competitive sport, but a code of chivalry and sportsmanship known as "mutual welfare and benefit" is taught in most judo clubs (dojos). Instructors and students seek "maximum efficiency with minimum effort," seeking their full potential through judo.

Competitions are often highlighted by spectacular throws. Timing, speed, and technique are the keys to a competitor's success.

To begin a contest, the competitors stand facing each other on a mark on the mat. They bow and take one step forward. The referee signals the start by calling out, "Hajime." Competitors try to score points by using various techniques to throw; or, when they fall to the mat, they use hold-downs (pins) on their opponent (see "Scoring"). The referee may temporarily halt a match, during which the competition clock stops, when

▪ one or both competitors go outside the competition area,

▪ a competitor performs a prohibited act (see "Prohibited Acts and Penalties"),

▪ a competitor is injured or ill, or

▪ the competitors are entangled on the ground and not making progress.

COMPETITION AREA

The competition area is a mat that is at least 14 meters by 14 meters (see figure 32.1). The mat is generally made of vinyl-covered foam and is placed on a resilient floor. The competition area is divided into two areas. The contest area is at least 8 by 8 meters with a maximum of 10 by 10 meters. The area outside and adjacent to the contest area is called the safety area. The safety area is a minimum of 3 meters wide. The safety area is generally another color, so it is easily distinguished from the contest area. There is also a free zone around the competition area that should be a minimum of 50 centimeters.

COMPETITORS

Judo competitors are grouped into various levels by gender, age, weight, and sometimes rank (skill) levels. The International Judo Federation does not allow individuals younger than age 15 to compete in official events. Age categories recognized by the organization are as follows:

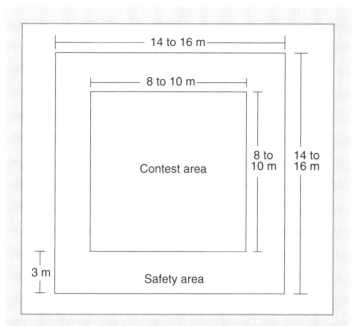

▶ **Figure 32.1** The dimensions and features of a judo competition area.

- Cadet: ages 15 through 17
- Junior: ages 15 through 20
- Senior: only has a lower age limit of 15

Each of the three age categories are then broken down by weight categories for both genders. There are 8 weight categories for each category listed above in male and female categories. These weight categories are as follows:

- Featherweight
- Extra-lightweight
- Half-lightweight
- Lightweight
- Half-middleweight
- Middleweight
- Half-heavyweight
- Heavyweight

EQUIPMENT

Judges use chairs, placed in opposite corners of the safety area just outside the contest area. A scoreboard is used to show points and penalty points for each contestant. Clocks are used to time the contest and to time the length of each osaekomi (hold-down).

Each contestant wears a white or blue judogi (uniform). The judogi jacket must be long enough to cover the thighs, and the arms of the jacket must reach the wrist joints when the arms are extended down. The trousers must reach to the ankle joints. Each contestant wears a belt, with the color corresponding to grade level, over the jacket. Fingernails and toenails must be cut short.

RULES

Competitors score points based on the techniques (throws and holds) they successfully execute and the penalties they incur.

Scoring

A competitor scores an ippon, worth 1 point and a victory, when he

- throws the opponent with speed and control, largely on the back with considerable force;
- holds (osaekomi) the opponent's back and at least one shoulder to the mat, and the opponent is unable to get away from this hold within 20 seconds; or
- employs a strangle technique or armlock from which the opponent submits (taps twice or more).

The judogi is integral to judo because most judo techniques require gripping the opponent's jacket or pants to execute a throw.

If a competitor is penalized hansoku-make (loss by violation of the rules), the opponent is awarded an ippon and the match.

Waza-ari is worth half a point (near point). A competitor scores waza-ari when he throws his opponent, but the technique is not deserving of ippon (e.g., it is partially lacking in one of the elements of control, being largely on the back and demonstrating force and speed).

A contestant also scores waza-ari when she holds her opponent's back and at least one shoulder to the mat, and the hold lasts 10 seconds but less than 20 seconds.

A wazia-ari is also awarded when a competitor throws her opponent but the technique is partially lacking in two of the elements necessary for ippon. For example, the opponent thrown may not be largely on her back, or the throw may have been lacking in speed or force.

Prohibited Acts and Penalties

There are two types of penalties:

▪ A shido is a minor infringement. There are 25 shido prohibited acts. Three shido add up to hansoku-make.

▪ A hansoku-make (loss by violation of the rules) is a very grave infringement. There are 13 direct hansoku-make prohibited acts.

A few examples of each type of infringement follow.

A shido may be called for noncombativity or preventing action (20 to 30 seconds of inactivity); adopting an excessively defensive posture (generally more than 5 seconds); false attack; applying leg scissors to the opponent's trunk, neck, or head; or bending back the opponent's fingers to break her grip.

A hansoku-make may be called against a competitor who dives headfirst onto the mat while performing, or attempting to perform, various techniques or who intentionally falls backward when an opponent is clinging to his back. Other examples include when a competitor applies joint locks (except for the elbow joints); acts in a way that could injure the opponent's neck or spinal cord; or lifts an opponent who is lying on the mat and slams her back onto the mat. Leg grabbing or grabbing the trousers shall be penalized first as shido and then, if it continues, as hansoku-make.

TERMS

Hajime ("Begin") is a call by the referee to start the contest.

Hansoku-make is a disqualification resulting from a major infraction.

Ippon is 1 point; **waza-ari** is half a point.

Mate ("Stop") is called by the referee to stop the contest.

Osaekomi is the call the referee makes when a hold-down is valid and the osaekomi clock is started.

A **shiai** is a judo tournament or championship, which is fought on a mat called a **tatami**.

In a judo competition, the attacker is called a **tori**. The thrown player is the **uke**.

A **shido** is a minor infraction.

Toketa is the call the referee makes when a hold is broken (when the uke escapes the hold-down). The osaekomi clock is stopped.

OFFICIALS

One referee and two judges conduct the contests. They are assisted by contest recorders (scoreboard operators), timekeepers, and pool sheet writers (match setters).

ORGANIZATIONS

International Judo Federation
www.ijf.org

United States Judo Association
One Olympic Plaza
Colorado Springs, CO 80909
719-866-4730
www.teamusa.org/usa-judo

United States Judo Federation
P.O. Box 338
Ontario, OR 97914
541-889-8753
www.usjf.com

33

Ju-Jitsu

Mireya Acierto/Taxi/Getty Images

Ju-jitsu is an ancient Japanese martial art that has been practiced for more than 2,500 years. In feudal Japan, samurai used the martial art to defend themselves against armed opponents. From the early 1600s to the late 1800s, more than 700 systems of ju-jitsu existed.

Although there are many variations of ju-jitsu, it consists primarily of grappling techniques that are based on using an attacker's energy against him. Methods of combat include striking, throwing, restraining, and weaponry. Defensive tactics include blocking, evading, off-balancing, blending, and escaping.

Many other martial arts were spawned from ju-jitsu, including judo and aikido.

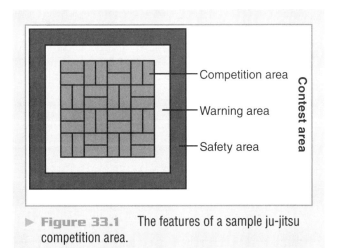

▶ **Figure 33.1**   The features of a sample ju-jitsu competition area.

OVERVIEW

Under the Ju-Jitsu International Federation (JJIF), competitions occur in a two-part system. The first part is the fighting system and the second part is duo competition. Depending on the size and nature of the competition, competitors are placed in divisions by gender, age, weight, or grade. Matches in the fighting system are 3 minutes, and competitors earn points based on the techniques they execute. In duo competitions, two couples perform three attacks in each of four series. The couple who receives the highest total score wins.

COMPETITION AREA

International competitions are held on a 12-meter by 12-meter tatami (see figure 33.1). The competition area is the center 8 meters by 8 meters, surrounded by a 1-meter warning area of a different color. National competitions are held on a 10-meter by 10-meter tatami with a 6-meter by 6-meter competition area and a 1-meter warning area. The outside meter of the tatami is a safety area.

COMPETITORS

There are different divisions for males and females, and various tournaments and championships use weight, age, and grade categories to open the competitions to more fighters.

Female competitors compete in these weight categories:

- Less than 55 kilograms (121 pounds)
- 55 to 62 kilograms (121-136 pounds)

- 62 to 70 kilograms (136-154 pounds)
- 70+ kilograms (154+ pounds)

Males compete in these weight categories:

- Less than 62 kilograms (136 pounds)
- 62 to 69 kilograms (136-152 pounds)
- 69 to 77 kilograms (152-169 pounds)
- 77 to 85 kilograms (169-187 pounds)
- 85 to 94 kilograms (187-207 pounds)
- 94+ kilograms (207+ pounds)

EQUIPMENT

Competitors wear ju-jitsu gi without rolling up the sleeves or trousers. The gi should be completely white, royal blue, or black. No other colors are permitted. The gi jacket must cover the hips and half of the forearms; pants must fit loosely. Gi pants must not fall higher than 5 centimeters above the ankle bone.

One competitor wears a blue belt; the other wears a red belt. Female competitors also wear a white T-shirt. Women must wear an elastic shirt, one-piece bathing suit, or gymnastics suit that hugs the body beneath the gi. All competitors wear light, soft, short-hand protectors as well as soft foot and shinbone protectors and mouthpieces.

FIGHTING SYSTEM RULES

In the JJIF fighting system, opponents compete using blocks, punches, kicks, locks, strangulations, throws, and takedowns. Matches consist of three distinct parts:

- First part: punches, strikes, and kicks
- Second part: throws, takedowns, locks, and strangulations
- Third part: floor techniques, locks, and strangulations

Fighters must be technically active in all three parts and earn points in each part of the 3-minute match. Those who are not technically active receive a passivity penalty. Fighting is continuous; the match is stopped only for injury, for penalty, or when points are scored for an *osaekomi* (hold-down) or a tapping (giving in to a lock, bar, or strangle).

The winner of the match advances to further rounds of competition. In the JJIF fighting system, competitions can be single elimination, double elimination, or various other systems of competition.

Conduct of Competition

The mat referee (MR), within the competition area, calls for a standing bow and signals the start by announcing, "Hajime" ("Begin"). Part one of the 3-minute match begins with competitors trying to score with strikes, blows, and kicks. As soon as one competitor has the other in a hold, part two begins, and blows, strikes, and kicks are not allowed unless they are simultaneous with the grab. When a competitor is taken down or thrown down, part three begins. If contact is lost either in part two or in part three, the competitors return to part one to continue the fight.

If the MR needs to stop the contest, she announces, "Matte" ("Stop"). The call "Yoshi" restarts the clock and the match. The match is continuous and is stopped only in the following cases:

- When one or both contestants go outside the contest area, perform a forbidden act, or are injured or become ill
- When the contact is lost in part two or part three
- When a competitor cannot make a tapping because of a strangulation or lock
- When the mat referee or side referees find it necessary
- When the referee announces, "Sonomama," for a technical penalty

- When osaekomi (hold-down) time is over
- When a competitor stays more than 5 seconds in the warning area

A sonomama occurs when a passivity warning or another technical penalty is warranted. When the MR calls a sonomama, the competitors freeze their positions; when the match is restarted, they begin in those same positions.

If a competitor inadvertently loses contact with her opponent in part two and is about to fight as in part one of the match, the MR will call, "Matte." If the competitor has intentionally lost contact in either part two or part three, he can be assessed a passivity penalty.

Two side referees (SRs) move along two opposing sides of the tatami, observing the competitors as the match goes on. A table referee (TR) also observes from a table located beyond the safety area.

During the match, the MR and SRs signal when points have been scored. At the end of the match, the MR announces the winner and signals for a standing bow.

Winner

The competitor with the most points wins. If a contestant has scored 2- or 3-point techniques in all three parts of the match in the same round, she wins by a full ippon. If a contestant earns 14 points more than his opponent at the end of the first round, he is declared the winner.

If competitors are tied, the competitor with more 2- or 3-point techniques wins. If the competitors are still tied after this, a hikiwake (draw, or tie) is called. In this case, the competitors fight an additional 2-minute rounds until a winner can be determined.

A contestant can also win by fusen-gachi (walkover) if her opponent does not appear for the match and by kiken-gachi (withdrawal) if her opponent withdraws from the contest during the match. Such wins earn 14 points.

Scoring

Points are awarded in this way when a competitor shows good balance and control:

Part One

- Unblocked blow, strike, or kick—2 points
- Partly blocked blow, strike, or kick—1 point

Part Two

- ▪ Perfect throw or perfect takedown—2 points
- ▪ Strangulation or a lock with tapping—2 points
- ▪ Less than perfect throw or takedown—1 point

Part Three

- ▪ Efficient ground control, announced as osaekomi—2 points for 15 seconds of control, 1 point for 10 seconds of control
- ▪ Strangulation or lock with tapping—3 points

The target area of the body is from the end of the throat to the groin. A competitor receives no points for blows, strikes, or kicks to the legs, and he may not strike or kick once an opponent has grabbed him or when his opponent is lying down.

Circular kicks and circular blows or strikes are allowed to the head. Unblocked kick attacks to the back are scored ippon (2 points).

Strangulations are not allowed with the hands or fingers, and locks on fingers and toes are not permitted. Likewise, cross-legged locks around the kidneys are not allowed.

To receive a score, a majority of the referees (two of the three among the SRs and the MR) must agree. If the three referees each give a different score, the middle score is used. If only two referees give a score, and they are different, the lower score is awarded.

Penalties

For a penalty to be given for a forbidden act, at least two of the three referees must agree. Penalties include the following:

- ▪ Shido—light forbidden acts such as passivity, minor technical infringements, and making further action after matte has been announced. Such acts give 1 point to the opponent.
- ▪ Chui—uncontrolled actions; attacks such as kicking, pushing, punching, and hitting the opponent in a hard way; disregarding the MR's instructions. These penalties give the opponent 2 points.
- ▪ Hansoku-make—heavy forbidden acts that could injure an opponent, including making any lock to the spinal column while in movement or any lock to the neck whatsoever. These penalties result in 14 points and the match being awarded to the opponent.

Injury and Illness

Each contestant has a total of 2 minutes in a match to recuperate from injury and resume the match. When a contestant is unable to continue because of injury, illness, or accident, the match is determined as follows:

- ▪ When the cause of the injury is attributed to the injured contestant, she loses the contest with 0 points, and the opponent gets a minimum of 14 points (more if she had already scored points).
- ▪ If the injury is attributed to the opponent, the opponent loses the contest.
- ▪ If it is impossible to attribute the cause of the injury, the uninjured contestant wins with whatever points he has achieved, and the injured opponent scores 0 points.
- ▪ If a contestant becomes ill and cannot complete the match, her opponent wins 14-0.

TERMS

Chui is a forbidden act.

Fusen-gachi refers to a loss that occurs when a competitor quits a match.

Hajime means begin.

Hansoku refers to two forbidden acts.

Ippon is a score of 2 points (3 points with tapping in part three).

Kiken-gachi is a loss that occurs when a competitor does not appear for a match.

Matte means stop.

Osaekomi means hold-down.

Shido is a light forbidden act.

Sonomama is an announcement to the competitors to freeze in position and hold position to receive a penalty or warning. They will restart from that position in which they froze.

Toketa signals that a hold has been broken in less than 20 seconds.

Waza-ari is a score of 1 point.

Yoshi or **joshi** means continue the match (in the same part).

OFFICIALS

Referees and judges are separately certified for fighting and duo competition and must meet stipulated rank requirements. At competitions, referees and judges must be fair and impartial and must independently make their own judgments. Gray trousers and socks, white shirt (long or short sleeve depending on the season), blue tie and jacket, and JJIF badges are required of all referees and judges. Failure of referees and judges to follow the rules of officiating can cause the loss of their license to officiate.

MODIFICATIONS

A variation of the fighting system is the ne-waza or grappling rules. Events often have both gi (must wear a ju-jitsu uniform) and no-gi divisions. The rules are similar to parts two and three of the fighting match, but points are accumulated for mounts, back control, passing the guard, takedowns, and sweeps and advantage points. Should a competitor tap out, he shall lose the match.

Another type of ju-jitsu is the JJIF duo competition. In these competitions, pairs of partners ("couples") demonstrate vigorous attacks and intense, controlled defends in response to those attacks. Couples are matched against each other two at a time. Points are given based on a comparison of their performances.

Divisions

There are three duo divisions in international competition: male, female, and mixed. Athletes making up a duo can be any age, weight, or grade. Either partner can be the attacker (uke) or defender (tori), and they can change roles at any time during the competition. Various national tournaments and championships can use age, weight, and grade categories to expand competition opportunities.

Uniforms and Competition Areas

The uniforms and competition areas are the same as in the ju-jitsu fighting system.

Conduct of Competition

The MR draws three cards for each series and gives them to each couple shortly before the start of the series. The MR announces the order of the attack to be performed for that series; this order is different for each couple. One couple is in red belts; the other couple is in blue belts.

The MR calls for a standing bow and announces "Hajime" to start each couple's series. The red couple competes first. Couples perform three attacks from each series and receive scores at the completion of each series. The red couple and the blue couple alternate the order of performance for each of the four series they compete in.

The couples focus on these attacks in each series:

- Series 1—gripping attacks
- Series 2—embracing and neck-lock attacks
- Series 3—punches, blows, and kicking attacks
- Series 4—weapon attacks

The MR calls for hantei (the judges' scores) at the end of each couple's performance after indicating to the jury (which consists of five referees) if the correct attacks were made. At the signal of hantei, the judges display their individual scores by holding up scorecards. Scores are whole numbers between 0 and 10 (or 5 through 10, with half points given). The high and low scores are disregarded; the middle three scores are added together to yield the couple's score.

Winner

The winner is the couple with the most cumulative points from the four series. Wins can also be gained by fusen-gachi (when the other couple does not show up) or kiken-gachi (if the other couple withdraws). If there is a tie, the couples repeat the series one at a time until the tie is broken.

Injury

A duo couple has a total of 5 minutes of injury time during a competition. If their injury time runs out, or if they cannot continue because of injury, they lose the match by kiken-gachi.

Judging

The judging jury scores duo performances based on these six criteria:

- Attitude
- Effectivity
- Speed
- Control
- Powerful attack
- Realism

The scores from 0 through 10 do not represent the values of the techniques but offer a comparison between the two couples. Each judge starts with an average score and then adds or subtracts points based on the performance. Judges often use a 6 or 7 for an average presentation and deduct or add points as necessary. The score for the first couple is then compared with the second couple's score, with the better overall performance getting the higher score.

Analyzing the Duo Performance

There are three parts to the performance of duo competitions: the attack and initial breaking of the opponent's attack, the off-balancing, and the end control and exit. Judges evaluate each part of the performance. The attack and initial defense account for about 40 percent of the score, the off-balancing for about 40 percent, and the ending and exit for about 20 percent.

ORGANIZATIONS

American Ju-Jitsu Association
www.americanjujitsuassociation.org

Ju-Jitsu International Federation
www.jjif.info

United States Ju-Jitsu Federation
www.usjjf.org

34

Karate

HECTOR RETAMAL/AFP/Getty Images

The origins of karate are somewhat obscure, but the martial art dates back to at least the 17th century in the Okinawa Prefecture of Japan. In its early stages, karate was an indigenous form of closed-fist fighting; *kara* means "empty" and *te* means "hand." Karate conditions both body and mind, and its many styles are enjoyed by people of all ages and skill levels. Competition as we know it today began in the 1950s. People as young as 4 years old can compete in karate in various age, weight, and experience categories; karate is popular among youths and young adults in America. It is estimated that more than 3.5 million people participate in karate in the United States.

OVERVIEW

Objective: In kumite competition, the objective is to score ippon (3 points), waza-ari (2 points), or yuko (1 point) by performing techniques according to specific criteria. The contestant with the highest score wins. In kata or weapons kata, the objective is to receive the highest score from the judges or, in the case of a bracketed kata event, the majority decision of the judges.

Scoring: In kumite, the first contestant to score 8 points above her opponent wins. In kata and weapons kata, contestants are judged and awarded points based on their performance and mastery of the requisite skills or, in the case of a bracketed division, based on the majority decision of the judges.

COMPETITION AREA

The kumite competition area is a matted square, 8 meters on each side (see figure 34.1) with an additional minimum of 1 meter on all sides as a safety area. The area may be raised up to 1 meter above the floor. If it is elevated, it should measure 12 meters on each side with the outer 2 meters being a safety area. The safety border must be in a different color from the rest of the matted area. Two parallel lines, each 1 meter long, are 1.5 meters from the center of the competition area. The contestants are positioned on these lines. A line 0.5 meter long and perpendicular to the contestants' lines is 2 meters from the center of

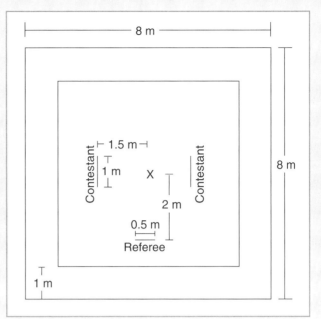

▶ **Figure 34.1** The dimensions and features of a karate competition area.

the competition area. This is the referee's line. A warning line is drawn 1 meter inside the edges of the mat on all four sides.

COMPETITORS

Competitions may be held according to age group, experience level, and weight.

Age Group

Competitors are categorized according to age, where most events consider the following groups or a variation of this:

- Junior: ages 5 or under to 17
- Adult: 18 and over
- Senior: 35 and over
- Senior, advanced male and female: ages 35 to 44 and ages 45 and over

In weapons kata, age groups may be combined. Male and female contestants may not compete against each other except in younger age groups.

Experience Level

There are four levels of experience:

- Beginner: not more than 1 year of experience (7th to 10th kyu or equivalent)
- Novice: 1 to 2 years of experience (green belt, or 4th to 6th kyu or equivalent)
- Intermediate: 2 to 3 years of experience (brown belt, or 1st to 3rd kyu or equivalent)
- Advanced: 3 or more years of experience or black belt

Weight

The weight classes are as follows:

- Junior age group: may be divided into divisions at the discretion of the tournament director
- Adult, advanced; male: under 132 pounds (60 kilograms); 132 pounds (60 kilograms) to 143 pounds (65 kilograms); 143 pounds (65 kilograms) to 154 pounds (70 kilograms); 154 pounds (70 kilograms) to 165 pounds (75 kilograms); 165 pounds (75 kilograms) to 176 pounds (80 kilograms); and 176 pounds (80 kilograms) and over
- Adult, beginner, novice, and intermediate; male: under 154 pounds (70 kilograms); over 154 pounds (70 kilograms)
- Adult, advanced; female: under 117 pounds (53 kilograms); 117 pounds (53 kilograms) to 132 pounds (60 kilograms); 132 pounds (60 kilograms) and over; open weight (no limitation)
- Adult, beginner, novice, and intermediate; female: under 132 pounds (60 kilograms); 132 pounds (60 kilograms) and over

EQUIPMENT

Each contestant wears a white unmarked karate gi. The back of the gi may be numbered. The jacket must cover the hips, but it must cover no more than three-quarters of the thigh. The jacket sleeves may not reach less than halfway down the forearm but must not extend beyond the wrists. The pants must cover at least two-thirds of the shins. One contestant wears a plain red belt and the other a plain blue belt. The belts must be about 5 centimeters wide and must allow for 15 centimeters of length on either side of the knot. The extra length

beyond the knot should not exceed three-quarters of the contestant's thigh length. Men wear groin cups. Approved mitts and mouth guards are mandatory in kumite; soft shin pads are allowed.

RULES

The sport includes competition in *kumite* (free fighting), *kata* (forms), and *weapons kata* (forms with weapons). Both team and individual competitions are held. A tournament may consist of kumite, kata, weapons kata, or all three. Individual matches are divided by the weight classifications mentioned previously. In kumite team matches, the coach determines her team's fighting order (from one to five) before the match begins. A kata team consists of three people performing in synchronization. Rules and guidelines for each follow here.

Kumite

The referee, judges, and contestants take their positions and exchange bows in the prescribed manner, and then the match begins. When a referee sees a scoring technique or a penalty, he stops the match, orders the contestants to take their original positions, and awards a score or penalty before restarting the bout. A score is awarded to a contestant who has performed a punch or strike to an approved scoring area according to these criteria: good form, sporting attitude, vigorous attitude, good timing, correct distance, and awareness (zanchin).

When a contestant scores 8 points above her opponent, the referee stops the bout and declares her the winner. Whether or not a contestant has scored 8 points, each bout between adult males is finished after 3 minutes; women's and junior bouts are limited to 2 minutes, and younger age groups may be as low as 1 minute 30 seconds. If the score is tied at the end, an overtime period begins. The first contestant to score wins. If there is no winner at the end of the overtime, a vote, or hantei, is taken, and the referee and judges declare a winner.

A contestant wins a match by scoring ippon, waza-ari, or yuko, or a combination thereof, to attain 8 points more than his opponent or by leading at the end of the match.

No technique can score if a contestant delivers it outside the competition area. Similarly, effective scoring techniques delivered simultaneously by both contestants cancel each other out. A referee temporarily stops a bout when there is a penalty or a score; when either or both of the contestants are out of the competition area; when a contestant needs to adjust her uniform or equipment; when a contestant breaks, or is about to break, a rule; when a contestant grabs his opponent but does not immediately execute an effective technique; when a contestant falls or is thrown and no effective techniques occur; when a contestant is injured or ill and cannot continue; or when as otherwise needed during the competition.

In team kumite, each team member takes a turn competing against a member from the opposing team, and the team that wins more matches wins the team competition. Although this is the most common team scoring method, there is also the option of adding together all team members' points from each match. The team with the most points would be considered the winner.

Legal and Illegal Acts

A contestant may attack an opponent in the head, face, neck, abdomen, chest, back (excluding shoulders), and side, but penalties can occur. The following penalty acts are in two categories, and each category accumulates separately:

Category 1

- Excessive contact to the head, face, or neck; attacks to these (and all) areas must be controlled
- Contact to the throat
- Attacks to the arms, legs, groin, joints, or instep
- Open-hand attacks to the face
- Dangerous throws that cause injury

Category 2

- Faking or exaggerating injury to gain an advantage
- Repeated exits from the competition area (jogai)

- Reckless actions that endanger either opponent
- Wrestling, pushing, or grabbing without immediately executing a technique
- Direct attacks to the arms and legs or attacks with the head, knees, or elbows
- Goading the opponent or failing to obey the orders of the referee

Such acts are penalized on the following scale:

- A *chukoku* is a warning called for minor infractions.
- A *keikoku* may be imposed for minor infractions for which a contestant has been previously warned. An ippon is added to the opponent's score.
- A *hansoku-chui* is usually imposed for a major infraction or for an infraction in which a keikoku has been previously issued. A nihon is added to the opponent's score.
- A *hansoku* is a very serious infraction that raises the opponent's score to 8 points (victory) and reduces the competitor's score to 0 points. Hansoku may be imposed for an infraction for which a hansoku-chui has previously been imposed.
- A *shikkaku* is a disqualification from the match, with the victory going to the opponent. Shikkaku may be called when a contestant takes an action that harms the honor and prestige of karate.

Note: The referee can award any of these penalties for the first penalty. Each succeeding penalty in a category must be awarded at a higher level, even if it is a less-serious infraction.

Kata

Individual bracketed method. Each round of kata pairs contestants up against each other, with the winner advancing to the next round. *Repechage* is commonly used to chart rounds. This means that each opponent who was previously defeated by the finalist in their pool or bracket gets the opportunity to compete for third place.

When the competitor's name is called, she stands on the designated line, bows to the panel of judges, and announces the name of the kata she will perform. She then performs the kata. When she is finished, her opponent performs her kata. At the end of the second kata, both return to the mat area to await the decision of the judging panel.

In the first round, the competitor performs a kata from the approved compulsory list. In the second round, she may be required to perform a different kata from the compulsory list, and in the remaining rounds, she may perform any kata from the approved list not previously performed. Style differences are permitted. Some open events allow any kata to be performed.

In kata, the contestants are judged according to both technical performance and athletic performance.

Technical performance includes performing stances and techniques according to the style of the kata, the use of transitional movements, timing and synchronization, correct breathing, and focus (kime). Consideration is given for technical difficulty and conformance—consistency in the performance of the kihon of the style (ryu-ha) in the kata.

Athletic performance includes the strength, speed, balance, and rhythm of the competitor.

For many national competitions, the kata division is judged as a group. Each person does her individual kata and is scored numerically between 0 and 10 with decimal points. The winner is the performer with the highest score of the group.

In team kata, movements are synchronized—otherwise, points are deducted—but the kata should neither be altered in rhythm or timing for the sake of synchronization nor should external cues be used. In either individual or team kata, if a contestant interrupts or varies a kata, the contestant (or team) is disqualified. Points are also deducted for momentary imbalances and brief pauses. If a contestant completely loses balance, falls, or comes to a distinct halt, he is disqualified.

Weapons Kata

Weapons kata is judged using the same criteria as open-hand kata, with the additional criterion of demonstrating the characteristics of the weapon used. A contestant must perform a kata that does not endanger people or property; loss of control of the weapon results in disqualification. Weapons are inspected before the competition to ensure that they are in good shape and are of authentic design and proper weight. Weapons include the following:

- Bo: A hardwood staff, either the height of the contestant or 6 feet.
- Ieku: An oar, about 5.50 feet long, with a handle about 3.25 feet long and a blade about 2.25 feet long.
- Kama: A bladed weapon, like a scythe; the blade is at least 6 inches long. The handle may not have a rope or cord attached to it.
- Kuwa: A garden hoe with a round or oval-shaped 4-foot-long handle with a 4-inch by 10-inch rectangular curved blade at one end.
- Nunchaku: Two hardwood sticks held together by a cord the length of the competitor's wrist.
- Nunti: A 6-foot bo with a manji sai attached to one end.
- Sai: A metal club with blunt edges and a sharp point; two hooks face outward from the grip. When held hooked between the thumb and forefinger, this piece should extend beyond the tip of the elbow 1 to 2 inches.
- Tonfa: Two hardwood sticks, round or square, with a handle off one side about 6 inches from the end.

TERMS

Hajime is the command to start a match and to continue the match after a command to stop.

A **hansoku** is a foul that results in a victory for the contestant fouled.

An **ippon** is worth 3 points. It is awarded for face kicks and scoring techniques delivered on a thrown or fallen opponent.

Kihon refers to the fundamentals required to perform advanced martial arts techniques. It typically refers to proper breathing and body positioning and form while executing basic stances, kicks, punches, and other foundational movements.

A win by **kiken** is awarded to a contestant if his opponent is absent, withdraws, or is withdrawn.

Kyu is a commonly used ranking system where 1 represents the highest rank and 10 represents the lowest.

Shikkaku means "disqualification" and can cause removal from the competition. A contestant is awarded the victory if her opponent commits an act leading to shikkaku.

A **waza-ari** is worth 2 points. It is awarded for middle-level kicks.

A **yuko** has a value of 1 point. It may be awarded for middle-body-level punches or strikes.

Yame is the command to stop. Yame may be called at any necessary time during the bout.

OFFICIALS

Matches are officiated by a match area referee, judges, arbitrators, and a scorekeeper.

ORGANIZATIONS

International Karate Association
3301 N. Verdugo Rd.
Glendale, CA 91208
818-541-1240
www.ikakarate.com

USA Karate Federation
1300 Kenmore Blvd.
Akron, OH 44314
330-753-3114
www.usakarate.org

35

Kung Fu

Xavier Cailhol / Icon Sport via Getty Images

Chinese martial arts is an enormous umbrella for hundreds of martial art forms originating in China, some of them dating back thousands of years. There are three different types of kung fu: traditional, wushu, and Tai Chi. For the purpose of this chapter, traditional and wushu methods will be the primary focus. Wushu was developed in 1949 and gained mainstream popularity after several action films about shaolin monks and kung fu were aired by Paramount and Warner Brothers. Obviously, the choreographed fighting in the movies wasn't a realistic depiction of kung fu, but it sparked a fire in pop culture, and soon several Chinese martial art schools in the Western world were formed. Though wushu's various forms of practice each have their own focus and goals, including health, well-being, and preserving traditional culture and skills, more recently wushu has developed into a globally practiced sport recognized by the International Olympic Committee with a combination of ancient practices and modern sport principles. It has not yet been included in the Olympic program. Athletes perform choreographed routines that highlight athletic strengths based on specific rules. These routines can be done barehanded or using weaponry. Traditionally, taolu (form) routines were used to develop and maintain the techniques and tactics of a particular lineage or system. As techniques were practiced, flexibility, stamina, strength, speed, balance, and coordination improved.

OVERVIEW

Objective: To score points using great technique, speed, and timing in the chosen competition. Sport wushu has two main categories—taolu (routines) and sanda (free-fighting).

Scoring: A panel of three judges awards points or charges penalty points to participants. The participant with the most points at the end of the match wins.

Contest Lengths: The length of the contest differs between variations. On average, a round takes 2 minutes, and most matches consists of two rounds. The contest ends when the contest time expires. A competitor can also win because of default (opponent not showing up), disqualification, or withdrawal.

COMPETITION AREA

The regular competition area for most kung fu styles is a rectangle measuring 12 meters by 8 meters. There are variations based on kung fu style and also on the age of participants. For Kung Fu Light Juniors, for example, the competition area measures 6 meters by 6 meters. In most of the variations, the area is a flat surface without any obstructing projections or obstacles.

RULES

The objective of almost every official kung fu match is to score points from judges who assess the technique of the variation of kung fu being practiced.

Scoring

All scoring starts with an average of 9 and can rise and fall depending on the competitor's demonstration of skill. The score is clamped in a range of 2 full points in most forms, and skill levels are clamped between 8.00 and 9.99. For children, this range can be lower. The scoring varies between different versions of the sport, but generally competitors are scored on accuracy, tightness, control, and elegance in the performance of a certain move or form.

Penalties

In all styles, any kind of force that is executed without control or restraint, any kicks to the knees or other attacks on joints, any head butting, and any kicks to the groin will result in disqualification.

A form must end in the same quadrant of the competition ring that it started in unless the chief judge agrees to an exception. A violation results in a 0.5-point deduction.

Re-performing a form due to sloppiness or forgetfulness results in a 0.5-point deduction. The same deduction applies with broken and dropped weapons.

The following are brief descriptions of the many variations of kung fu-wushu.

Sanda

Sanda is unarmed combat derived from traditional wushu techniques. Full-contact bouts are free flowing and include punching, kicking, throwing, wrestling, and defensive techniques. In competition, participants carry out their bout on a raised platform topped by high-density foam with a canvas cover. This competition area is called a *lei tai*, and it is 80 centimeters high, 8 meters wide, and 8 meters long. There must be protective mats around the competition area. These mats must be 30 centimeters high and 2 meters wide. Equipment worn by the competitors include a head guard, a chest protector, gloves, a mouth guard, and a jockstrap.

Competition bouts are three rounds of 2 minutes (1 minute 30 seconds for juniors). Competitors receive points for striking areas on the opponent such as the head, chest, abdomen, waist, back, and legs. The person who wins two out of the three rounds of a bout is declared the winner. The other way to win a bout is to knock out the opponent.

Sanda adult competitions include 11 categories for men and 7 categories for women.

- Adult male: 48, 52, 56, 60, 65, 70, 75, 80, 85, 90, and over 90 kilograms
- Adult female: 48, 52, 56, 60, 65, 70, and 75 kilograms
- Junior male: 48, 52, 56, 60, 65, 70, 75, and 80 kilograms
- Junior female: 48, 52, 56, and 60 kilograms

Taolu

This is a style of wushu in which a contestant executes a routine of choreographed techniques. These techniques include hand and leg movements, jumps, sweeps, stances, footwork, seizing, throwing, and wrestling. Taolu includes compulsory routines and choreographed individual and group routines, as well as partner/duel routines with two or more participants. Routines are appraised by a panel of judges who evaluate the quality of the movements, overall performance, and degree of difficulty.

Taolu competition arenas are 8 meters by 14 meters and consist of high-density foam covered by a low-static carpet. At official World Wushu Championships, the main taolu event categories include:

Chang Quan (Long Fist)   This style, originating in the areas north of the Yangtze River, is fast and dynamic. It uses a wide range of leg techniques and is defined by open and long-range strikes. Chang quan is an exciting style because of its use of acrobatic, high-speed techniques.

Nan Quan (Southern Fist)   This style, originating in the areas south of the Yangtze River, is intense and powerful. Contestants use low stances with fewer leg techniques. The focus is instead on performing short, powerful arm strikes while maintaining stability. Nan quan features fewer acrobatics due to its emphasis on maintaining a solid stance and its concentration on intricate hand techniques.

Taiji Quan (Tai Chi Chuan)   This is the most widely practiced and popular martial art in the world today, mostly due to its health benefits. Taiji quan is exemplified by its slow and graceful motions, coupled at times with explosive bursts of force. The combination of both types of techniques requires synchronization of motion and breath, concentration, and coordination of the entire body.

Taiji Jian (Tai Chi Straight Sword)   Taiji jian couples the use of a double-edged straight sword with the principles and characteristics of taiji quan.

Daoshu (Broadsword)   This style of taolu was widely practiced throughout Chinese history, and it requires fierce and powerful movements. The sword has a curved, single-edged blade, and the style is illustrated by vigorous attack and defensive techniques, such as hacking, upper-cutting, slashing, blocking, thrusting, and circling.

Jianshu (Straight Sword)   The straight sword was one of the most widely used short-bladed weapons in Chinese history, and it has deep cultural significance. Participants in jianshu should exhibit naturally flowing motions. These movements are to be graceful, elegant, brisk, and agile. Jianshu focuses on a balance between hard and soft techniques. Techniques include thrusting, pointing, tilting, shearing, and sweeping combined with intricate footwork and flexible body work, which should include changes in speed.

Gunshu (Cudgel) The long cudgel style is fast paced and focuses on sweeping, chopping, butting, smashing, and rotating techniques. It combines offensive and defensive techniques in quick and heavy movements.

Qiangshu (Spear) The spear is the major long-shafted weapon whose use is practiced widely throughout China. Qiangshu is illustrated by agile footwork, flexible body work, smooth transitions, and fast and precise techniques, both short and long range. Thrusting is the primary technique, but qiangshu also includes coiling, circling, circular blocking, and slamming movements.

Nandao (Southern Broadsword) Nandao is the collective term given for all the different types of broadsword styles most commonly practiced in southern parts of China. Nandao is similar to daoshu, and it uses the principles and style of nan quan. It features short and sharp bursts of power with the broadsword close to the body in order to apply defensive hand techniques.

Nangun (Southern Cudgel) Nangun is the collective term given for all the different types of cudgel styles that are typically practiced in the southern parts of China. Nangun has a fast-paced rhythm and uses double-handed techniques with extension and withdrawal methods.

Duilian (Choreographed Sparring/Duel) This is a choreographed routine that includes two or more participants. Bare-handed combat and weaponry are used to simulate a combat situation. This method requires accuracy and high-level techniques in both offensive and defensive applications. Common techniques demonstrated in duilan include quick leaping, jumping, tumbling, and falling, and it is visually entertaining.

Baguazhang (Eight Trigrams Palm) Baguazhang foundational training consists of circle walking, and its techniques emphasize horizontal and vertical crossing as well as walking while modifying techniques. This emphasizes the contestants' ability to adjust as situations change.

Shuang Jian (Double Straight Swords) Shuang jian demonstrates coordination between the hands as the person uses straight sword techniques. Coordination and fluidity between the weapons and the body of the performer are also very important.

Chun Qiu Da Dao (Spring and Autumn Halberd) This method is popularly referred to as guan dao. Common techniques include continuous circular slicing and various slashing actions that use the momentum of the heavy blade. This requires significant body work from the participant.

Xingyi Quan (Shape and Intent Fist) Xingyi quan is derived from the traditional Chinese concepts of yin and yang. It uses the law of motion in the five element techniques and the 12 animal forms and their corresponding characteristics. The result is a powerful exertion of force in practical attack and defense techniques.

EQUIPMENT

In every official match and tournament, as well as in most training sessions, kung fu uniforms are acceptable, and they should be clean and ironed. Participants may wear a personal sash.

In various kung fu styles, such as Kung Fu Light, the fighter is also fitted with head and dental protection in the form of a helmet and a gum shield, respectively, and sometimes other forms of protective materials such as groin shields, shin guards, and boots to cover the entire foot to protect the fighter from serious injury. Chest protectors are optional.

TRADITIONAL KUNG FU TOURNAMENT FORMATS

Nearly all traditional kung fu styles use the same official formats and methods of competition. The contestants are grouped into weight classes, and no contestant can participate in more than one weight class at the same tournament. According to the official rules for international competitions, every weight class must have at least four contestants.

Kung Fu Light

The Kung Fu Light format allows young fighters (children ages 12 to 18) to compete with no risk of serious injury under safety rules. In this format, the scoring is done in a lighter fashion than in Kung Fu Full, and any strong contact that results in a knockdown is penalized by a disqualification. All preliminary matches for children up to age 15 are conducted in two rounds of 1 minute 30 seconds with a 1-minute break between rounds. For children between ages 15 and 18, this is two rounds of 2 minutes.

Kung Fu Full

This form allows fighters to use all types and forms of throwing (as long as they are performed in 3 seconds), low kicks, reverse kicks to the body or the head, spinning back kicks, and foot sweeps. All preliminary matches are conducted in two rounds of 2 minutes with a 1-minute break between rounds. The final matches are conducted in three rounds of 2 minutes with the same break.

Tueishou

Also called push hands, tueishou is based purely on balance. In this style, opponents do not punch or kick each other but try to cause each other to lose their balance by pushing each other. There is no weight limit in this category. Points are awarded based on the level of imbalance that is achieved against the opponent.

TERMS

Kai shi is a command meaning "Begin" [the match].

Kow tow is the Chinese word for bow, which is a procedure performed by contestants before and after the end of the contest to show respect to the opponent and the referee.

Kung fu is a skill achieved through effort and hard work.

A **lei tai** is an elevated platform cover where bouts take place.

Sanda is combat between unarmed participants that was developed from traditional wushu techniques.

Taolu refers to the set routine component of wushu, which includes a large number of individual and group variations.

Tueishou is a style of kung fu that focuses on putting the opponent off balance through pushes and redirecting forces.

Wushu is a form of kung fu that includes various types of exhibitions or full contact contests using hands or weapons to accumulate points from a panel of judges.

OFFICIALS

The referee regulates the match flow in an unbiased manner and ensures the use of fair play. When rules are violated, the referee can give a warning, a penalty point, or a disqualification to a fighter or a coach.

In most cases, three judges positioned equally at the sidelines of the competition area award points (or penalty points) to participants. The number of judges can vary based on the kung fu style.

The timing of the match, timeouts, and suspension periods are done by the recorder. He also records the points awarded and deducted. In some cases, the recorder also operates the video recorder, a device set to record an official match.

Lastly, every official tournament will have an inspector. Her responsibility is to inspect the contestants' protective equipment in order to ensure their safety.

MODIFICATIONS

At this time, no official modifications are recognized by either the International Kung Fu Federation (IKF) or the International Wushu Federation (IWF).

ORGANIZATIONS

International Kung Fu Federation
29 Block, Metbuat Avenue
AZ1073 Baku
Azerbaijan
www.internationalkungfu.com

International Wushu Federation
Avenue de Rumine 7
Lausanne
Switzerland
www.iwuf.org

Lacrosse

Lacrosse originated in North America, where it was played by Native Americans in what is now Canada and New York. French missionaries playing the game thought the sticks they used resembled the bishop's staff, or crozier; thus they called it "la crosse." Certainly the biggest rule change from its early days centers on the length of the game and field: When Native Americans played the sport, a game stretched on for days and the goals could be 15 miles apart!

The men's and women's games are among the most rapidly growing sports in the United States. Other countries in which lacrosse is popular include Canada, Japan, Australia, and England.

Major League Lacrosse is an outdoor professional league that debuted in 2001; the National Lacrosse League, an indoor professional league, began in the mid-1980s. More than 40,000 men and women play lacrosse in college. Some 300,000 boys and girls play lacrosse in high school. About 400,000 youths participate in recreational lacrosse programs across the country.

OVERVIEW

Objective: To score more goals than the opponents.

Number of Players: 12 per side for women; 10 per side for men.

Length of Game: Two 25-minute halves for women (30-minute halves for collegiate women); four 12-minute quarters for men (four 15-minute quarters for collegiate men).

Scoring: 1 point for each goal (see "Scoring"). Players use long-handled sticks to throw, catch, and scoop the ball and to try to throw the ball into the opponents' goal. Women's rules limit stick contact and prohibit extensive body contact; men's rules allow some stick and body contact. Lacrosse is a combination of basketball, soccer, and hockey and requires quickness, speed, and endurance.

WOMEN'S LACROSSE

Women's lacrosse is distinctly different from the men's version of the game. One main difference is that in the women's game, body checking is prohibited and stick contact is limited. Women, therefore, don't require protective gear beyond mouth guards and eyewear. Headgear specifi-

cally designed for women's lacrosse is optional. The much more physical game played by the men requires male players to wear helmets and protective padding.

The stick, or crosse, has a much shallower pocket for women, requiring them to cradle the ball to keep it from falling out as they run up the field. (The men's crosse has a deep pocket that allows them to run easily downfield with the ball.) A full sized field; in women's lacrosse is 10 yards longer and 10 yards wider than a traditional men's lacrosse field. Women play with 12 players per team on the field and men with 10.

Field

An area measuring 120 yards by 70 yards is desirable. The goals are 90 to 100 yards apart, with 10 to 20 yards of playing space behind each goal line, running the width of the field. Minimum width is 60 yards. The goal circles, 8-meter arcs, 12-meter fans, and center circle are as shown in figure 36.1.

The goals are of wood or metal, 6 feet high and 6 feet wide. A goal line is marked between the two goal posts. Netting is attached to the posts and is firmly pegged to the ground 6 feet behind the center of the goal line.

Players

Twelve players for each team may be on the field at one time. Players wear composition or rubber-soled shoes; spikes are not allowed. Goalkeepers may wear padding on the hands, arms, legs, shoulders, and chest; they must wear helmets with face masks, throat protectors, and chest protectors. All players must wear protective eyewear and mouth guards. Headgear is optional. Substitutions are unlimited. Players may reenter the game.

Equipment

The ball is rubber; it is solid yellow and not less than 20 centimeters or more than 20.3 centimeters in circumference. It weighs between 142 and 149 grams.

The field crosse is made of aluminum, fiberglass, gut, leather, nylon, plastic, rubber, or wood; the head of the crosse is triangular. The crosse is 36 to 44 inches long. The head is 7 to 9 inches wide and 10 to 12 inches long. Its pocket may have a maximum depth of 2.5 inches. Maximum overall

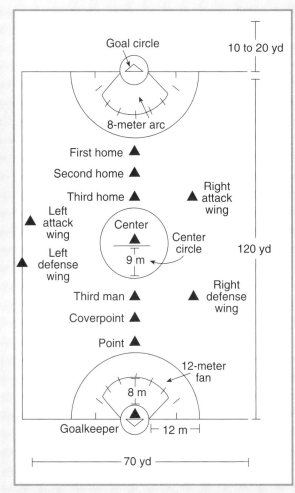

▶ **Figure 36.1** The dimensions, features, and player positions of a women's lacrosse field.

weight is 20 ounces. The goalkeeper's crosse is 36 to 48 inches long and may weigh a maximum of 26 ounces.

Rules

The maximum regulation playing time is 50 minutes (60 minutes in college play), split into halves with up to a 10-minute halftime. The clock stops after a goal is scored and on every whistle in the last 2 minutes of each half. If a team is leading by 10 or more goals, the clock does not stop after a goal. A game starts with a draw—two opposing players toeing the center line, their crosses held in the air, parallel to the center line. The umpire places the ball between the players, calls, "Ready," and blows the whistle. The players pull their sticks

up and away, lifting the ball into the air. All other players must be outside of the center circle during the draw. The team that has the ball tries to score a goal by advancing the ball down the field by carrying, throwing, rolling, or batting it.

Only one player (the goalkeeper or her deputy) may be in the goal circle (see figure 36.1). Within the goal circle, the goalkeeper must clear the ball within 10 seconds. She may use her hands and body to stop the ball, as well as using her crosse. She may also use her crosse to reach out and bring the ball into the goal circle, provided no part of her body is grounded outside the circle. When the goalkeeper leaves the goal circle, she loses all goalkeeping privileges.

Scoring

A team scores a goal when the ball passes completely over the goal line, between the posts, and under the crossbar of the opponents' goal. A goal counts if it bounces off a defender and goes into the goal.

If, however, the ball is last touched by an attacking player, it must be propelled by the player's crosse; a goal does not count if the ball bounces off an attacking player and goes into the goal. A goal may also be disallowed if the ball enters the goal after the whistle has blown, if the attacking player or her crosse breaks the plane of the goal circle, or if any other attacking player is in the goal circle. In addition, a goal may be disallowed if an attacking player interferes with the goalkeeper or if the umpire rules the shot or follow-through dangerous.

Fouls

Players may be called for major, minor, or goal circle fouls. Major fouls include

- rough or reckless checking or tackling;
- slashing;
- holding a crosse around the face or throat of an opponent;
- hooking an opponent's crosse;
- blocking;
- remaining in the 8-meter arc for more than 3 seconds, unless marking an opponent within a stick's length;
- detaining or tripping an opponent, or charging or backing into an opponent; and
- shooting dangerously.

Minor fouls include

- guarding a ground ball with the player's foot or crosse,

- touching the ball by hand (by anyone other than the goalkeeper),

- throwing a crosse,

- drawing illegally,

- taking part in the game without holding a crosse,

- intentionally delaying the game, and

- deliberately causing the ball to go out of bounds.

Goal circle fouls may be called when

- a field player enters the goal circle or holds her crosse over the goal circle line,

- the goalkeeper allows the ball to remain within the circle for more than 10 seconds,

- the goalkeeper reaches beyond the circle to play the ball,

- the goalkeeper draws the ball into the circle while she is partially grounded outside the circle, or

- the goalkeeper steps back into the circle while she has the ball.

A player may be given a misconduct or suspension for playing in a rough, dangerous, or unsporting manner. The penalty for a misconduct or suspension violation is the same as for major fouls (see "Penalties").

Penalties

The penalty for major and minor fouls is a free position awarded to the player who was fouled. The player with the free position may run with the ball or throw it with her crosse. All other players must be at least 4 meters away.

When a defender commits a major foul within the 8-meter arc, the free position is awarded at the spot of the foul. When a defender commits a minor foul within the 12-meter fan, the player fouled takes the free position at the nearest spot, with her defender at least 4 meters away. This is an indirect free position, and the player taking this position may not take a shot until another player has played the ball.

The penalty for a goal circle foul by the defense is an indirect free position taken 12 meters out to

either side, level with the goal line. The exception here is for an illegal deputy; this is treated as a major foul.

A slow whistle can occur on a major foul; the referee throws a signal flag and allows the attacking players to continue a scoring play in the critical scoring area. If the attackers score a goal, the referee does not assess the foul; if the attackers don't score, the referee assesses the foul.

MEN'S LACROSSE

Men's lacrosse is very different from—and much more physical than—the women's game. For a few of the basic differences, refer back to "Women's Lacrosse."

Field

The field is 110 yards long by 60 yards wide (see figure 36.2). A center line runs across midfield.

The two goals have openings 6 feet wide and 6 feet high. Goal posts are made of metal pipe and joined by a crossbar. Each goal is centered between the sidelines and is 15 yards from the nearest end line; the goals are 80 yards apart. Each goal has a mesh net fastened to the posts, crossbar, and ground 7 feet behind the center of the goal. Each goal has a goal crease—a circle with a 9-foot radius—drawn around it. The center of the crease is the midpoint of the goal line. The goal areas are marked at each end of the field by lines 40 yards long, centered on the goal and parallel to and 20 yards from the goal line at that end of the field.

Players

A team is made up of 10 players in the following designations: goalkeeper, defense, midfield, and attack. Four players at most, not counting the goalkeeper, may use long crosses 4.5 to 6 feet long.

A team may play with fewer than 10 players if some players have been injured or expelled, as long as onside provisions are maintained. Substitutes may enter the game when officials have suspended play or they may enter "on the fly," with one player entering the field from the table area after the player he is replacing has left the field by the table area.

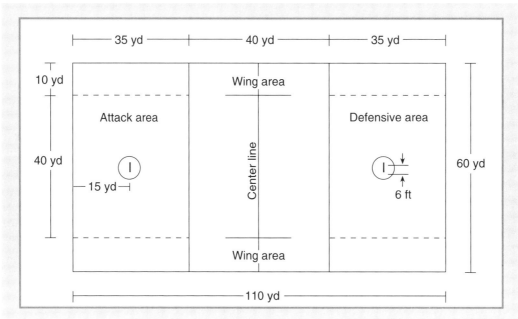

► **Figure 36.2** The dimensions and features of a men's lacrosse field.

Equipment

The ball is solid rubber, weighing between 5 and 5.25 ounces and having a circumference between 7.75 and 8 inches. The crosse is made of wood or synthetic material. It is 40 to 42 inches long for a short crosse and 52 to 72 inches long for a long crosse. The goalkeeper's crosse may be 72 inches or less. The circumference of the crosse handle may be no greater than 3.5 inches; the head at its widest point is between 6.5 and 10 inches. The head for the goalkeeper's crosse may range from 10 to 12 inches in width.

All players must wear protective helmets and mouthpieces. They must also wear protective gloves, arm pads, shoulder pads, shoes, and jerseys. The goalkeeper must wear protective goalkeeper equipment.

Rules

A game lasts 60 minutes (four 15-minute quarters). Intervals of 2 minutes separate the first and second quarters and the third and fourth quarters; halftime lasts 10 minutes. After each period in regulation time, the teams change goals. Each team gets two timeouts per half. If the game is tied at the end of regulation, sudden-death overtime is played in 4-minute periods until a goal is scored. Teams get one timeout each per sudden-death period.

The ball is put into play at the beginning of the game and after each goal is scored with a face-off between two opposing players at the center of the field. The referee places the ball between the two players' crosses and blows a whistle to begin the action, and the two players try to take control of the ball.

After gaining possession of the ball in its defensive area (see figure 36.2), a team must advance the ball past the midline within 20 seconds or turn the ball over to its opponents.

After crossing the center line in possession of the ball, the attacking team must advance the ball into the attack area within 10 seconds. Once the ball is in the attack area, players may take it back outside that area, unless warned to "keep it in" (this warning occurs automatically in the final 2 minutes of regulation if the team in possession is winning by four goals or less). A team that has advanced the ball into the attack area may not carry or propel the ball past the midline.

A player may body check an opponent who has the ball or who is within 5 yards of a loose ball. The check must be from the front or side, above the waist, and below the neck.

When a player who has the ball steps on or outside a boundary line, or when his crosse touches on or beyond the boundary line, the ball is out of bounds and is awarded to the opponents. On a restart, no player may be within 5 yards of the player with the ball.

The team that wins the coin toss to begin the game gets the option of choosing which goal to defend or first alternate possession if the official cannot determine which team should be awarded the ball.

If the ball becomes caught in a player's uniform or equipment other than his crosse, the ball is immediately awarded in accordance with the alternate-possession rule.

A team is offside when it has more than six men in its attack half of the field when on offense or more than seven men in its defensive half of the field when on defense. In such cases, a technical foul (see "Fouls") is called against the offending team.

Within the goal crease area, the goalkeeper may stop the ball with any part of his crosse or body, including batting it with his hands; however, he may not catch the ball with his hands. If the ball is outside the crease area, he may not touch the ball with his hands, even if he is within the crease area. No opponent may make contact with the goalkeeper while he is in the crease area, whether or not the goalkeeper has the ball. An attacking player may not be in the crease area at any time. A defending player with possession of the ball outside of the crease, including the goalkeeper, may not enter the crease area. If a defending player gains possession of the ball within the crease area, he must get rid of the ball or leave the crease area within 4 seconds.

Scoring A team scores a goal when the ball passes from the front and completely through the imaginary plane formed by the rear edges of the opponents' goal line, the goal posts, and the crossbar.

A goal does not count when

- it passes the goal's plane while an attacking player is in the goal crease area,
- the attacking team has more than 10 men on the field (including the penalty area),
- the attacking team is offside as the goal is scored, or

- an official has whistled the play dead for any reason.

Fouls Players may be called for personal, technical, and expulsion fouls. Personal fouls include illegal body checking, slashing, cross-checking, tripping, unnecessary roughness, unsportsmanlike conduct, and using an illegal crosse. A player committing a personal foul is suspended for 1 to 3 minutes, depending on the severity of the foul. The ball is given to the team fouled. A player who commits five personal fouls in a game is disqualified and may be replaced by a substitute when any penalty time for the fifth foul is over. If the ball was not possessed at the time of a technical foul, there is no penalty time given and the team that is fouled is given the ball to start play.

Technical fouls are less serious than personal fouls. They include violations of rules that aren't covered under personal fouls and expulsion fouls. Examples of technical fouls include holding, pushing, offside, crease violations, illegal offensive screening, interference, and stalling. A player must serve a 30-second penalty if his opponents had possession of the ball at the time of his foul; if his team had possession of the ball, the ball is awarded to the opponents for a technical foul.

MEN'S INDOOR LACROSSE

Indoor lacrosse, also known as box lacrosse, boxla, or just box, is played on an ice hockey rink where the ice has been removed and play is on a concrete, wood, or turf carpet surface.

The Arena

Turf carpet is the typical indoor playing surface laid to cover a hockey ice surface. When turf is unavailable, a concrete floor with dasher board ranging from 3.5 to 4.0 feet above the floor is used.

The playing area consists of a defensive zone, a center (also known as neutral) zone, and an offensive zone. Two lines separate the three zones, making it clear where each zone begins and ends.

The goal posts and goal line are located 12 feet from the ends of the playing surface and are centered within the width of the area.

A goal crease is marked clearly with a circle, and it should be marked using the midpoint of the goal as the middle of the circle. The radius of the goal crease must be 9.25 feet, which must include the entire area, including the outside edge of the circle.

Length of Game

The game is 15-minute quarters with a 2-minute interval between both the first and second quarters and the third and fourth quarters and a 12-minute interval at halftime. There are no tie games in professional indoor lacrosse; a game that is tied at the end of regulation is decided in sudden-death overtime. Teams exchange goals after each quarter ends. Each team receives one timeout of 45 seconds for each half.

Players

Each team has five runners (forwards, transition players, and defensemen) and a goaltender on the floor during the game. A full team dresses 18 players (16 runners, two goaltenders) per game, with players rotating on and off the floor in shifts, similar to ice hockey. Each team should have just one captain to discuss questions that arise during the game. All players should wear a uniform with identifying numbers at least 10 inches high on their backs.

Equipment

A ball may be rubber with a smooth surface and a solid color with a circumference between 7.75 and 8.00 inches and weighing between 5.0 and 5.25 ounces. Players' lacrosse sticks may be 40 to 42 inches long and 4.5 inches to 7.0 inches wide at their widest point, except the goalkeeper's, the head of whose stick may not exceed 16.5 inches in length and 13 inches in width.

All players are required to wear:

- a protective helmet;
- intra-oral mouth guard;
- facemask and chinstrap;
- protective gloves;
- shoulder and vest pads; and
- rib pads.

Rules

The rules primarily follow those of men's outdoor lacrosse. There are a few special rules to accommodate the smaller playing area. An 8-second violation occurs when the offense fails to advance the ball past midfield within that amount of time after taking possession on their own end. A 30-second clock begins counting down when a team assumes possession of the ball. A shot on goal must be taken within the 30 seconds. If a shot is taken and missed but the offensive team recovers possession, the clock is reset for a new 30 seconds.

TERMS

Blocking occurs when a player moves into the path of an opponent who has the ball without giving the opponent a chance to stop or change direction without contact.

Body checking occurs when a defender moves with an opponent without making body contact but causing her to slow, change direction, or pass off.

The **critical scoring area** is at each end of the field, where the attacking team shoots for a goal. It runs from approximately 15 meters in front of the goal circle to 9 meters behind the goal circle and 15 meters to either side of the goal circle. It is not marked on the field.

Cross-checking is stick checking an opponent with the portion of the handle that is between both hands.

A **deputy** is a player on the defensive goalkeeper's team who may enter the goal circle when her team is in possession of the ball and the goalkeeper is out of the goal circle.

Marking is the term used to describe guarding an opponent within a stick's length.

A **pick** is a technique used by a player without the ball to force an opponent to take a different direction. The player must give the opponent time to see the pick and react to it.

Slashing is viciously or recklessly swinging a crosse at an opponent's crosse or body. Contact doesn't have to be made for the umpire to call a foul.

A **slow whistle** occurs when an attacking team is fouled on a scoring play within the critical scoring area; the play is finished and the umpire assesses a foul only if the attacking team does not score a goal.

OFFICIALS

In women's lacrosse, an umpire, a scorer, and a timer officiate the game. Otherwise, a referee, umpire, and field judge control the game. At least two officials must be used; a fourth may be used as a chief bench official.

ORGANIZATIONS

Federation of International Lacrosse
www.filacrosse.com

U.S. Lacrosse
113 W. University Parkway
Baltimore, MD 21210
410-235-6882
www.lacrosse.org

37

Netball

Netball seems to have evolved from an early version of basketball (i.e., scoring when the ball was successfully thrown into a basket placed in a higher position than the players at each end of a court area). The game developed in the United States and England shortly after basketball was invented in 1891. Originally the game was known as nine-a-side basketball, and it became most popular in Australia and New Zealand. It is the most popular women's sport in Australia with an estimated one million participants. The game was then played outdoors, with rings on the goal posts instead of baskets.

Today netball is played by more than 20 million people in more than 80 countries, including Commonwealth countries. In 1960 an international code of play was introduced, and in 1963 the first world championships were held in England, where Australia and New Zealand established themselves as the dominant teams. Australians have been the world champions for almost all of the years since 1963.

Netball is predominantly a game for women, but men also play in mixed and men-only teams. Players' ages range from 5 years to masters, with most of those participating between the ages of 15 and 40.

OVERVIEW

Objective: To score more goals than the opponents.

Number of Players: Seven on the court per team.

Scoring: A goal may be scored by one of two scoring players on each side.

Match Length: A match consists of four quarters, each 15 minutes long, with an interval of 3 minutes between the first and second and between the third and fourth quarters. Halftime is 5 to 12 minutes, determined by the agreement of the event organizer and both teams.

The game starts (and restarts after every goal) with a center pass taken alternately by the opposing center players from the center circle in the middle of the center third of the court. The center pass and all subsequent passes must be caught or touched by a player who is standing or who lands in whichever third the ball is in (the ball must not pass over a complete third without being touched).

COURT

The court is 100 feet long and 50 feet wide. It is divided into three equal areas, called thirds (see figure 37.1), which regulates where players are allowed to move. There are scoring hoops, or rings, at both ends of the court. The longer sides of the court are sidelines, and the shorter lines are goal lines. A center circle is located in the center of the court.

At each end of the court, there is a semicircular shooting circle, or goal circle, within which all scoring shots must be taken. The goal posts are 3.05 meters high from the top of the ring to the ground and 65 to 100 millimeters (2.5 to 4.0 inches) in diameter and have no backboards.

PLAYERS

Each team consists of up to 12 players, 7 of whom are on the court at the same time. All players on the court wear identification letters front and back that show their playing positions and the areas of the court into which they may move. These are the court areas in which each player is allowed:

- Goal shooter (GS): 1, 2
- Goal attack (GA): 1, 2, 3
- Wing attack (WA): 2, 3
- Center (C): 2, 3, 4
- Wing defense (WD): 3, 4
- Goal defense (GD): 3, 4, 5
- Goal keeper (GK): 4, 5

EQUIPMENT

The ball may be made of leather, rubber, or similar material and is spherical in shape. It measures 27 to 28 inches in circumference, weighs 14 to 16 ounces, and is inflated to 11 to 12 psi.

RULES

At the start of play, all players must be in their respective goal thirds and are free to move; the defending center is in the center third and free to move; and the attacking center is in the center circle, ready to pass the ball.

The attacking center may throw to one of four teammates who are allowed, by virtue of their

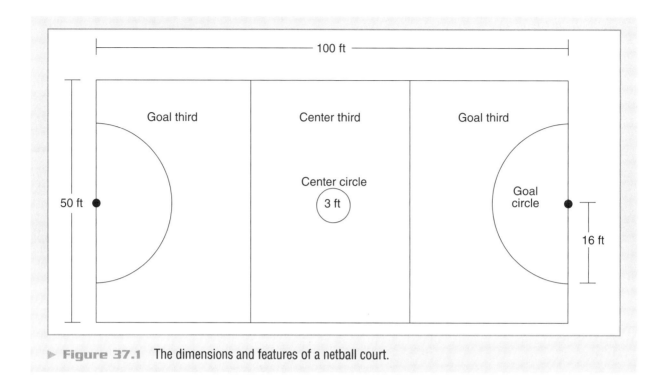

▶ **Figure 37.1** The dimensions and features of a netball court.

playing positions, to enter the center third. Those players are the wing attack, goal attack, wing defense, and goal defense. The attacking team then tries to move the ball downcourt into the goal circle, where one of two players—the goal attack or the goal shooter—tries to score a goal. Only these two players may attempt to shoot goals and then only from within the goal circle, which is a semicircle centered on the goal line with a radius of 16 feet.

Footwork

When a player catches the ball, she must pass it within 3 seconds and obey the footwork rule. Footwork is one of the most important of the netball skills. The player with the ball is not allowed to reground the grounded foot once it has been lifted unless the ball has been released (thrown).

Skilled players who jump to catch the ball while in the air can land on one foot, step onto the other foot, lift the first foot, and then throw the ball before that foot is placed on the floor. That sequence could read something like this: Land on the left foot, step onto the right foot, lift the left foot, throw the ball, and put the left foot back onto the floor.

Passing

There are many passing options, including the bounce, the lob, the two-hand pass (chest pass), and the single-hand shoulder pass (the most common). If a ball goes out of court, it is returned to play by any member of the nonoffending team who is allowed in the area from where the ball is to be thrown in.

Injury or Illness and Blood

The umpires hold time for injury or illness upon appeal from an on-court player or for blood when it is noticed.

When play is stopped for a team during a quarter for an injured, ill, or bleeding player, the player must leave the court within 30 seconds and receive any treatment off the court. Only primary care persons are permitted on the court to assess the player's medical condition and to help the player off the court. During the stoppage, both teams may make substitutions or team changes, provided these are completed within the time allowed for the stoppage.

If no substitution is made for the injured or ill player, or for a player who is bleeding, play may resume with the position left vacant. If the player is the center and no substitution is made, another player must move to the center position to allow the match to continue. If a position is left vacant, the player concerned or a substitute may take the court immediately after one of the following: a goal is scored; a stoppage occurs for injury, illness, or blood; or an interval between periods occurs.

There is no limit to the number of substitutions that may be made, provided the players used are in the starting 12 listed at the beginning of the game.

Scoring

A goal is scored when the ball is thrown over and completely through the goal ring by either the goal shooter or the goal attack. The 10-foot goal post has a goal ring with a 15-inch diameter, which is projected horizontally 6 inches from the post. The post is centered on the goal line. Should any player other than the goal shooter or goal attack throw the ball through the goal ring, no goal is scored, and play continues.

Infringements and Sanctions

Netball infringements are classified into two main groups: minor infringements and major infringements. The minor infringements include not releasing the ball within 3 seconds of receipt, throwing the ball over more than a third of the court, using incorrect footwork, moving offside into an area that is not part of a player's designated playing area, moving out of court, and breaking at a center pass. The sanction for minor infringements is a free pass taken by any member of the nonoffending team who is allowed in the area where the infringement occurred.

The major infringements include obstruction and contact and are penalized with a penalty pass. A goal shooter or goal attack who takes a penalty pass in the goal circle may either pass or shoot for goal. For this penalty, the offending player must stand out of play until the ball has been released. This penalty is taken from where the infringer was standing; the ball must be released within 3 seconds, and the footwork rule must be obeyed. The umpire may conduct a toss-up if there is a simultaneous infringement or action by any two opposing players.

One of the major infringements, obstruction, has three elements: distance, arms, and interference. Players must be 3 feet from the player with the ball if they wish to use their arms to defend. If they do not use their arms, they may be within that 3-foot distance. It is possible for both attacking and defending players to infringe this rule. If there is the legal distance between an attacking and a defending player and the attacking player lessens the distance, there is no obstruction infringement. Players may use outstretched arms to catch a thrown ball, to try to catch a feint pass, or to rebound a shot at goal.

There are also rules regarding contact. When attacking, defending, or playing the ball, opposing players may come into physical contact with each other. Provided that they do not interfere with each other's play or use their bodies to gain an unfair advantage over their opponents, it is deemed to be "contest," and play continues. "Contact" occurs when a player's actions interfere with an opponent's play, whether these are accidental or deliberate.

Leaning on an opponent, pushing, tripping, or any similar type of physical contact is illegal.

Players and officials are expected to uphold the rules and the spirit of the game at all times. Should players infringe in this area, they may be penalized with an appropriate sanction, which may include an on-court sanction, a caution, a warning, a suspension, or an ordering off, depending on the severity of the infringement.

OFFICIALS

Match officials are the two umpires and the reserve. Technical officials are the scorers and timekeepers. Team officials include the coach, manager, captain, and up to three other personnel, at least one of whom must be a primary care person who is qualified to diagnose and treat injury and illness (e.g., a doctor or physiotherapist).

MODIFICATIONS

Sometimes teams play netball using a basketball hoop. In this case, if the ball contacts the backboard, the ball is out of play. Goals that are scored off the backboard do not count.

A variation of this rule allows a goal to be scored from a backboard rebound if a player catches it and throws it in without the ball touching the ground.

ORGANIZATIONS

International Federation of Netball Associations
INF Secretariat, Albion Wharf
19 Albion St.
Manchester M1 5LN
England
440-161-234-6515
www.netball.org

USA Netball Association
Bowling Green Station
P.O. Box 1105
New York, NY 10274
561-738-3174
www.usanetball.org

Pickleball

YinYang/E+/Getty Images

Right after the sport of pickleball was invented in the summer of 1965 in Bainbridge Island, Washington, as a sort of "mini-tennis," it gained significant popularity because of the many competitions that were organized in the United States at local, state, and national levels. The game revolves around hitting a plastic ball (very similar to a whiffle ball) back and forth over a net with a paddle, and it can be played with two or four players. It took nearly a decade for other countries to gain interest in the sport, a landmark that was characterized mainly by the national associations that were formed around the world. The USA Pickleball Association reports an estimated 3.1 million pickleball players in the United States. The activity skews heavily to an older demographic. Sixty-six percent of participants are over age 60; however, according to the association, player participation is now trending younger.

OVERVIEW

Objective: The objective is to score more points than your opponent. Typically, a game is won when one player or team accumulates 11 points, leading by 2 points. As a sport, the objective of pickleball is to introduce people to other racquet sports with greater ease. Because of its accessibility, it's a popular way for people of all abilities to engage in a racquet sport.

Scoring: A person or team can only score a point when they are serving the ball. A point is scored when the ball bounces twice after it is hit over the net to the opponents' side, when the opponents hit the ball against their side of the net, or when the opponents hit the ball outside the court lines. The first side to score 11 points while leading by a margin of at least 2 points wins the game. If one player or team reaches a score of 11 points but is not 2 points ahead, then the game continues until one of the teams achieves a 2-point lead. In tournament play, games may be played to 15 or 21, still with the requirement of winning by at least 2 points.

Number of Players: Pickleball can be played in singles and doubles matches.

COURT

For both singles and doubles matches, the court has a width of 20 feet (6.10 meters) and a length of 44 feet (13.41 meters). The net is placed in the middle of the long side, dividing the court into two sides. A rectangular non-volley zone (7 feet from the net) is marked by one line on each side of the net; players are prohibited from entering this 7-foot-wide (2.13 meters) zone when contacting the ball on a volley.

The net dividing the court into two separate sides is made of any open, meshed material. It must be at least 21.75 feet (6.63 meters) long, extending from one post to the other (see figure 38.1). The net height should be at least 30 inches (0.76 meters) from top to bottom. The net is suspended over the center of the court. Specifically it must reach a height of 36 inches (91.44 cm) high at the posts on the sidelines and 34 inches (86.36 cm) high at the center of the court. The net's mesh must be small enough to prevent a ball from passing through it.

EQUIPMENT

Equipment consists mainly of the ball and the paddles that the players are using. Balls used must be 2.87 inches (7.30 cm) to 2.97 inches (7.55 cm) in diameter, uniform in color, and made from a durable material that is free of texturing (i.e., they have a smooth surface). The ball may have a slight ridge at the seam, as long as it does not significantly impact the ball's flight characteristics.

The paddles are made from relatively rigid, noncompressible materials, such as graphite or carbon fiber, and they may not have rough textures, holes, indentations, tape, or any material that can be used to impart additional spin on the ball. The combined length and width of the paddles used can be up to 24 inches (60.96 cm), and the length cannot exceed 17 inches (43.18 cm).

TOURNAMENT FORMATS

In official pickleball tournaments, there are four formats that may be used to regulate the tournament flow. Specifics for each one follow.

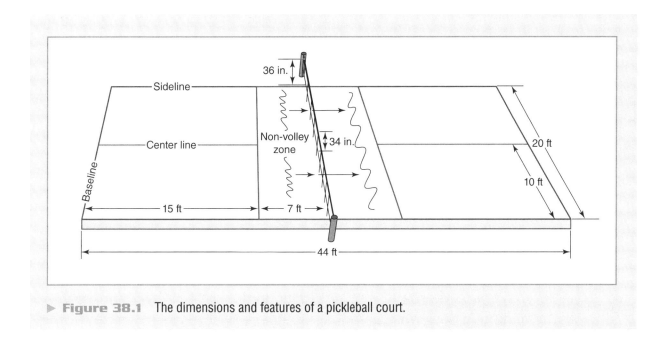

▶ **Figure 38.1** The dimensions and features of a pickleball court.

Single Elimination With Consolation

This method means that the tournament is divided into brackets representing the stages of progression. Losers from all rounds go into a consolation bracket playing for the bronze medal/third place and are eliminated after a second loss. The final two players or teams in the winners bracket play for the gold/first place and sliver/second place.

Double Elimination

This format is the most popular choice of the USA Pickleball Association. A loss places the loser into a lower bracket. The winner of the lower bracket plays the winner of the top bracket for the championship. A tie-breaker match must be played when the winner of the lower bracket wins.

Round Robin

All players or teams play each other, and all matches have the same set of conditions or rules. After all matches have been played, the player or team that won the most matches is declared the winner. When there is a tie, the first tie-breaker is head to head; and the second tie-breaker is point differential of all games played.

Pool Play

This format is a combination of two formats mentioned earlier. The participants are divided into two or more pools, and each pool plays a round-robin to determine the qualifiers that get into a single-elimination or double-elimination playoff.

RULES

Pickleball resembles other popular racquet sports, with similar objectives and scoring methods. There are, however, many unique components to the game, and these are described in the following sections to provide an overview of how pickleball should be played.

Serving

A game of pickleball begins with a coin toss or any other fair method to decide which side may serve first.

When serving, the ball is always served underhand and diagonally to the other court. The ball must clear the net and land within the opposition's playing area during a serve. When returning the serve, the receiver must let the ball bounce before returning. The serving team must then let the ball bounce once on its first return. After both sides have returned with one bounce, they may hit either off one bounce or with no bounces. When playing doubles, only the correct receiver can return the ball. As long as the server holds serve, after each point the server will alternate serving from the right and left sides of the court. Both players on a team will serve before a side out is declared, except at the start of each game, when only the starting first server will serve.

In singles, the server serves from the right or even court when the score is even and from the left or odd court when the score is odd.

Doubles is the most common format for pickleball. The service sequence for doubles varies considerably from tennis rules. The sequence is as follows:

- Both players on the serving doubles team have the opportunity to serve and score points until they commit a fault, except for the first service sequence of each new game, when only one partner on the serving team has the opportunity to serve before faulting.

- The first serve of each sideout is made from the right or even court.

- If a point is scored, the server switches sides, and the server initiates the next serve from the left or odd court.

- As subsequent points are scored, the server continues switching back and forth until a fault is committed and the first server loses the serve.

- When the first server loses the serve, the partner then serves from his correct side of the court (except for the first service sequence of the game).

- The second server continues serving until his team commits a fault and loses the serve to the opposing team.

- Once the service goes to the opposition (at sideout), the first serve is from the right or even court, and both players on that team have the opportunity to serve and score points until their team commits two faults.

Non-Volley Zone

The non-volley zone is the court area within 7 feet of the net on both sides where volleying is prohibited. This rule prevents players from executing smashes. It is a fault if, when volleying a ball, the player steps on the non-volley zone or the line or the player's momentum carries her into the non-volley zone. It is a fault even if the volleyed ball is declared dead before this happens.

A serve that contacts the non-volley zone line is short and a fault.

Faults

A fault is any action that stops play because of a rule violation. When the receiving team faults, it results in a point for the serving team. When the serving team faults, it results in the server's loss of serve (i.e., a sideout).

TERMS

A **carry** occurs when hitting the ball in such a way that it does not bounce away from the paddle but tends to be carried along on the face of the paddle during its forward motion.

Cross-court is the area of the court diagonally opposite from the court area you're currently standing in.

A **dink** shot is a soft shot that arcs just over the net and lands in the non-volley zone.

A **double hit** occurs when one player or team hits the ball twice before it is returned.

A **drop shot** is a groundstroke shot that falls short of the opponent's position on the opponent's side of the court.

A **fault** is a loss of rally, resulting in a point for the opposing team, a loss of serve (from first serve to second serve), or a side out.

A **groundstroke** is hitting the ball after it bounces once.

A **hinder** is any occurrence that affects play.

Let is called on a serve or rally that must be replayed for any reason

A **rally** is continuous play after the serve and before a fault.

The **two-bounce rule** eliminates the serve and volley advantage and extends rallies. When the ball is served, the receiving team must let it bounce before returning it, and then the serving team must let it bounce before returning, thus two bounces.

After the ball has bounced once in each team's court, both teams may either volley the ball (hit the ball before it bounces) or play it off a bounce (groundstroke).

A **volley** is when the ball is hit, during a rally, before it bounces on the court.

OFFICIALS

The tournament director is the manager of the tournament. She is responsible for designating the officials and delegating their responsibilities. If a player or a team misbehaves, she can expel them from the tournament. The officials check on the preparation of the court before a match and regulate the matches. In the final tournament matches, also called medal matches, it is recommended that the tournament director assign line judges as well. These officials have the responsibility to call all line faults within their area of jurisdiction.

MODIFICATIONS

Special rules apply for matches with players who use a wheelchair. In this case, the wheelchair is considered part of the player's body. A major rule change is that the ball is now allowed to bounce twice on his side of the net. The second bounce can be anywhere inside or outside of the court boundaries. When a wheelchair player is playing with or against a standing person in singles or doubles, the rules for wheelchair players apply to wheelchair players and the regular rules apply for all standing players.

ORGANIZATIONS

USAPA (USA Pickleball Association)
P.O. Box 7354
Surprise, AZ 85374

International Federation of Pickleball (IFP)
16772 West Bell Rd., Ste. 110-488
Surprise, AZ 85374
http://ifpickleball.org

Racquetball

Racquetball is a fast-paced game played with a hollow rubber ball and strung racquets. It was created in 1949 by combining the rules of squash and handball. By 1970 about 50,000 people were playing regularly in the United States. That figure has grown today to about four million Americans and about 14 million people worldwide.

OVERVIEW

Objective: To win rallies and (if serving) score points by striking the ball so that the opponent cannot keep the ball in play.

Number of Players: Two, three, or four.

Scoring: Points are scored only by the serving player or team; a rally is won when one player or team cannot return the ball to the front wall before it hits the floor twice, when a player or team returns a ball that hits the floor before it hits the front wall, or when a penalty hinder is called.

Length of Match: The best two of three games.

Length of Game: The first two games are played to 15 points; if a third game is necessary, it is played to 11 points. The first player or team to reach the requisite score wins.

The winner of a coin toss chooses to serve or receive to begin the first game. The player or team that begins the first game as server begins the second game as the receiver. To begin a third game, the player or team that scored the most points during the first two games gets the choice to serve or receive. If the point totals are equal, another coin toss is required.

In singles, the server continues to serve if she wins the rally. She earns 1 point for each rally won. When she loses a rally, her opponent gains the serve.

In doubles, to begin a game, player 1 of team A serves until his team loses a rally. Team B then gains the serve. From then on, when the first server of a team loses the serve, it is called a hand-out, and the serve goes to the second player on the team. When the second server loses the serve, it is a sideout, and the opponents gain the serve.

COURT

The court is 20 feet wide by 40 feet long (see figure 39.1). The court is 20 feet high, with a back wall at least 12 feet high. The short line is midway between the front and back walls. The service line is 5 feet in front of the short line. The service zone is the space between these two lines.

Service boxes are on either end of the service zone; they are 18 inches wide. Drive serve lines are marked by lines parallel to the side walls; these lines denote the drive serve zone, which is 36 inches wide. The receiving line is 5 feet behind the short line. The safety zone is that space between the receiving line and the short line.

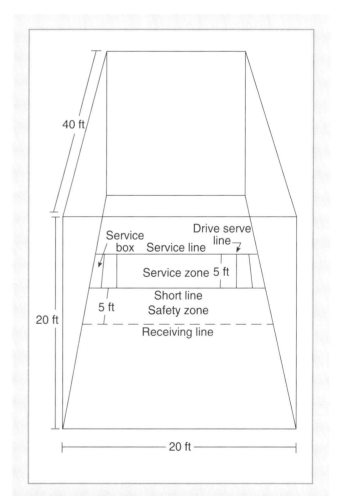

▶ **Figure 39.1** The dimensions and features of a racquetball court.

PLAYERS

Players may play in singles matches (two players) or doubles (four players). A nontournament game consisting of three players—called cutthroat—may also be played. In this version, the server often plays against the other two players; the serve rotates among the three players. There are many variations of this three-player game.

EQUIPMENT

The ball is 2.25 inches in diameter and weighs about 1.4 ounces. The racquet may not exceed 22 inches in length; it must have an attached wrist cord. The racquet may be made of any material deemed to be safe. It is strung with gut, nylon, or a combination of materials.

Players are required to wear protective eyewear designed for racquetball; it must meet or exceed ASTM F803 standards. Shoes must have soles that do not mark or damage the floor.

RULES

The rules of play fall into these categories: serving, return of serve, rallies, hinders, and timeouts.

Serving

The server has 10 seconds to serve once the score or "second serve" has been called. It is the server's responsibility to make sure the receiver is ready before she serves. A receiver may signal she is not ready by raising her racquet above her head or by turning her back to the server. These are the only two acceptable signals.

The server serves from any place within the service zone except for certain drive zones. Neither the ball nor any part of either foot may be beyond the service zone lines when the server begins his motion. The server may step beyond the front service line if no portion of either foot is placed fully beyond the service line until the served ball passes the short line.

Once the server begins the motion, they must bounce the ball once and hit it with their racquet. The ball must strike the front wall first and then strike the floor on its first bounce beyond the back

edge of the short line. A serve can hit one of the side walls before hitting the floor.

A player may hit a drive serve between himself and the side wall nearest to them only if he remains outside of the 3-foot drive service zone until the served ball crosses the short line.

In doubles, players may change their order of serve each time their team gains the serve.

The nonserving partner in doubles must stand with her back to the side wall and with both feet within the service box until the ball passes the short line. A violation results in a foot fault unless the partner enters the safety zone (the area between the short line and the receiving line); in this case, the server loses the serve.

A dead-ball serve results in no penalty; the server is given another serve. Dead-ball serves include court hinders (e.g., the served ball bounces irregularly because it hit a wet spot or irregular surface) when a ball breaks on the serve.

Two consecutive fault serves result in a handout or a sideout. Types of fault serves include foot faults (by either the server or the partner), short serves (those that hit the floor on or in front of the short line), three-wall serves (those that hit the front wall and both side walls before striking the floor), ceiling serves (those that hit the front wall and then the ceiling, with or without touching a side wall), and long serves (those that hit the back wall before hitting the floor or go directly out of the court).

Out serves, which result in an immediate handout or a sideout, may be called for a number of occasions, including when the server executes two consecutive fault serves; when the server totally misses an attempted serve; when a served ball rebounds and touches the server or the server's racquet; and when a served ball is stopped or caught by the server or the server's partner. Other instances in which an out serve is called include when the served ball strikes any surface other than the front wall first; when a player hits a "crotch serve"—one that hits the juncture of the front wall and any vertical surface, front wall and side wall, or front wall and ceiling; and when a player serves out of order (any points scored by the player serving out of order are subtracted).

Return of Serve

The receiver may not enter the safety zone until the ball bounces or crosses the receiving line. The receiver may try to return the ball before it strikes the floor, but the ball must pass the plane of the receiving line first. So, the receiver's racquet or body on such a return may break the plane of the receiving line on the follow-through.

A receiver may not intentionally catch or touch an apparently long serve until the referee has made the call or the ball bounces twice. Violation results in a point for the server. A receiver must return a serve before it strikes the floor twice. The return must hit the front wall before it touches the floor. However, it may hit any combination of walls and ceiling beforehand.

Rallies

During a rally—all the play that follows the return of serve—a player may hit the ball only with the head of the racquet, which may be held in one or both hands. Removing the wrist thong during play to switch the racquet from one hand to the other, results in a loss of the rally. Other losses of rally result when a player

- touches the ball more than once on a return;
- intentionally carries the ball (slings or throws it rather than hitting it);
- fails to return the ball before it bounces twice or rolls out;
- fails to hit the front wall on the return, before the return strikes the floor;
- hits himself or his partner with the ball;
- commits a penalty hinder (see "Hinders"); or
- hits the ball out of the court unless the ball has first hit the floor.

The ball remains in play until it touches the floor a second time, no matter how many walls the ball hits, including the front wall. A player may swing more than once at a ball and miss in a return attempt as long as they hit it before it bounces on the floor twice.

In doubles, both partners may try to return the ball; no alternating is necessary. However, only one player may strike the ball on a return. If a return strikes the front wall, bounces on the floor, and goes into the gallery or through any other court opening, the ball is dead, and the server receives two serves. Whenever a rally is replayed, the server begins with two serves.

If a ball breaks during a rally, the rally is replayed. If a foreign object enters the court during a rally, play is stopped and the rally is replayed.

Hinders

A replay hinder results in a simple replay of the rally with no penalty; the server receives two serves. The receiver must make a reasonable effort and have a reasonable chance to make a return before a referee will call a hinder. Some examples of replay hinders include when the ball hits a doorknob or bounces irregularly off a rough surface, when the ball hits an opponent (unless it's obvious the ball would not have reached the front wall), when incidental body contact occurs (if the contact prevents a player from being able to make a reasonable return), and when an offensive player is screened from the ball passing close to a defensive player.

A penalty hinder results in loss of the rally. A penalty hinder does not necessarily mean the act was intentional. Examples of penalty hinders include when a player does not move enough to allow her opponent a shot straight at the front wall as well as a cross-court shot; when a player's movement, or lack of movement, impedes her opponent's swing; when a player's position blocks her opponent from reaching or returning a ball; and when a player moves into the path of, and is struck by, a ball just hit by an opponent.

Timeouts

Each player or team may take up to three 30-second timeouts in games to 15 and two 30-second timeouts in games to 11. If a timeout is called after the serve has begun, or when the player or team has none left, a technical foul (loss of point) is called for delay of game. A player is awarded up to 15 cumulative minutes of injury timeout.

The referee may award a player or team a timeout of up to 2 minutes, if all regular timeouts have been used, to change or adjust equipment. A 2-minute break is allowed between the first two games; a 5-minute break is allowed between games two and three. Professional and international rules allow players or teams to call equipment timeouts without being charged.

TERMS

A **crotch serve** is one that hits the juncture of the front wall and vertical surface at the same time. This serve results in an out.

A **dead-ball serve**—such as from a court hinder or a broken ball—is replayed, but no previous fault serve is canceled.

The **drive serve lines** are 3 feet from and parallel to each side wall within the service zone. Along with the side walls, they define a 17-foot drive serve zone (see figure 39.1).

Fault serves result from a variety of violations: foot faults, short serves, three-wall serves, ceiling serves, long serves, screen serves, and so on. Two consecutive fault serves result in an out.

A **game** is normally played to 15 points.

A **match** is the best two of three games. Tiebreaker games are played to 11 points

Out serves result from various defective serves, including two consecutive fault serves, missed serve attempts, fakes, and touched serves. The player loses her serve on an out serve.

A **penalty hinder**—such as blocking an opponent or impeding an opponent's return—results in the loss of the rally.

A **rally** is all the play after a successful the return of serve to the front wall.

The **receiving line** is a broken line parallel to, and 5 feet behind, the short line.

A **replay hinder**—such as when a ball that would have otherwise reached the front wall on the fly hits an opponent or when body contact hinders a return—results in a replay, with no penalty. The server receives two serves after such a hinder. This also includes *court hinder* such as when the ball hits the lights and bounces poorly or hits the door latch.

The **safety zone** is the 5-foot area between the receiving line and the short line. The receiver may not enter this zone (i.e., break the plane of the receiving line) until the served ball has either bounced on the floor inside the zone or else crossed over the receiving line.

Service boxes are at the end of each service zone; they are marked by lines parallel with the side walls. The boxes are 18 inches wide.

The **service line** is parallel to, and 5 feet in front of, the short line. The space between and including the service line and the short line is known as the Service Zone.

The **service zone** is the 5-foot area between the short line and the service line.

The **short line** is midway between, and parallel to, the front and back walls.

A **sideout** occurs when a player or side loses the serve to the opponent.

A **technical foul** may be called for a variety of unsporting actions, including profanity, excessive arguing, and slamming the racquet on a wall or floor. A technical foul results in a point being taken away from the offender.

A **technical warning** is given for any lesser unsporting actions that the referee does not think warrants the deduction of a point.

A **tiebreaker** game, to 11 points, is played if the opponents split the first two games of a match.

OFFICIALS

A referee is in charge of the match; two line judges and a scorekeeper may assist the referee. The referee makes all decisions regarding rules, but may receive assistance on appealed plays from line judges.

MODIFICATIONS

This section highlights major rule modifications affecting play for various groups and divisions.

Multi-Bounce

The multi-bounce game is for young (usually 8 years old and under) players with limited experience. The ball remains in play until it stops bouncing and begins to roll, with the following stipulations: A player may swing at it only once and must hit it before it crosses the short line on the way back to the front wall. If the ball travels from the front wall to the back wall on the fly, it may be hit from anywhere on the court, including beyond the short line.

Tape is used to mark two parallel lines on the front wall: one 3 feet above the floor and the other 1 foot above the floor (measuring from the bottom of the lines). A ball that hits between the 1- and 3-foot lines must be returned before it bounces three times. A ball that hits below the 1-foot line must be returned before it bounces twice. A ball that hits on or above the 3-foot line can be returned on any bounce. All games are played to 11 points.

One-Wall

The front wall is usually 20 feet wide and 20 feet high. The floor is 20 feet wide and 40 feet to the back edge of the long line. The court should extend 3 to 6 feet beyond the long line and the sidelines for the safety of the players.

The back edge of the short line is 20 feet from the front wall. The service zone is the entire area between and including the short line, sidelines, and service line. The receiving zone is the entire area behind the short line, including the sidelines and the long line.

Three-Wall

Three-wall can be played with either a short side wall or a long side wall. With a short side wall, the front wall is 20 feet wide and 20 feet high; side walls are 20 feet long and 20 feet high, tapering to 12 feet high at the back end of the court. The rest of the court dimensions are the same size as for a four-wall court.

With a long side wall, the court is 40 feet long. The walls may taper from 20 feet high to 12 feet high by the back end of the court. All other markings and dimensions are the same as for a four-wall court. A serve that goes beyond the side walls on the fly is an out. A serve that goes long, but is within the side walls, is a fault.

Wheelchair

The standard rules generally apply, with the following exceptions:

- Body contact includes wheelchair contact. Such contact may be either a replay or penalty hinder.
- The ball is not dead until the third bounce.
- If a player intentionally leaves his chair, he automatically loses the rally.

- Maintenance delays for chair repair may not take more than 5 minutes. A player may have two maintenance delays per match.
- In multi-bounce play, the ball may bounce any number of times, but the player may swing at it only once. The ball must be struck before it crosses the short line on its way back to the front wall. The receiver cannot cross the short line once the ball hits the back wall.

Other Rule Modifications

In addition to the preceding modifications, there are also modifications that apply to both men and women professionals as well as visually and hearing-impaired players.

Online Rulebook

To view the complete rulebook for standard four-wall racquetball and its many variations, please go to www.teamusa.org/USA-Racquetball/rules.

ORGANIZATIONS

International Racquetball Tour
201 W. Main St.
Washington, MO 63090
www.irt-tour.com

USA Racquetball
2812 W. Colorado Ave., Ste. 200
Colorado Springs, CO 80904-2921
719-635-5396
www.teamusa.org/USA-Racquetball

Racquetball Canada
145 Pacific Ave.
Winnipeg, MB R3B 2Z6
www.racquetball.ca

Rowing

Comstock

The oldest known reference to a regatta was found in a document dating from 1274 in Venice, Italy. Racing was common in Venice in the 1300s, and it began in London in the 1700s. The first race in the United States took place in New York in 1756; in 1852, Harvard defeated Yale in an eights race in the first intercollegiate contest of any sport in America.

Rowing became an Olympic sport in 1896 although Olympic rowing races were first contested in 1900, and recreational rowing came into its own in the United States with the more-durable and seaworthy shells of the 1970s. Rowing is most popular in the collegiate Northeast and Pacific Northwest, but it is gaining in popularity throughout the United States, especially in the East and Midwest, and it is gaining force as a high school sport as well.

OVERVIEW

Objective: To finish with the fastest time.

Number of Lanes: From two to eight.

Number of Rowers: Depends on the race.

Length of Course: 2,000 meters for sprint races; 1,000 meters for masters courses; head races vary in distance.

Rowing races (other than head races) are ideally held on courses that have no bends or turns. Head races are longer races (generally 2 to 4 miles) held primarily on rivers; the courses include the bends in the river. A rowing crew consists of one, two, four, or eight rowers. Some crews also have a coxswain who steers the boat and provides feedback for the rowers but does not actively row. Rowers sit with their backs to the forward movement of the boat.

Competitions, known as regattas, include sculling events (single, double, quadruple), in which each rower uses two oars, and sweep rowing races (pair, four, and eight), in which each rower uses one oar. A head race is contested by crews who start a few seconds apart and race the clock. Events may be categorized by type of boat, gender, age, weight, or skill level.

COURSE

A standard race course is 2,000 meters long (except for masters courses, which are 1,000 meters long) and is wide enough to hold two to eight lanes. If a buoy system is used—which is called "Albano system"—each lane is 12.5 to 15 meters wide; without a buoy system, each lane is 15 to 20 meters wide; a lane width of 15 meters is recommended.

According to the rules of the International Rowing Federation (FISA), a Class A course must have a minimum straight length of 2,120 meters and no or only slight stream; at least six lanes—if the course is built after 2001, it must have eight lanes—and a water depth of at least 2 meters throughout all racing lanes if the depth of the course is equal at all points, or 3 meters at the shallowest point if the depth over the course is unequal. It also must have

- at least a width of 105 meters (i.e., 15 meters + (6 lanes x 12.5 meters each) + 15 meters = 105 meters) with no obstacles at the side of the course that could influence the wind in the different lanes;

- a buoy system for lanes, with buoys marking the lanes every 10.0 to 12.5 meters (the first 100 meters and the last 250 meters use different-colored buoys, and the first 100 meters buoys must be marking the lanes every 5 meters);

- a starting pontoon covering all lanes and a start tower with a number of technical installations that provide fair starting conditions for all competitors;

- distance markers every 250 meters on both sides of the course; and

- finish installations including a finish tower that allows accurate measurement of the times to the 1/100 second when the boats cross the finish line.

The international rowing federation FISA defines all courses who do not meet A course standards as B courses. US Rowing however defines also B and C courses: A Class B course is the same as a Class A course, with the following exceptions. Water current may not exceed 6 meters per minute; there must be a minimum of four lanes; water depth must be sufficient to ensure safe racing; and obstacles nearer than 5 meters from the perimeter must be marked. Other distinctions of a Class B course include the following:

- Fixed obstructions must not interfere with, or create a hazard for, a crew.

■ A buoy system is not required, but overhead lane markers every 250 meters define the lane boundaries.

■ A single marker may be used for steering markers.

■ Distance markers are placed every 500 meters; these may consist of painted stripes on the shore.

A Class C course does not meet the standards for a Class A or B course but does meet the requirements for length, width, and uniform conditions for all crews.

CREWS

Each member of a crew wears identical clothing, although headgear is optional for each competitor. Junior competition is for those ages 18 and younger; a junior B competition may be held for those ages 16 and younger. Most masters competition is for those ages 27 and older, broken into age groups, although some regattas offer race opportunities for masters of ages 24 and older. Age for masters competition is determined by averaging the ages of the crew members, excluding the coxswain. Each rower must be of master`s age but need not fall into the specific age category.

Male coxswains may compete in female events and vice versa. In the United States, a coxswain for a men's crew must weigh at least 120 pounds; for a women's crew, a coxswain must weigh at least 110 pounds. Coxswains who do not meet the weight requirement may carry dead weight, placed as close to their torso as possible, to meet the requirement.

Competitions may also be categorized by skill (intermediate, senior, and elite). In addition, lightweight crews may compete against similar crews, with each rower not weighing more than 160 pounds in men's crews. For women, each rower cannot weigh more than 130 pounds.

EQUIPMENT

All load-bearing parts of a boat must be firmly fixed to the boat, although the rowers' seats may move along the boat's axis. Sliding riggers, where the oar's support is not fixed in one place, are forbidden in normal competition. For boat categories, see table 40.1.

Each boat must have a supple or plastic ball, 4 centimeters in diameter, of a white or fluorescent color, on its bow to protect against injury and to provide visibility. A sweep oar must be at least 5 millimeters thick, measured 3 millimeters from

TABLE 40.1

Boat Categories

Number	Boat name/oar	Coxswain	Abbreviation	Minimum weight (lb)	Minimum weight (kg)
1	Single/scull	No	1x	30.86	14
2	Double/scull	No	2x	59.53	27
2	Pair-without/sweep	No	2–	59.53	27
2	Pair-with/sweep	Yes	2+	70.55	32
4	Four-without/sweep	No	4–	110.23	50
4	Four-with/sweep	Yes	4+	112.44	51
4	Quad/scull	No	4x	114.64	52
4	Quad-with/scull	Yes	4x+	116.85	53
8	Eight/sweep	Yes	8+	211.64	96
8	Octuple/scull	Yes	8x	213.85	97

Adapted by permission from The United States Rowing Association, *Rules of Rowing*, 2018. Available: http://www.usrowing.org/wp-content/uploads/2018/02/Rules_Of_Rowing_2018_FINAL_v2.pdf.

the blade's tip; a scull oar must be at least 3 millimeters thick, measured 2 millimeters from the tip. Each boat must have footgear that allows for quick release with no delay in case the boat capsizes.

In a race, each boat has a numbered card attached to its bow. The number indicates its race lane. If equipment breaks before a crew passes the 100-meter starting area, the crew may signal the referee, who will stop the race. The referee will restart the race after the crew has had time to repair equipment.

RULES

Racing rules can be categorized by those concerning the start, the race in progress, and the finish.

Start

Crews are required to be at their starting stations 2 minutes before the start. The aligning judge makes sure that each boat is aligned with the starting line's plane. When the judge at start is satisfied with the alignment, he or she shall so indicate by any of the following methods: (1) raising and keeping aloft a white flag, (2) raising and keeping aloft a fluorescent green flag, (3) causing a white light to be illuminated.

Once aligned, crews are polled individually by the starter to make sure they are ready. After the crews are polled, ready, and aligned, the starter raises a red flag overhead and gives the command to begin—a verbal "Attention!" and then "Go!" accompanied by a down-sweep of the flag. If a starting light system is in place the starter presses after calling, "Attention!" a button (or switch) that turns the traffic lights red, and then after a distinct and variable pause, the starter will give the starting command by pressing a button that changes the red light to green and make an audible signal through the loudspeakers at the same moment.

Depending on weather or when conditions prevent from normal starting procedure, a starter also may use a quick start, dispensing with the polling procedures. When the starter determines that the race may be safely and fairly started, the Starter shall call out, "Quick Start!" followed by the starting procedure with flag or lights; the starter will not recognize a crew signaling that it is not ready.

Once a crew rows out of the starting area, which is 100 meters long, the crew may not protest the start as unfair. If a crew's bow crosses the starting line before the signal to begin is given, it is assessed a false start. More than one crew may be assessed false starts on one start. The race is recalled, the offending crews are warned, and the race is restarted. If a crew commits two false starts in one race, it is excluded from the race.

Race in Progress

Crews that row out of their assigned lanes do so at their own risk. If they are out of their own lane and interfere with a crew in its proper lane, the referee will tell the offending crew to alter its course. A crew that does not alter its course may be asked to stop. If a crew interferes with another crew while out of its lane (clashing oars, washing the opposing crew, or forcing the other crew to alter its course to avoid collision), the interfering crew may be excluded. If the interference was slight and did not alter the race results, the referee may issue a lesser penalty.

A crew must maintain its racing cadence as indicated by strokes per minute. It may be penalized for not maintaining the cadence if so instructed by the referee. A crew may not receive outside assistance or coaching during a race. Such assistance may result in exclusion. The referee can stop the race, if, due to interference or unfair condition, it is likely that a crew in contention has been deprived of its opportunity of winning, placing, or advancing and if further continuance of the race would be of no further competitive value.

If the referee believes a crew has not had a fair chance to win, place, or advance, either because of interference or unfair course conditions, the referee may elect to advance the crew or to rerow the race with some or all of the participants.

Officials may impose the following penalties on a crew:

- Reprimand: This is an informal caution and has no immediate effect on the crew.
- Warning: A crew that has been given two warnings in the same race is excluded. A false start counts as a warning.
- Exclusion: Officials may rule that a crew is excluded from the event but may compete in other events.

▪ Disqualification: A crew that is disqualified is removed from the event and from all remaining events in the same regatta. This occurs when a crew flagrantly or intentionally breaks the rules.

▪ Relegation: The penalty of relegation shall consist of placing a crew in last place in a race and is reserved for violations of equipment specifications (e.g., minimum weight of boats).

Finish

A crew finishes a race when the boat's bow or any part of its hull touches the plane of the finish line. If the judges are unable to determine the order of finish with reasonable certainty, it shall be considered a dead heat if two or more crews finish the race simultaneously. Depending on the circumstances (heat or final, weather, etc.) the crews in the dead heat may be ordered to rest and then rerow to determine places or a tie is awarded without a rerow. If a tie occurs in a race that advances crews to the next level of racing, the referee allows all the crews that tied to advance, if possible; if not, they must rerow after a rest.

TERMS

A **coxswain** is a competitor who does not row or physically participate in propelling the boat forward except to steer.

A **crew** consists of all competitors in the boat, including the coxswain.

A **head race** pits crews who race on a course at different times against one another. Their finish times determine their placement.

A **regatta** is a combination of different rowing events that are considered a single race.

A **scull** refers to the shell in which rowers use two oars. It also refers to the events in which each rower uses two oars.

The **starting area** is the first 100 meters of the course.

Sweep refers to a shell or an event in which each rower uses a single oar.

A crew **washes** another crew when the water turbulence from the oars and the wake of the leading shell affect the progress of the trailing crew.

OFFICIALS

Officials who oversee rowing competitions include a chief referee, a referee, a starter, a judge at start, a chief judge, and other judges. A jury made up of the chief referee and four other officials hears and decides any protests.

Each race is followed by at least one referee (the primary judge), who may be aided by additional referees. These additional referees may withdraw if the primary judge is satisfied with how the race is proceeding. The primary judge must remain with the race, however, to oversee the fair and safe competition, to keep the total elapsed time and to declare the race to be official..

ORGANIZATIONS

International Rowing Federation
Maison du Sport International
Av. de Rhodanie 54
CH-1007 Lausanne
Switzerland
+41 21 6178373
info@fisa.org
www.worldrowing.com

Rowing Canada Aviron
321-4371 Interurban Rd.
Victoria, BC V9E 2C5
877-722-4769
rca@rowingcanada.org
www.rowingcanada.org

U.S. Rowing
2 Wall St.
Princeton, NJ 08540
800-314-4ROW (4769)
members@usrowing.org
www.usrowing.org

Rugby Union

karaboux/fotolia.com

Rugby union began in 1823 when a young man named William Webb Ellis of Rugby School in England broke the rules of foot-the-ball (soccer) by picking up the ball and running with it. About half the players on both sides stopped playing because this clearly was in violation of the rules. But the other half took no heed, and as Ellis recklessly made his way down the field toward his opponents' goal, many defenders became among the first to try to tackle a ball carrier, and many teammates became among the first to move alongside the ball carrier, hoping to catch a pass.

Cambridge University immediately adopted the new sport, making local rules, but Rugby School itself did not officially consent to play the game until 1841—18 years after Ellis picked up the ball and ran with it. By 1871, however, laws for rugby union were in place, and the game was quickly spreading. Today it is a worldwide sport, popular in England, Wales, Scotland, France, and other European countries as well as Australia, New Zealand, and South Africa. In 2016, rugby was played by 3.2 million registered players and 5.3 million nonregistered players across more than 100 countries. The Rugby World Cup, held every 4 years, attracted a television audience of more than four billion in 2015. With the addition of Rugby Sevens to the Olympics in 2016, the sport continues to be in growth mode, especially among women and children. Almost two million children were introduced to the sport via World Rugby's Get Into Rugby program in 2016.

OVERVIEW

Objective: To score the most points.

Number of Players: 15 players per side; 7 for Rugby Sevens.

Scoring: 5 points for a try; 2 points for a conversion kick scored after a try; 3 points for a goal scored from a penalty kick; 3 points for a dropped goal. (This is scored using a drop kick and cannot be scored using a punk kick.)

Length of Game: 80 minutes—two 40-minute halves with a 10-minute halftime. For Tens, 10 minute halves and a 2-minute halftime. For Sevens, 14 minutes—two 7-minute halves with a 2-minute halftime.

The team that kicks off makes a dropkick from the center of the halfway line, while the receiving team stands on or behind its 10-meter line. If the ball doesn't reach the 10-meter line, the receiving team may choose either to field another kickoff or to form a scrum at the center. In a game of Sevens, the receiving team has a free kick at center to restart the play.

The teams try to score by carrying, passing, kicking, and grounding the ball in in-goal. After the kickoff, any player who is onside (whose progress is not ahead of the ball) may catch or pick up the ball and run with it; pass it to another player; kick; tackle an opponent holding it; fall on it; take part in a scrum, ruck, maul, or line-out; or ground the ball in in-goal.

FIELD

The field of play is rectangular; it is not wider than 70 meters and not longer than 100 meters from goal line to goal line (see figure 41.1). The in-goal areas are each between 6 meters and 25 meters deep. A halfway line runs the width of the field at the center of the field. On both sides of the halfway line, 10-meter lines are marked in broken lines, 10 meters from the halfway line. Broken 5-meter lines run parallel to, and 5 meters inside, the touchlines (sidelines). Two solid 22-meter lines are on either end of the field, each 22 meters from a goal line.

Solid lines 15 meters inside the touchlines intersect the goal lines, the 22-meter lines, and the halfway line. The top edge of the goal's crossbar is 3 meters high; the goal posts are 5.6 meters apart and at least 3.4 meters high.

PLAYERS

Players may not wear anything with dangerous projections, such as buckles or rings. They may only wear equipment and clothing approved by World Rugby Board. They may wear circular studs on their shoes not exceeding 18 millimeters in length or 13 millimeters in diameter at the base. Players may wear shin guards and elastic knee and elbow pads. They may also wear scrum caps to protect their ears.

No more than eight players per team may be replaced with exceptions made for temporary replacements for blood and front row injuries.

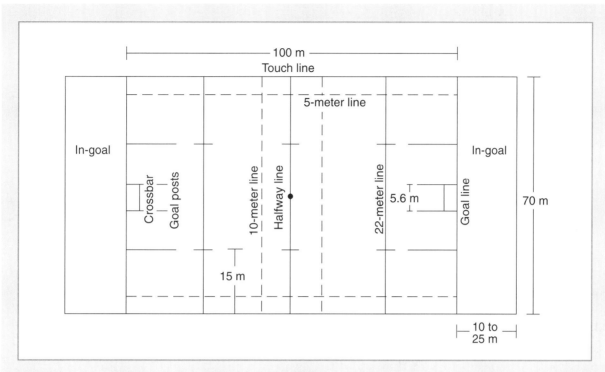

▶ **Figure 41.1** The dimensions and features of a rugby field.

EQUIPMENT

The ball must be oval, made of leather or suitable synthetic material, and made of four panels. The ball is 280 to 300 millimeters long. It is 740 to 770 millimeters in circumference, from end to end, and 580 to 620 millimeters in circumference around the middle. Weight should be 410 to 460 grams. The ball may be treated to make it water-resistant and easier to grip.

RULES

Most of the fundamental rules of play are covered in tackling, scrums, line-outs, rucks, and mauls.

Tackling

A player is tackled when he is brought and held to the ground. If one or both of the player's knees are on the ground or if he is on top of another player who is on the ground, the ball carrier is considered tackled. Once tackled, a player must immediately release or pass the ball and move away.

Once a player is tackled, the next player to play the ball must be on her feet. A player who goes to the ground to get the ball must immediately get up or pass or release the ball. Failure to do so may result in a penalty. It is illegal to prevent a tackled player from passing or releasing the ball or to impede him from moving away from the ball after he has passed or released it. It is also illegal to fall intentionally on a tackled player who possesses the ball or to fall intentionally on other players lying on the ground near the ball.

Scrum

A scrum is a set play where one team puts the ball into play between two groups of players. A scrum is formed at the place of infringement. Eight players from each team are involved in a scrum—at least three in the front row and two in the second row. The players must be stationary, and the middle line must be parallel to the goal lines until the ball is put into play.

The middle player in each front row is the hooker; the players on either side of her are the props. Each front row crouches with heads and shoulders no lower than the hips and not farther than an arm's length from their opponents' shoulders. The players bind to each other, hooking arms around the bodies of the teammates next to them.

The team not responsible for the infraction puts the ball into play, or, if no infraction occurred, the ball is put into play by the team that was advancing the ball. The player putting the ball into play stands 1 meter from the scrum, between the two front rows. She holds the ball with both hands between her knees and ankles, and with a single forward movement, she puts the ball into play between the two front rows. Once the ball enters the "tunnel" between the front rows, the hookers try to gain possession of it with their feet. If the ball comes out of either end of the tunnel, it is put in again by the same team.

Line-Out

A line-out is a set play that occurs when a ball has gone in touch (out of bounds). The ball is thrown in by a member of the team whose opponents last touched the ball before it went in touch. A member of one team throws the ball in bounds between two lines of players—one line consisting of his teammates and the other of his opponents. The team throwing the ball in determines the maximum number of players on the line. The two lines stand a meter apart. On the throw-in, the ball must be thrown 5 meters before it can be played. Players may not charge an opponent in the lineout, except to tackle him or play the ball once it has been thrown in, and they may not hold, push, or obstruct an opponent not carrying the ball.

The line-out ends when a ruck or maul forms and all the players' feet move beyond the original line on which the ball was thrown in; when a ball carrier leaves the line-out; when the ball is passed, knocked back, or kicked from the line-out; or when the ball becomes unplayable.

Ruck

Each player joining a ruck must bind with at least one arm around the body of a teammate; failure to do so results in a free kick for the opponents. A player in a ruck may not

- return the ball into the ruck,
- pick up the ball with hands or legs,

- intentionally collapse the ruck or jump on other players,
- intentionally fall or kneel in the ruck, or
- interfere with the ball while lying on the ground.

If the ball becomes unplayable in a ruck, a scrum is ordered.

Maul

The players in a maul must be on their feet, they must be in physical contact with each other, and their heads and shoulders must be no lower than their hips. A player in a maul may not jump on top of other players in the maul, collapse the maul, or try to drag a player out of the maul. To be in the maul, a player must be bound to it and not merely alongside it.

Scoring

A try (5 points) is scored when a player grounds the ball in her opponents' in-goal. A try may be scored in a scrum or ruck if a team pushes its opponents over its goal line and the ball is grounded in-goal by an attacking player. A try is awarded when the ball is grounded while held on the goal line or when a held ball is in contact with the ground and a goal post. A try may also be awarded if a team probably would have scored a try except for a foul by its opponents.

After a try, a team can take a conversion kick, either through a placekick or dropkick, worth 2 points. The kick is made anywhere on a line opposite where the try was scored. (Thus, it's an advantage to score near the center of the goal line, so that the kick's angle is not too sharp.) The kicker's team must be behind the ball when it is kicked. The opponents must stay behind the goal line until the kicker approaches the ball; at that point they may try to block the kick. In the game of Sevens, however, when a drop kick is necessary, opponents are required to move away from the kicker toward the 10 meter line.

A penalty kick, taken by any player of the offended team, is taken with the kicker's teammates behind the ball, except for the placer. The kicking team may kick for goal, kick for touch, or kick ahead for possession or territorial advantage. If the kick at goal goes over the crossbar and between the goal posts, it is worth 3 points. The opponents may not interfere with the kick and must retreat 10 meters from the mark where the kick is being taken.

Penalties

Penalties may be called for obstruction, unfair play, misconduct, dangerous play, unsporting behavior, retaliation, or repeated infringements. If the nonoffending team has an advantage, the referee does not have to whistle for the foul.

Obstruction occurs when a player running for the ball pushes or shoves an opponent also going for the ball; shoulder-to-shoulder contact is not considered obstruction. Obstruction is also the call when an offside player willfully blocks or prevents an opponent from reaching a teammate carrying the ball. A penalty kick is awarded for obstruction.

Unfair play and repeated infringements occur when a player deliberately wastes time or knocks or throws the ball into touch, into touch-in-goal, or over the dead-ball line. These infractions result in free kicks. The opponents of a player who deliberately plays unfairly or repeatedly breaks the law of the game are awarded a penalty kick.

Misconduct and dangerous play include

- striking, kicking, tripping, or trampling an opponent;
- tackling early, late, or dangerously;
- charging or obstructing an opponent who has just kicked the ball;
- holding, pushing, or obstructing an opponent who is not holding a ball, except in a scrum, ruck, or maul; and
- intentionally collapsing a scrum, ruck, or maul.

A player guilty of misconduct or dangerous play is cautioned or given a yellow card and ordered off the field for 10 minutes, meaning his team is one player short for the 10 minutes. A cautioned player who repeats the offense must be given a red card and ordered off and may not play anymore in the match, meaning his team is one player short for the remainder of the match.

Offside

When a player of the team in possession of the ball is closer to the opponents' goal line than the ball is, that player is offside. This means she may not take part in the play and faces a possible pen-

alty. A player can also be offside in scrums, rucks, mauls, and line-outs. A player may be penalized while in an offside position if she plays the ball or obstructs an opponent.

A player is offside in the following situations:

- A player is offside during a ruck if he joins the ruck from the opponents' side; if he doesn't retire behind the offside line at the hindmost foot of his teammates in the ruck or to his goal line, whichever is nearer; or if he places a foot in front of the offside line.
- In situations not involving a line-out, a player is offside if she joins the ruck or maul from her opponents' side; joins it in front of her hindmost teammate; or unbinds from it but fails to retire behind the offside line without delay; or advances beyond the offside line but doesn't join the ruck or maul.
- When a ruck or maul takes place at a lineout, a player is offside if he joins the ruck or maul from his opponents' side, joins it in front of his hindmost teammate, or is in the line-out but is not in the ruck or maul and does not retire behind the offside line (his hindmost teammate in the ruck or maul).
- A player participating in a line-out is offside if she advances beyond the line-of-touch before the ball has touched a player or the ground. After the ball has touched a player or the ground, a player is offside if she is not carrying the ball and advances beyond the ball, unless she is trying to tackle the ball carrier. A player who is not participating in the line-out is offside if she goes beyond the offside line before the line-out ends.
- If the ball has been kicked forward, a player is offside if he started in front of the kicker and moves toward the opponent waiting to play the ball before being put onside or if he comes within 10 meters of the opponent or the ball.

Onside

Except for a player who is within 10 meters of an opponent waiting to catch a kick, a player who is offside is made onside when he retires behind the teammate who last kicked, touched, or carried the ball; when the teammate carrying the ball runs in front of him; or when a teammate runs in front of him after coming from the place or behind the place where the ball was kicked. A player who is offside may also be made onside when an opponent carrying the ball has run 5 meters, when an opponent kicks or passes the ball, or when an opponent intentionally touches the ball and does not catch or gather it.

Knock-On and Throw-Forward

A knock-on occurs when the ball is propelled toward the opponents' goal line after a player loses possession of it or strikes it with her hand or arm. A throw-forward occurs when the ball carrier passes the ball forward toward the opponents' goal line. A knock-on or a throw-forward results in a scrum to the nonoffending team at the place of the infringement.

In-Goal

Touch-in-goal occurs when the ball touches a corner post, a touch-in-goal line, or the ground or a person on or beyond the line. The flag is not part of the corner post. When the ball becomes dead in in-goal by the attacking team, the defending team may either form a scrum where the ball was kicked or have a drop out on or behind the 22 meter line. If a player carries the ball into in-goal but is held and cannot ground it, the ball is dead. The ball is also dead if a defender kicks, knocks, or carries the ball into his own in-goal area and the ball becomes dead.

In Touch

The ball is in touch (out of bounds) when it touches on or beyond a touchline or when it is carried by a player who touches on or beyond a touchline. A player who catches or is holding the ball can also be in touch if they are already touching the touch in goal line or touchline. The ball is not in touch if it re-enters the playing area in any manner, even if it reaches the plane of touch. Additionally, a ball is not in touch if a player is in touch and kicks or knocks the ball but cannot hold it and it hasn't yet reached the plane of touch.

Ball or Player Touching Referee

If the ball or a ball carrier touches a referee, play continues unless the referee believes a team has gained an advantage. In this case he orders a scrum, and the team that last played the ball puts it in. If a player carrying the ball touches the ref-

eree while in her opponents' in-goal, before she can ground the ball, she is awarded a try.

TERMS

The **dead-ball line** is the line at the end of the in-goal area.

A **drop out** is a dropkick taken on or behind the 22-meter line; the opponents may not cross the line until the kick is made.

A **mark** may be made by a player within his 22-meter area or his in-goal. He must catch the kick and shout, "Mark!" He is awarded a free kick for a mark.

A **free kick** is awarded to a team after a mark or minor infringement. The team may not score a dropped goal from a free kick.

In-goal is the area bounded by the goal line, the touch-in-goal lines, and the dead-ball line. It includes the goal line and goal posts but excludes the touch-in-goal lines and dead-ball line.

A **knock-on** occurs when the ball travels toward the opponents' dead-ball line after a player loses possession of it or propels or strikes it with her hand or arm, or when the ball strikes a player's hand or arm and touches the ground or another player before it is recovered.

A **line-out** is a set play with a member of one team throwing the ball in bounds between two lines of players, with each line defending its own goal.

A **maul** is formed by players from both teams, on their feet and converging on the ball carrier. It ends successfully when the ball is on the ground and is immediately available or when a ball carrier emerges from the maul. The maul ends unsuccessfully when the ball is not made available, and the referee calls for a scrum.

A player is **offside** in general play when his team is in possession of the ball and he is in front of it. He may not take part in the play, but he is not penalized unless he plays the ball or obstructs an opponent.

A player is **onside** in general play when she is behind the ball. She may take part in the play when she is onside.

A **penalty kick** may be taken by any player of the offended team. The kick must be taken at or behind the prescribed mark. When awarded a penalty kick, a team may opt to kick for goal, to kick for touch and have a line-out, to put the ball in a scrum, or to tap the ball and play. The opponents may not interfere with a penalty kick.

A **ruck** occurs when the ball is on the ground and players from each team are on their feet, in physical contact, driving over the ball from a position originating behind the ball. If the ball becomes unplayable, a scrum is ordered.

A **scrum** is a set play where one team puts the ball into play between players from both teams after a minor infringement, such as a knock-on. The non-infringing team puts the ball into the scrum.

A **throw-forward** occurs when the ball carrier passes the ball forward toward the opponents' dead-ball line.

The ball is in **touch** when it touches on or beyond a touchline (out-of-bounds line) or is carried by a player on or beyond a touchline.

A **touch-down occurs** when a player grounds the ball (touches the ball to the ground) in his in-goal.

A **try**, worth 5 points, is scored when a player grounds the ball in her opponents' in-goal.

OFFICIALS

A referee is in charge of the match. Two assistant referees, one on each side of the field, assist the referee.

MODIFICATIONS

Rugby Sevens, also called simply *Sevens*, generally follows the same rules as the 15-person game, including playing on the same-sized field. There are several rule variations, most notably seven players per side, designated as three forwards and four backs. Five substitutions are allowed, and scrums are with three players. The two halves are just 7 minutes long, with a halftime of just 2 minutes. (This quick pace allows whole tournaments to be played in a weekend or a day, and it creates a more festive atmosphere at these "festivals".)

All conversion attempts must be drop-kicked in Sevens, and they must be taken within 30 seconds of scoring a try. On kickoffs in Sevens, the team that scored kicks off rather than the team that was just scored upon, as is the case in 15-per-side rugby. Yellow cards result in a 2-minute suspension, and in major competitions, additional in-goal touch judges are employed so the game is not delayed waiting for touch judges to move into position for the conversion attempts.

Rugby league football is similar to rugby union football. The main differences include the following:

- Each side has 13 players per side instead of 15.
- A try is worth 4 points; a conversion is worth 2. A penalty goal nets 2 points, and a drop goal counts for 1 point.
- A tackled player is allowed to retain possession of the ball temporarily.
- Ground gained by a kick into touch does not count, unless the ball lands in the field of play before it bounces into touch.

ORGANIZATIONS

World Rugby
www.worldrugby.org

USA Rugby
2655 Crescent Dr., Unit A
Lafayette, CO 80026
303-539-0300
www.usarugby.org

Ruby Canada
30 East Beaver Creek Rd., Ste. 110
Richmond Hill, Ontario L4B 1J2
905 707-8998
https://rugby.ca/en

42

Shooting

Scott Barbour/Getty Images

International shooting competition was introduced at the 1896 Summer Olympics, and the first world championships were held in 1897. In 1907, eight national federations founded the Union Internationale de Tir (French for the International Shooting Union), the international governing body for the sport. In 1998, the union's name was changed to the International Shooting Sport Federation (ISSF).

OVERVIEW

The sport of shooting has a number of events, each with its own detailed technical rules. The ISSF recognizes 19 events for men and junior men and 12 for women and junior women in the world championships. In Olympic competition, men and women have six events. There are also three mixed events, one in each discipline of rifle, pistol, and shotgun where one male and one female team up to represent their country.

The objective is to score points by hitting targets. Rules for this chapter come from USA Shooting, the national governing body for the sport; for more detailed information on each event, contact USA Shooting (see "Organizations"). Only general rules are provided here.

RANGE

A range has a line of targets and a firing line. Firing points or shooting stations are behind the firing line. The firing point is equipped with a removable or adjustable bench. Ranges have walls, electronic targets or paper and backing targets, and a pellet trap, bullet trap, or berm to collect or stop the spent rounds.

Wind flags are placed as close to the bullets' flight path as possible (10 meters and 30 meters forward of the firing line) without interfering with the shooting. They aid the shooters in determining the wind's likely effects on a bullet's flight path. Ranges for air gun competitions are located indoors.

Shooting distances are measured from the firing line to the target face.

Targets have 10 rings, with the innermost ring counting 10 points and the outermost 1 point; the width of the rings depends on the event. For the events specified, the proper heights of the target centers are as follows:

- 10-meter and 25-meter ranges; 10-meter and 50-meter running targets: 1.4 meters
- 50-meter ranges: 0.75 meter

SHOOTERS

In USA Shooting competitions, shooters compete in one of the following categories:

- J1 intermediate: 18 to 20 years of age
- J2 junior: 15 to 17 years of age
- J3 sub juniors: 14 years of age and under
- Collegiate: undergraduate students carrying a minimum of 12 credit hours
- Senior: 50 to 59 years of age
- Intermediate senior: 60 to 69 years of age
- Senior veteran: 70+ years of age and older

Shooters are further grouped within a shooting discipline by shooting precision classifications, ranging from AA (highest classification) to D (lowest).

EQUIPMENT

Specifications for air rifles are

- length of front sight tunnel: 50 millimeters,
- diameter of front sight tunnel: 25 millimeters,
- heel-to-toe length of butt plate: 153 millimeters,
- weight with sights and hand stop: 5.5 kilograms, and
- the front sight may not extend beyond the muzzle.

For pistol specifications, see table 42.1.

RULES

Men's and women's events recognized by the International Olympic Committee are shown in tables 42.2 and 42.3.

Scoring

For rifle and pistol events, ISSF matches are all shot on electronic targets. The shots are detected by sound as they go through either paper or

TABLE 42.1

Pistol Specifications

Pistol	Maximum weight	Maximum barrel length	Caliber
Rapid fire	1,400 g	Box size only	.22
Center fire	1,400 g	153 mm	.30-.38
Sport and standard	1,400 g	153 mm	.22
Free	No restriction	No restriction	.22
Air	1,500 g	Box size only	.177

Adapted from International Shooting Sport Federation, *Official Rules and Regulations* (Munich: ISSFR, 2008). Available: issf-sports.org/documents/rules/2017/ISSFRuleBook2017-2ndPrintV1.1-ENG.pdf.

TABLE 42.2

Men's Olympic Events

Event	Shots	Final with eliminations
50 m rifle, 3 positions	3 × 40 shots	3 × 15 shots max
10 m air rifle	60 shots standing	24 shots max
25 m rapid-fire pistol	60 shots	8 × 5 shots max
10 m air pistol	60 shots	24 shots max
Trap	125 targets	50 targets max
Skeet	125 targets	60 targets max

From International Olympic Committee.

TABLE 42.3

Women's Olympic Events

Event	Shots	Finals with eliminations
50 m rifle, 3 positions	3 × 40 shots	3 × 15 shots max
10 m air rifle	60 shots standing	24 shots max
25 m pistol	30 × 30 shots	10 × 5 shots max
10 m air pistol	60 shots	24 shots max
Skeet	125 targets	60 targets max
Trap	125 targets	50 targets max

From International Olympic Committee.

rubber and the electronic computer program will analyze where the shot is located on an XY access. The electronic targets are programed for each event and use the correct target on the monitor where the shooter can see each shots placement. Shooters can see their shots in 10 shot strings, or all the way up to 60 shots together in the air rifle and pistol events.

Each target has 10 rings, with scoring values ranging from 1 on the outside to 10 for the inner ring. For paper targets, scoring officials hand score each bullseye on the target where shooters shoot one shot per bull and ten bullseyes per target for rifle events, 5 shots per target in pistol events.

Deciding Ties

Ties are required to be broken in the 10, 25, 50, and 300 meter events. In the event of a tie, the following steps are following in attempt to break the tie:

- The individual with the highest number of inner tens would be successful in the tie.

- By working backwards by 10 shot series' the highest score of the last ten in full ring scoring would be the successor.

- If a tie still remains, the participants' scores get compared shot by shot starting with inner tens and then moving to outer tens if needed. This methods begins with the last shot taken and then the second to last, third to last, etc. until the tie is broken.

- If electronic targets were used and a tie still remains the scores are analyzed by the decimal ring scores. This is also done on a shot by shot basis following the same shot procedure as mentioned above.

- If still a tie is evident, the shooters are given the same ranking and are listed in order by the Latin alphabet and listed by their family names.

- In 10 m air rifle and 50 m rifle prone elimination competitions or qualifiers, ties can be broken using the highest decimal scores of the last ten shot series. This is only when decimal scoring is used and the shot scoring procedure is the same as mentioned above.

TERMS

An **air pistol** is one with a .177 caliber; it is a compressed air pistol that may be loaded with one pellet only.

An **air rifle** is one using compressed air; its caliber is .177 millimeter.

A **double** consists of two skeet clay targets thrown at the same time, one from each house; in the case of double trap, a double is two targets thrown from the machines in front of station 3.

Dry firing means the release of the cocked trigger mechanism of an unloaded firearm, or the release of the trigger mechanism of an air gun fitted with a device that allows the trigger to operate without releasing the propelling charge.

A **free pistol** is one with a .22 caliber; it can be loaded with only one cartridge.

An **irregular double** in skeet shooting occurs when one or both targets of a double are irregular (they don't conform to the normal standards) or when only one target is thrown.

A clay target is **lost** when it is not hit in flight, is hit outside the shooting boundaries, or is "dusted" but no visible piece falls from it.

A **no-bird double** is called when both clay targets are not thrown according to the rules.

A **rapid-fire pistol** is a .22 caliber semiautomatic firearm.

A **regular double** in skeet shooting occurs when regular targets are thrown simultaneously from each house.

Sights are metallic and without optics other than optional colored lenses attached to the rifle or pistol or another means of sighting. Sights not containing corrective lenses are permitted.

A **smallbore free rifle** is one with a .22 caliber.

A **smallbore sport rifle** also has a .22 caliber.

A **sport pistol** is chambered for long-rifle .22 cartridges and is a semiautomatic firearm capable for firing five shots.

A **standard pistol** is chambered for long-rifle .22 cartridges.

OFFICIALS

Competition officials include a chief range officer (one appointed for each range), who is in charge of the competition at the range and in charge of the range officers, who give the commands to the shooters. Scoring officers ensure that targets are rapidly changed, scored, and marked.

ORGANIZATIONS

USA Shooting
Colorado Springs, CO 80909
719-866-4670
www.usashooting.org

Amateur Trapshooting Association
P.O. Box 519
1105 E. Broadway
Sparta, IL 62286
618-449-2224
www.shootata.com

International Practical Shooting Confederation
P.O. Box 15661
1001 NA Amsterdam
The Netherlands
31 20 2440600
www.ipsc.org

International Shooting Sport Federation
Bavariaring 21
80336 Munich
Germany
+49 89 544 355 0
munich@issf-sports.org
www.issf-sports.org

National Rifle Association of America
11250 Waples Mill Rd.
Fairfax, VA 22030
703-267-1000
www.nra.org/home.aspx

National Skeet Shooting Association and National
  Sporting Clays Association
5931 Roft Rd.
San Antonio, TX 78253
210-688-3371
www.nssa-nsca.com

43

Skateboarding

In 1958, Bill Richards from North Hollywood, California, saw some boys riding surfboards they'd attached to wheels. He ordered some wheels from a roller skate company, attached them to boards, and began selling them as "sidewalk surfboards." A hit song by Jan and Dean gave the new sport nationwide exposure, and the first national skateboard championship took place in 1965.

In 1971, Richard Stevenson designed the kicktail (the upward curve on the back of the board), making it easier to control, and 2 years later Richard Nasworthy created the polyurethane wheel, offering better traction. In 1978, Alan "Ollie" Gelfand discovered he could go airborne by standing on the tail of his skateboard to jump curbs, rails, and other obstacles.

In 1981, the National Skateboarding Association was formed; it became World Cup Skateboarding in 1993. By 2000, skateboarding was the sixth most popular participant sport in the United States (third in the 6 to 18 age bracket). There are more than 10 million skateboarders in the United States and more than 50 million worldwide.

OVERVIEW

Disciplines recognized by World Cup Skateboarding (WCS) include street style or park, mini ramp, vert ramp, and pool or bowl. WCS also recognizes special events such as vert doubles, highest air, and best trick. The rules in this chapter are from the WCS.

SKATERS

WCS suggests the following divisions and age groups for amateur contests. However, contest organizers set the final age groups and divisions.

Divisions

Beginner: Skater who has never entered a skateboard competition or has some experience in competition but has never placed in the top three in the beginner class.

Intermediate: Skater who has placed in the top three in the beginner class, has competition experience, has performed tricks beyond the scope of a beginner, or is considered by the judges to skate at the intermediate level.

Advanced: Skater who has been placing in the top three in the intermediate level or is considered by the judges to skate above the intermediate level.

Age Groups

At amateur events, there are three major age groups of skaters: preteens, teens, and young adults. Preteen groups include ages 10 and under and ages 11 to 12. Teenager groups can be divided into ages 13 to 14, 15 to 16, and 17 to 18. Young adults are 19 and over. Sometimes there is also a masters group for ages 27 and over. For high-level amateur competitions, the recommended age divisions are 14 and under and 15 and over.

Professional events are considered open age, but skaters under age 16 should prove their abilities as top-level amateurs before turning pro. Pro masters division skaters are age 40 and older. Legend division skaters were top pros in their younger years; most are over 40 years of age.

EQUIPMENT

Helmets should be required for all events. For vert ramp and mini ramp events, helmets, elbow pads, and knee pads should be required. The condition of personal skateboard equipment is the responsibility of the competitor.

RULES

The following rules apply to competitions and practices before competitions.

Practice

Every skater is allowed equal practice time on the ramp or street course. If a skater disrupts a practice session, he can lose practice privileges. Making up a missed practice heat is at the discretion of the competition director.

Contest Structure Failure

If the competition director or the head judge deems that the skating surface is defective, the surface will be repaired and the heat will be restarted at the point when it was deemed unskateable.

Equipment Failure

If a skateboard breakdown occurs during the elimination phase of a contest and before any seeding process has been used, the skater is allowed two runs at the end of her division's session. If a breakdown occurs before a skater's first or second run or during the first 30 seconds of a run, the skater will skate at the end of the heat.

If the failure occurs after 30 seconds of the skater's run has elapsed, the run will be scored as a completed run. The option to place the skater in the next heat is up to the contest director. If the breakdown occurs during the finals, the skater will skate second to last.

Interference

Interference can be caused by a spectator, photographer, another competitor, failure of the skating surface, or an object dropped in the skating area. If any of these occur, the skater should immediately raise his hand.

If the competition director or head judge determines that interference did indeed occur and the skater was less than 30 seconds into his run, he will be allowed to restart his run. However, if 30 seconds of the run had elapsed, his run will be scored as a completed run with no penalty.

Missed Heat or Run

If a skater misses a heat or a run, the contest director will decide if the skater can still compete. The skater can pay a fee and protest the contest director's decision. The contest jury will then make the decision.

GENERAL JUDGING AND SCORING GUIDELINES

The minimum number of judges for an amateur event is three; the minimum is five for professional events. Seven judges can be used for professional events.

Scoring is based on a 1 to 100 point scale, with a suggested low of 40. The head judge sets the suggested average or base scores. Following is a suggested scale:

- Amazing run: 90-100
- Above average run: 80-89
- Average run: 70-79
- Below average run: 60-69
- Poor run: 50-59
- Very poor run: 30-49
- No tricks or few tricks completed: 0-29

The judges' high and low scores are discarded, and the remaining scores are added. The total is then averaged, giving the skater's score.

Ties are broken in this manner and in this order:

1. All judges' scores from the best run are averaged.
2. The other run's score is used to break the tie.
3. All judges' scores from the other run are averaged.
4. The lowest run score for each rider breaks the tie.

All judges' scores from the lowest run score are averaged.

VERT RAMP AND MINI RAMP COMPETITIONS

This section provides standards and competition formats for vert ramps and mini ramps.

Vert Ramps

The following standards are minimum requirements for a safe and sound structure to be used in any WCS-sanctioned event. The overall size of the ramp can vary but should be within the following limits:

Width: 48 to 100 feet

Transitions: 10.5 to 11.5 feet

Vert: 1.5 to 2 feet

Flat bottom: 14 to 16 feet

Extensions: 1 to 2 feet

Platforms on sides of ramp: 8 to 12 feet

Mini Ramps

The mini ramp should have at least two small back-to-back halfpipes and a spine, preferably with a double pipe along the top of the spine. The basic size of a mini ramp is as follows:

Width: 24 to 40 feet

Height: 4 to 7 feet

Transitions: 6 to 9 feet

Flat bottom: 8 to 12 feet

Competition Formats

All vert ramp and mini ramp contests are conducted in three phases: eliminations, semifinals, and finals. For competition runs, the clock or stopwatch starts at the competitor's first trick. A 15-second warning is announced, and the judges stop scoring the run at the end of the allotted time.

Judging for Vert Ramp and Mini Ramp Competitions

In judging the routine's composition routine or line for vert ramp or mini ramp competitions, judges consider the following:

- How many maneuvers the skater makes
- How many areas of the ramp the skater uses
- Whether the skater avoids wasted setup walls
- Whether the skater performs the routine to the limit while maintaining control

Judging criteria include

- degree of difficulty;
- bionics or amplitude (height of airs, length of grinds, and so on);
- variety of maneuvers and lines;
- linking of tricks;
- originality and style;
- continuity of run and consistency;
- use of the ramp or pool, including extensions, hips, channels, and corners; and
- aggressive execution of maneuvers.

Judges assess a penalty for falls. The severity of the penalty depends on what the skater was attempting when the fall or step-off occurred and how the fall affected the overall run.

STREETSTYLE AND PARK COMPETITIONS

Streetstyle and park courses include obstacles that resemble natural street skating elements, such as ledges, handrails, banks, quarter pipes, hips, centerpieces, and pyramids. The course should be a minimum of 100 by 150 feet and should offer a variety of skateable lines.

Competition Formats

All streetstyle and park contests are conducted in three phases: eliminations, semifinals, and finals. For competition runs, the clock or stopwatch starts at the competitor's first trick. A 15-second warning is announced, and the judges stop scoring the run at the end of the allotted time.

Judging for Streetstyle and Park Competitions

Judges' criteria for streetstyle and park competitions include the following:

- The routine's content: the number, difficulty, originality, and variety of tricks successfully performed
- The aggressive execution of maneuvers performed
- The style of the routine: the fluid linking of individual tricks
- The use of the street course and ramps, boxes, handrails, and so on

Judges take falls into consideration, assessing penalties based on what the skater was attempting when the fall or step-off occurred, how the fall affected the run's fluidity, and how the skater was able to recover and continue the run.

OFFICIALS

Each WCS-sanctioned competition has a contest jury composed of a contest director, a contest promoter representative, a head judge, and a riders' representative. Each member of the contest jury has voting rights.

The contest jury is responsible for maintaining and enforcing the rules, dealing with protests, and making necessary decisions regarding any problems that arise.

ORGANIZATIONS

World Skate
www.rollersports.org

USA Skateboarding
josh.friedberg@usaskateboarding.net

World Cup Skateboarding
10460 Frontier Trail
Cherry Valley, CA 92223
530-888-0696
www.wcsk8.com

World Freestyle Skateboard Association
www.wfsafreestyle.org

World Skateboarding Federation
http://worldskateboardingfederation.org

Snowboarding

Krzysztof Tkacz/fotolia.com

Snowboarding offers several forms of competition. First developed in the United States in the 1960s, the sport combines elements of skiing, surfing, and skateboarding. Snowboarding's popularity caught on in the 1970s and 1980s; in 1985, the first World Cup for the sport was held in Zurs, Austria. The International Snowboard Association was founded in 1994, and snowboarding became an Olympic sport in 1998. Today, most of the ski areas in North America and Europe allow snowboarding. Some four million Americans snowboard, with 78 percent being under the age of 34.

OVERVIEW

Snowboard competitions consist of alpine racing events (slalom, parallel slalom, giant slalom, parallel giant slalom), freestyle events (halfpipe, slopestyle, big air), and snowboard cross.

▪ In the slalom races, riders race downhill through gates with tight turns that require significant technical skill. In giant slalom races, gates are set farther apart on longer courses, and riders gain more speed on these courses.

▪ In halfpipe competitions, competitors perform tricks in the air while going from side to side on a semicircular U shaped ditch or ramp. They receive scores from judges for their performances.

▪ In slopestyle competitions, competitors perform tricks while moving around, over, across, or down terrain features, such as jumps and rails, again receiving scores from judges for doing so.

▪ In snowboard cross, four to six riders race on a downhill course with jumps, berms, and other obstacles, with the first two or three riders, respectively advancing to the next round. The overall winner is the rider who finishes first in the final round.

COURSES

Following are descriptions of courses for competitions in these events: slalom, giant slalom, parallel events, halfpipe, snowboard cross, and slopestyle.

Slalom

Slalom courses include a series of turns that allow competitors to combine maximum speed with precise turns. The courses are between 400 and 600 meters long with a vertical drop of between 120 and 180 meters. They must be at least 30 meters wide if two runs are set on the same slope and at least 20 meters wide if the second run is set on the first track. The finish must be at least 8 meters wide.

Slalom courses allow for fluent runs with changes of direction with very different radii. Gates are set so that some full turns are required, interspersed with traverses. Slalom gates alternate red and blue. Each gate has between 10 and 14 meters from turning pole to turning pole. Snowboarders negotiate at least 35 gates on the course but could reach up to a maximum of 55 gates. Padding, nets, or other safety measures are put in place where riders might encounter danger.

Giant Slalom

Giant slalom courses present a variety of long, medium, and short turns. The courses have a vertical drop of between 200 and 400 meters and are at least 40 meters wide, assuming both males and females are using the same course.

Gates alternate red and blue except for double gates, which are the same color. The nearest poles of two successive gates must be at least 10 meters. Riders must navigate at least 20 gates over undulating and hilly terrain that is topped by compact, hard snow. Padding, nets, or other safety measures are put in place where riders might encounter danger.

Triple Slalom Event

The Triple S consists of three individuals competing on side-by-side courses. Slalom courses described above are typically used with some slight variations. The length of the courses are between 250 and 450 meters with a vertical drop of between 80 and 120 meters. Courses are recommended to consist of approximately 25 gates, and the course requires a minimum of a 40 meter width. Each course receives their own color of gates. The left course is marked with red, the middle with blue, and the right with yellow.

Parallel Events

In parallel events—parallel slalom and parallel giant slalom—two competitors ride simultaneously side-by-side down two courses, which are configured and prepared to be as identical as possible, posing the same challenges for each competitor. The left course (looking from the top) is set with red gate poles and flags, and the right course is set with blue poles and flags. Courses are set to have a variety of turns and to cause changes in rhythm.

Parallel slalom courses have a vertical drop between 80 and 120 meters and are between 250 and 450 meters long. They have an average steepness of 14 to 18 degrees and a distance between gates of 10 to 14 meters. These courses require a minimum of 18 gates but are recommended to have between 23 and 30. The distance between the two parallel slalom courses is between 8 and 10 meters.

Parallel giant slalom courses have a vertical drop of 120 to 200 meters, with a length of 400-700 meters. The distance between gates is 20 to 27 meters and courses are recommended to have 18 to 25 gates per course. The distance between the two parallel giant slalom courses is between 9 and 12 meters. The competitors each take one run on each course head to head and the winner of the combined times, or differential on the second run advance.

Halfpipe

Halfpipe courses are channels constructed in snow. Courses are as hard and even as possible, and the tops of each wall are clearly marked with color. The length of a halfpipe course ranges from 100 to 120 meters, and its width is from 15 to 22 meters, with a wall height of 3.5 to 7 meters.

Snowboard Cross

Snowboard cross courses include banked turns, jumps, berms, drops, and steep and flat sections that challenge riders' ability to stay in control. The courses measure between 100 and 260 meters in vertical drop, with the average slope incline between 8 and 12 degrees. The slope should be at least 40 meters wide in most cases, although for short sections of the course it can drop to as low as 20 meters wide. The finish must be at least 15 meters wide.

Gates are placed along the course so competitors can distinguish them clearly and quickly at high speeds.

Slopestyle

Slopestyle courses are a minimum of 30 meters wide and include a minimum of 50 to 150 meters of vertical drop depending on the competitor's level. The slopes should 12 degrees or steeper and contain a variety of hits, with two or more lines that competitors may choose to perform. Each course includes at least two features and a minimum number of jumps and judged hits predetermined by the competitor's level. Courses are designed to be technically challenging while allowing riders to set up for the next feature.

RIDERS

In the United States of American Snowboard and Freeski Association (USASA) competitions, riders compete in these divisions:

- Ruggie: 7 and under
- Grommet: 8 to 9
- Menehune: 10 to 11
- Breakers: 12 to 13
- Youth: 14 to 15
- Juniors: 16 to 17
- Jams: 18 to 22
- Senior: 23 to 29
- Master: 30 to 39
- Legend: 40 to 49
- Kahuna: 50 to 59
- Methuselah: 60 and over
- Open class
- ID snowboard
- Adaptive snowboard
- Adaptive freeski

EQUIPMENT

On riders' bibs, the number must be at least 12 centimeters high and easily legible. Safety leashes are optional, unless required by the organizer or the ski area. Snowboards with a gliding surface of up to 135 centimeters must have a minimum width of 14 centimeters; boards with a gliding surface greater than 135 centimeters must have a minimum width of 16 centimeters. Bindings must be fixed diagonally on the long axis of the board, and boots cannot overlap each other. Participants are required to wear helmets for all training and competition events. Competitors are not allowed to use any kind of device that can support their balance or reduce or accelerate their speed.

RULES

The rules for this chapter are derived from the U.S. Ski and Snowboard Association. Each course has its own set of rules.

Slalom

The slalom start takes place at irregular intervals; a competitor does not have to finish the course before the next competitor begins. The starter says, "Ready," and then, a few seconds later, gives the signal to "Go!" The competitor has 10 seconds to start after this signal.

A slalom is decided by two runs, each run on a different course. All riders go on one course, and then all move over to the second course. The competition committee can reduce the number of competitors in the second run to half, provided that such notice was given before the race started.

In the slalom, as with all snowboarding events, helmets are required for all competitors.

Giant Slalom

Competitors usually start at 60-second intervals (sometimes shorter or longer intervals are used). The starter gives the competitor a 10-second warning and then at 5 seconds counts, "5, 4, 3, 2, 1, Go!"

A giant slalom is decided by two runs; typically these runs are made on the same day. The second run can be held on the same course, but the gates must be reset.

Parallel Events

In parallel events, competitors are allowed to inspect the course, but they cannot ride down the prepared course or through the gates. Instead, they can slide down the sides of the course.

Competitors start side by side in two separate start gates that open simultaneously. Any start system can be used, as long as it guarantees a simultaneous start. Starts take place at irregular intervals; riders need not have crossed the finish line before the next set of competitors begins.

A competitor is disqualified if he manipulates the starting gate or tries to pass the starting gate before the start signal has been given.

Competitors are also disqualified if they change from one course to another; disturb or interfere with the opponent, whether voluntarily or not; or incorrectly pass a gate. Competitors who are disqualified in the first run start the second run with the maximum penalty time of 5 percent; if they are disqualified in the second run, they are eliminated from the competition.

The finish lines for each competitor are symmetrical and are each at least 8 meters wide.

Each race between two competitors consists of two runs, with each competitor going once on each side of the course.

Halfpipe

The starter gives a "Ready" command to a competitor and then says, "Go." The competitor can leave anytime after the command. Once a competitor starts, she is not allowed to restart.

Competitions can be held in best of two runs, in best of three runs, and in modified formats. In the best of two runs, competitors get two runs in the halfpipe, going in the same order as they went in the first run. Judges score each run, and the better score of the two runs is the only score that counts toward the final placing. The same approach works for the best of three runs.

Three to six judges are used at halfpipe events, and they evaluate the runs on the following criteria:

- Standard airs: These include tricks and airs that are less than 360 degrees. Tricks that are performed well increase scores for execution. Judges emphasize variety, difficulty, and execution of tricks.

- Rotations: These are maneuvers that include a rotation of 360 degrees or more. Judges look for smooth, precise, under-control rotating and take into account the variety, difficulty, and execution of the tricks.

- Amplitude: This measures the height of maneuvers. The amplitude score is derived from the sum of all hits, divided by the number of hits taken. The value of each hit is equal to the number of feet between the pipe's lip (top) and the rider's center of mass.

- Overall impression: This includes how a rider designs his run to show a variety of tricks that are well executed and difficult.

If two competitors are tied, the rider with the higher score from the other run wins. If both runs are tied, then the rider with the highest combined overall impression score wins.

Snowboard Cross

Snowboard cross competitions are generally run according to a single-elimination format; sometimes a double-knockout format is used.

Competitors choose their lane positions in order of their qualifying times. Riders are disqualified if they intentionally push or pull another rider or otherwise cause a competitor to slow down, although unavoidable and casual contact can be okay. Course judges determine whether the contact is acceptable.

Place of finish is determined by the first part of the body or snowboard that crosses the finish line. In case of a tie, the two riders who tied run again.

Slopestyle

Competitors take two runs, with only their high score counting toward the final ranking. Judging is based on overall impression. Judges look at trick difficulty, execution, and amplitude of tricks as well as the sequence of tricks.

Scoring can be based on an overall scoring system, in which each judge scores each rider on a scale of 0 to 10, using one decimal, or on a scale of 0 to 100 with no decimals. Scoring can also be determined by a ranking system, in which riders are ranked for various tricks and their rankings are added up to determine places.

TERMS

Chatter is the vibration of the snowboard as a result of high speed, tight turns, or icy conditions.

The length of a snowboard's metal edge that makes contact with the snow is the **effective edge**.

The part of the halfpipe between the two walls is the **flat bottom**.

Freestyle snowboarding is usually associated with riding a halfpipe but encompasses any kind of riding that includes tricks.

Riding with the right foot closest to the nose of the snowboard is **goofy footed**.

A **halfpipe** is a vertical U-shaped structure used in freestyle snowboarding. As for a skateboarding halfpipe, riders use the opposing walls to get air and perform tricks as they travel down the fall line of the slope.

The edge of the snowboard where the heels sit is called the **heel edge**.

The top edge of the halfpipe wall is the **lip**.

In a term borrowed from skateboarding, to **Ollie** is to get air by first lifting the front foot, springing off the back foot, then landing on both feet.

A **quarter-pipe** is designed like a halfpipe but with only one wall.

Riding with the left foot closest to the nose of the snowboard is **regular footed**.

Rocker is the opposite of camber. It occurs when the snowboard is placed on a flat surface and rests only on the center portion.

The horizontal part of the halfpipe wall that serves as a vantage point, waiting area, or walkway to the uphill end of the pipe is the **rollout deck**.

Sliding sideways quickly to slow down before a jump or other situation where speed control is necessary is called a **speed check**.

The **transition** (also known as *tranny*) is the initial curved part of a halfpipe wall between the flat of the bottom and the vertical section of the wall.

As in skiing, to **traverse** is to ride perpendicular to the fall line of the slope. In the halfpipe, a freestyle rider traverses the flat bottom to perform tricks on either wall.

A snowboard whose nose and tail are shaped identically so that the board will ride equally well in either direction is a **twin tip**.

The topmost portion of the walls of a halfpipe is called a **vertical** (also known as *vert*). Verticals allow riders to fly straight up from the halfpipe wall.

The opposing sections of the halfpipe are the **walls**. A wall is made up of a transition (where the rider begins the ascent) and a vertical section (where the rider launches and performs a trick).

OFFICIALS

Officials for snowboarding events include

- a jury, which monitors rule adherence and course preparation, among other things;
- a technical delegate (TD or technical supervisor [TS]), who ensures that the rules are followed and the event runs smoothly;
- referees, gate judges, and course setters for alpine events; and
- judges for freestyle events.

ORGANIZATIONS

International Ski Federation
Marc Hodler House
Blochstrasse 2
CH-3653 Oberhofen
Switzerland
41-033-244-6161
www.fis-ski.com

United States of America Snowboard and Freeski
   Association
P.O. Box 15500
South Lake Tahoe, CA 96151
800-404-9213
www.usasa.org

U.S. Ski and Snowboard Association
P.O. Box 100
1 Victory Ln.
Park City, UT 84060
435-649-9090
www.usskiandsnowboard.org

Soccer

Klaus Vedfel/DigitalVision/Getty Images

Soccer is based on 17 laws, which have been refined since the game's modern beginnings in Great Britain in 1863. The sport was first known in Britain as association football; this was shortened to A-soc and, finally, soccer. The sport's popularity in the United States lagged until the 1970s, when youth leagues began to flourish. Soccer is a popular sport worldwide, especially in Argentina, Brazil, England, Germany, and Italy. In the United States, it is second only to basketball in youth participation (about 7.7 million U.S. youths play soccer). About 18 million people play soccer at least once a year in the United States, nearly half of those regularly in soccer leagues. The game is popular in the United States both recreationally and at youth and high school levels.

OVERVIEW

Objective: To score as many goals as possible by putting the ball into the opponents' goal.

Number of Players: 11 per side (for short-sided games, see "Modifications").

Scoring: A goal is scored when the ball completely crosses the goal line under the crossbar and between the goal posts.

Length of Game: Two 45-minute halves with a 10- to 15-minute halftime. Youth matches are played in equal halves of lesser times (20 to 40 minutes), depending on the age of the players.

Players must use their feet, head, or chest to play the ball. With the exception of the goalkeeper (and a player taking a *throw-in*), players may not use their hands or arms. The player who begins the game by kicking off may not touch the ball again until it has been touched by any other player. The game proceeds with each team trying to control the ball, move it down the field, and score a goal.

FIELD

See figure 45.1 for the components and dimensions of a soccer field. The field length is 100 to 130 yards, and it is marked by a halfway line that divides the field in half and contains a circle with a radius of 10 yards around it. Goals are 8 yards wide and 8 feet high. There is a penalty mark 12 yards from the midpoint between the goalposts in each of the penalty areas. There is also an arc of a circle with a 10-yard radius from the center of each penalty mark drawn outside each penalty area.

PLAYERS

Each team has up to 11 players, one of whom must be the goalkeeper. The other players are known as defenders, midfielders, and forwards (or strikers). A match may not start or continue if either team has fewer than seven players. The number of substitutes, up to a maximum of five, may be used in any official competition under the

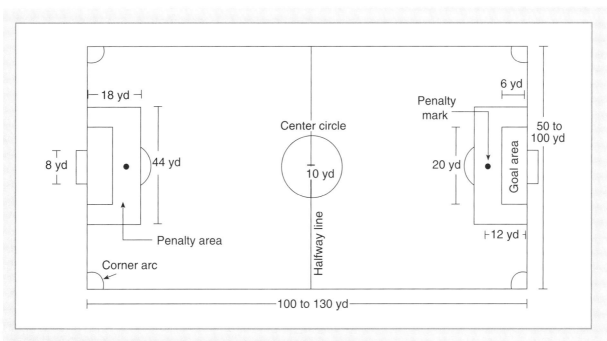

▶ **Figure 45.1** The dimensions and features of a soccer field.

Fédération Internationale de Football Association (FIFA), the confederation, or the national football association. In some top division leagues, a maximum of three substitutes might be allowed. In youth play, unlimited substitution is generally permissible. When play is stopped, any player, with the referee's approval, may change places with the goalkeeper.

A substitute must be summoned onto the field by the referee and must enter the field at the halfway line after the player being replaced has left the field. Once players have been replaced, they may not return to the game. (Different soccer associations have variations of this substitution rule for youth, women's, and senior competitions.)

EQUIPMENT

The ball is round, is covered in leather or other suitable material, and is a number 5 ball, which is between 27 and 28 inches in circumference (a smaller ball is used in younger youth matches).

Players must dress in matching shirts, shorts, and socks, and they must also wear shin guards and shoes. Shoes may have studs if they are rounded with no sharp edges. Goalkeepers often wear elbow and knee pads and gloves. A goalkeeper must wear a different-colored uniform from that of any other player, which includes teammates, opponents, and the opposing goalkeeper. Any equipment deemed dangerous to players may not be worn. All items of jewelry are forbidden and must be removed. Using tape to cover jewelry is not permitted.

RULES

Some of the basic play is governed by the rules concerning offside, free kicks, and goalkeeping.

Offside

A player is in an offside position if he is closer to the opponents' goal line than the ball, unless the player is still in his own half of the field or is not closer to the opponents' goal line than the last two opponents. The offside offense is determined by the player's position at the moment a teammate plays or touches the ball, not at the moment the player receives the ball.

A player is not called offside for merely being in an offside position. To be ruled offside, the player must be actively participating in the play by interfering with play, interfering with an opponent, or gaining an advantage. The player is still subject to being declared offside even after the ball deflects off the goal, the goalkeeper, or any defender. When a player is declared offside, the opposing team is awarded an indirect free kick (IFK) at the point of the infraction.

A player in an offside position is not offside upon receiving a ball directly from a goal kick, corner kick, or throw-in or playing a ball that was last played by an opponent who had possession of the ball.

Free Kicks

There are two types of free kicks: direct free kicks (DFKs), awarded for any of 10 major fouls committed by the opposing team, and indirect free kicks (IFKs), awarded for other violations made by either team. Opposing players must be at least 10 yards from the ball during the taking of any free kick. A free kick awarded to the defending team within its own goal area may be taken from any point within the goal area. An IFK awarded to the attacking team within the opponents' goal area is taken from the goal-area line nearest to the point where the infraction occurred. A goal may be scored on any DFK with only the initial kicker touching the ball. On an IFK, another player from either team must also touch the ball before a goal can be scored.

A DFK is awarded to a team's opponents when that team

- kicks (or attempts to kick), trips (or attempts to trip), or pushes an opponent;
- jumps at an opponent;
- violently or dangerously charges an opponent, or charges an opponent from behind;
- strikes (or attempts to strike) an opponent with the hand, arm, or elbow;
- spits at an opponent;
- holds an opponent's body or clothing;
- tackles an opponent to gain possession of the ball and makes contact with the opponent before touching the ball; or
- deliberately plays the ball with any part of the hand or arm (from the shoulder to the

fingertips) unless the player is the goal-keeper.

An IFK is awarded to the opposing team when a player

- is declared offside,
- deliberately impedes the progress of an opponent by blocking her path instead of playing the ball,
- plays in a dangerous manner,
- behaves in an unsporting manner,
- fair charges an opponent when the ball is not within playing distance, or
- prevents the goalkeeper from releasing the ball back into play.

An IFK is also awarded when goalkeepers take more than 6 seconds before releasing the ball from their hands.

Goalkeeping

These rules address the use of hands and of time-delaying tactics. Goalkeepers must release the ball back into play within 6 seconds after gaining possession of the ball. A goalkeeper may not delay the game by holding the ball before punting. (Penalty: An IFK is taken from the spot of the violation, or, if it occurred within the goal area, the kick is taken from the goal-area line that runs parallel to the goal line, nearest the spot of the infraction.)

Once the ball has been released into play, goal-keepers may not touch the ball again with their hands before an opponent touches it anywhere on the field or another teammate touches it outside of the penalty area.

Goalkeepers may use their hands to field a ball that has been deliberately headed, chested, or kneed to them by a teammate, but they may not use their hands to field a ball that has been intentionally kicked to them by a teammate or upon receiving a ball directly from a throw-in by a teammate.

TERMS

An **advantage** refers to a situation in which the referee calls, "Play on!" despite a foul having been committed—because the team that would be given a free kick already has a greater advantage of a scoring or passing opportunity.

A referee may issue a player a **caution** (yellow card) for misconduct or **send off** a player (red card) for violent conduct, serious foul play, or abusive language.

A **corner kick** is awarded to the opposing team when a player last touches the ball over his own goal line. For a corner kick, the ball is placed in the corner arc, and all opposing players must be at least 10 yards away.

A **direct free kick (DFK)** is awarded for any of the 10 major fouls.

A **fair charge** occurs when a player makes shoulder-to-shoulder contact with an opposing player in a nonviolent manner while trying to gain possession of the ball. For a fair charge to be legal, players must be within playing distance of the ball, and each player must have at least one foot on the ground.

A **foul** results in a DFK or an IFK for the opposing team at the spot of the offense.

A **goal** may not be scored directly from a throw-in. A goal may be scored directly from an opposing player's corner kick, kickoff, or goal kick or from an opposing goalkeeper's punt. Attacking players may not use their hands or arms to throw, carry, or propel the ball across the goal line.

A **goal kick** occurs after a player last touches the ball over the opposing team's goal line. The opposing team is awarded a goal kick, in which the ball may be placed anywhere within the goal area. Opposing players must be outside the penalty area, and the ball may be kicked by either the goalkeeper or another player. It must be kicked beyond the penalty area to be put into play. The player who initially kicks the ball may not touch the ball again until it has been touched by another player.

Players **head the ball** by hitting it with their head.

An **indirect free kick (IFK)** is awarded for minor fouls and other various violations.

A player is **offside** if she is closer to the opponents' goal line than the ball, unless the player is still in her own half of the field or is not closer to the opponents' goal line than the last two opponents.

The ball is not **out of play** (out of bounds) until the entire ball has crossed entirely over the outside edge of the touchline or goal line. The ball is also considered out of play whenever the referee blows his whistle to stop the game. A player may go off the field of play (out of bounds) to keep the ball in play. A ball remains in play if it bounces back onto the field after hitting a goal post, crossbar, or corner post or if it does not completely leave the field after it hits an official.

A team is awarded a **penalty kick** when an opposing player commits a major foul within her own penalty area. All players except the kicker and the goalkeeper must stand outside the penalty area, behind the ball, and at least 10 yards from the ball. The goalkeeper must stand on the goal line and not move off the goal line until the kick is made. If the ball is stopped by the goalkeeper and rebounds onto the field, play continues. If a goal is not scored and the ball goes over the goal line after being touched by the goalkeeper, the attacking team gets a corner kick.

A **sliding tackle** occurs when a player slides on the ground in an attempt to kick the ball away from an opponent.

A team is awarded a **throw-in** when the ball goes over the touchline (sideline), having last been touched by an opposing player. A player throws the ball in from over her head, with both feet on the ground at the moment of release. At least part of each foot must be on or behind the touchline. If the throw-in is done incorrectly, the opposing team is awarded a throw-in.

OFFICIALS

One referee and two assistant referees control the game. The referee is responsible for enforcing the rules; keeping the time and score; and issuing warnings, cautions, and send-offs to players and coaches. The referee signals the start and end of the game.

The assistant referees indicate when and where a ball leaves the field of play, and they determine which team is awarded a throw-in, goal kick, or corner kick. They also indicate offside offenses and signal with the flag other violations that the referee is not able to see.

MODIFICATIONS

Different organizations modify the sport in different ways. Younger players generally do not play 11 v 11 but play short-sided games ranging from 4 v 4 through 9 v 9. Ball size is dependent on the age of the players, with a number 4 ball being used for U12 through U9 players and a number 3 ball for U8 through U6 players. Following are general recommendations that are used as is or are further modified for youngsters playing soccer.

9 v 9

This is often played by 12-and-under leagues. A goalkeeper is required for this level. Field size is 70 to 80 yards long by 45 to 55 yards wide. The goals are 7 feet high by 21 feet wide. Game length is two 30-minute halves with a 10-minute halftime. The basic rules of the game remain the same except deliberate heading is not allowed until players reach the U12 level.

7 v 7

This is often played by 10-and-under leagues. Goalkeepers are allowed. Field size is 55 to 65 yards long by 35 to 45 yards wide. The goals are 6.5 feet high by 18.5 feet wide but can be modified to 12 feet wide based on the age and ability of the participants. The field also has built out lines on both sides of the field equidistant from the midline and the goal line. These lines help to keep track of offside calls. Specifically, offside is not allowed to be called between the midline and the build out line, but they can be called between the build out line and the goal line. The build out line requires players to stay behind it while the ball is put into play by the goaltender, allowing for the ball to be played under less offensive pressure. Once the ball is in play the opposing team can cross the build out line. Game length is two 25-minute halves with a 10-minute halftime. Heading is not allowed in 7 vs 7 games.

4 v 4

This is often played by 8-and-under leagues. Goalkeepers are not allowed. Field size is 25 to 35 yards long by 15 to 25 yards wide. The goals are 4 feet high by 6 feet wide. The game length is four 10-minute periods with 5-minute breaks between quarters. The basic rules are the same, except for the following differences:

- On kickoffs, goal kicks, corner kicks, and free kicks, opponents should be at least 10 feet away from the ball.
- Offside is not called.
- All kicks are IFKs.
- There are no penalty kicks.
- Heading is prohibited.

ORGANIZATIONS

American Youth Soccer Organization
19750 S. Vermont Ave., Ste. 200
Torrance, CA 90502
800-872-2976
www.soccer.org

Fédération Internationale de Football
    Association (FIFA)
FIFA-Strasse 20
8044 Zurich
Switzerland
41 (0) 43 222 7777

www.fifa.com

National Soccer Coaches Association of America
30 W. Pershing Rd., Ste. 350
Kansas City, MO 64108-2463
816-471-1941
www.nscaa.com

Soccer Association for Youth USA
11490 Springfield Pike
Cincinnati, Ohio 45246
800-233-7291
www.saysoccer.org

United States Soccer Federation
11490 Springfield Pike
Cincinnati, OH 45246
800-233-7291
www.ussoccer.com

46

Softball

Softball was first played in Chicago in 1887, indoors, with a 17-inch ball. An outdoor version of the game was played with a 12-inch ball in Minneapolis in 1895. The game was standardized in 1923, and today there are many variations, including fastpitch, slowpitch, 16-inch slowpitch, and coed play. These variations make softball a widely accessible sport, played by young and old alike. The bulk of this chapter focuses on the slowpitch game.

OVERVIEW

Objective: To score the most runs.

Scoring: A player scores a run when she safely touches first, second, third, and home before her team makes three outs.

Number of Players: 10 per team (11 if using an extra player who bats but does not field; only 10 are on the field).

Number of Innings: Seven.

Number of Outs per Inning: Three outs for each team.

The defense fields 10 players. The extra player is optional, but if one is used, he must be in the starting lineup and be used for the entire game. Each team has a batting order that it must adhere to, although substitutions may be made. Once a player is removed from the game, she can reenter the game once. The visiting team bats first, in the top half of the inning; the home team bats in the bottom half of the inning. The pitcher pitches and tries to get the batter out; the batter tries to get on base and eventually score. The most common ways to record outs are by strikeout, force out, tag out, and fly out.

FIELD

Figure 46.1 shows the dimensions of a softball field for adult slowpitch. Home plate is five-sided, 17 inches wide across the edge facing the pitcher, 8.5 inches long on sides parallel to the batter's box, and 12 inches long on the sides of the point facing the catcher. Bases are 15 inches square and no more than 5 inches thick. A double base, 15 inches by 30 inches, can be used at first base. Half the base is in fair territory and is white; the other half is in foul territory and is orange.

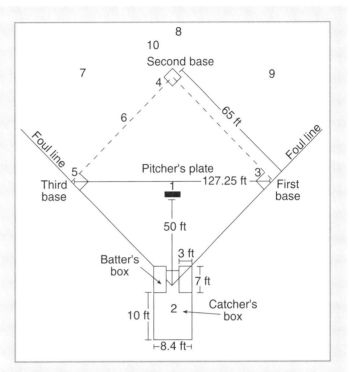

▶ **Figure 46.1** The dimensions, features, and player positions of a softball field.

The pitcher's plate is 24 inches long by 6 inches wide; its front is 50 feet from the back point of home plate.

The outfield fence varies in distance from home plate, from 265 to 275 feet for women to 275 to 325 feet for men. In coed play, the fences are 275 to 300 feet. A dead-ball area is drawn with chalk outside the field of play. The line itself is in play, but if a fielder has either foot on the ground completely over the line, the ball is dead and no play can be made. If a fielder intentionally carries a live ball into the dead-ball area, any runners are awarded two bases beyond the last bases they legally touched. If the act is unintentional, each runner is awarded one base.

PLAYERS

In slowpitch, a team has 10 fielders:

▪ Pitcher
▪ Catcher
▪ First baseman
▪ Second baseman
▪ Third baseman

▪ Shortstop

▪ Left fielder

▪ Center fielder

▪ Right fielder

▪ Extra fielder

A team may also have an extra player (EP) who bats but does not field. The EP is optional, but if one is used, he must be in the starting lineup and must be used for the entire game. With an EP, all 11 players must bat, and any 10 may play defense. Defensive positions may be switched, but the batting order must remain constant.

All players, including the EP, may be replaced and may reenter the game once. The starting player and the substitute cannot be in the lineup at the same time; each player must occupy his same position in the batting order. A substitute may enter a game only once. A starting pitcher who is removed from the game may reenter the game once at any position except pitcher.

Under the short-handed rule, a team may start with 10 or 11 players and continue with one fewer player when a player leaves a game for any reason other than ejection. If the player leaving the game is a base runner, she is called out; when her turn at bat comes, an automatic out is declared. The player may not return to the lineup unless she has left for the blood rule, which stipulates that a player who is bleeding or who has blood on her uniform must receive appropriate treatment before continuing to play. Play may be momentarily suspended while the player receives treatment, or the player may be required to at least temporarily leave the game.

A player or coach who is ejected may stay on the bench unless the offense is flagrant, in which case the ejected person must leave the grounds. If an ejected player continues to participate or reenters the game, the contest is forfeited to the other team.

EQUIPMENT

The ball is smooth-seamed, flat-surfaced, and pebble or dimple-textured, with concealed stitches. Its core is cork, rubber, or a polyurethane mix, covered with horsehide or cowhide. The 11-inch ball weighs between 5.9 and 6.1 ounces. The 12-inch ball weighs between 6.25 and 7.00 ounces.

The bat is made of hardwood, metal, graphite, or other approved material. It may not be longer than 34 inches or weigh more than 38 ounces. It may not exceed 2.25 inches in diameter. A safety grip must be between 10 and 15 inches long and must not extend more than 15 inches from the bottom of the bat. Metal bats may be angular.

Gloves may be worn by any player, but only the catcher and first baseman may wear mitts, with thumb and body sections. Webbing on any glove or mitt may not exceed 5 inches. Pants, sliding pants, and shirts should be of the same design. Caps are optional; if they are worn, they must be of the same design. Exposed jewelry may not be worn. Shoes may have soft or hard rubber cleats or be smooth. In adult play, metal soles or heel plates may be used if the spikes do not extend more than 0.75 inch. Shoes with round metal spikes are illegal.

RULES

The bulk of this chapter focuses on slowpitch rules. Most of these rules also apply to fastpitch and 16-inch slowpitch; for differences, see the "Modifications" section. The basics of softball are found in the rules for pitching, batting, base running, runners advancing safely, runners being put out, and recording wins.

Pitching

The pitcher must come to a complete stop for at least 1 second while facing the batter and then release the ball within 10 seconds. One foot must be in contact with the pitcher's plate throughout the delivery. A pitcher may use any continuous windup but must deliver the ball on the first forward swing of the arm past the hip and toward home plate. All pitches must be thrown underhand and must reach an arc between 6 and 12 feet high. The pitcher may not continue her windup after releasing the ball.

At the beginning of each half inning, and when a relief pitcher enters the game, the pitcher has 1 minute to complete no more than three warm-up pitches. A team manager may go out to the pitcher's mound for a conference with the pitcher, but the pitcher must be removed on the second conference in an inning. Shouting instructions from the bench is not considered a conference. A starting pitcher is credited with a win when she has pitched at least four innings and her team has a lead that it does not give up when she leaves the game. In a game shortened to five innings, the pitcher must pitch at least three innings to be credited with a victory. A pitcher is charged with a loss when he leaves the game with his team trailing and his team fails to tie the score or gain the lead.

An umpire calls "no pitch" when play is suspended, when a runner leaves his base before the pitch reaches home or is hit, when a runner has not yet retouched her base after a foul or dead ball, or when the ball slips from the pitcher's hand during his windup or backswing.

Batting

Players must hit in the batting order on their lineup card. The batter must stand in the batter's box (the lines are part of the box); no part of her feet may be outside the lines. The batter may not hinder the catcher from throwing while standing in the batter's box.

Batter Out

A batter is out when he swings and misses at a third strike or fouls a third strike; when his fair or foul fly ball is caught in the air by a fielder; when, on a ground ball, a defensive player who possesses the ball touches first base before he does; or when he switches boxes after the pitcher begins to pitch.

A batter is also out when he has an entire foot on the ground out of the batter's box and he hits a fair or foul ball; when any part of his foot touches home plate and he hits a fair or foul ball; when he is caught using an illegal or altered bat; or when he bunts or chops the ball. Other instances in which batters are out include these:

- After the batter hits the ball in fair territory, the bat strikes the ball again (unless the umpire rules this contact was unintentional).

- A batted ball in fair territory strikes the batter outside of the batter's box.

- A base runner interferes with a fielder before the batter reaches first base.

- The batter-runner runs outside the 3-foot lane after hitting a fair ball and interferes with the fielder taking the throw at first base. (The batter-runner may, however, run outside the 3-foot lane to avoid a fielder attempting to field a ball.)

- The batter-runner interferes with a fielder attempting to field the ball.

- The batter-runner rounds first base on a hit, turns toward second, and is tagged.

Base Running

A base runner must touch the bases in legal order. A runner is entitled to an unoccupied base if she reaches it before she is put out. Two runners may not occupy the same base. The runner who arrives first is entitled to the base, unless forced to advance; the other runner may be tagged out with the ball. If the first runner was forced to advance, she may be tagged out.

A run does not count if the third out is made by the batter, by a runner being forced out at a base, or by a runner being tagged out before another runner touches home plate.

A runner must tag up before advancing on a caught fly ball. The runner may not leave her base until the ball is touched by the fielder. In slowpitch play, a runner may not steal. A runner hit by a batted ball is out unless she is on a base when the ball hits her. If the closest defensive player is in front of the base the runner is on, the ball is live. If the closest defender is behind the base, the ball is dead.

Runner Advancement

A runner may advance, without the risk of being put out, when he is forced to vacate a base because the batter is walked, when a fielder is called for obstructing the runner, when the ball is overthrown (runners advance two bases from where they were when the ball left the thrower's hand), and when the ball is blocked by equipment not involved in the game (unless it is blocked by the offensive team's equipment, in which case the runner closest to home is called out).

Other situations in which runners may advance without the risk of being put out include when the batter hits an over-the-fence home run, when the batter hits a ground-rule double, when a fielder unintentionally carries a live ball into dead-ball territory (one base), or when a fielder intentionally causes a live ball to go into dead-ball territory (two bases).

A runner may advance but risks being put out, when the batter hits the ball, when a fly ball is first touched, or when a fair ball strikes the umpire or another runner after having passed an infielder other than the pitcher.

A runner must return to his base when the batter hits a foul ball, when an illegal hit is declared by the umpire, when the batter or another runner is called for interference, when a pitch is not hit by the batter, or when the umpire rules that a fielder intentionally dropped a ball.

Runner Out

The runner is out when she runs out of the baseline to avoid being tagged out; when she is tagged with a live ball while not on a base; when a fielder in possession of the ball touches the base to which the runner is forced to advance; when she passes a runner ahead of her; when she leaves her base before a caught fly ball is first touched and the play is appealed; or when she misses a base and the play is appealed.

A runner is also out when she interferes with a fielder trying to field or throw a ball; when she is hit by a batted ball while not on base; when she purposely kicks the ball or runs the bases backward to confuse the defense; or when the third-base coach runs toward home to draw a throw (the runner closest to home is out).

In addition, a runner is out when a coach or team member intentionally interferes with a thrown ball while in the coach's box; when the runner stays on her feet and deliberately crashes into a fielder who has the ball; when she leaves her base before the pitch reaches home plate, touches the ground, or is hit; or when she doesn't return immediately to her base when the pitcher receives the ball after a pitch while in the 8-foot radius of the pitcher's mound (fastpitch only).

Runner Safe

A runner is not out when he runs out of the baseline to avoid interfering with a fielder; when he is hit by a fair, untouched batted ball and the umpire rules that no fielder had a chance to make an out; when he cannot avoid contact with a fair ball that is touched by any fielder; when he is tagged with a ball that is not held securely by the fielder; and when he overruns first base and returns to the base without turning toward second base.

In addition, a runner is not out when he is on base while hit by a batted ball or when he dislodges a base while sliding into it.

Recording a Win

A win may be recorded in a variety of ways:

- Seven-inning win for the visitors: If the visitors are ahead after seven complete innings, the game is over.
- Seven-inning win for the home team: If the home team is ahead after the visitors bat in the top half of the seventh inning, the game is over; if the home team scores the winning run in the bottom of the seventh, the game is over when the run scores.
- Extra-inning victory: A game tied at the end of seven innings goes into extra innings and is played until one team has scored more than the other at the end of a complete inning or until the home team scores the winning run.
- Shortened game: A game stopped by rain or darkness or for other reasons is considered complete if after five innings one team has scored more runs than the other team. The game is considered complete if after four and a half innings the home team has scored more runs than the visitors.
- Forfeit: The umpire may call a forfeit for a number of reasons, which include a team's failing to show up or refusing to begin a game, noticeably delaying or hastening the game, or willfully breaking the rules. If an ejected player does not leave within 1 minute, that, too, is reason to call a forfeit. The score of a forfeited game is always 7-0.

TERMS

Note: The following list includes terms that are specific to fastpitch as well as slowpitch.

An **altered bat** is illegal. This includes inserting material inside the bat, applying more than two layers of tape to the grip, or attaching a "flare" or "cone" grip to the bat.

An **appeal play** is one in which the umpire does not have to make a decision unless requested by a coach or player. The appeal must be made before the next pitch or before the pitcher and infielders have crossed the foul line on their way to the bench.

An **assist** is credited to a fielder when her throw leads to the putout of a runner. Two or more fielders can receive assists on the same play.

A batter is credited with a **base hit** (single) when he reaches first base safely on a hit without the aid of an *error*, a fielder's choice, or a force play at another base.

A batter receives a **base on balls** when the umpire calls four pitches "balls" (outside the strike zone and not swung at by the batter). This allows the batter to reach first base safely. In slowpitch, the pitcher can notify the umpire if he wants to issue an intentional base on balls (also called a *walk*); the batter then may go to first base without getting any pitches.

The **base path** extends 3 feet on either side of a direct line between bases. A runner is out when she runs outside the base path, except to avoid interfering with a fielder fielding a batted ball.

A **catch** means a fielder has secured the ball with his hands or glove. Regarding a catch that results in a putout—such as an outfielder catching a fly ball or a first baseman catching a throw on a force out from an infielder—the catch is good if the player has complete control of the ball but then drops it in the act of removing it from his glove or throwing it. A fly ball is not considered caught if the fielder simultaneously falls or collides with another player or the fence and the ball is dislodged.

A **chopped ball** occurs in slowpitch when the batter strikes the ball downward to bounce the ball high in the air intentionally. This is illegal and the batter is ruled out.

A **crow hop** is executed in fastpitch play by a pitcher who steps or hops off the front of the pitcher's plate, replants her pivot foot, and pushes off from this new starting point as she completes her delivery.

A **dead ball** is a ball that is not in play. A **delayed dead ball** remains live until the play is finished; at that point the proper call is made. A delayed dead ball may be called for an illegal pitch, catcher's obstruction, plate umpire interference, obstruction, or a batted or thrown ball hit with detached equipment.

A **double** is a hit in which the batter safely reaches second base.

A **double play** is recorded by the defense when two outs are made on the same play.

An **error** is charged to a fielder who misplays a ball (e.g., dropping a fly ball or throw, or fumbling a ground ball), thus prolonging an at bat for the batter or the life of a base runner, or permitting a runner to advance one or more bases. An error may be charged even if the fielder does not touch the ball (e.g., for a ground ball that goes between the legs).

Fair territory and **foul territory** are marked by two foul lines. Each line extends from home plate. One line creates a third baseline and left field line, stopping at the left field fence; the other creates a first baseline and right field line, stopping at the right field fence. Anything on or in between the foul lines is considered fair territory; anything outside the foul lines is considered foul territory.

A **fake tag** is a form of obstruction of a runner by a fielder who neither has the ball nor is about to receive it. The umpire awards the runner the base he would have made, in the umpire's judgment, had the obstruction not occurred.

A **force play** occurs when a runner is forced to advance to the next base because the batter becomes a runner. When a batter hits a ground ball with a runner on first, the runner is forced to run to second. If a fielder touches second base with the ball in her possession before the runner reaches second, the runner is "forced out" at second. If a runner is on second when a ground ball is hit, she is not forced to advance if first base is unoccupied.

A **foul ball** is any ball hit into foul territory.

A **ground-rule double** is awarded a batter when his fair ball bounces over or passes through or under the outfield fence.

A **home run** is recorded when a batter hits a fair ball over the fence or circles the bases on an inside-the-park hit without being thrown out.

An **illegally batted ball** occurs when a ball is hit and the batter's entire foot is on the ground completely outside the lines of the batter's box, or when any part of the foot is touching home plate. It also occurs when an illegal bat is used.

The **infield** refers to that portion of the field containing the four bases. In terms of players, the infield is made up of the first, second, and third basemen and the shortstop. The pitcher and the catcher (called the *battery*) are also positioned in the infield.

The **infield fly rule** prohibits an infielder from intentionally dropping a fair fly ball that can be caught with normal effort. This rule is in effect with either first and second or first, second, and third bases occupied before two are out. When an umpire calls an infield fly rule, the batter is automatically out and runners may advance at their own risk. Any defensive player positioned in the infield at the start of the play is considered an infielder for the purpose of this rule.

Interference occurs when an offensive player impedes or confuses a defensive player as he is trying to make a play. Interference can be physical or verbal. Defensive players must be given the chance to play the ball. In fastpitch, a batter may be called for interference if he impedes the catcher in his throw on an attempted steal. A base runner may be called for interference if he is hit by a batted ball while he is not on a base and the ball has not passed an infielder, excluding the pitcher. It is not interference, however, if the batted ball was first touched by a defensive player or if no infielder had a chance to make an out on the ball.

A runner may **lead off** a base in fastpitch once the ball has left the pitcher's hand. In slowpitch, a runner may not leave her base until the ball is batted, touches the ground, or reaches home plate, and she must return to her base if the ball is not hit.

Leaping is the term used in fastpitch when the pitcher goes airborne as he delivers the ball. With this delivery, the ball is released as the pitcher's feet return to the ground. This is legal in men's fastpitch but illegal in women's fastpitch.

A **legal touch**, resulting in an out, is made by a defensive player who tags a runner with the ball while the runner is not on a base. The ball may not be juggled or dropped by the fielder, unless the runner knocks the ball from the fielder's hands or glove after the tag.

A defensive player may be called for **obstruction** if she hinders a batter from hitting the ball or impedes a base runner while the fielder does not have the ball and is not about to receive the ball.

An **out** may be recorded in a variety of ways, including strikeout, force out, tag out, and fly out.

The **outfield** is that portion of fair territory between the infield and the fence. In terms of players, the outfield consists of the left fielder, the center fielder, the right fielder, and, in slowpitch, an extra fielder.

A batter-runner may **over-slide** first base and not be put out, but a runner over-sliding second or third base is in jeopardy of being tagged out.

In fastpitch, a **passed ball** is charged to the catcher when she fails to control a pitch that should have been caught or contained with normal effort and a base runner or base runners advance.

A **quick return pitch** is one made by a pitcher before the batter is set.

A batter is credited with the appropriate number of **runs batted in (RBIs)** when his hit is responsible for one or more runners scoring. RBIs are not tallied for runs scored as a result of errors or if a run scores as the batter grounds into a double play.

A **sacrifice fly** is credited to a batter whose caught fly ball results in a runner on third base tagging up and scoring. A sacrifice fly does not count as a time at bat. A run must score for a sacrifice fly to be recorded.

In fastpitch, a runner may attempt to **steal** a base during a pitch to the batter. In slowpitch, no stealing is allowed.

A pitched ball is in a batter's **strike zone** when it is over any part of home plate between her armpits and the top of her knees in fastpitch play, or between her back shoulder and front knee in slowpitch play.

A batter is credited with a **triple** when he reaches third base safely on his hit.

A **triple play** is credited to the defense when it records three outs on the same play.

In fastpitch, a **wild pitch** occurs when a pitch eludes the catcher, allowing one or more runners to advance a base. A wild pitch is judged to be the pitcher's fault, not the catcher's. A ball that bounces in the dirt and allows any base runners to advance is automatically a wild pitch.

OFFICIALS

Umpires govern the game of softball. The home plate umpire stands behind the catcher. She controls the game and calls balls and strikes. She also calls plays involving the batter, fair and foul balls, and plays at the plate. The base umpire assists the home plate umpire in making calls and makes decisions at the bases. See figure 46.2 for officials' signals.

MODIFICATIONS

The following modifications explain some of the major differences between the rules just presented and the rules for fastpitch, 16-inch slowpitch, coed, and senior play.

Fastpitch

A team has nine players, with an optional designated player (DP) who can hit for one of the nine players. If the DP plays defense for the player he's hitting for, that player is considered to have left the game. The DP can play defense for any other player, and that player can still hit. Other differences include the following:

▪ Pitching: The pitcher's hand may go past his hip twice if there are not two complete revo-

Timeout

Strike

Player is out

Runner is safe

▶ **Figure 46.2** Common officials' signals in softball.

lutions in the windup. In men's and boys' Junior Olympic competition, the pitcher needs to have only one foot in contact with the pitcher's plate. In women's and girls' Junior Olympic competition, both feet must be in contact with the pitcher's plate.

▪ One step must be taken forward in releasing the ball. Male adult and Junior Olympic pitchers may have both feet in the air during this step. Female adult and Junior Olympic pitchers must drag the foot or push off the pitcher's plate with the pivot foot; the leap is not legal in female competition. For both males and females, the delivery is underhanded, with the hand below the hip and the wrist not farther from the body than the elbow.

▪ After the pitcher has taken her position, she may not throw to a base without stepping back off the pitcher's plate before throwing. Failure to step

off the pitcher's plate results in a ball being called and any runners advancing one base. "No pitch" is called when the umpire judges that the pitcher is trying to "quick pitch" a batter who is not set.

▪ Ball in play: The ball is in play when a ball or strike is called. The ball is also live during an intentional walk.

▪ Batter safe: A batter is not out on a third strike that is a foul ball, unless it is a bunt. A batter hit by a pitch—even if it bounces—that is not a strike and that he tries to elude is awarded first base.

▪ Third strike: In Junior Olympic 10-and-under play, the batter is out on the third strike, whether or not the ball is caught.

▪ Base running: Runners must maintain contact with their bases until the ball leaves the pitcher's hand or they will be called out. Stealing is allowed at all levels except for Junior Olympic 10 and under. In Junior Olympic 10 and under, runners may leave base when the ball leaves the pitcher's hand but must return to the base if the ball is not hit.

▪ A runner off her base after a pitch must advance immediately to the next base or return to her base once the pitcher has the ball within the 8-foot circle. Failure to do so results in her being called out.

▪ Runners advance one base when the umpire calls an illegal pitch. On a wild pitch or passed ball lodged in or under the backstop, runners are entitled to advance one base.

▪ Breaking ties: In Junior Olympic girls' and women's fastpitch, if the score is tied after nine innings, the offensive team begins its half inning with the batter who had made the last out in the previous inning placed on second base.

16-Inch Slowpitch

A strike is live, but runners cannot advance. Runners may lead off their bases, but they risk being picked off by the pitcher or catcher. (A pickoff attempt occurs when the pitcher or catcher throws the ball to a defensive player near the runner in an effort to tag the runner while she is off the base.) Runners may not advance on an overthrown pickoff attempt.

Coed

The lineup consists of five males and five females, batting in alternating order. Two males and two females play in both the infield and the outfield; one male and one female split duties as pitcher and catcher. The lineups can also have two EPs, one male and one female. Any 10 players may play defense if the proper mix is kept. If a male batter is walked, whether intentionally or not, the next female batter has the option of walking also. The 11-inch ball is pitched to women; the 12-inch ball is pitched to men.

Senior

One or two EPs may be used. Unlimited courtesy runners are allowed; any player in the batting order may be used as a runner. A player may be used as a courtesy runner only once an inning; if it's his time at bat and he is on base, he is called out. A second home plate is placed 8 feet from the back tip of home plate, on the first baseline extended. Runners must touch this second home plate to score. If the runner touches the original home plate, he may be called out on an appeal play. Once a runner crosses a line 20 feet from home plate, he may not return to third base. He will be called out if he does so. A runner may be put out at home in a nonforce situation without being tagged; if a defensive player steps on the original home plate while holding the ball before the runner touches the second home plate, the runner is out.

ORGANIZATIONS

World Baseball Softball Confederation
Maison du Sport International
Avenue de Rhodanie 54
CH-1007 Lausanne
Switzerland
41-21-318-8240
www.wbsc.org

National Softball Association
P.O. Box 7
Nicholasville, KY 40340
859-887-4114
www.playnsa.com

USA Softball
2801 NE 50th St.
Oklahoma City, OK 73111
405-424-5266
www.usasoftball.org

47

Speed Skating

Photodisc

Ice skates used for hunting and made of wood, bone, antlers, and leather straps first appeared in Europe in the 4th century. Iron skates were crafted in Scotland in 1572, and competitions began to take place soon after that, with racing becoming more popular across Europe in the 18th century. In 1850, the first all-steel skates were made in America, and in 1889 the Netherlands hosted the first world championships. Speed skating events for men became part of the first Winter Olympics in 1924; women began Olympic competition in 1960.

OVERVIEW

Objective: To skate the fastest time.

Competitors: The number of skaters in a competition varies from two to large packs, depending on the race.

Distances: Ranges from 500 to 5,000 meters for short track and 500 to 10,000 meters for long track, with longer distances for marathon events.

Skaters compete in *short-track* events, *long-track* events, *relays*, and *marathons*. Skaters compete in pack-style racing in groups of four to eight skaters, where the first skater who crosses the finish line wins the race, or in long-track metric style (Olympic) head-to-head racing, where the best time of all competitors in a distance is the winner.

Olympic-style, long-track speed skaters reach speeds exceeding 40 miles per hour; short-track speed skaters lean into the turns at a 65-degree angle to maintain speeds of up to 35 miles per hour. The world record for 10,000 meters is 27.6 miles per hour. Skaters also compete in relay and marathon competitions.

RINK

A short-track course is a 111.12-meter oval within an Olympic-sized hockey rink (30 by 60 meters). A long-track course is a 400-meter oval. Survey lines (or points) define track lanes (see figure 47.1). Lines are blocks set on the ice for long track. The skater's path is considered to be 0.5 meter outside

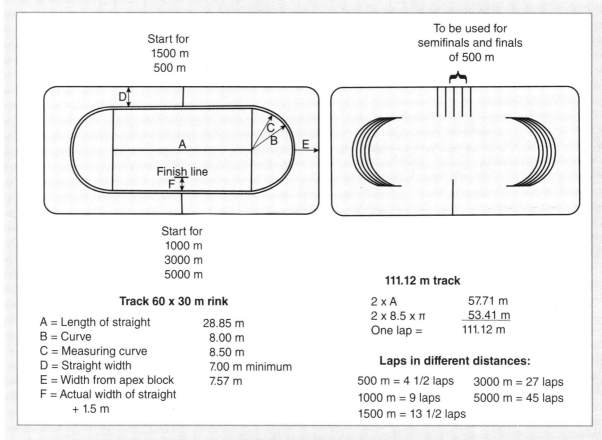

▶ **Figure 47.1** The dimensions and features of a speed skating rink.

the survey line. This path is used in determining the distance.

The tracks have start and finish lines marked in the ice. Long-track courses also have a fall-down mark 10 meters beyond the starting line. Short-track courses have safety padding covering the walls all the way around both ends of the rink.

SKATERS

Skaters compete in age classes:

- Junior E: 9 to 10
- Junior D 11 to 12
- Junior C: 13 to 14
- Junior B: 15 to 16
- Junior A: 17 to 18
- Neo-senior: 19 to 20
- Senior: 21+

EQUIPMENT

In short track, skaters wear safety helmets, shin guards, neck protection, gloves, and skates. There are no requirements for skates, but the boots are usually made of leather and composite materials and have steel blades 12 to 18 inches long. Long-track skates have light, low-cut boots with thin blades that are only slightly curved on the bottom and not fixed on the boot of the skate. These allow for longer pushes and are called clap-skates. Short-track skates have sturdy, high-cut boots with thicker, adjustable blades that have more curvature on the bottom to negotiate the sharper turns and more pronounced leans. Short track skaters are required to wear cut resistant suits under their team suits. Finally, for mass start events in long track, the same protective equipment is required as in short track, including the cut resistant suit.

RULES

If a skater falls within the first 10 meters of a long-track race or in the apex of the corner in a short-track race, the starter may recall the race with a second shot. If the fall was not caused by interference and does not impede other skaters, the starter won't recall the race. Falls are not called back in metric-style racing.

A skater may make one false start, after which the race is restarted. If a second false start is made, the racer is disqualified from that event. In pack style, competitors may not cross to the inner edge of the track unless they can do so without interfering with other skaters. Skaters must skate in a straight line once they enter the homestretch unless they can change lanes without interfering with another skater.

In metric-style racing, the skater who starts on the inner track changes to the outer track at the crossing straight, and the skater who started on the outer track changes to the inner one. The change in tracks occurs each time the skaters come to the crossing straight. The skater coming from the inner track may not hinder the skater coming from the outer track on the crossing straight.

In long-track races, a skater with inside or pole position must be passed on the right side unless the skater leaves enough room on the left for a skater to pass. It is the responsibility of the skater who is passing to avoid a collision, although the skater being passed may not act improperly and intentionally cause a collision. In short-track races, skaters may pass on the left or right side. Again, the responsibility for avoiding a collision falls on the passing skater. Skaters may be disqualified for

- impeding, charging, or pushing another skater;
- skating inside the corner markers;
- endangering other skaters by kicking out one's blade or throwing one's body across the finish line;
- unsporting conduct, including foul language and fighting; and
- loafing, competing to lose, or coaching during a race.

TERMS

Assistance is a foul called when a skater gives or receives assistance during a race. This does not apply to relay races.

Impeding is a foul called in short-track speed skating when a skater deliberately impedes, charges, or pushes another competitor with any part of the body.

Kicking out is a foul called when a skater deliberately kicks out his skate, thereby causing danger. This includes kicking out at the finish line and throwing the body across the finish line.

Off track is a foul called when a skater shortens the distance to be skated with one or both skates on the left side of the curve, which is marked by track-marking blocks.

OFFICIALS

Large competitions include a chief referee, assistant referees, competitor stewards, starters, finish judges, timers, scorers, and a lap counter. The chief referee has overall authority, including deciding all protests.

MODIFICATIONS

Speed skating events include the following:

　Short track: Individual and relay events are contested on a 111.12-meter track. In individual events, four to eight skaters (the pack) start on the line; the first to cross the finish line with the leading tip of her skate blade wins. International distances for individual competitions are 500 meters, 1,000 meters, and 1,500 meters for both men and women.

　Long track: Events are contested on a 400-meter oval using one of two formats: metric (also known as Olympic style) or pack style. In metric style, two skaters compete at a time, in separate lanes, racing against the clock; the distances are 500 meters, 1,000 meters, 1,500 meters, 5,000 meters, and 10,000 meters for men and 500 meters, 1,000 meters, 1,500 meters, 3,000 meters, and 5,000 meters for women. In pack style, up to eight skaters compete at once; they are not confined to lanes, and they can use drafting and race strategies.

　Relay: Teams of four skaters compete at varying distances; the national championship distance is 3,000 meters for women and 5,000 meters for men. Each member must take part in the race. A skater finishing a portion must touch the team member who is taking over. Relay exchanges may take place at any time except during the final two laps.

　Marathon: These events are contested over distances of 25 kilometers and 50 kilometers.

ORGANIZATIONS

International Skating Union
Avenue Juste-Oliver 172
CH-1006 Lausanne
Switzerland
www.isu.org

Speed Skating Canada
House of Sport – RA Centre
2451 Riverside Dr.
Ottawa, ON K1H 7X7
613-260-3669
www.speedskating.ca

U.S. Speedskating
5662 South Cougar Lane
Kearns, UT 84118
801-417-5360
www.teamusa.org/US-Speedskating

Squash

Fuse/Corbis/Getty Images

Variations of squash originated in England in the early 1800s when the use of a softer ball—one that could be "squashed" by a racket— gave rise to the game's name. Squash was introduced to the United States in the 1880s. There are two versions of the game: one using a soft ball and one using a hard ball and a smaller court. The international version is played with the soft ball; the American version—played also in parts of Canada and Mexico—uses a hard ball, although in the 1990s the soft ball gained in popularity in the United States, with more than 95 percent of the games in the United States being played with the soft ball.

Squash's popularity has spread to many countries—it is now played by 20 million people in more than 185 countries. Recently the game has increased in popularity in South America, eastern Europe, the Far East, and especially in the United States, where participation has grown by 66 percent since 2010 to a total of 1.71 million players.

There are two types of squash courts (International and American) and two types of squash match (singles and doubles). Squash on an international court is played with a soft ball, and squash on an American court is played with a hard ball. This chapter will cover only the rules of soft ball singles, because of its overwhelming popularity. Although the court is considered to be an International squash court, it is still the predominant court and squash type played in the United States.

OVERVIEW

Objective: To win rallies and ultimately the game by scoring more points than the opponent.

Number of Players: Two players (1 vs 1) is by far the dominant way the game is played. Doubles is occasionally played on a different-size court.

Scoring: Soft-ball singles currently uses the point-a-rally (PAR) scoring system. Under this scoring system, the winner of a rally scores 1 point and then serves to begin the next rally. Each game is played to 11 points. The player who scores 11 points first wins the game except that if the score reaches 10-10, the game continues until one player wins by two points. Either

player may score points. Match: A match is the best of five games, or best of three.

Players hit a small rubber ball against the front wall, above the tin and within the out-of-court lines, attempting to score points by hitting the ball in such a way that the opponent cannot return it before it bounces twice. When a good serve is delivered, the opponent tries to return the serve. Play is continuous throughout the game, except for equipment changes approved by the referee or for injury. There is a 90-second break between games.

COURT

The dimensions and markings of a squash court are shown in figure 48.1. The court is 21 feet wide by 32 feet long. The short line is 18 feet from the front wall.

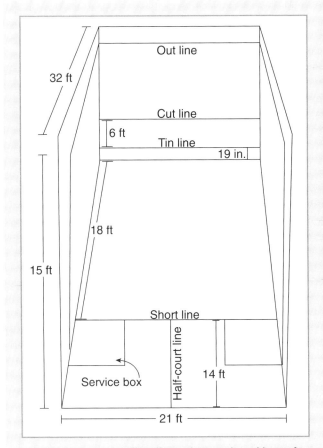

▶ **Figure 48.1** The dimensions and markings of a soft-ball squash court.

PLAYERS

Players may only be coached only during the 90-second breaks between games. A referee may penalize any behavior deemed to be offensive or intimidating. This may include obscene language and gestures, abuse of racquet or ball, arguing with the marker or referee, unnecessary physical contact, excessive racket swing, and dangerous play. It is recommended that all squash players wear protective eyewear.

EQUIPMENT

The ball has a diameter of 1.56 to 1.59 inches and weighs 0.8 to 0.9 ounce (23-25 grams). It is made of rubber or butyl, or a combination; it's hollow and, appropriately enough, "squashy." Racquets are commonly made from titanium and graphite composites. They may be no more than 27 inches long and 8.5 inches wide with a maximum strung area of 77.5 square inches and a maximum weight of 9 ounces (255 grams).

RULES

The fundamental rules of squash are found in its rules for serving and for playing out rallies.

Serving

At the beginning of each and when the service changes from one player to another, the server may choose to serve from either service box (see figure 48.1). Part of one foot must be on the floor in the service box, with no part of the foot touching the service box line, when the server strikes the ball. The server throws the ball in the air to begin the serve. The served ball may not hit any surface before striking the front wall. It must strike the front wall between the service line and the outline so that it reaches the floor within the quarter court opposite the server's box (unless volleyed by the opponent).

A server continues to serve until he loses a rally. As long as he holds serve, he alternates boxes. If a rally ends in a let (an undecided point), he serves again from the same service box.

When the receiving player wins a point, they become the server and may choose which service box to serve from. At the beginning of the second and subsequent games, the winner of the previous game serves first. A server loses the point if the serve is not successful. A serve is deemed to be out when

- the serve hits a side wall, floor, or ceiling before reaching the front wall;
- the server's foot is not on the floor in the server's box, with no part of that foot on the box line when the server strikes the ball; or
- the ball bounces on or outside the short or half-court line of the quarter court opposite the service box.

A serve is also lost when a server

- tries and fails to make contact with the ball,
- does not strike the ball correctly (e.g., hits the ball more than once or carries the ball with the racquet),
- serves the ball out,
- serves onto or below the service line, or
- is struck by her own serve before the opponent can strike at it.

Rallies

A good serve may be returned before the ball strikes the ground or after it bounces once. It must hit the front wall above the tin before touching the ground. It may not touch any part of the striker's body or clothing or any part of the opponent's body, clothing, or racket.

If a striker hits an opponent with the ball, the striker wins the point if the return would have struck the front wall, within the boundaries of the court, without first touching any other surface.

If a striker hits an opponent with the ball, and the ball would have hit the side wall before reaching the front wall, a let is played (replay the point). In both cases, if the striker hit his opponent with the ball and the referee determines that the return would not have been good, the striker loses the rally.

A striker may make contact with the squash ball only once on a return but may make any number of attempts to hit the ball before it bounces twice. If a striker swings at and misses a ball which then hits the opponent, her clothing, or her racket, the referee will call a let if he believes the striker could have made a good return. The striker loses the rally if the referee believes she could not have made a good return.

A player who hits the ball must try to provide his opponent with unobstructed direct access to the ball, a fair view of the ball, space to complete a swing at the ball, and freedom to play the ball directly to any part of the front wall. The player retrieving a ball must also make every effort to get to the ball.

At any time during a rally, a striker who believes that interference has occurred may stop and request a let by saying, "Let, please." That request must be made without undue delay. The referee then decides on the request by awarding the striker a let, stroke, or no let.

A player, finding his opponent interfering with the play, can accept the interference and play on, or stop the rally. It is preferable to stop play if there is a possibility of colliding with the opponent or of hitting the opponent with the racquet or ball. If the player retrieving a ball stops play due to interference, the referee will decide to play a let stroke or no let. The player attempting to retrieve the ball is entitled to a let (replay the point) if he or she could have returned the ball and the opponent has made every effort to avoid the interference. The player attempting to retrieve the ball receives a no let (loses point) if he or she would have been unable to retrieve the ball, played through the interference, or if the interference was so minimal that the player's access to the ball was not affected. The player attempting to retrieve the ball is awarded a stroke (wins the point) if the opponent did not make every effort to avoid the interference, if the retrieving player would have hit a winning return, or if the retrieving player would have struck the opponent with the ball going directly to the front wall.

A let is always allowed if one player refrains from striking the ball because of a reasonable fear of striking her opponent with the ball or with the racket. This is the case even if no interference actually occurred.

In addition to previous mentions of lets, rallies may be replayed when

- the striker doesn't hit the ball in order to ensure the safety of his opponent,
- a player is distracted by an occurrence on or off the court,

- the receiver is not ready for the serve and doesn't try to return it,
- the ball breaks during play, or
- court conditions affect play.

TERMS

Down is the expression used when a shot strikes the tin or fails to reach the front wall.

Game ball means that the server needs 1 point to win the game.

The **half-court line** runs parallel to the side walls, dividing the court into two equal parts, intersecting the short line to form a T.

A **handout** means that the serve is changing hands.

Match ball means that the server needs 1 point to win the match.

Not up is the term used when the ball has not been struck according to the rules.

The **out line** is a continuous line comprising the front wall line, both side wall lines, and the back wall line. This line marks the top boundaries of the court. Unlike in tennis, if the ball touches any part of the line, it is considered out. If there are no side wall or back wall lines, the boundaries are the tops of the walls. If a ball strikes part of the horizontal top surface of such an unlined wall, it is out, even if it rebounds into the court.

A **quarter court** is one-half of the back part of the court, which is divided into two equal parts by the half-court line.

A **rally** is the play that begins with the serve and ends when the ball is no longer in play.

A **service box** is in each quarter court, bounded by the side wall, the short line, and two other lines. The server serves from this box.

The **service line** is a horizontal line across the front wall 6 feet above the floor.

The **short line** is parallel to and 18 feet from the front wall.

The **striker** is the player whose turn it is to hit the ball.

A **stroke** is gained by the player who wins a rally because of interference. A stroke results in either a point scored for the server or a change of hand.

The **tin** is between the board and the floor, running the length of the floor. It makes a distinctive noise when the ball hits it. It is 19 inches tall (17 inches in professional matches).

OFFICIALS

A referee controls the match, sometimes assisted by a marker. The referee makes all major calls and decisions; the marker calls the play, calls the score, and calls faults, downs, outs, and handouts.

ORGANIZATIONS

U.S. Squash
555 8th Ave., Ste. 1102
New York, NY 10018-4311
212-268-4090
www.ussquash.com

World Squash Federation
25 Russell St., Hastings
East Sussex, TN34 1QU
United Kingdom
44-01424-447440
www.worldsquash.org

Stand Up Paddle Boarding

Cameron Spencer/Getty Images

Stand up paddle boarding, more commonly known as SUPing, is one of the fastest-growing sports among water enthusiasts globally, and it narrowly missed being added to the 2020 Summer Olympics. Many cultures around the globe have used similar styles of paddling watercraft such as canoes, rafts, and boards for centuries, but there is no doubt that SUPing has its roots in surfing. Today's style of stand up paddle boarding can be attributed to Duke Kahanamoku, as can much of modern surfing, and his compatriot Bobby Ah Choy, who used this style of stand up paddling to get a better vantage point to see incoming swells. Today SUPing contains many different styles from traditional wave riding, racing, and downwinding. The basic components of SUPing have remained the same: a surf-style "watercraft," as defined by the U.S. Coast Guard, and a single-bladed paddle used to push the board through the water. This differs from more traditional prone paddle boarding or surfing because of this second component, the paddle.

OVERVIEW

Objective: Cover the prescribed distance (short or long course, or elite) in the race format (surf slalom, triangle, downwind, or out-and-back) faster than the other competitors. While there are some SUPing competitions related to wave riding, the more common competitions involve racing.

Length of Course: Varies from two to five-plus miles, based on course setup and the experience levels of competitors.

COURSE

In addition to class, which primarily affects the equipment participants can use, races are organized by skill level. Skill levels are determined by the participants' past results in SUP races: short course (2-4 miles), long course (5+ miles), and elite or experienced participant races. Short-course participants are typically new or inexperienced racers. Long-course participants are able to navigate more challenging terrain such as waves, currents, and open ocean conditions. Elite and experienced racers have a proven track record in long-course races, have often placed within the top three in short-course races, or have regularly placed within the top 10 in long-course races.

In addition to being classified based on the participants' skills, races occur in four different categories: surf slalom, triangle, downwind, and out-and-back.

Surf Slalom race courses typically take place within the surf zone and require racers to navigate the surf to various buoys placed beyond and within the surf zone.

Triangle races typically require racers to face a headwind, a tailwind, and a side wind, and they can feature multiple loops, depending on the length of each section within the triangle.

Downwind courses usually require participants to travel downwind to a designated location. These races are typically much longer than other races because they do not require racers to head upwind.

Out-and-back races typically require participants to travel upwind or downwind and return in the opposite direction. Race directors may choose to conduct a combination of these race types, depending on conditions, and they are required to provide racers with notice of changes to the course at least 30 minutes before the race.

CLASSES

Races fall into four different classes for both men and women: Unlimited, 14-feet, 12-feet, 6 inches, and Surfboard (12 feet, 2 inches) class. Junior age categories (8 and under, 9 to 11, 12 to 14, and 15 to 18) compete on a board 12 feet, 6 inches and under.

Race directors should offer all of the stated categories in order to provide points for World Paddle Association (WPA) rankings, but they have the option to omit categories depending on factors such as number of entrants, conditions, and length of race.

EQUIPMENT

Equipment may vary depending on class:

SUP Unlimited class, where there are no restrictions beyond using a surf-style watercraft and single-bladed paddle.

SUP 14-feet class, with no restriction on board weight or design but a maximum length of 14 feet.

SUP 12 feet, 6 inches and SUP Surfboard class are similar to SUP 14-foot class in that they both have regulations on size (12 feet, 6 inches and 12 feet, 2 inches, respectively). However, SUP Surfboard class requires that boards must be designed in a surfing style with a nose at least 17 inches wide and 12 inches back from the nose, a 14-inch minimum tail size, and a maximum 5-inch thickness. Board design and shape influence how the board floats and moves through the water.

Other regulations include that multihull boards are not allowed except in the SUP Unlimited class. Center fins must be symmetrical and may not be multipointed (i.e., no hydrofoils) except in the SUP Unlimited class, and rudders are only permitted in specified races.

As of summer 2016, all race participants must use a leash or short cord connecting the participant to his or her watercraft, and a personal flotation device (PFD). PFDs are required due to U.S. Coast Guard regulations, which characterize stand up paddle boards as watercraft. Children under age 13 must wear a PFD at all times while on a watercraft.

Typically, single-bladed paddles resemble paddles that would be used for canoeing but are much longer so they may be used while standing upright on the board.

RULES

Paddlers are given a three minute warning prior to the start of the race. The race director will then start the fastest water craft and there is typically a one minute interval between racers, in order to cut down on start line congestion. Races can have a beach start or a water start. During races, all competitors must be standing while paddling from the start of the race until they cross the finish line. Competitors are not required to stand the entire time; they may sit or kneel to rest, but they may not make forward progress in this position. Competitors may be penalized if they choose to take more than five paddle strokes in a position other than standing. The only exception to this rule is if the competitor must change positions specifically for safety purposes. In addition, the only source of forward momentum during races must come directly from paddling, wind, or waves. Racers may not use any outside force or specific clothing meant to catch wind in order to gain an advantage over other competitors. It is the race director's decision as to whether drafting will be permitted within a race. If drafting is permitted, the racer is considered drafting when they are within 3 meters of another racer. The World Paddle Association suggests that a racer may only draft a competitor in the same board class, gender, and number on a board. A competitor is able to pass another competitor without being penalized, however, the maximum amount of time to draft is one minute.

If a mark or a buoy needs to be moved during the race to ensure a distance is met, all participants must be notified prior to the start of the race, and it must be moved before the first competitor reaches the area.

TERMS

A **watercraft** is any boat or vessel that travels on water.

A **stand up paddle board (SUP)** is characterized as a watercraft by the U.S. Coast Guard.

A **leash** is a short cord used to connect the paddler to his watercraft. These must be worn at all times during competitive events.

A **personal flotation device (PFD)** is a traditional life jacket. Some PFDs have been modified for races and may be carried in a small bag around the racer's waist or attached to the paddle board.

A **center fin** is a long, narrow strip of plastic or fiberglass that is extended beneath the center of the board at the tail. This helps the board to have a forward trajectory in the water and helps to reduce **yaw** or side motion.

A **foil** is a fin that is angled more than 30 degrees perpendicular to the bottom of the board. This provides lift and reduces drag on the board. **Foils** are permitted in SUP Unlimited races but are not permitted in other race types.

A **rudder** is any fin or foil that pivots beneath the board as a means to steer the board. This is typically controlled by the racer from the top of the board.

A **multihull** is defined as more than a single hull, two or more, attached together at the bottom of a board. This includes any board with a concave bottom surface of greater than 2 inches.

Length is measured from the **nose,** or front of the board, to the **tail,** or back of the board.

A **paddle** is a single-bladed shaft with a handle on one end and a wide blade at the other end.

The paddle is used to project the board forward through the water. Typically, paddle lengths are adjustable, and they should be the height of the racer's extended arm at a 90-degree angle upward from her body.

OFFICIALS

Race directors act as officials during SUP races and are regulated by the WPA SUP event rules and guidelines. This includes a variety of requirements, including the submission of applications, obtaining liability insurance, the signing of liability releases by participating competitors, and the submission of race results. In addition to ensuring that races follow general WPA rules and guidelines, race directors are responsible for making sure that the racers' safety is not compromised. This includes providing a minimum of two water safety crafts and one safety boat with at least six safety personnel, one of whom is lifeguard-certified. Directors are responsible for posting results, which should include the race location; time; and racer's age, division, and gender. Race directors are subject to a committee, which is referred to in the event that competitors contest race results. Committees should include three or five people (not four, to avoid tie voting). Race directors must facilitate a prerace meeting with competitors at least 10 minutes before the race. At the meeting, they are required by the WPA to post the following information:

- Race course, times, and award times and the location where results will be posted. Results should include age, gender, board size, and race class (i.e., SUP Surfboard, 12 feet, 6 inches, 14 feet, or SUP Unlimited)
- A copy of the WPA SUP rules and guidelines
- Drafting rules and any other local regulations
- Safety requirements (PFD and leash requirements) and location of race safety boats
- Starting sequence, location, and finishing areas

MODIFICATIONS

There may be general safety modifications based on the region in which the race is held, the race class, and the race age group. Depending on the race class, the distances of races may vary. Typically, the 12 feet, 6 inch class is 4 to 6 miles, 14 feet is 6 to 9 miles, and SUP Unlimited is 6 to 9 or more miles.

ORGANIZATIONS

Stand Up Paddle Athletes Association
http://supathletes.com

World Paddle Association
888-972-4959
info@worldpaddleassociation.com
http://worldpaddleassociation.com

50

Surfing

Warren Bolster/The Image Bank/Getty Images

Surfing, while often claimed by Californians, Australians, and South Americans, undeniably derives its roots from Polynesian culture. The Native Hawaiians practiced surfing on large wooden planks shaped from the koa tree, first documented by Captain Cook in 1778 when he arrived on the Hawaiian Islands as the first Westerner to observe wave riding. Surfing was practiced by royalty and common people alike in Native Hawaiian society. While today surfing is considered primarily a leisure activity, the Native Hawaiians used surfing as a means to stay in peak physical condition and to commune with the ocean. In addition, Native Hawaiians used competitive surfing as a means to resolve conflicts and settle scores of wealth, pride, and love.

Surfing was almost lost with the arrival of white missionaries on the Hawaiian Islands. Christian missionaries associated surfing with pagan practices and quickly went about trying to wipe the practice from Hawaiian culture. Maintained by a small group of dedicated Hawaiians, surfing arrived on the west coast of the United States in the early 1900s and was quickly adopted by groups often considered outsiders. Today, surfing is a global sport and a billion-dollar industry.

Equipment design has changed in recent years. Fourteen- to fifteen-foot wooden boards have given way to shorter boards made of foam and fiberglass that promote buoyancy, maneuverability, and accessibility for a global community of surfers. Given this and other technological advancements—notably the human-made wave pool—surfing was chosen to debut at the 2020 Summer Olympics.

Kelly Slater, one of the most renowned professional surfers in the modern era, once described professional surfing as a combination of gymnastics, dance, and sport. While there are a number of organizations that facilitate surfing competitions, the professionally recognized organization is the International Surfing Association (ISA). The ISA has been in existence since 1964 and includes competitors from 100 countries across five continents.

OVERVIEW

Objective: To reach the highest point total in a field of competitors based on a surfer's two highest-scoring waves.

Scoring: Surfers are judged on their two highest-scoring waves out of 10 to 15 waves caught. See "Judging and Points."

Length of Competition: Heats and finals are 20 to 30 minutes long as chosen by the contest director after consultation with the head judge. Variations to heat times can be made when there isn't enough time to complete an event.

COURSE

The venues for professional surfing events vary from nation to nation. Typically, surfers are given a certain location within a surf break to compete in. This is dependent on the type of wave, such as beach break, reef break, or point break.

EQUIPMENT

Typical surfing equipment consists of a board, a leash, and occasionally a wetsuit, a helmet, and a personal flotation device (PFD). Boards used during world championship events typically feature a tapered nose, a wide beam with a sharp, angled, or curved "rail" or side, and fins located at a tapered tail used for maneuvering the surfboard. For most professional surfing competitions, there is no regulation of board design. During specific competitions, such as longboard, stand up paddle boarding (see chapter 49), kneeboard (must be ridden on knees), or bodyboard (flexible with soft exterior skin, no more than 5 feet long, fins optional), there are board design specifications that must be taken into account. Longboards must be at least 9 feet from nose to tail, with a minimum width of 47 inches. Width is regulated within 12 inches of the nose and tail of the longboard.

RULES

Professional surfing has fewer rules than most high-performance sports, but the rules that are in place help to ensure the safety of the athletes, the fairness of competition, and the promotion of elite surfing.

Flow of Competition

A minimum of 18 inches (0.5 meters) of wave height is needed for surf to be contestable, but on the last day of competition, if there is a lower wave that is rideable, an allowance may be given.

All heats begin from either a designated marshalling area out in the water or from the beach under the contest director's supervision. The marshalling area must be clear of the take-off zone. If a water start is used, competitors have a limited amount of time to paddle out to the marshalling area while staying clear of the heat in progress.

Judges' decisions regarding allowable waves in and around the buffer zone—an area used to separate two podiums (where judges are able to view the wave without obstruction) where no competition is to be held—are final, and no appeal is allowed. Buffer zones should be at least 100 meters wide and limited by lines of sight between a beach flag and a contest buoy set in the water. A surfer may catch a wave in the direction of the podium from near the buffer zone line or in its edge, but if the ride goes into the buffer zone, it is not required to be scored. Any surfing in the wrong podium may result in the participant receiving an interference penalty or a fine or both.

Sirens are used to signal the start (one blast) and finish (two blasts) of each heat. A visual warning and a public-address system warning are given when five minutes remain in a heat.

Judging and Points

Surf competitions are made up of rounds, and each round consists of multiple heats where, depending on location, two to four surfers compete at any given time, with each looking to lock in their two highest-scoring waves. A minimum of 50 percent of surfers in a heat advance to the next round. Heats are typically between 20 and 30 minutes long. Scoring is based on a 10-point scale with a total of 20 possible points available in each heat. Performances are scored by a panel of five judges. To reach a competitor's score for each wave, the highest and lowest scores from the judging panel are omitted, and the three remaining scores are averaged. The two highest-scoring waves are added together to become the participant's heat total.

Judges analyze the commitment, degree of difficulty, innovation, progression, combination, variety, speed, power, and flow of all maneuvers.

Performances are scored on the following scale:

- Poor wave ride: 0.0–1.9
- Fair wave ride: 2.0–3.9
- Average wave ride: 4.0–5.9
- Good wave ride: 6.0–7.9
- Excellent wave ride: 8.0–10.0

Longboard surfing is judged on the same criteria and point-scoring system. Judges determine if the surfer can perform controlled traditional maneuvers with the highest degree of difficulty in the most critical sections of the wave. Judges want to see if the surfer uses the entire board, and nose riding, trimming, and footwork are taken into consideration.

Rankings

Rankings from multiple surf competitions are added together to determine a surfer's placement in the competitive tour. Surfers are awarded points following their events. A surfer's placing and current performance determine the number of points she receives.

Priority

Wave priority is allocated to one person during a heat. The surfer who is given priority has the right of way to catch any wave. Other surfers in the heat are permitted to paddle for and catch the same wave, but only if they do not interfere with the scoring potential of the competitor with priority. A surfer can lose priority by missing the wave or taking off closest to the peak. If two or more surfers catch the same wave, the surfer to make it to the take-off zone first is given priority.

Interference

A surfer who hinders the scoring potential of another surfer who has priority over him receives an interference penalty. In most situations, this means that the penalized surfer's heat score will only consist of the best wave value. If the same surfer interferes twice during a heat, he is disqualified from that heat.

Other Penalties

Surfers may only proceed when the previous heat has ended; otherwise, they face a penalty.

It is considered an advantage if a participant reaches the takeoff area before her competitors. If this occurs, the surfer is banned from riding until the first wave is caught by one of the other competitors.

If a surfer in competition rides a wave out of his designated area, the judges may use their discretion to either score the entire ride or only to score a portion of it. In this situation, the surfer may not protest. Surfers may not ride during other heats, and they may be penalized with a fine or disqualification or both. Waves caught during dead time between heats are not scored, but no penalty or fine is applied.

A competitor is responsible for the number of waves caught. If she has caught more than the maximum number of waves permitted within the time limit, she is penalized for each additional wave caught. A surfer is also penalized if an additional wave clearly deprives another competitor of an available ride.

If a caddy rides a wave, the surfer the caddy is supporting may be penalized. If the caddy interferes with any of the other surfers in any way, interference is charged to the surfer for whom he is caddying.

Heat Restart

If no one catches a wave halfway through a heat, then the head judge can restart the heat.

TERMS

A **barrel** (also known as a **tube**) develops when the wave is hollow when it is breaking.

A **board** is the craft on which a surfer rides waves during competition.

A **break** is the location where waves accumulate and form. They vary based on surf conditions, air conditions (wind), and terrain conditions (such as the ocean floor topography and the depth of the water).

A **buffer zone** is an area of noncompetition between two podiums.

Fins are typically small fiberglass fixtures attached to the bottom of the board to promote stability and maneuverability.

A **floater** is riding over the whitewater back onto the shoulder of the wave.

Hanging five means five toes hang over the nose of the board.

Hanging ten is a maneuver, usually done on a heavy longboard, where the surfer ensures that the wave covers the back of the board. The surfer walks to the front of the board and hangs all 10 toes over the nose of the board.

A **heat** is the amount of time that a surfer is given to compete during a given **round** (finals, semifinals, qualifiers, etc.)

A **leash** is a device used to connect the surfer to the board. This does not allow the feet to remain connected to the board, but it keeps the board from being washed away during a **wipeout** or fall.

A **longboard** is a surfboard with a rounded nose.

Nose riding is a maneuver best performed on head-high waves. The board cuts through the water, and once the surfer is on the front end, the entire board behind becomes submerged beneath the water. The front of the board generates lift to counterbalance the weight of the surfer.

The **peak** is considered the highest point of the wave and is typically the first place where a wave breaks.

Point break refers to the place where a wave breaks as it hits a point of land jutting out from the coastline.

A **team** is a collection of surfers competing for the same nation or organization, depending on the rules of the competition.

Trimming the surfboard occurs when the competitor progressively positions herself on the board to get the most out of the wave.

OFFICIALS

The contest director oversees all judges and contest officials during ISA events. This includes the head judge or judges. All officials for professional surfing competitions are appointed directly by the ISA based on professional, international, and national criteria. While the contest director is responsible for overseeing the event with support from the head judge, enforcing competition rules, and seeding competing surfers, he is not directly responsible for judging individual surfers during heats. It is the responsibility of the head judge and associate judges to score individual surfers during events.

MODIFICATIONS

While most rules and regulations hold true for all world championship events (men's, women's, juniors, boys, and girls) there are some specific modifications, mostly in the form of team size. This is dependent on the individual ISA-sponsored event and location.

In extreme conditions, water caddies may be allowed to help surfers in a defined marshalling area. Once the heat begins, competitors are only permitted to use equipment from their own caddy. No communication is allowed between a competitor and the caddy unless it is a hand signal for an equipment change.

ORGANIZATIONS

International Surfing Association
5580 La Jolla Blvd. #145
La Jolla, CA 92037
858-551-8580
info@isasurf.org
www.isasurf.org

World Surf League (WSL)
www.worldsurfleague.com

European Surfing Federation (ESF)
16 Beacon Estate
Sancreed, Penzance
Cornwall TR20 8QR
United Kingdom
+44-7534-983046
www.eurosurfing.org

Pan American Surf Association
www.pasasurf.org

51

Swimming and Diving

Clive Rose/Getty Images

The origins of swimming as a sport are not known, although swimming championships were first held in Japan in the early 1600s. For a race in London in 1844, England's Swimming Society brought over several American Indians; these Native Americans dominated the race using a style unknown to the English, a style resembling today's freestyle stroke. Swimming has been an Olympic sport since the inception of the modern Olympics in 1896.

Diving as a sport consisted only of what is now known as the forward straight dive until the early 1800s, when Swedish and German gymnasts began performing acrobatic twists, turns, and jumps off the board. Diving became an Olympic sport for men in 1904 and for women in 1912. The United States has long been successful in international competition, although in the 1990s China emerged and has become a dominant force in the sport. Synchronized diving made its debut at the 1995 FINA World Cup in Atlanta, Georgia.

OVERVIEW

Objective: In swimming, the objective is to record the fastest time; in diving, it is to receive the highest score from judges.

Pool Swimming Distances:
Numerous distances, ranging from 50 to 1,500 meters. Open-water swimming was added as an event at the 2008 Summer Olympics. The Olympic competition, conducted separately for men and women, is over a distance of 10 kilometers. At the world championship level there are also 5, 10 and 25 kilometers open water races for both men and women, as well as a 5 kilometers mixed team event.

Diving Heights: Competitions are conducted from 1-meter and 3-meter springboards as well as 10-meter platforms,

which include team and synchronized events, as well.

In swimming, both individual and relay races are contested over varying distances using one stroke or a combination of strokes. Strokes used are the freestyle, backstroke, breaststroke, and butterfly. In team competitions, swimmers earn points for their teams according to where they place in the competition.

In diving, several components of the dive are judged. Each dive has a rating for degree of difficulty, which is multiplied by the judges' awards to obtain a total point score for the dive. Divers perform a series of dives in various body positions, with different degrees of difficulty depending on the level of competition.

SWIMMING POOL

A long-course pool is 50 meters long (see figure 51.1). In the US, a short-course pool is sometimes used for NCAA competition and is 25 meters long. The minimum lane width is 2.5 meters. For championship competitions using pools with starting blocks, the water depth is at least 1.35 meters.

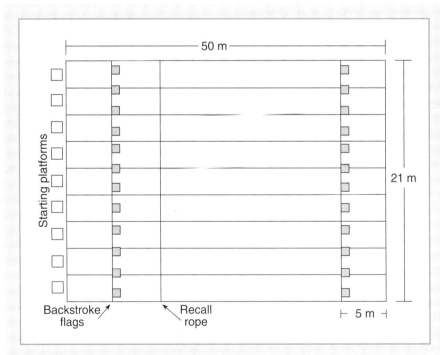

▶ **Figure 51.1**   The dimensions and features of a swimming pool.

Pool-bottom lane markers, 0.2 meters to a maximum of 0.3 meters wide, mark the middle of each lane. These markers terminate in a *T* 2 meters from the pool wall. End-wall targets, in the shape of a *T*, are in the center of the wall at the end of each lane, extending at least 1 meter below the surface.

Lanes are numbered from right to left as swimmers stand facing the pool. Lanes are separated by floating lane dividers with a diameter of 5 to 11 centimeters. The color of the floats from the wall to 5 meters out are different from the color for the rest of the course.

The starting platforms for a long-course pool are between 0.5 and 0.75 meter above the water. The front edge of the platforms is flush with the wall. The top surfaces of the platforms are square, at least 0.5 by 0.5 meter, and covered with a non-slip material.

Backstroke starting grips are between 1 and 2 feet above the water. The front edge of the grips is parallel with the water and flush with the face of the end wall. Two triangular backstroke flags are placed 5 meters from each end of the course, anywhere from 1.8 to 2.5 meters above the water.

A recall rope is used to recall swimmers after a false start. The rope is placed at the 15 meter mark and is suspended at a minimum of 1.2 meters above the water level. Water temperature is to be maintained at 77 to 82 degrees Fahrenheit (25 to 28 degrees Celsius).

SWIMMERS

Swimmers compete in freestyle, backstroke, breaststroke, butterfly, and individual medley, which is a combination of all four strokes. They swim in different age groups. Traditionally recognized age groups are 10 and under, 11 to 12, 13 to 14, 15 to 16, and 17 to 18. Many local meets feature 8 and under, single-age groups, or senior and master level events.

SWIMMING EQUIPMENT

Races are timed with automatic, semiautomatic, or manual timing systems. Automatic systems are activated by electric impulse, and the timing stops when the swimmer touches the touchpad. Semiautomatic systems are activated by electric impulse and are stopped by human timers who push buttons when racers finish. Manual timing is usually done with handheld stopwatches.

SWIMMING RULES

Swimmers are seeded in preliminary heats according to their fastest times. The fastest swimmers in each heat are placed in center lanes of the pool. In finals heats, the slowest swimmers swim first and the fastest swimmers swim last. Some events, such as the Olympic Games and world championships, have semifinals, from which the fastest eight competitors qualify for the finals. Swimmers who record the same time tie for that event.

To begin a race, competitors are called to their starting blocks. After the referee's whistle, swimmers "take their mark." When they are motionless, the starter signals the start by shooting a gun or sounding a horn. If a swimmer leaves too early, he is disqualified at the end of the race. A swimmer is not charged with a false start if it was caused by the motion of another swimmer.

Competitors must stay in their own lanes. Swimmers may be disqualified for swimming out of their lanes or otherwise obstructing other swimmers. Grabbing lane dividers to assist forward motion is prohibited. A swimmer is disqualified for standing on the bottom of the pool, except during a freestyle race. A swimmer may not walk or spring from the bottom of the pool or leave the pool. A swimmer who is not entered in a race but enters the pool while a race is under way is disqualified from the next event in which they were scheduled to participate.

Freestyle

A swimmer uses a forward start. Any style of stroke may be used. To make a turn, a swimmer must touch the wall with any part of their body; to complete the race, the swimmer must touch the wall at the prescribed distance.

Backstroke

The swimmer begins in the pool with both feet on the starting wall and with both hands holding onto the starting grips, pulling themselves toward the starting block, facing the starting end. The swimmer pushes off on their back and must remain on their back for the entirety of the distance with the exception of the turns. Part of the swimmer's body must break the water's surface throughout the race, except during the turns. At the start and during turns, a swimmer may be underwater for up to 15 meters.

To make a turn, some part of the swimmer's body must touch the wall. During the turn, the swimmer may turn over onto their breast. Once the swimmer has turned past vertical, they may use a single or double arm pull to begin the turn. Upon leaving the wall, the swimmer must be in a position on their back. The swimmer finishes the race by touching the wall while on their back.

Breaststroke

Swimmers use a forward start from blocks. In the water, both shoulders must be in line with the water surface, and the arms must move in the same horizontal plane. The hands are pushed forward together from the breast and brought back under the water's surface; the elbows must be underwater at all times, except for the final stroke of each length. The hands may not be brought beyond the hips, except during the first stroke after the start and after each turn. At least part of the swimmer's head must break the water's surface at least once on each complete stroke cycle, except after the start and turns, during which the swimmer may take one complete arm stroke, one dolphin kick, and one breaststroke leg kick while submerged. The feet must be turned outward during the propelling part of the kick; scissors or flutter kicks are not permitted.

At turns, a swimmer must touch the wall with both hands simultaneously at, above, or below the surface. Once the touch is made, a swimmer may complete the turn in any way he desires. At the finish, a swimmer must touch the wall with both hands simultaneously at, above, or below the water surface.

Butterfly

The swimmer uses a forward start and keeps their shoulders in line with the water's surface at or past the vertical toward their breast on each stroke. A swimmer may use only one arm pull underwater per stroke, but they may use two dolphin kicks. Both arms must be brought forward and the swimmer's elbows must come

out of the water and then pulled back together. The legs must kick in unison. A swimmer may not use a scissors or breaststroke kick.

At turns, the body must be on the breast. Both hands must touch the wall simultaneously at, above, or below the surface. After the touch, the swimmer may complete the turn any way they want. The swimmer's shoulders must be at or past vertical toward the breast when they leave the wall. At the finish, a swimmer must touch the wall with both hands simultaneously at, above, or below the surface, with their shoulders in line with the surface.

Individual Medley

This event consists of four equal portions, with strokes used in this order: butterfly, backstroke, breaststroke, and freestyle. It is important to note that the swimmer can choose any style of swimming during the freestyle portion, as long as it is not one of the previous three styles completed. Swimmers use a forward start and must complete each portion according to the rules for the appropriate strokes. When changing from one stroke to the next, the swimmer follows the turn rules for the stroke just completed, except for the backstroke, where a swimmer must touch the wall as if they were finishing a backstroke race. As with the freestyle finish, a swimmer completes this race when any part of their body touches the final wall.

Relays

In a freestyle relay, four swimmers each swim one-quarter of the distance, using the freestyle rules. In a medley relay, four swimmers each swim one-quarter of the distance, with the first swimmer using the backstroke; the second, breaststroke; the third, butterfly; and the fourth, freestyle.

No swimmer may swim more than one leg in a relay. Each swimmer must touch the touch-plate or pad in their lane before their teammate begins. A team is disqualified for violating this rule.

Scoring

In dual meets, scoring for individual events is on a 5-3-1-0 basis; that is, the winner gets 5 points, the swimmer placing second gets 3 points, the third-place swimmer gets 1 point, and all other competitors get no points. Scoring for relays is on a 7-0 basis. For triangular meets, scoring for individual events is on a 6-4-3-2-1-0 basis; for relays, it's 8-4-0. Scoring for most other meets, with point values doubled for relay events, is as follows:

- 4-lane pools: 5-3-2-1
- 5-lane pools: 6-4-3-2-1
- 6-lane pools: 7-5-4-3-2-1
- 7-lane pools: 8-6-5-4-3-2-1
- 8-lane pools: 9-7-6-5-4-3-2-1
- 9-lane pools: 10-8-7-6-5-4-3-2-1
- 10-lane pools: 11-9-8-7-6-5-4-3-2-1

In case of a tie between swimmers, the points for the tied place and the following place are added and divided in two; each swimmer is credited with the same points. For example, in a 10-lane pool, two swimmers tying for first would receive 10 points each (11 for first, 9 for second; divide that total of 20 by 2).

SWIMMING TERMS

Body refers to the torso, including the shoulders and hips.

A **forward start** is a forward entry taken facing the water.

Heats and semifinals are competitions used to pare the field to a manageable number for a final event.

A **lane** is the area in which each swimmer swims. Lanes are separated by **lane lines**, which are floating markers, and they are marked on the bottom of the pool by **lane markings**.

Long course refers to events held in 50-meter pools.

Short course refers to events held in 25-meter pools.

Timed finals are competitions in which heats are swum and final placements are determined by times recorded in the heats.

SWIMMING OFFICIALS

Officials include a referee, a starter, stroke judges and turn judges. Three timers per lane are used; they are presided over by a chief timer. Other officials, in applicable situations, include place judges and relay takeoff judges.

SWIMMING ORGANIZATIONS

Fédération Internationale de Natation
Av. de l'Avant-Poste 4
CH-1005 Lausanne
Switzerland
41-21-310-4710
www.fina.org

United States Masters Swimming
P.O. Box 185
Londonderry, NH 03053-0185
800-550-7946
www.usms.org

USA Swimming
1 Olympic Plaza
Colorado Springs, CO 80909-5778
719-866-4578
www.usaswimming.org

DIVING POOL

The competition springboard is made of flexible material and has a nonskid surface. It is 20 inches wide and 16 feet long, set at either 1 or 3 meters above the water's surface. The 3-meter springboard should have guardrails extending to at least the pool's edge; boards should project at least 1.5 meters, and preferably 1.8 meters, beyond the pool's edge and over the water.

The platform is solid and nonflexible and has a nonslip surface. It is at least 19.69 feet long and 9.83 feet wide. The platform height is 10 meters; intermediate platforms can be set from 5 to 7.5 meters. For synchronized diving events, the 10-meter platform should be at least 8 feet wide but preferably 9.83 feet wide. The water depth varies, depending on the height of the platform.

DIVERS

Divers compete in three divisions:

- Junior: For divers 18 and under, there are three junior programs—learn to dive, novice, and competitive.
- Senior: For divers of any age, although typically senior divers are ages 16 to 28.

They must meet competitive requirements in terms of number of dives and difficulty.

■ Masters: for 21 and older.

DIVING RULES

The order of diving is decided by random draw. The diver's name, the dive, and its degree of difficulty are announced before each dive. After each dive, the judges, without communicating with each other, immediately and simultaneously flash their awards.

A diver is responsible for ensuring that the correct dives are marked on the diving sheet used by the announcer to indicate which dive will be performed. If the announcer makes a mistake while describing the type of dive that will be performed and the diver executes the dive written on the dive sheet, they are permitted to score the dive. However, a diver may neither perform a dive other than what is announced (doing so results in a failed dive, with no score awarded), if it is correctly recorded on the dive sheet, nor repeat the same dive, even in a different body position. In competitions other than national championships, a diver may elect not to perform a dive and take no points. This is to ensure the safety of the participants. There are six types of dives that may be performed.

1. Forward dive: The diver begins facing forward toward the water and rotates toward the water.
2. Backward dive: The diver begins standing backward on the end of the springboard or platform and rotates toward the water.
3. Reverse dive: The diver begins facing forward toward the water and rotates toward the springboard or platform.
4. Inward: The diver begins standing backward on the end of the springboard or platform and rotates toward the springboard or platform.
5. Arm-stand dive: The diver begins from a handstand on the end of the platform. This dive is performed only in platform diving.
6. Twisting dive: The diver includes a twist in any of the previous five groups of dives. This is the largest group of dives.

Divers may execute dives in four body positions:

1. Straight: no bending at the knees or hips; feet together and toes pointed
2. Pike: bent at the hips with legs straight; feet together and toes pointed
3. Tuck: bent at the hips and knees; feet and knees together and toes pointed
4. Free: any combination of the other three positions when executing a twisting dive

Three categories of dives may be performed, and the requirements for each are specified by the level of competition:

1. Required dives: A specific dive or body position—or both—is designated. All divers in the contest must perform a required dive.
2. Voluntary dives with limit: Divers perform a number of dives from different groups. The dive choice is up to the diver, but the total degree of difficulty of all dives cannot exceed a predetermined limit.
3. Voluntary dives without limit: The diver performs a number of dives from different groups. There is no limit on the total degree of difficulty. These dives are commonly referred to as optional dives.

Scoring

A dive is judged on five parts:

1. Approach: the walk or run to the end of the springboard or platform, which begins forward, reverse, and some twisting dives
2. Takeoff: springing and jumping from the end of the springboard or platform to begin a dive
3. Flight: the dive must follow the direct line of flight and results in one of the aforementioned body positions
4. Entry: the angle of entry, which should be vertical; the straightness of the body; the amount of splash; the distance out from the springboard or platform; and whether the dive was in front of the springboard or platform or off to one side

Judges award points in half-point increments based on the following scale:

- Excellent: 10.0 points
- Very good: 8.5 to 9.5 points
- Good: 7.0 to 8.0 points
- Satisfactory: 5 to 6.5 points
- Deficient: 2.5 to 4.5 points
- Unsatisfactory: 0.5 to 2.0 points
- Completely failed: 0.0 points

When seven or nine judges are used, the two highest and the two lowest awards are cancelled. When five judges are used, the high and low awards are cancelled. When nine judges are used, the sum of the remaining awards is multiplied by the degree of difficulty and then by 0.6 to obtain the equivalent of a three-judge score. When seven or five judges are used, the sum of the remaining three awards is multiplied by the dive's degree of difficulty.

JUDGING

The starting position for dives with an approach is assumed when the diver is ready to take the first step. For standing dives, the starting position is assumed when the diver stands still on the front end of the springboard or platform, with head erect and body and arms straight.

If the diver begins the approach or press and stops, a balk has been committed. A preparatory movement of the arms may be made before the approach or press without a balk being called. The first balk results in 2 points being deducted from each judge's award. A second balk on the same dive results in a failed dive. Any action before the diver takes the starting position does not count. The forward approach should be smooth, straight, and graceful and shall be not less than three steps and a hurdle. The takeoff for the hurdle—the jump to the end of the springboard—must be from one foot only.

In running dives, the takeoff from the springboard must be from both feet simultaneously. Springboard dives with a forward takeoff may be performed either standing or with an approach. In running platform dives, the diver must take at least three steps and a hop for a two-foot takeoff

and at least four steps for a one-foot takeoff. Two points are deducted from each judge's score for violations.

On a standing dive, the diver must not bounce on the board or rock it excessively before takeoff. Doing so results in a deduction of not more than 2 points from each judge, at the individual judge's discretion.

Touching the end of the board or diving to the side during the execution of the dive results in a deduction of points, up to the discretion of each judge. While the diver is in the air, the judges look for the following:

- In the straight position, points are deducted if the knees or hips are bent.
- In the pike position, the pike should be as compact as possible (the legs must be straight).
- In the tuck position, the tuck should be as compact as possible; 0.5 to 2.0 points are deducted for opening the knees.
- In the free position, any combination of the three other positions must conform to the criteria of those positions.
- A twist dive is considered failed if the twist is greater or less than 90 degrees of the announced twist.

As described earlier, the entry into the water for all dives must be vertical, with the body straight and the toes pointed. On headfirst entries, the arms should be stretched beyond the head in a line with the body, with the hands close together. If any part of the body below the waist enters the water before the hands, the dive is considered failed. On feet-first entries, the arms should be held close to the body, without bending at the elbows. (Novice divers performing certain dives are allowed to hold their arms straight overhead.)

DIVING OFFICIALS

A referee is in charge of the competition and oversees the judges (typically three for dual meets and five for regional meets). A secretary oversees the scoring table and verifies the results. The scoring table may consist of three or more personnel who record and calculate the scores.

DIVING ORGANIZATIONS

Fédération Internationale de Natation
Av. de l'Avant-Poste 4
CH-1005 Lausanne
Switzerland
41-21-310-4710
www.fina.org

USA Diving
1060 N. Capitol Ave., Ste. E-310
Indianapolis, IN 46204
317-237-5252
www.teamusa.org/USA-Diving

52

Synchronized Swimming

Clive Rose/Getty Images

ustralian Annette Kellerman attracted national attention by performing water ballet at the New York Hippodrome in 1907. The sport of synchronized swimming began in Canada in the 1920s and came to the United States in the 1930s (the first collegiate competition was in 1939). Esther Williams popularized synchronized swimming during and after World War II through Hollywood films. Synchronized swimming, which was renamed artistic swimming by the international governing body, FINA, in 2017, was an Olympic demonstration sport from 1948 to 1968 and became a full-medal Olympic sport in 1984. The United States led all international competitions through 1996. Since then, Russia has dominated at all Olympic and world championships, with other countries such as China, Japan, Ukraine, Canada, Italy, and Spain vying for top positions. Today more than 80 nations on 6 continents compete in the sport, and it includes men's competitions as well as women's.

OVERVIEW

Objective: To receive the highest score from the panel of judges.

Number of Competitors: Varies, depending on the event. Synchronized swimmers compete in solo, duet, mixed duet, trio, team, combination, and highlight events.

Routine Scoring: The range is from 0 to 10, based on execution, difficulty, and artistic impression for free routines and execution, elements, and impression for technical routines.

Synchronized swimmers perform figures and free routines or technical and free routines, dependent on the competition. Routines consist of a combination of figures, strokes, swimming, and propulsion techniques. Technical routines consist of specific elements that must be performed by all competitors at the same time. For upper-age-group and junior-level competitions, the score for the technical routine is added to that of the free routine for the final score. Free routines are open and do not have any regulations except for the limit of six acrobatic moves, routine and deck work times, and the restriction against touching the bottom. The highest score wins.

In larger events, preliminaries and semifinals in routine competition may be held first, followed by figure competition and then the finals in routine competition.

Figures are performed in front a panel of judges individually, and for the novice, intermediate, and lower age group competitions, their scores are added to the free routine scores to produce the final results.

COMPETITORS

Competitors may compete in the following classifications: senior (ages 15 and up), junior (ages 15 to 18), and age groups (12 and under, 13 to 15, 16 to 17, 18 to 19).

Competition is also held for designated skill levels, such as novice, intermediate, and age group. Competition is divided geographically (association, regional, zone, and national) to provide progressive opportunities for swimmers to qualify for each succeeding level. The rules for championships conducted at the local level may have minor adjustments to meet the needs of the participants.

RULES

Competitions are composed of various figures, technical routines, and free routines, with penalties figuring into the composite scores.

Figures

Figures are combinations of specific and precise movements, ranging in degrees of difficulty from 1.1 to 3.5. There are four categories of figures: ballet leg, dolphin, somersault, and diverse.

Figure competition is excluded at many international events, including the Olympic Games and the World Aquatic Championships. Figures are performed individually, without music, before panels of trained judges, and they are designed to determine the swimmer's ability to control movement and demonstrate balance, coordination, flexibility, and timing.

Figure competitions are made up of two compulsory and two optional figures. There are three sets of two optional figures from which the optional group is drawn 18 to 48 hours before the figure competition. For some competitions, the four figures are preselected and particular age groups, skill levels, and special programs—such as novice, 12 and under, collegiate, and masters—have specified required figures that are known throughout the season.

Judges, seated together in panels, individually award points from 0 to 10, in one-tenth of a point increments, as follows:

- Perfect: 10.0 points
- Near perfect: 9.5 to 9.9 points
- Excellent: 9.0 to 9.4 points
- Very good: 8.0 to 8.9 points
- Good: 7.0 to 7.9 points
- Competent: 6.0 to 6.9 points
- Satisfactory: 5.0 to 5.9 points
- Deficient: 4.0 to 4.9 points
- Weak: 3.0 to 3.9 points
- Very weak: 2.0 to 2.9 points
- Hardly recognizable: 0.1 to 1.9 points
- Completely failed: 0.0 points

Each performance is measured from the standpoint of perfection in design and control, as detailed in the figure description. Design is the assessment of the swimmer's precise definition of positions, the degree of full extension of the body and limbs, and the path of movement from one position to another. Control factors include the swimmer's stability, the support of weight above the water, the water lines achieved, and how smoothly and easily the figure is performed.

To determine the figure score for each competitor, the score for each of the four figures performed is determined by first dropping the highest and lowest scores awarded, then averaging the remaining scores and multiplying the result by that figure's assigned degree of difficulty. The four figure scores are then added together, divided by the degree of difficulty of the group of figures, and multiplied by 10 to obtain the final figure score. For duet, trio, and team events, the figure scores of the competitors performing the routine are averaged to determine the figure score for that routine.

Routines

There are six routine events recognized internationally: solo, duet (two swimmers), mixed duet (one male and one female), team (four to eight swimmers), free combination (10 swimmers), and highlight routines. U.S. novice and intermediate competitions usually include a trio (three swimmers) event.

Routine competition takes two different forms: the free and the technical programs. One or both may be included in a competition. The free program has no restrictions concerning music or choreography. The technical program contains at least five required elements, must be performed by all members simultaneously, and is shorter in duration.

Scores for free routines are awarded in three categories: execution, difficulty, and artistic impression. Each is worth a different percentage. Scores for technical routines are awarded in three categories: execution, elements, and impression, and each of these is worth a different percentage. The execution score is based on execution and synchronization. The difficulty score is based on the difficulty of all moves, and the artistic impression score is based on choreography, musical interpretation, and manner of presentation. For technical routines, the element score covers execution and synchronization of each of the required technical elements. The scoring range is the same as for figures; 0.0 to 10.0. There are no figure or technical routine scores added to the free combination or highlight routine scores.

Judges, seated at various vantage points around the pool, award points from 0.0 to 10.0 in one-tenth of a point increments. There are three panels of five judges, each judging one category. The highest and lowest scores are cancelled, and the scores are calculated by using a specific equation.

Time requirements are shown in table 52.1.

TABLE 52.1

Routine Time Requirements in Minutes

	Solos	Duets	Teams	Combos
12 and under	2:00	2:30	3:00	3:00
Ages 13-15	2:15	2:45	3:30	3:30
Junior/senior	2:30	3:00	4:00	4:00
Technical	2:00	2:20	2:50	

A variation of 15 seconds over or under the requirement is allowed. Routine time limits are reduced for younger and less-skilled competitors. A maximum of 10 seconds is allowed for deck movements, known as deck work. The timing begins and ends with the accompaniment, and the timing of the deck work ends when the last competitor enters the water. The competitors must perform the routine without stopping, and the routine must end in the water.

Penalties

Referees may assess penalties for infractions of the event rules and for deviation from or omission of designated movements. Following are examples of actions that can be penalized:

- Failing to begin or finish with the accompaniment
- Exceeding 10 seconds for deck movements or 30 seconds for deck walk-ons
- Exceeding the specified routine maximum or minimum time limits
- Interrupting deck movements to begin again (unless of technical nature)
- Not ending a routine in the water
- Deliberately walking on the pool bottom or using the pool bottom to assist another swimmer
- Deliberately touching the pool deck
- Failure to perform required technical elements or performing them incorrectly.

Composite Score

When only two events are included in the competitive program, the figure or the technical routine score and the free routine score from the preliminary swim are added together to determine who will advance to the finals. The score for the preliminary free routine swim is dropped and replaced by the final free routine swim to determine the winners. The figures or technical routine are weighted 50 percent, and the free routine is weighted 50 percent to determine the final score.

TERMS

Note: These terms refer to figure positions.

In a **back layout position**, the body extends on the back with the face, chest, thighs, and feet at the surface.

In a **ballet leg position**, the body and one leg are extended on a horizontal line either at or beneath the surface, with the other leg extended vertically, and with the water level as high as possible on the thigh.

In a **fishtail position**, the body and one leg are perpendicular to the surface, with the foot of the other leg at the surface.

In a **flamingo position**, one leg extends perpendicular to the surface and the other draws toward the chest, with the midcalf opposite the vertical leg and the foot and knee at and parallel to the surface.

In a **front layout position**, the body extends horizontally on the stomach with the head, upper back, buttocks, and heels at the surface.

In a **front pike position**, the hips are bent to form a 90-degree angle, with the legs together and fully extended at the surface. The head is extended in line with the trunk toward the bottom of the pool.

In a **split position**, both legs are fully extended at the surface, evenly split forward and backward, with the feet and thighs at the surface. The lower back is arched, with hips, shoulders, and head on a vertical line.

In a **tuck position**, the body is as compact as possible, heels pressed to buttocks, back rounded, knees to face, and legs together.

OFFICIALS

Up to 15 judges score routines and up to 7 judges score figures. An event referee has full jurisdiction over the event.

ORGANIZATIONS

Fédération Internationale de Natation
Av. de l'Avant-Poste 4
CH-1005 Lausanne
Switzerland
41-21-310-4710
www.fina.org

United States Synchronized Swimming
1 Olympic Plaza
Colorado Springs, CO 80909
719-866-2219
www.usasynchro.org

53

Table Tennis

Zhizhao Wu/Getty Images

Table tennis, originally known as ping-pong, is believed to have been developed in England in the late 1800s or early 1900s. The sport is growing in popularity in the United States with an estimated 16 million participants, but for decades the players from Asian and European countries have been dominant in international competition. Today the sport attracts more than 40 million competitive players worldwide, and many millions more play the sport recreationally.

OVERVIEW

Objective: To score points by hitting the ball across the net and onto the opponent's side of the table so that the opponent cannot return the ball successfully.

Number of Players: Two (singles) or four (doubles).

Length of Games and Matches: The first side to score 11 points wins unless the score is tied at 10 (deuce). Then the side that first gets ahead by 2 points wins. A match is the best of any odd number of games. Most tournament matches are best of five or best of seven games. Doubles matches are normally the best of five.

Scoring: A point is awarded for good hits not returned and in other circumstances (see "Scoring").

In singles, the server serves, the receiver returns, and the two continue to alternate hits until a point is scored. In doubles, the server serves, the receiver returns, the partner of the server returns, and the partner of the receiver returns. That sequence continues until a point is scored. In singles, after every 2 points, the server becomes the receiver, and the receiver becomes the server. In doubles, each player gets two serves at a time, in this repeating order:

- Player 1, team A (serving to player 1, team B)
- Player 1, team B (serving to player 2, team A)
- Player 2, team A (serving to player 2, team B)
- Player 2, team B (serving to player 1, team A)

When the score reaches 10-10 and beyond in both singles and doubles, the serve changes after each point.

TABLE

The table is 9 feet long and 5 feet wide (see figure 53.1). The playing surface is 30 inches above the floor. It may be made of any material that produces a uniform bounce. Normally the surface is dark green or blue, with a white line along each edge, forming two sidelines and two end lines. For doubles, a center line divides each court in half; the center line is regarded as part of each right-half court.

The playing surface includes the top edges of the table but not the sides below the edge. The net is 6 feet long and extends from the playing surface to 6 inches above it along its complete length. The minimum playing space should be 40 feet long, 20 feet wide, and 11.5 feet high. The floor is usually made of hard, nonslippery wood, concrete, or hard rubber.

PLAYERS

Players typically wear a short-sleeved shirt, shorts or skirt, socks, and soft-soled shoes. Clothing may be of any color, but the main color must be different from that of the ball in use.

EQUIPMENT

The ball is spherical, weighs 2.7 grams, and has a diameter of 40 millimeters. It is made of celluloid or similar plastic and may be white or orange and matte. The racket may be of any size, shape, and weight. The blade must be continuous, of even thickness, flat, and rigid. At least 85 percent of the blade's thickness must consist of natural wood. The color of the blade must be uniformly dark and matte. The sides of the blade used to strike the ball are covered with rubber. The blade should be black on one side and bright red on the other.

RULES

Play is continuous, although a player may ask for a 1-minute break between games. The referee may stop play for up to 10 minutes for an incapacitated player if the delay does not disadvantage the opposing player or team. Brief pauses at the end of every 6 points may be taken to towel off, to hydrate, or to perform a similar task.

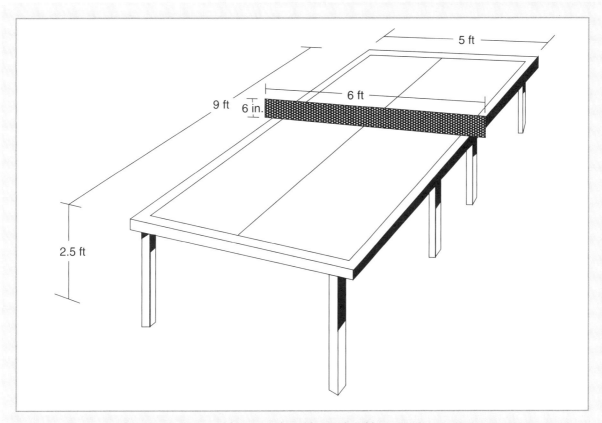

▶ **Figure 53.1**   The dimensions and features of a table tennis table.

Players or teams change ends at the end of every game. In the final game, sides change ends when either side scores 5 points. At this same point in a doubles match, the receiving team switches receiving order. The player or pair who served first in the preceding game receives first in the next game.

A ball is in play until it touches something other than the table, the net assembly, the racket, or the racket hand below the wrist, unless the ball is a let (a rally in which no point is scored).

A let occurs when a serve touches the net assembly and otherwise is a good serve, when a serve is made before the receiving team is ready, or when a disturbance outside the receiver's control occurs. A let is also called when an error occurs in the playing order or in the ends or when a player changes rackets without notifying the umpire and the opponent (the second time this occurs the player is disqualified). A let is usually announced by the umpire or a player raising a free hand and calling out, "Let!"

The expedite system is put into effect if a game exceeds 10 minutes, unless both sides have scored at least 9 points. In this system, the serve alternates after each point. If the receiver makes 13 good returns including the serve, the receiver wins a point. Once the expedite system is put into play, it stays in effect for the rest of the match, with the sides alternating serves after every point.

Serving

The server holds the ball on the open palm of his free hand. The ball must be stationary, above the table, and behind the serving end line. The server tosses the ball nearly vertically upward at least 6 inches without spinning it. The server strikes the ball on the descent with the racket behind the serving end line. The ball must touch the server's court first, pass over or around the net, and touch the receiver's court.

From the start of service until it is struck, the ball must be above the level of the playing surface and behind the server's end line, and it cannot be hidden from the receiver by any part of the body or clothing of the server or her doubles partner. In doubles, the served ball must hit on the server's right-half court and then the receiver's right-half court. If any player misses the ball while attempting to serve, the player loses a point.

Returns

A return is good when it passes over or around the net or its supports and then strikes the opponent's court. A return may touch the net or its supports as long as it lands in the opponent's court. The ball may not bounce twice on the same side or be hit twice on the same side before its return.

Scoring

A player scores a point when the opponent

- fails to make a good serve,
- fails to make a good return,
- obstructs the ball,
- allows the ball to bounce twice in her court,
- strikes the ball twice in making one return,
- moves the table while the ball is in play,
- touches the playing surface with the free hand,
- touches the net or its supports while the ball is in play,
- strikes the ball out of sequence in doubles play, or
- fails to return the serve and 12 successive returns under the expedite system.

TERMS

A **let** is a rally that is not scored.

The **net assembly** includes the net, the supporting cord, and the brackets and clamps.

Obstruction occurs when a player or a player's racket or clothing touches the ball in play when it is over his court or heading toward his court and when it has not touched his court since last being struck by his opponent.

A **rally** describes the time during which the ball is in play.

The **receiver** is the player who strikes the ball second in a rally.

The **server** is the player who strikes the ball to begin the rally.

The **stroke counter** is the person who counts strokes under the expedite system.

OFFICIALS

If available, an umpire or referee makes calls during the match.

MODIFICATIONS

Wheelchair competition follows the rules listed elsewhere in this chapter, except for the following modifications.

The table must not have any physical barrier that might hinder the normal and legal movements of a wheelchair. If the receiver does not strike a serve, and the served ball bounces twice on the receiver's court, the serve is a let. Players classified as IA, IB, or IC may toss the ball up with either hand, and they may touch the playing surface with the free hand while the ball is in play, but they may not use the free hand for support while hitting the ball.

Competitors' feet may not touch the floor during play, and competitors may not rise noticeably off their cushions during play. Their cushions may be of any size. Wheelchairs are not required to have back support.

When a standing player plays a wheelchair player, wheelchair service rules apply to both. In wheelchair doubles, team members don't have to alternate shots.

ORGANIZATIONS

International Table Tennis Federation
Ch. de la Roche 11
1020 Renens/Lausanne
Switzerland
41-21-340-7090
www.ittf.com

USA Table Tennis
4065 Sinton Rd., Ste. 120
Colorado Springs, CO 80907
719-866-4583
www.teamusa.org/USA-Table-Tennis

54

Taekwondo

Michael Steele/Getty Images

Taekwondo originated in Korea more than 20 centuries ago and is one of the most popular modern martial arts today. Tae means "to strike with the foot;" kwon means "fist" or "to strike with the hand;" do means "the way of" or "art of." Thus, taekwondo stands for "the art of kicking and punching."

Taekwondo was introduced to the United States in the 1950s and was officially recognized as a means of self-defense when many Korean martial artists unified their techniques under the style now known as taekwondo. There are now about five million practitioners of taekwondo in the United States, and the sport made its premier as a medal sport in the 2000 Summer Olympics.

OVERVIEW

Objective: To win the contest by either scoring the most points or knocking the opponent out.

Scoring: Scoring techniques to the body protector are worth 2 points; scoring techniques to the head are worth 3 points and an additional 2 points are awarded for spinning techniques.

Number of Competitors: Two per contest; only same-sex competitions are allowed.

Length of Contest: Three rounds that are 2 minutes each with a 1-minute rest period between rounds.

Competitors use fast, spinning kicks to score points by connecting in legal scoring areas on their opponents. They use no weapons, only their bare hands and feet. The competitor who knocks her opponent out or scores the most valid points wins.

Participants compete in weight categories and must weigh in the day before the competition. The contest begins with the referee's call of "shijak," which means "start." Each opponent then tries to score points in legal scoring areas of his opponent's trunk and head while also trying to prevent his opponent from scoring. At the end of the contest, the competitors bow to each other and then turn and bow to the head of court. The referee then raises the hand of the winner.

COMPETITION AREA

The competition area measures no less than 10 meters and no more than 12 meters square. It is covered with an elastic mat and may be on a platform raised 50 to 60 centimeters. The inner part of the competition area, measuring 8 meters square, is called the contest area; the surrounding area up to the boundary lines is called the alert area. See figure 54.1. If necessary, the competition area may also be installed on a platform 0.6 to 1 meter high.

COMPETITORS

Table 54.1 shows weight divisions for black belts in international, U.S. team trials, and U.S. national competitions.

Weight divisions for the world junior championships are shown in table 54.2.

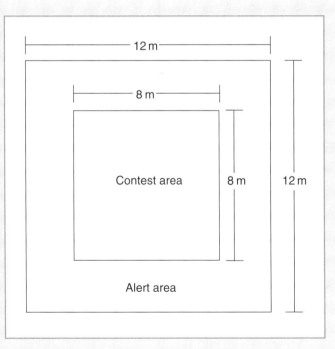

▶ **Figure 54.1** The dimensions and features of a taekwondo competition area.

TABLE 54.1

Weight Divisions for International and National Junior Divisions

Divisions	Men's weight	Women's weight
Fin	Not to exceed 45 kg (99.2 lb)	Not to exceed 42 kg (92.6 lb)
Fly	Over 45-48 kg (over 99.2-105.8 lb)	Over 42-44 kg (over 92.6-97.0 lb)
Bantam	Over 48-51 kg (over 105.8-112.4 lb)	Over 44-46 kg (over 97.0-101.4 lb)
Feather	Over 51-55 kg (over 112.4-121.3 lb)	Over 46-49 kg (over 101.4-108.0 lb)
Light	Over 55-59 kg (over 121.3-130.1 lb)	Over 49-52 kg (over 108.0-114.6 lb)
Welter	Over 59-63 kg (over 130.1-138.9 lb)	Over 52-55 kg (over 114.6-121.3 lb)
Light middle	Over 63-68 kg (over 138.9-149.9 lb)	Over 55-59 kg (over 121.3-130.1 lb)
Middle	Over 68-73 kg (over 149.9-160.9 lb)	Over 59-63 kg (over 130.1-138.9 lb)
Light heavy	Over 73-78 kg (over 160.9-172.0 lb)	Over 63-68 kg (over 138.9-149.9 lb)
Heavy	Over 78 kg (over 172.0 lb)	Over 68 kg (over 149.9 lb)

Data from The World Taekwondo Federation, *Competition Rules,* 2017, p. 13. Available: http://www.worldtaekwondo.org/wp-content/uploads/2017/01/WTF-Competition-Rules-Interpretation-Nov-15-2016-Burnaby-Canada.pdf.

TABLE 54.2

Weight Divisions for World Adult Championships

Divisions	Men's weight	Women's weight
Fin	Not to exceed 54 kg (119.0 lb)	Not to exceed 46 kg (101.4 lb)
Fly	Over 54-58 kg (over 119.0-127.9 lb)	Over 46-49 kg (over 101.4-108.0 lb)
Bantam	Over 58-63 kg (over 127.9-138.9 lb)	Over 49-53 kg (over 108.0-116.8 lb)
Feather	Over 63-68 kg (over 138.9-149.9 lb)	Over 53-57 kg (over 116.8-125.7 lb)
Light	Over 68-74 kg (over 149.9-163.1 lb)	Over 57-62 kg (over 125.7-136.7 lb)
Welter	Over 74-80 kg (over 163.1-176.4 lb)	Over 62-67 kg (over 136.7-147.7 lb)
Middle	Over 80-87 kg (over 176.4-191.8 lb)	Over 67-73 kg (over 147.7-160.9 lb)
Heavy	Over 87 kg (over 191.8 lb)	Over 73 kg (over 160.9 lb)

Data from The World Taekwondo Federation, *Competition Rules,* 2017, pg. 13. Available: http://www.worldtaekwondo.org/wp-content/uploads/2017/01/WTF-Competition-Rules-Interpretation-Nov-15-2016-Burnaby-Canada.pdf.

EQUIPMENT

Each competitor wears a uniform with protective gear, including a trunk protector, head protector, mouth guard, groin guard, and forearm and shin guards.

RULES

A contestant may use the knuckle portion of their clenched fist to deliver a fist technique. They may deliver a foot technique by using any portion of their foot below the ankle bone. Legal scoring areas include all areas of the body protector (front and back) that are colored red or blue and the entire head that is above the bottom line of the head protector. A contestant may attack an opponent's trunk with feet or hands but may attack the head only with feet. A closed fist is required to make contact with the hands; opponents are allowed to push each other with open palms.

A contestant scores a point each time he accurately and powerfully delivers a permitted technique in a legal scoring area. Each scoring technique is worth 2 points, with the exception of a kick to the head, for which 3 points are awarded. If a contestant touches the floor with any body part other than their feet, they receive a one point deduction. This is represented on the score board by giving the opponent an additional point. A point is not valid if the contestant used any prohibited act in delivering the attack.

Scoring

Kicks are generally emphasized more than punches in scoring. Punches are aimed at the torso, while kicks can hit the trunk protector or the head. A valid punch to the trunk protector is worth 1 point, but if the kick incorporates a spinning technique, it can score 2 points. Kicks to the head are worth 3 points, but if they incorporate a spinning technique, they are instead worth 5 points. One point is deducted from a participant's score when called for gam-jeom. If one fighter gains a 20-point lead at the end of the second round, then the bout is ended at the end of that round, except in a semi-final or final match.

Knockdowns

A knockdown occurs when any part of the body other than the sole of the foot touches the floor as a result of an opponent's delivered technique. A contestant is also judged to be knocked down if he is staggering and unable to continue the match.

When a knockdown occurs, the referee calls for a break and counts from 1 to 10 at 1-second intervals. If the downed contestant rises, the referee counts up to 8, and if he believes the contestant can continue, he calls for the match to resume. If the contestant does not rise or does not appear able to continue by the count of 8, the referee will declare the opponent the victor.

Decisions

If the score is tied at the end of three rounds and one contestant has had more points deducted than the other, the contestant who was awarded the most total points wins. If the score is tied and the point deduction totals are also the same, the match goes to a sudden-death round. In this fourth round of 1 minutes, the first athlete to score a valid point, called a "golden point," wins the match. If the match is still tied at the end of the sudden-death round, then the referee decides the winner based on touches on the electronic scoring device that didn't initially score. A contestant may register a win by knockout, by the referee stopping the contest, by score or superiority, by withdrawal or disqualification, or by the referee's punitive declaration.

The referee may suspend a contest for injury to one or both contestants. The injured contestant may be treated for 1 minute. If a contestant does not demonstrate the will to continue after such an injury, then he loses the contest, unless the injury was caused by a gam-jeom prohibited act. If this is the case, a one point deduction is given for the penalty.

TERMS

The **alert area** is the area between the outer boundary line and the **contest area** (the inner part of the competition area measuring 10 meters square). The total competition area measures 12 meters on each side.

A **gam-jeom** penalty is a deduction penalty. A contestant who commits a gam-jeom penalty has 1 point deducted.

Kalyeo means break. The referee calls this to keep an attacker from a downed opponent.

Keuman means stop. The referee calls this to end each round.

Keysok means continue. The referee calls this when a downed contestant is ready to resume.

The **permitted area** on a contestant, where attacks using permitted techniques may be delivered, is the trunk and the face.

Permitted techniques include using the fist and the foot to deliver blows.

Shijak means start. The referee calls this to begin a contest.

A **valid point** is scored when a permitted technique is scored to a legal scoring area on the trunk or face.

OFFICIALS

The referee controls the match. Judges record points using an electronic scoring system. The head of court has overall control of the competition area and confirms the match decision.

ORGANIZATIONS

International TaeKwon-Do Association
P.O. Box 281
Grand Blanc, MI 48480
810-235-8594
www.itatkd.com

International Taekwon-Do Federation
Yiewsley Leisure Centre
Otterfield Rd.
Yiewsley UB7 8PE
United Kingdom
44-1895-459946
www.itf-administration.com

USA Taekwondo
1 Olympic Plaza
Colorado Springs, CO 80909
719-866-4632
www.teamusa.org/usa-taekwondo

55

Team Handball

skynesher/iStock/Getty Images

Team handball originated in Europe at the end of the 19th century and was introduced to the United States in the late 1920s. Interest lagged in the United States until the late 1950s, when the U.S. Team Handball Federation was formed from a group of clubs in New York and New Jersey. The field version of handball made its first appearance in the 1936 Summer Olympics as an outdoor sport with 11 players per side. The United States was one of a handful of teams that fielded a team in Berlin. In 1972, men's handball was reintroduced as an Olympic sport, played on a court with seven players per side; women's competition was added in 1976. The sport is now played in more than 200 nations. The International Handball Federation (IHF) is responsible for all major international tournaments.

OVERVIEW

Objective: To score the most goals.

Number of Players: Seven players per side may be on the court at once.

Length of Game: A game consists of two 30-minute halves, with a 10-minute intermission. In international competition the half time can be up to 15 minutes. The playing clock normally runs continuously but is on occasion stopped (see "Keeping Time"). Normal playing time for youth teams is two 25-minute halves for ages 12 to 16 and two 20-minute halves for ages 8 to 12, both with a 10-minute halftime.

Scoring: A goal is scored when the entire ball crosses the goal line.

The game begins with a throw-off at center court. All players must be on their own half of the court when the throw is made, with the opponents at least 3 meters from the thrower. The throw-off to begin the second half is taken by the team that defended the first throw-off.

Team handball is a fast-moving, exciting game that combines running, jumping, catching, and throwing. Elements of soccer, basketball, water polo, and hockey can be seen as players try to maneuver past opponents and throw the ball past the goalkeeper and into the goal to score.

COURT

The court is 40 meters long and 20 meters wide (see figure 55.1). It has two goal areas and a playing area. The lines marking the boundaries on the sides of the field are called sidelines; the shorter boundary lines are called goal lines for the portion between the goal posts and outer goal lines for the portions on either side of the goal.

Each goal is netted and is 3 meters wide and 2 meters high. The goal area is marked by a goal-area line that fans in a semicircle 6 meters away from the goal post. The free-throw line, or 9-meter line, is a broken line fanning in a semicircle 9 meters from the goal post. The 7-meter line is 1 meter long. It is parallel to, and 7 meters from, the rear edge of the goal line, and it is directly in front of the goal. The goalkeeper's restraining line (the 4-meter line) is 15 centimeters long and 4 meters from the rear edge of the goal line, directly in front of the goal. The center line runs the width of the court at midcourt, dividing the court into equal halves.

PLAYERS

A team consists of 14 players, seven of whom may be on the court at one time. In international play a team can consist of up to 16 players. A team must have at least five players to begin a game, but the game may continue if a team is later reduced to fewer than five players on the court. A team may choose to remove the goalkeeper and add an additional court player for an offensive advantage. Otherwise, all players except the goalkeeper wear the same color uniform, with numbers at least 20 centimeters high on the back of the shirt and at least 10 centimeters high on the front. Goalkeepers are not allowed to wear gloves or a helmet.

Substitutes may enter the game at any time and for an unlimited number of times. The timekeeper does not need to be notified, but the player the substitute is replacing must be off the field completely before the substitute enters. Substitutes must enter a game at the substitute line, which is near midcourt. A faulty substitution results in a 2-minute suspension for the offending player.

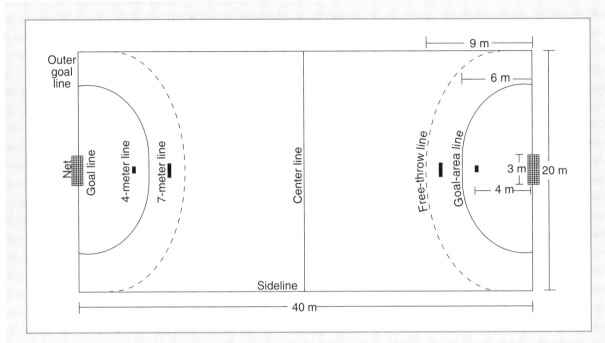

▶ **Figure 55.1** The dimensions and features of a team handball court.

Teams use different offensive sets and have different names for positions, but one basic offensive set is to have three players (left back, center back, and right back, just beyond the free-throw line and three others (left wing, circle runner, and right wing) between the free-throw line and the goal-area line. Wing players tend to be smaller and quicker players who can shoot from difficult angles. Circle runners, or pivots, are often directly in front of the goal, are larger and aggressive, and may set picks and screens for the backcourt players. Centers are like quarterbacks, directing the offense. The other backcourt players tend to be taller, with the ability to jump and shoot powerful shots over the defense from the backcourt.

EQUIPMENT

The ball is spherical, is made of leather or synthetic material, and has an inflated rubber bladder. It has the following dimensions:

- ░ Men over 16 (size 3): 58 to 60 centimeters in circumference, weighing 425 to 475 grams

- ░ Women over 14 and male youth ages 12 to 16 (size 2): 54 to 56 centimeters in circumference, weighing 325 to 400 grams

- ░ Female youth ages 8 to 14 and male youth ages 8 to 12 (size 1): 50 to 52 centimeters in circumference, weighing 290 to 330 grams

RULES

Most of the rules of play are understood through the regulations for keeping time, advancing the ball, approaching an opponent, goalkeeping, and throws.

Keeping Time

The clock is always stopped when a referee gives a 2-minute suspension, disqualifies or excludes a player. Time may be stopped for a 7-meter throw, but it is at the referee's discretion (see "Throws"). Each team has 3 time outs per game. They may use a maximum of 2 time outs per half, however, they may not use two time outs in the last five minutes of the game. The clock may also be stopped for extraordinary incidents (spectators or objects on the court, goal damaged, and so on), consultations between the referees and the timekeeper or scorekeeper, injuries, and delays in executing a formal throw. In addition, the clock stops for goalkeeper substitutions during a 7-meter throw.

Advancing the Ball

Players may throw, catch, stop, push, or hit the ball, using their open or closed hands, arms, heads, torsos, thighs, and knees. A player may hold a ball for a maximum of 3 seconds. A player may

- take a maximum of three steps with the ball,
- transfer the ball from one hand to the other,
- play the ball from sitting, kneeling or lying on the court, as long as a part of a foot is touching the court at all times,
- roll the ball and catch it or pick it up while standing or running,
- bounce the ball once and catch it while standing or running, and
- dribble the ball and then catch it.

If a player is holding the ball, they must dribble, pass, or shoot it within 3 seconds or after taking three steps. They may dribble it continuously an unlimited number of times, but once the player has picked up their dribble they may not begin dribbling again unless another player touches the ball. The player may take three steps, and then dribble, and then take three more steps; at this point they must pass or shoot the ball within 3 seconds.

Offensive players are not allowed to touch the ball with any part of the body below the knee (unless the ball has been thrown at the player by an opponent); doing so may result in a 2-minute suspension for kicking. They also cannot carry the ball while dribbling, play the ball intentionally out of bounds (except for the goalkeeper, in blocking a shot), or "stall" without the intent of scoring (this is passive play, and the defensive team is awarded a free throw at the point where the ball was when play was interrupted).

Approaching an Opponent

A player may use their arms and hands to try to gain possession of the ball, and they may use their torso to obstruct an opponent either with or without the ball. But the player may not

- obstruct an opponent by using their arms, hands, or legs;
- pull or hit the ball with one or both hands out of the hands of an opponent;
- use their fist to hit the ball from an opponent;
- endanger an opponent with the ball or endanger the goalkeeper; or
- hold, trip, run into, hit, or intentionally jump onto an opponent.

Less serious infractions merit first a warning and then a suspension (in which the offending player sits out 2 minutes). More serious infractions result in disqualification. Also, three 2-minute suspensions result in a player disqualification.

Goalkeeping

Only the goalkeeper may be in the goal area. A court player may not play the ball when it is stationary or rolling in the goal area. A court player may, however, play the ball when it is in the air above the goal area if they are not in the goal area themselves as long as they are throwing the ball before they land. A goalkeeper throw is awarded to the opposing team when a court player enters the goal area in possession of the ball, steps on the 6-meter line before throwing the ball at the goal, or enters the goal area without the ball.

A 7-meter throw is given when a clear chance of scoring is illegally destroyed anywhere on the court by a player. For example, a 7-meter throw is given when a defending court player enters the goal area and gains an illegal advantage over a player with the ball. No 7-meter throw is awarded if a player enters the goal area without the ball and gains no advantage.

If a defending player intentionally plays the ball into their own goal area with their feet inside the goalie area, the opponents are awarded a free throw. If this occurs unintentionally, the referee will determine where the ball went out of play and how it will reenter (goalie ball or throw in).

The goalkeeper may

- touch the ball with any part of their body while inside the goal area;

- move with the ball inside the goal area, with no restrictions;

- leave the goal area without the ball, at which time they become subject to the rules applying to all players in the playing area; and

- leave the goal area without control of the ball and play it in the playing area if they have not been able to control it.

A goalkeeper may not endanger an opponent, intentionally play the ball out over the goal line after gaining control of the ball, leave the goal area while in control of the ball, or touch the ball outside the goal area after making a goalkeeper throw, unless another player has since touched the ball.

In addition, a goalkeeper may not touch the ball in contact with the floor outside the goal area when they are inside the goal area, pick up the ball outside the goal area and bring it inside the goal area, touch the ball with any part of their body below the knee if they are not in the act of defending goal, or cross the 4-meter line before the thrower has thrown the ball in taking a 7-meter throw.

Throws

The following throws may be made during a game.

- A throw-off is used to begin a half and to resume play after a goal from center court. Each team is on its own side of the court when the half begins. After a goal, only the team that has to execute the throw-off must be on its own side of the court until the whistle is blown by the referee. Opponents must be at least 3 meters from the thrower. The referee whistles; the thrower has 3 seconds to throw.

- A throw-in is used when the ball has gone out of bounds. The referee doesn't whistle but indicates possession by indicating a direction; a player on the team awarded the ball throws the ball in with one foot on the sideline until the ball leaves their hand. They may not play the ball in to themselves. Opponents must stand at least 3 meters away, although they may stand outside their goal line, even if it's less than 3 meters away.

- A goalkeeper's throw is used when a shooter steps on the outer goal-area line, when an attacker behind the goal line (and the ball was not deviated by a defender), or when the ball is thrown by an attacker and the ball is deviated by the goalkeeper behind the goal line. If the goalkeeper throws the ball over the goal-area line, the referee does not whistle. A goalkeeper's throw also is used if the ball comes to rest in the goal area, the goalkeeper controls the ball in the goal area, or when the opposing team rolls the ball into the goal area.

- A free throw is used for numerous violations, including goalkeeper infractions, court player infractions in the goal area, infractions when playing the ball, passive play, and infractions connected with other throws. The ball is thrown either from where the infraction occurred or, if the violation occurred between the 9-meter line and the goal-area line, from the nearest point immediately outside the 9-meter line. After a whistle, the player takes the throw with opponents at least 3 meters away. Teammates may not be on the 9-meter line or between it and the 6-meter line before the player takes the throw.

- A corner throw is awarded to the attacking team when the ball is thrown toward the goal by an attacker, and it is deviated behind the goal line by a defender (not the goalkeeper).

- A 7-meter throw is used when a clear chance of scoring is destroyed by a defensive player's illegal action or a referee's inadvertent whistle, when a goalkeeper enters their own goal area with the ball, or when a court player enters their own goal area while playing defense. The ball is thrown at the 7-meter line. A referee blows their whistle, and the player has 3 seconds to take a shot on goal from behind the 7-meter line. The player must not touch on or beyond the line before the ball leaves their hand. Just the goalkeeper and the thrower are initially involved; the ball is not played again until it has touched the goalkeeper or goal. All other players must be beyond the 9-meter line or at least 3 meters away from the player when they take the throw. The throw is retaken if a defensive player violates this positioning (unless the player scored a goal); the player may also throw again if the goalkeeper moves beyond the 4-meter line before they release the ball.

Scoring

A team scores a goal when the entire ball crosses the entire width of the goal line and enters the goal, and the scoring team has not committed an infraction on the play. If the game is tied at the end of regulation time and a winner must be determined, teams play an overtime period: two halves of 5 minutes each. A coin toss determines who throws in.

If the score is still tied at the end of the first overtime, the teams play a second overtime period. If a tie exists at the end of the second overtime period, a penalty shootout occurs. Each team selects five shooters who alternate shooting from the penalty line. If a tie still exists at the end of each team's five penalty shots, individual penalty shots continue until a winner is determined. Only players who have not been suspended, disqualified, or excluded at the end of regulation time may participate in the penalty shots.

Punishments

A referee may warn, suspend, disqualify, or exclude a player. Warnings result from less serious infractions, such as those noted in "Approaching an Opponent." They also may result from violations that occur when a player is executing a formal throw and from unsportsmanlike conduct. The referee indicates a warning by holding up a yellow card.

Suspensions occur for repeated infractions, for faulty substitutions, and for failure to put the ball on the floor when the referee makes a decision. Suspensions last 2 minutes and are indicated by the referee's holding up their hand with two fingers extended. The team may not replace that player during the suspension but is free to substitute others. A player can receive another 2-minute suspension (4 minutes total) if they immediately repeats an infraction (e.g., keeps arguing with the referee).

Disqualifications occur when a player not entitled to participate enters the court, when there are serious infractions and repeated events of unsporting conduct, or when a player receives their third suspension. The team may not replace the disqualified player for 2 minutes. The disqualified player must leave the field of play and cannot return for the remainder of the match. A referee indicates a disqualification by holding up a red card.

A disqualification can also result from an assault that occurs either on or outside the court against another player, a referee, another official, or anyone in the area. Spitting is regarded as assault. As noted above a disqualification results in a player or team official leaving and not returning to the game, but in this circumstance the reduction in players on the field will only occur for 4 minutes. Due to the seriousness of the offense these types of suspensions are reported in writing to the appropriate authorities and receive further attention. For this reason referees show a blue card after showing the red card.

TERMS

The **center line** runs the width of the court, dividing the court into equal halves.

A **free throw** is awarded for goalkeeper infractions and other violations (see "Throws"); the player taking the free throw takes it from the point of infraction or, if the violation occurred between the 9-meter line and the goal-area line, from the nearest point outside the 9-meter, or free-throw, line.

The **free-throw line** is also known as the 9-meter line. It is a broken, nearly semicircular line drawn 3 meters from and parallel to the goal-area line.

The **goal area** is defined by the goal-area line, which is drawn 6 meters in front of the goal line in front of the goal and 6 meters from the goal post on each side of the goal. The line is a semicircle, with each end touching the goal line on either side of the goal.

The **goalkeeper's restraining line** is also known as the 4-meter line. It is 4 meters from the rear edge of the goal line, directly in front of the goal.

A **goalkeeper's throw** is awarded to the goalkeeper when the ball crosses the outer goal line. The goalkeeper must throw the ball from the goal area and beyond the goal-area line.

The **7-meter line** is 1 meter long. It is directly in front of the goal, 7 meters away from the rear edge of the goal line.

A **7-meter throw** is awarded in various situations (see "Throws") and is taken by a player who may not step on or beyond the 7-meter line before they throw the ball. The foremost foot cannot slide forward, backward, or side to side.

The **substitution area** may contain a maximum of four team officials and seven substitutes. Any players disqualified or excluded are not allowed in this area.

A **substitution line** allows players to leave and enter the court at any time over their own team's substitution line.

A **throw-in** is taken to put the ball back into play after it has gone out of bounds. It is taken where the ball went out of bounds or, if it crossed the outer goal line, from the intersection of the goal line and the sideline nearest where it went out of bounds.

A **throw-off** is used to begin each half and to resume play after a team has scored a goal. The team in possession of the ball must be on its own side during a throw-off, which takes place at center court. To put the ball in play, one player must place their foot on the center line while maintaining possession of the ball and wait until the referee has blown the whistle before making the throw-off.

OFFICIALS

Two referees with equal authority are in charge of the game. A timekeeper and a scorekeeper assist the referees.

ORGANIZATIONS

European Handball Federation
www.eurohandball.com

International Handball Federation
Peter Merian-Strasse 23
CH-4052 Basel
Switzerland
41-61-228-9040
www.ihf.info

USA Team Handball
1 Olympic Plaza
Colorado Springs, CO 80909
719-866-2203
www.teamusa.org/USA-Team-Handball

56

Tennis

FEFERBERG/AFP/Getty Images

Tennis can trace its roots back to 13th-century France, where players hit a ball over a net with their hands. The game was brought to Wales, where it evolved into lawn tennis, with players using rackets. The game became popular in 19th century England; the first Wimbledon championships were held in 1877.

Tennis was also introduced in the United States in the 19th century, but it didn't catch on as a major sport, either professionally or recreationally, until the 1960s. Recreational play in the United States peaked in the mid-1970s, with 34 million playing at least once per year. The number of those who play in the United States is on the rise, from 7.3 million in 1995 to nearly 18 million now.

OVERVIEW

Objective: To hit the ball over the net into the opponent's court so that the opponent cannot return the ball.

Number of Players: Either two (singles) or four (doubles).

Scoring: A point is scored in a variety of ways; see "Scoring."

Length of Games, Sets, and Matches: The first player to have a 2-point advantage and to have scored at least 4 points wins the game. The first player or side to win six games and lead by two games wins the set. A match is composed of the best two of three sets or the best three of five.

Each game begins at 0-0, or love. The first point scored is 15, the second is 30, the third is 40, and the fourth is game point. Game point wins the game unless the score was a deuce (40-40). If the server scores in deuce, she gains the advantage, or ad; if she scores the next point, she wins. If her opponent scores the next point, it is again deuce. A player must win by 2 points. When the server has the advantage, it is called ad-in; when the receiver has the advantage, it is called ad-out.

If a set is 6-6, a tiebreaker is often used to determine the winner. Players play 12 points; the first player to reach at least 7 points and be ahead by 2 points wins the tiebreaker and the set. If the score is 6-6, every 6 points, the players change ends and resume play until one is ahead by 2 points.

COURT

A court is 78 feet long by 27 feet wide for singles play or 36 feet wide for doubles play (see figure 56.1). It is divided in half by a net, made of cord, 36 inches high in the center and 42 inches high at the two supporting side posts. Service lines are parallel to and 21 feet from the net. They are 18 feet in front of the baselines, which are also parallel to the net and mark the outer boundary of each side of the court.

A center service line, parallel to the sideline, intersects the net and divides the service courts into two sections on both sides of the net. The center service line connects the two service lines. There are two service courts on each side of the net, covering the area between the net, the service line, the center service line, and the sideline. Each service court is 21 feet long by 13.5 feet wide. This area is also called the forecourt.

The backcourt is the area between the service line and the baseline. It is 18 feet long by 27 feet wide for singles play or 36 feet wide for doubles play. The court surface is clay, grass, or hardcourts made of asphalt or cement.

PLAYERS

Tennis is played in singles matches (two players) or doubles matches (four players). The following rules apply to doubles matches:

- Doubles use the widest portion of the court (36 feet).
- For serving, the same-size service courts are used as in singles.
- Teams alternate serves after each game, as in singles play; team A serves the first game, team B the second, and so on.
- Each team's players alternate serving complete games. Player 1 on team A serves game 1; player 2 on team A serves game 3, and so on.
- Players also alternate receiving serves. Player that receives the serve on either the deuce court or ad court must remain on that side for the whole match.
- If a player is discovered to have served out of turn, all prior points are counted and the mistake is immediately corrected with the

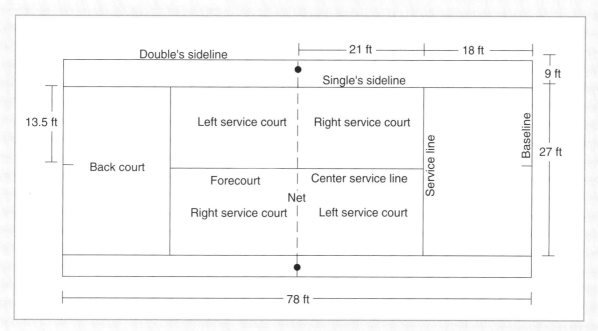

▶ **Figure 56.1** The dimensions and features of a tennis court.

right person serving next. If a team is discovered to have changed its receiving order, this order must remain until the end of the game, at which time the team resumes its normal receiving order.

- Doubles partners do not have to alternate hits.

EQUIPMENT

The ball is hollow rubber, either white or yellow. It is between 2.57 and 2.87 inches in diameter and weighs between 1.975 and 2.095 ounces. The racket may be up to 32 inches long and 12.5 inches wide. The strung surface, a pattern of crossed strings, may not be more than 15.5 inches long and 11.5 inches wide. Rackets are made of various materials; they may be of any weight. The net, when fully extended, should extend beyond the doubles playing area, and it should be held down by a white strap in the center. A white band should be spread across the full length of the top of the net. The mesh should be small enough so that the ball cannot pass through it.

RULES

The basics of tennis can be understood through its rules for serving, returning serve, and playing.

Serving

Players alternate serves: In singles, player 1 serves the first game, player 2 the second, and so on. In doubles, player 1 of team A serves the first game and player 2 of team A serves the third game; player 1 of team B serves the second game and player 2 of team B serves the fourth game, and so on. They also alternate the sides of the court they serve from, beginning each game on the right side. The serve is made into the service court diagonally opposite the side the server is standing on. Players switch ends of the court at the end of the first, third, fifth, and subsequent alternate games.

Play is continuous; the receiver must play to the reasonable pace of the server and must be ready to receive serve when the server is ready to serve. When changing ends, a maximum of 1 minute 30 seconds may elapse from the time the ball went out of play to end the previous game to the time the first serve begins the next game. Twenty seconds is allowed between points. Following the first game of each set and during tiebreakers, players change ends but with no rest. After each set there is a 2-minute break.

The server must stand with both her feet behind the baseline (see figure 56.1) and within the imaginary continuations of the center line and sideline. When the receiver is ready, the server tosses the ball in the air and hits it with her racket before it hits the ground. The ball must pass over the net and hit within the receiver's proper service court.

If the ball strikes the net and lands inside the proper service court, the play is called a let. A let may also be called for an interruption of play. A service fault occurs when the server swings and misses, hits the ball into the net, or hits the ball outside the opponent's proper service court.

A foot fault occurs when the server steps on or beyond the baseline or over the imaginary extensions of the center line or sideline while serving. Once the racket strikes the ball, the server may step on or over the baseline, center line, or sideline.

A server is allowed one fault (either service or foot). The player serves from behind the same half of the court on the second serve. If the player faults on his second serve, this is called a double fault, and his opponent wins the point.

In a tiebreaker, the player whose turn it is to serve serves one time. Her opponent serves the next two serves. It continues with each player serving twice until the set has been decided. Players change ends every 6 points. An alternative to using a tiebreaker is to continue the set until one player has a two-game lead, which system is used is up to the tournament officials. The points that decide the result of a game, set, or match are called game point, set point, and match point, respectively.

The server's score is always given first.

Returning Serve and Playing

The receiver must return the serve on the first bounce, hitting it over the net and into her opponent's court. A ball striking a boundary line is in play. During a *rally*—that is, a series of hits by the players—the ball may hit the net if the ball crosses and lands inbounds in the opponent's court. A let

occurs only during the serve (or when a point is inadvertently interrupted).

After the serve is returned, players may volley by hitting the ball before it bounces on their side or use ground strokes to return the ball after one bounce. A player's racket may cross over the net after he has returned (made contact with) the ball.

If a player intentionally hinders an opponent from making a stroke, the hindered player receives a point. If the action is unintentional, the point is replayed.

Scoring

The server scores a point if he hits an ace (a serve that the receiver cannot return) or if his serve hits his opponent. The receiver scores a point if the server double-faults. A player loses a point if she

- cannot return a ball before it bounces twice on her side,
- returns the ball out of bounds,
- hits the ball into the net,
- carries or catches the ball on her racket or deliberately touches the ball with her racket more than once,
- touches the net or posts,
- hits the ball by throwing her racket, or
- hits the ball before it has crossed the net.

TERMS

An **ace** (1 point) is scored by a server whose good serve is not touched.

A server commits a **fault** when he hits the ball into the net or outside his opponent's service court (service fault) or when he steps on or over the baseline before he hits his serve.

A **game** is won by the first player to score 4 points and be ahead by 2.

Game point is the point that can decide the game.

Hindrance may be called when a player is hindered by either her opponent or a spectator. Depending on the situation, hindrance results in a let, a playover, or a point awarded to the player hindered.

A **let** occurs on a serve when the ball strikes the net and lands in the opponent's proper service court, or it can occur when play is interrupted. A let requires that the point be replayed.

A **match** is won by the player who wins the best two of three or three of five sets.

Match point is the point that can decide the match.

A **rally** is a series of hits between players.

The **serve** is the play (the stroke or shot) that begins each point.

A **set** is won by the player who wins six games and is ahead by two games or who wins a tiebreaker.

Set point is the point that can decide the set.

A **volley** is a hit before the ball strikes the ground.

OFFICIALS

Matches are typically officiated by an umpire, whose decision is final; by net-cord judges, who place their fingers on the net to detect lets on serves; by linesmen, who make boundary decisions; and by foot-fault judges, who call foot faults. In many tournaments where umpires and linesmen are not available, however, players call their own lines.

MODIFICATIONS

Wheelchair tennis is played the same as regular tennis except that wheelchair players are allowed two bounces of the ball. The first bounce must be within the court, but the second bounce may be outside the court boundaries and still be in play.

The server may not roll or spin his chair while serving nor have any wheel touching on or beyond the baseline or imaginary extensions of the center line and sideline. A server may not use any part of his lower extremities to brake or stabilize himself while serving. Doing so results in a fault.

If a player is physically unable to serve in a conventional manner, another person may drop the ball to begin the player's serve. The wheelchair is considered part of the body. As such, if the ball touches a chair, that player loses a point. A player also loses a point if

- she hits her own partner with a ball;
- she uses any part of her feet or lower extremities to brake or stabilize while serving, stroking a ball, turning, or stopping; or
- she fails to keep one buttock in contact with her chair while hitting a ball.

ORGANIZATIONS

International Tennis Federation
Bank Lane
Roehampton
London SW15 5XZ
United Kingdom
www.itftennis.com

Professional Tennis Registry
P.O. Box 4739
Hilton Head, SC 29938
843-785-7244
www.ptrtennis.org

United States Professional Tennis Association
11961 Performance Dr.
Orlando, FL 32827
800-877-8248
www.uspta.org

United States Tennis Association
70 W. Red Oak Ln.
White Plains, NY 10604
914-696-7000
www.usta.com

57

Track and Field (Athletics)

Stockbyte

Competition in track and field events dates back to the 7th century BC. Modern track and field (or athletics, as it is known internationally) sprang from university events in England in the 19th century. Today the sport is popular worldwide and is one of the headline sports at the Olympic Games. In the United States, it is very popular at the youth and high school levels.

OVERVIEW

Objective: Depending on the event, to run the fastest, throw the farthest, or jump the highest or farthest.

Events: Running events include the sprints (60 meters, indoor only; 100, 200, and 400 meters); the hurdles (60 meters, indoor only; 100 meters for women, 110 meters for men, and 400 meters for both); and the middle-distance and distance events (from 800 to 10,000 meters). There are also throwing events (discus, hammer, javelin, shot put, and weight throw) and jumping events (high jump, long jump, triple jump, and pole vault). Walking events are also contested at 3 kilometers, 5 kilometers, and 10 kilometers.

In some competitions, team scores are kept; others are geared to individual (nonteam) competition. The rules in the main body of this chapter pertain to the senior classification (ages 18 and older). The sport is modified widely for groups of various ages and abilities; toward the end of the chapter, some of these modifications are highlighted.

COMPETITION AREA

Outdoor competition takes place on and around a 400-meter oval track (see figure 57.1). A track has six to nine lanes measuring between 1.22 meters and 1.25 meters in width. The surface is usually a synthetic composition.

Running events take place on the track; field events take place on the field inside the track or in a field away from the track. Indoor tracks vary in size; many are 200 meters in length. They usually have banked turns and are made of synthetic materials.

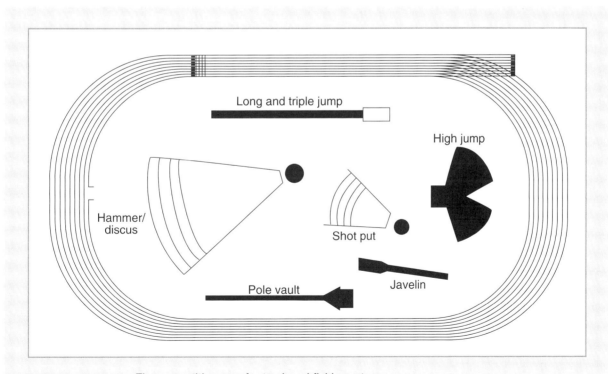

▷ **Figure 57.1** The competition area for track and field events.

ATHLETES

Athletes typically wear a bib on their front and sometimes only a hip sticker is needed to identify an athlete within a heat or a section. In the jumping events, only one bib is required, on the front or on the back. The bib should include a number, but the athlete's name or other identification is acceptable if permission is granted. The number is assigned by the meet organizer and provided to the athletes prior to competition.

RULES

Athletes compete in a variety of running events, jumping events, and throwing events.

Running events include hurdles, steeplechase, sprints (100, 200, and 400 meters), relays, and middle-distance and distance events. Jumping events include long jump, triple jump, high jump, and pole vault. Throwing events include shot put, hammer, weight throw, javelin, and discus. Athletes also compete in combined events—the decathlon and the heptathlon.

Running Events

Runners in events up to and including the 400-meter dash use starting blocks to protect the track. Both runner's feet must be in contact with the blocks, which often are equipped with a device that helps starters detect false starts. Many races are recorded by electronic timers, which register times to a hundredth of a second. Most events allow athletes to wear spiked footwear, with up to 11 spikes.

A runner's left hand is always toward the inside of the track; races are run counterclockwise. Many meets have heats, or qualifying rounds, through which runners must advance to get to the finals. Runners are either randomly assigned lanes or according to their seed time that is submitted by coaches or an electronic database in the first round; after that, their performance determines in which lane they will run.

Sprinters (competitors in races of 400 meters or less) run in the same lane the whole race. In the 200-meter and 400-meter events, where sprinters must race around curves, the starting places are staggered so that each runner runs the same distance.

In 800-meter events, runners run in lanes until after the first turn, when they can cut to the inside lane. Races beyond 800 meters are not run in lanes.

Start All competitors must be completely behind the starting line, with no parts of their bodies touching it or extending beyond it. For races of 400 meters or less, the commands are "On your marks" and "Set." When all competitors are set and completely motionless in the starting position, the starter fires a starting pistol. For races beyond 400 meters, the command is "On your marks," and when runners are ready, the gun is fired. All competitors must immediately follow the commands; delaying in getting set, or resetting once a runner is set, will result in a false start.

No false start may be assessed generally to the field; each one must be charged to an individual. In the event a race has to be recalled because of a false start, the starter fires the pistol again. In races where starting blocks are used (up to and including the 400 meters), false-start detection apparatuses may be hooked up to the blocks.

A distance race can be recalled in case of a fall within the first turn.

Race Any runner who jostles or impedes another runner may be disqualified. In races run entirely in lanes, competitors must stay in their lanes or be disqualified. In races begun in lanes, runners must remain in their lanes until the break-line mark. A runner who leaves the track (crossing over the inside boundary line of the first lane without being pushed off) is out of the race.

Finish A runner officially ends the race when their torso reaches the finish line. The head, neck, arms, hands, legs, and feet do not count. In case of a tie, times are given down the thousandths to determine the winner.

Hurdles Hurdle events include the 60-meter (indoors only), 100-meter, 110-meter, and 400-meter races. Youth competitions can also include a 300 meters event.

Hurdle races are run entirely in lanes. A runner must clear the hurdle with both legs. The runner is disqualified if either leg dips lower than the horizontal plane of the hurdle. This means that the leg must go over the top of the hurdle and is not allowed to go around or beside it. Hurdlers are not disqualified, however, for unintentionally knocking over hurdles.

The top bar of the hurdle is made of wood or plastic. The hurdle is durable enough that it is not easily broken by a competitor hitting it. Heights of hurdles and distances between hurdles are shown in table 57.1.

Steeplechase The 3,000-meter steeplechase has 28 hurdle jumps and 7 water jumps (5 jumps per lap, with the water jump as the fourth jump). Runners run the first 200 meters without taking a hurdle; from there on they take five hurdles per lap.

The 2,000-meter steeplechase, run in some junior events, has 18 hurdle jumps and 5 water jumps.

The height of the men's hurdles is 36 inches; women's hurdles are 30 inches. The hurdles are 13 feet wide, and the bar on top of each hurdle is 5 inches square. The water jump is 12 feet long. The water is 27.5 inches deep at the beginning of the jump, nearest the hurdle; it slopes to the level of the field at the end of the jump.

A runner is disqualified if they don't fully clear a hurdle. Runners may not trail a leg or foot lower than the horizontal plane of the top of the hurdle. Runners may clear a hurdle by jumping over it without touching it or by placing a foot on the hurdle and vaulting over it.

Relays The relay is contested over 400, 800, 1,600, and 3,200 meters. There are various medleys as well, which are made up of a variety of distances. A relay race is made up of teams of four runners each. Each runner runs a set distance before passing a baton to a teammate. A baton is a hollow tube, usually made of metal, not longer than 30 centimeters and weighing no less than 50 grams.

The baton handoff must take place in a 20-meter takeover zone, with the starting line in the middle of this zone. If the handoff occurs outside of this zone, the team is disqualified. It is the baton's position, and not that of the runners, that determines whether the handoff was legal or not.

For races where lanes cease to be used, waiting runners move to an inside position to receive the handoff as their incoming teammates arrive. For races where lanes are used, runners who have finished their leg must remain in their lanes after handing off to avoid interfering with other runners.

In outdoor relays, runners of either 100-meter or 200-meter segments may use a 10-meter acceleration zone before the exchange zone. In indoor relays, such an acceleration zone is not used.

The 400-meter and 800-meter relays are run entirely in lanes. In the 800-meter medley relay, the first, second, and third runners run in lanes, with the fourth runner moving to the inside. In the 4 × 400 relay, the first runner runs entirely in their lane, while the second runner runs the curve to a break line before moving to the inside. In the 4 × 800 relay, the first runner runs the curve in their lane to a break line before moving to the inside.

TABLE 57.1

Hurdle Specifications

Hurdle event	No. of hurdles	Height of hurdles (in.)	Distance between hurdles (m)
Women's 60 m	5	33	8.50
Men's 60 m	5	42	9.14
Women's 100 m	10	33	8.50
Men's 110 m	10	42	9.14
Women's 400 m	10	30	35.0
Men's 400 m	10	36	35.0

Adapted by permission from USA Track and Field, *2018 USATF Competition Rules* (Indianapolis, IN: USA Track and Field, 2018, 77. Available: http://www.usatf.org/usatf/files/72/72d219cf-4410-4631-923b-5cbda90b79f7.pdf.

Jumping Events

Jumping events include

- the high jump, where competitors try to jump over a crossbar;
- the pole vault, where competitors use a flexible pole in trying to vault over a crossbar;
- the long jump, where competitors sprint to a takeoff board and try to leap the farthest into a sand pit; and
- the triple jump, where competitors sprint to a takeoff board and take a hop, step, and jump into a sand pit.

In all jumping events, competitors have a fixed amount of time after they are called to complete their jump. It is customary in vertical jumps that if a competitor passes on three consecutive heights, they are allowed one warm-up jump without the crossbar in place.

It is common practice for an athlete to compete in various events during a competition. Typically, an athlete will prioritize a track event and therefore the athlete can leave the jump area to compete in another event but must notify a jump official and report back at the required time.

High Jump   The apron surrounding the high jump pit is a 15-meter semicircle. In championship events, a 20-meter runway is suggested. The high jump standards (the uprights and posts) are rigid. The crossbar is typically constructed of fiberglass, its cross-section is circular and may be up to 3 centimeters in diameter. The bar may sag a maximum of 2 centimeters.

The landing pit of cushioned foam rubber is 5 meters long by 4 meters wide. The height of a jump is measured from the ground to the lowest portion of the crossbar. Jumpers may use one or two markers to assist in their run-up and takeoff.

Jumpers compete in the order drawn. A competitor may choose to pass at any height but may not later attempt a jump at that height, except in a jump-off to break a first-place tie.

If the jumper knocks the bar off the standards, or touches an area beyond the uprights before going over the bar, the jump is a failure. After three consecutive missed jumps at any height, the competitor is finished. A jumper may fail at one height and then pass on their next turn, waiting for the next height.

At the end of each round, the bar is raised at least 2 centimeters. Rounds continue until only one competitor remains in the competition. That jumper may attempt greater heights. If two jumpers are tied, the jumper with the fewest attempts at the winning height wins. If the jumpers are still tied, the competitor with the fewest overall misses wins.

Pole Vault   The suggested runway for the pole vault is 40 to 45 meters. The takeoff box, where the vaulter plants their pole after the run-up, is about 61 centimeters wide by 99 centimeters long, sinking into the ground at 105 degrees in front of the standard's uprights, which are rigid and can be manipulated by up to 80 centimeters away from the takeoff box. The crossbar is similar to that for the high jump but slightly heavier and longer, as the standard's uprights are farther apart than those of the high jump.

The landing area is cushioned foam rubber, 5 meters square. The pole may be of any material, length, and diameter, but its basic surface must be smooth. A vaulter may use one or two layers of adhesive tape on the pole and may use resin or an adhesive substance on their hands for a better grip. A vaulter may use one or two markers alongside the runway to assist in their run-up, and, as with the high jump, the measurement is from the ground to the highest portion of the crossbar.

The competitive procedure is similar to that for the high jump: A vaulter may pass at any height and is out of the competition after three consecutive misses. Depending upon the amount of athletes left in the competition, as well as the predetermined increments, the bar is moved up at least 2 inches after each completed height. A jump is recorded as a miss if the vaulter knocks the bar off the standards; if the athlete or the pole touches an area beyond the uprights before they clear the bar; or if the competitor, while in the air, moves their lower hand above their upper hand or moves their upper hand off the pole. Competition continues until the last vaulter has recorded three misses, or until that vaulter decides to retire once their competitors have been eliminated from the competition. Ties are broken, as in the high jump, with a jump-off for the first place ranking and through a count back for the lesser rankings. If a pole is broken during an attempt, the attempt does not count against the competitor.

Long Jump   There is no maximum limit on the run-up; a competitor is limited only by the actual length of the runway. Competitors may place one or two markers along the runway to assist in their steps on the run-up. On the run-up, the jumper approaches the takeoff board, made of wood and about 8 inches wide by 4 feet long. The jumper's foot must not mark beyond the takeoff line at the far end of the board. Beyond this board is a plasticine board, about 4 inches wide, on which athletes' footprints may be spotted.

A windsock is placed near the takeoff board so that jumpers can determine the approximate direction and strength of the wind. The landing area is a sand pit, 3 meters wide by approximately 10 to 11 meters long extending from the board. The sand must be level with the takeoff board.

In competitions with more than eight jumpers, each competitor takes three jumps, in rotating order. Each competitor counts their best jump. The eight best marks advance; these eight athletes get three more jumps. The longest jump wins. In competitions with eight or fewer athletes, each jumper gets six jumps and counts their best legal jump. The measurement is taken from the takeoff line to the nearest sand broken by the competitor. A jump is a foul when the athlete

- touches the ground beyond the takeoff line,
- takes off beyond either side of the takeoff board (whether or not behind the line),
- touches the ground outside the landing area closer to the takeoff line than to the nearest mark made in the pit, or
- walks back through the landing area.

Triple Jump   The jumping area is the same as for the long jump. The placement of the takeoff board depends on the caliber of competition. In major competitions, the distance between the board and the landing area should be at least 13 meters for men and 10 meters for women. The recommended distance between the takeoff board and the end of the landing area is 21 meters.

The competitor sprints down the runway, takes off on either foot from the takeoff board, lands on that same foot, takes a long step and lands on the opposite foot, and jumps into the landing area.

It is not a foul if the jumper touches the "off" leg or foot on the ground during the jump. All other rules and procedures for the triple jump are the same as for the long jump.

Throwing Events

Athletes compete against each other to record the longest throw of various implements in the discus throw, the hammer throw, the javelin throw, the shot put, and the weight throw. These general rules apply to all throwing events: In throws from a circle, the athlete must begin from a stationary position. The competitor may touch the inside of the band or stop-board but not the top. Failing to start from a stationary position and touching the top of the stop-board are fouls.

Other fouls include touching any surface outside the circle, improperly releasing the implement, failing to leave the circle from the back, and leaving the circle before the implement lands.

Except in the hammer and weight throws, or to cover an open cut, athletes may not tape their fingers. They may use a substance on their hands to improve their grip, and they may wear belts to protect their backs from injury. Competitors have a given time to begin their trials once their names are called by the event official. As in the jumping events, they must check out when leaving the area for another event and must report back on time.

Except for the hammer and weight throws, no gloves are allowed. No flags or markers may be placed in the landing sector, which fans out in two lines from the throwing circle at a 40-degree angle. A throw is not valid if it does not land within the landing sector marked on the ground.

If a competitor misses their turn, that turn is lost, but they may still use any subsequent turns they have coming to them. In a field of nine or more competitors, each athlete gets three attempts, and the eight individuals with the best attempts advance. In a field of eight or fewer, all competitors get six throws. The best legal throw for each competitor is used to determine final standings.

For the discus, hammer, shot put, and weight throw, the measurement is made from the inside of the circle's circumference along a line to the nearest point of the mark made by the implement. For the javelin, the measurement is made from the inside edge of the throwing arc on a line to the point where the ground was broken by the tip of the javelin.

Shot Put   The shot is a solid metal ball. Contestants "put" (throw) the shot from a circle with a 7 foot diameter. The shot is put from the shoulder, with one hand. The hand holds the shot close to the chin; it may not be dropped from its position during the put. The shot may not be brought behind the line of the shoulders.

Discus   The discus is a smooth implement, usually wood with a metal rim. It is thrown from a circle that is 2.5 meters in diameter. Contestants may not wear spiked shoes. A cage surrounds the throwing area to protect spectators.

Javelin   The javelin is a slender metal shaft thrown from behind a curved arc at the end of a runway, which is between 30.0 and 36.5 meters long and 4 meters wide. The arc is white, typically made of wood or metal, and has a radius of 8 meters. The men's javelin is 8.8 feet long; the women's javelin is 7.5 feet long. Tape may not be used on the javelin. The surface and finish must be smooth. A nonslip grip is placed in the middle of the shaft. Competitors may wear spiked shoes.

The javelin is thrown into a landing sector, which begins 8 meters behind the arc and extends out in a 29-degree angle. The javelin must be held with one hand and thrown over the shoulder. The tip of the javelin must strike the ground first for the throw to be valid. Other fouls are recorded when

- the competitor turns their back to the throwing area after preparing to throw;
- the throw does not land completely in the landing sector;
- the competitor touches the arc, the ground beyond the arc, or the boundary lines; or
- the competitor leaves the runway before the javelin touches the ground.

Javelin throwers may place one or two marks along the runway to assist in the run-up.

More states at the high school level are now competing in the Turbojav than in the regular javelin. The Turbojav is much safer because it is made out of plastic and has a foam tip.

Hammer   The hammer consists of three parts: a solid metal head, a wire about 4 feet long, and a single or double-loop grip. This event is only contested outdoors. The senior men's hammer weighs 16.0 pounds; the women's hammer weighs 8.8 pounds. The hammer thrower may wear gloves. The thrower may rest the head of the hammer either inside or outside the throwing circle. The thrower grips the hammer with both hands.

It is not a foul if the hammer touches the ground or the top of the iron band in the throwing circle as the competitor is making their turns in preparing to throw. It is a foul, however, if the hammer touches the ground or iron band and the hammer thrower stops their throw. If the hammer breaks during the throw or while in the air, it is not considered an attempt. The competitor may throw another hammer.

Weight Throw   The weight throw is only contested indoors. The weight consists of three parts: a solid metal head, a handle of round metal, and a steel link connection. Men throw a 35-pound weight; women throw a 20-pound weight. In making the throw, a competitor uses both hands, holding the weight by the handle, assuming any position they choose.

Combined Events

Men and women have several combined events to compete in, both indoors and out. The most common combined event for men is the decathlon, which consists of 10 events over 2 days. On day 1, men compete in the 100-meter dash, the long jump, the shot put, the high jump, and the 400-meter dash. On day 2, they compete in the 110-meter hurdles, the discus throw, the pole vault, the javelin throw, and the 1,500-meter run. Men compete in the heptathlon indoors, over two days. On the first day, they contest the 60 meters, long jump, shot put, and high jump, and on the second day, the 60-meter hurdles, the pole vault, and the 1,000 meters.

The most common women's combined event is the heptathlon, which consists of seven events over 2 days. On day 1, women compete in the 100-meter hurdles, the high jump, the shot put, and the 200-meter dash. On day 2, they compete in the long jump, the javelin throw, and the 800-meter run. Indoors, women can compete in the pentathlon, which consists of five events on 1 day: the 60-meter hurdles, high jump, shot put, long jump, and 800 meters.

Rules for combined events generally are the same as for the individual events, with the following exceptions:

- Competitors get three trials each in the long jump, shot put, discus throw, and javelin throw.

- A competitor is disqualified in the hurdles or running events after a second false start. The first false start will be charged to the field, and any subsequent false start may result in disqualification. The allowable wind reading in combined events is +4 meters per second.

- An athlete who does not start one event is disqualified from the competition, but starting and not finishing does not remove the athlete from competition (though it will significantly affect the score).

- Points are awarded for times and distances recorded for each event. The highest score wins.

TERMS

A **false start** occurs when a runner begins a race before the starting pistol is fired. A competitor is disqualified for either one or two false starts, depending on the level of competition.

FAT is an acronym for **f**ully **a**utomatic **t**iming, in which the timing device starts automatically when the starter's pistol goes off. It automatically records when each torso crosses the finish line.

Some competitions have **heats**, or qualifying rounds, to narrow the field and advance runners to the finals.

A **photo finish** is the term used when a finish uses a photographic system to determine the winner of a race.

A **wind-aided effort** refers to running events up to and including the 200-meter race, as well as the long jump and triple jump, where the velocity of the wind exceeds 2 meters per second in the direction of the competition. Records set on a wind-aided effort are not recognized.

OFFICIALS

The number of officials needed to conduct a track and field meet varies with the size and type of meet being conducted. For large meets, these officials are typically in place:

- General officials—games committee, meet director, marshals, announcers, press steward, medical doctor or certified trainer, records coordinator, meet referees, juries, scorers, and custodian of awards

- Track events officials—clerks of course, finish judges, manual timers, starters, running referee, umpires, hurdle setters and block setters, wind gauge operators, lap counters, head finish evaluator (fully automatic timing), and timing device operators (fully automatic timing)

- Field events officials—head field judge, field judges, markers, measurers, implement inspector, wind gauge operators, throwing referee, jumping referee

MODIFICATIONS

This section contains some of the basic rules that modify the sport for youth, masters, and race walking.

Junior

Junior track is divided into 1- or 2-year age divisions up through age 19. These divisions are based on the athlete's birth year.

Important modifications of rules for these classifications include the following:

- In competitions for younger athletes, starting blocks are not necessary, although runners may choose to use them.

- Youth athletes run a 2,000-meter steeplechase. In field events, in lieu of three attempts in a preliminary round and three attempts in a final round, competitors may have one round with four attempts.

In the javelin, the measurement is made from the center of the circle to the first point of contact the javelin makes with the ground in the landing sector. The contact may be with any part of the javelin.

Masters

Masters competition is split into 5-year age groups, beginning with 30 to 34 (submasters). Starting blocks are not required, but competitors may use them. Competitors are disqualified after one false start.

In the high jump and pole vault, athletes who pass on three consecutive heights are allowed one warm-up jump without the crossbar in place. Hurdle heights are increasingly lowered as competitors reach older age groups. Implement weights (for the shot put, discus, javelin, and so on) are lowered as well.

Race Walking

Race walking may take place on either road or track. The main rules include the following:

- Unbroken contact must be maintained with the ground (the lead foot must touch the ground before the back foot leaves the ground).
- The support leg must be straightened for at least a moment. One warning is given for a violation; a second occurrence means disqualification.

ORGANIZATIONS

Amateur Athletic Union
P.O. Box 22409
Lake Buena Vista, FL 32830
407-934-7200
www.aauathletics.org

International Association of Athletics Federations
17 rue Princesse Florestine
BP 359
MC-98007
Monaco
377 93 10 8888
www.iaaf.org

Road Runners Club of America
1501 Lee Hwy., Ste. 140
Arlington, VA 22209
703-525-3890
www.rrca.org

USA Track & Field
132 E. Washington St., Ste. 800
Indianapolis, IN 46204
317-261-0500
www.usatf.org

58

Triathlon

AMR Image/iStock/Getty Images

The first known triathlon—a three-part swimming, cycling, and running event—was held in 1974 in San Diego, California. John Collins, a U.S. naval officer, who competed in this first informal triathlon, brought the sport to Hawaii, helping to create the Ironman Triathlon from three separate endurance events already in existence there. The first Ironman was held in 1978, with 12 men finishing; the next year, 13 men and 1 woman finished.

The sport began to take off in the early 1980s; now nearly 2,000 athletes compete in the Ironman World Championship, with another 1,500 competing in the National Age Group Championship presented by USA Triathlon. Triathlon races of varying distances are held throughout the United States and internationally. There are nearly four million active triathletes in the United States. The sport made its Olympic Games debut at the 2000 Summer Olympics in Sydney, Australia.

OVERVIEW

Objective: To complete the course with the fastest time while keeping within the rules.

Although a triathlon is composed of a single race with swimming, bicycling, and running events, in that order, USA Triathlon is the national governing body for all disciplines of multisport—generally triathlon, duathlon, aquathlon, off-road triathlon, aquabike, and winter triathlon. The specific information in this chapter, however, pertains to swimming, biking, and running—in other words, to triathlon.

USA Triathlon recognizes four distance categories: short, intermediate, long, and ultra. The distances may vary somewhat, but the basic categories are shown in table 58.1.

TABLE 58.1

Triathlon Distances

Type	Swim (mi)	Bike (mi)	Run (mi)
Short	0.2-0.6	5.0-18.6	1.0-3.9
Intermediate	0.7-1.2	18.7-31.0	4.0-8.0
Long	1.3-1.9	31.1-62.0	8.0-18.6
Ultra	2.0+	62.1+	18.7+

From USA Triathlon.

FIELD

Depending on the size of the field, a triathlon begins with either a mass start, in which all athletes begin at once, or a wave start, in which triathletes are grouped and begin at different times. After completing the swim, triathletes enter the transition area, where they don helmets and shoes, get on their bikes, and begin the cycling course. Upon finishing the cycling phase, they again enter a transition area, replace their bikes in the designated corral, and begin the running phase. Once they complete the run, the race is over.

TRIATHLETES

Triathletes generally compete in appropriate age groups based on their age as of December 31 each year. Competitors may be assessed variable time penalties for a variety of rules infractions, including drafting, improper position on the bike course, passing on the right of another cyclist, littering, and receiving unauthorized assistance such as pacing or aid from a nonparticipant. They may exit a race course, but they must reenter at the point they exited or be assessed a variable time penalty. The rules of the sport were established to provide a consistent foundation of safety and fairness in competition; helmets must always be worn during the event and while at any location within the race venue, and personal audio devices cannot be worn during competition.

EQUIPMENT

Swimmers must wear either the official race cap or a brightly colored swim cap. They may wear goggles or face masks, but these are not required.

They may not wear fins, paddles, gloves, floating devices, or any artificial propulsion device.

Cyclists must wear helmets that are approved by the Consumer Product Safety Commission (CPSC) and bear the CPSC sticker. They must fasten their chin straps before they mount their bikes, and they may not unfasten them until after they dismount.

Bicycles may not exceed 2 meters in length or 75 centimeters in width. The distance between the center of the chainwheel axle and the ground must be at least 24 centimeters. Bikes may not have any wind resistance shields or devices attached anywhere. The front wheel of the bike must be of spoke construction; the rear wheel may be either spoke or solid. Each wheel must have one working brake.

RULES

Following are the basic rules for each of the three phases of a triathlon.

Swimming

Swimmers may use any stroke; they may tread water, float, or stand on the bottom to rest. They may also hold onto buoys, boats, ropes, or other objects to rest, but they may not make forward progress while holding onto an object.

Swimmers may wear wetsuits in water temperatures up to and including 78 degrees Fahrenheit (25.6 degrees Celsius). They may wear wetsuits when the water temperature is between 78 and 84 degrees Fahrenheit, but they are not eligible for prizes or awards. When the water temperature is 84 degrees Fahrenheit (28.9 degrees Celsius) or greater, they may not wear wetsuits.

Cycling

Cyclists must obey all traffic laws unless directed to do otherwise by a race official. Cyclists must use only their own force in propelling their bikes. Forward progress on the bike course must be made with the bicycle in the participant's possession. Cyclists assume sole responsibility for knowing the course. Neither race directors nor officials will adjust race times if cyclists get off course.

Cyclists who endanger themselves or others are disqualified. They may not wear or carry personal audio devices such as music players or other items deemed dangerous by race officials. They may carry a cell phone as long as it is stored out of sight. They must wear approved helmets with fastened chin straps.

Cyclists may not work together to improve performance or team position. No cyclist may be in the drafting zone of another cyclist or of a motor vehicle, except if he is passing. A cyclist's drafting zone is 7 meters long and 2 meters wide, with the length beginning at the front of the front wheel. A motor vehicle's drafting zone is 15 meters wide and 30 meters long. Cyclists must keep to the right of the course unless passing.

They may not attempt to pass unless they have adequate space to do so.

A cyclist is generally entitled to a position on the course if she gained it without touching another cyclist. Although cyclists who have established the right of way may not obstruct the progress of other cyclists, a cyclist who is overtaking another cyclist bears the primary responsibility for avoiding a positioning foul, even if the cyclist ahead decreases speed. A cyclist overtakes another cyclist when her front wheel goes beyond the front wheel of the other cyclist.

When a cyclist overtakes another cyclist, the overtaken cyclist bears primary responsibility for avoiding a positioning foul. An overtaken cyclist must move completely out of the drafting zone of the cyclist who has just passed her before she tries to pass that cyclist. A cyclist may be in the drafting zone of another cyclist only

- when it takes 15 seconds or less to overtake the cyclist;
- for safety reasons, course blockage, in transition areas, or when making a turn of 90 degrees or greater; or
- when race officials allow it because of narrow lanes.

A cyclist who violates a positioning rule is assessed a variable time penalty for each of the first two violations and is disqualified after the third violation.

Elite athletes at the Olympic Games and certain international competitions are allowed to draft on the bicycling leg of the race, which provides very exciting racing conditions.

Running

Triathletes must run or walk the course. As with the cycling portion of the race course, contestants are responsible for knowing and following the course. They may not wear or carry personal audio devices such as music players. They may carry a cell phone as long as it is stored out of sight.

TERMS

A **variable time penalty** is assessed for fouls such as obstruction and unfair advantage. The time penalized depends on the race distance.

- Short: 2 minutes
- Intermediate: 2 minutes
- Long: 4 minutes
- Ultra: 8 minutes

OFFICIALS

Race officials consist of a head referee, marshals, judges, and a head timer. The decisions of the head referee are final and binding with respect to all competition matters, and the final results reflect those rule enforcement and penalty decisions.

ORGANIZATIONS

British Triathlon
P.O. Box 25
Loughborough LE11 3WX
United Kingdom
44 01509 226 161
www.britishtriathlon.org

International Triathlon Union
Maison du Sport International
Av. de Rhodanie 54
CH-1007 Lausanne
Switzerland
41-21-614-6030
www.triathlon.org

USA Triathlon
5825 Delmonico Dr., Ste. 200
Colorado Springs, CO 80919
719-955-2807
www.usatriathlon.org

59

Ultimate

Ultimate arose from a game invented by students at Columbia High School in Maplewood, New Jersey, in 1968. It is now played in more than 80 countries by 7 million people, with as many as 3.6 million people estimated to play in the United States alone, and it is the most popular flying-disc sport. This fast-growing sport is played at club, high school, college, community, and corporate levels. It holds competitions for mixed gender, men's, women's, youth, and masters play.

OVERVIEW

Objective: To score the most goals, typically reaching a target goal (most often 15) before a time cap.

Scoring: A goal is scored when any player catches a legal pass in the end zone of attack; the player's first point of contact with the ground must be completely in the end zone.

Number of Players: Seven per team on-field, often with offensive and defensive roles and lines.

Size of Field: 40 yards wide by 70 yards long, with 20- or 25-yard end zones on either end.

Disc: For championship levels, 175-gram models approved by the USA Ultimate Disc Standards Review Process; for informal play, any flying disc that is acceptable to both team captains.

Length of Game: Until one team reaches or exceeds a set target number of goals, 15, typically with a certain time capped period and is ahead of any other team by two or more goals.

Ultimate is a noncontact disc sport, meaning intentional contact is not allowed per the rules, although incidental contact that does not affect the outcome of a play nor endanger player safety is not against the rules. The disc is advanced by passing it to other players; self passes are not legal. Players are not allowed to continue running after catching a pass and must make efforts to come to a stop and set a point of pivot. The disc may be passed and caught in any direction on the playing field. Any time a pass is incomplete, intercepted, or knocked down or contacts an out-of-bounds area, a turnover occurs and results in an immediate change of team possession with no required time delay.

FIELD

The standard field of play is a rectangular area with dimensions of 40 by 120 yards, as shown in figure 59.1. More recent standards of play at championship levels are utilizing a slightly shorter field of 110 total yards and 20-yard end zones, in order to decrease the common offensive advantage and ease of scoring, as well as to make more field spaces viable. The brick mark is 20 yards towards midfield from each end zone, midway between the sidelines. The playing field proper is the playing field excluding the end zones. The corners of the playing field proper and the end zones are typically marked by cones or pylons, with sidelines, endlines, and goal lines marked by paint of chalk.

PLAYERS

Player roles include throwers, markers, receivers, and receiver defenders. Following are the essential rules governing play for each of these types of players.

Thrower

The thrower is the offensive player in possession of the disc or the player who has just released the disc. Once an offensive player has picked up the disc, that player is required to put the disc into play. If the disc is on the playing field proper, an offensive player must put the disc in play within 10 seconds. If the disc is not on the playing field proper, an offensive player must put the disc in play within 20 seconds. The thrower can pivot in any direction, but once the defensive marker has established a legitimate stationary position, the thrower may not pivot into the marker's body. The thrower cannot change the pivot until the throw is released.

Marker

Only one defensive player may guard the thrower within 3 meters of distance from the thrower's pivot spot at any one time; that player is the marker. No other defensive player can establish a position within 3 meters of the thrower's pivot unless that defender is guarding and reacting primarily to another offensive player receiver in that area. There must be at least one disc diameter

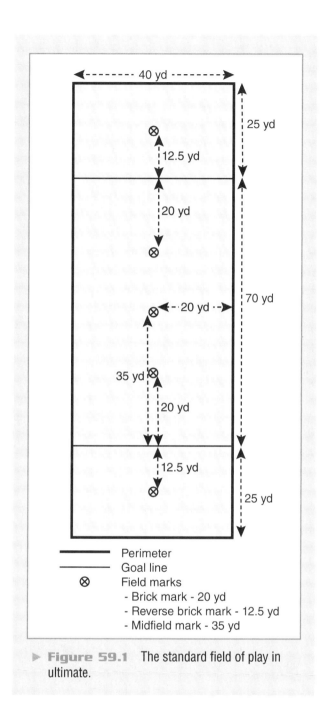

▶ **Figure 59.1** The standard field of play in ultimate.

from reaching a receiver after the disc has left the thrower's hand.

After establishing controlled possession of a nonspinning disc, the thrower is allowed 10 seconds to throw, which is timed by the marker's audible stall count. The marker loudly announces, "Stalling," and counts from 1 to 10 (in 1-second intervals) loudly enough for the thrower to hear. Only a marker within 3 meters of the thrower's point of ground contact may initiate or continue a stall count.

If the defense switches markers, the new marker must restart the stall count. A marker leaving the 3-meter radius and returning is considered a new marker.

The marker may not straddle (place one foot on either side of) the thrower's pivot or deliberately block the thrower's vision.

Receiver

The receiver is any offensive player either in the act of catching the disc or not in possession of the disc. If a receiver speeds up, changes direction, or obviously takes more steps than are required to stop after catching a pass and before establishing a pivot, that player has traveled. If a receiver catches a pass on the run and then releases a pass after the third ground contact before coming to a complete stop, that player has traveled. Bobbling to gain control of the disc is permitted, but purposeful, controlled bobbling to oneself to advance the disc in any direction is considered traveling.

If the disc is caught simultaneously by offensive and defensive players, the offense retains possession. If an airborne player catches the disc and is contacted by an opposing player before landing, and that contact causes the receiver to land out of bounds, the receiver may call a blocking foul and retain possession at the spot of the foul.

between the upper bodies of the thrower and the marker at all times. If a line between any two points on the marker touches the thrower or is less than one disc diameter away from the torso or pivot of the thrower, it is a disc space violation. However, if this situation is caused solely by movement of the thrower, it is not a violation. The marker typically attempts to block a throw

EQUIPMENT

Any flying disc may be used as long as it is acceptable to both team captains and the event organizer. If the captains cannot agree, the current official disc of USA Ultimate should be used. Cleats with any dangerous parts, such as metallic baseball cleats, track spikes, or worn or broken studs with sharp edges, are not allowed.

RULES

The purpose of the rules of ultimate is to provide a guideline describing the way the game is played. It assumed that no ultimate player will intentionally violate the rules; thus there are no harsh penalties for inadvertent infractions but rather a method for resuming play in a manner that simulates what would most likely have occurred had there been no infraction.

Spirit of the Game

In ultimate, an intentional foul is considered cheating and a gross offense against the spirit of the game. Often a player is in a position where it is clearly to a player's advantage to foul or commit some infraction, but that player is morally bound to abide by the rules. The integrity of ultimate depends on each player's responsibility to uphold the spirit of the game, and this responsibility should not be taken lightly. Ultimate relies upon the spirit of sportsmanship that places the responsibility for fair play on the player. Highly competitive play is encouraged but never at the expense of mutual respect among competitors, adherence to the agreed upon rules, or the basic joy of play. Protection of these vital elements serves to eliminate unsportsmanlike conduct from the ultimate field. Such actions as taunting opposing players, dangerous aggression, belligerent intimidation, intentional infractions, or other win-at-all-costs behavior are contrary to the spirit of the game and must be avoided by all players.

Much of the basics of ultimate can be understood through its rules regarding length of game, pulls, inbounds and out of bounds, end zone possession, and violations and fouls.

Length of Game

A standard game is played until one team reaches or exceeds 15 goals with a margin of at least two goals over its opponent. (Halftime occurs when one team first reaches or exceeds half the game total needed to win.) There are variations on that length, however, including

- a point cap, which is a maximum score limit imposed before the event;
- a soft time cap, which is a maximum score limit imposed during the game once a predetermined time of play has elapsed and after the current scoring attempt is completed; and
- a hard time cap, which is the ending of the game once a predetermined time of play has elapsed and after the current scoring attempt is completed. If the score is tied, play continues until one additional goal is scored.

Note: A soft time cap creates a new cap to the game score that didn't exist at the start of the game. For example, suppose a game score is 11-10 and the time slot for a particular round of play is expiring. A reduced winning score can be set to ensure completion of the game. In general, it is the current higher score plus 1 or 2 points. A hard time cap ensures the end of the game is imminent because the time slot for a particular round of play has expired. This cap means that whoever is ahead at the completion of the current scoring attempt has won the game, unless the score is tied in which case 1 additional point must be played.

Time caps are used to control the logistics of tournament play to ensure that all games are played.

Pulls

Play starts at the beginning of each half and after each goal with a pull, where a player on the pulling team throws the disc to the opposing team. The players on the pulling team are free to move anywhere in their end zone, but they may not cross the goal line until the disc is released. The players on the receiving team must stand with one foot on the goal line they are defending without changing position relative to one another. As soon as the disc is released, it is in play and all players may move in any direction. Other rules governing pulling and restarting play include the following:

- If a pull hits and remains inbounds, it is put into play at the spot where it came to rest.
- If the disc initially hits inbounds and then becomes out of bounds before being touched by the receiving team, it is put into play at the spot on the playing field proper (i.e., excluding the end zones) nearest to where it first crossed the perimeter line to become out of bounds. If the disc initially hits inbounds and then becomes out of bounds after being touched by the receiving

team, it is put into play at the spot on the playing field nearest to where it first crossed the perimeter line to become out of bounds.

■ If a pull initially hits the ground out of bounds, the receiving team has the option of putting the disc into play at a spot closest to where the disc last crossed the perimeter line in flight or, after signaling for a brick or middle, before gaining possession of the disc.

■ If the pull is caught, the disc is put into play on the playing field nearest to where the disc was caught. If the pull is dropped by the receiving team, it is a turnover.

■ Each time a goal is scored, the teams switch the direction of their attack, and the team that scored pulls to the opposing team.

■ All offensive players must establish a stationary position by the end of a timeout, and the defense has up to 20 seconds to check the disc into play.

■ When any call or event stops play, all players must come to a stop as quickly as possible and remain in their respective positions until play is restarted.

■ When play is to be restarted with a check but no marker is near enough to touch the disc in the thrower's hand, play is restarted using an offensive self-check. When play is to be restarted with a check but no offensive player is near enough to take possession of the disc at the appropriate spot, play is restarted using a defensive self-check.

Inbounds and Out of Bounds

The entire playing field is inbounds. The perimeter lines are not part of the playing field and are out of bounds. For a player to be considered inbounds after gaining possession of the disc, that player's first point of ground contact with any area must be completely inbounds.

An airborne player whose last ground contact was with an out-of-bounds area is out of bounds. Exceptions include the following:

■ When momentum carries a player out of bounds after that player has gained possession of an inbounds disc and landed inbounds, the player is considered inbounds. The disc is put into play at the spot on the perimeter line where the player went out of bounds.

■ The thrower may contact an out-of-bounds area while pivoting, provided that the pivot remains in contact with the playing field.

■ Contact between players does not confer the state of being inbounds or out of bounds from one to the other.

End Zone Possession

If a team gains possession in the end zone it is defending after a turnover, the player taking possession must immediately decide to put the disc into play at that spot or to carry the disc to the closest point on the goal line and put it into play there.

If a player catches a pass from a teammate in the end zone while defending, that player does not have a choice of advancing the disc to the goal line.

If a team gains possession other than by interception of a pass in the end zone it is attacking, which is a goal, the player taking possession must carry the disc directly to the closest spot on the goal line and put the disc into play from there.

Violations and Fouls

A foul is the result of physical contact between opposing players that affects the outcome of the play. It is the responsibility of all players to avoid contact in every way possible. In general, the player initiating contact is guilty of a foul. A foul can be called only by the player who has been fouled and must be announced by loudly calling out, "Foul!" immediately after the foul has occurred.

Whenever a call is made, play continues until the thrower in possession acknowledges the call. If the disc is in the air or the thrower is in the act of throwing at the time of the call, play continues until the outcome of that pass is determined.

In general, when a foul or violation stops play, players must resume their respective positions at the time the foul or violation was called. If a dispute arises concerning a foul, violation, or the outcome of a play, and the teams cannot come to a satisfactory resolution, the disc is returned to the thrower and put into play with a check, with the count the same or at 6 if over 5. (That is, if the count was at 8, it begins again at 6.)

If offsetting infractions are called by offensive and defensive players on the same play, the disc reverts to the thrower, with the count the same or at 6 if over 5, and play restarts with a check. A throwing foul may be called when there is contact between the thrower and the marker. The disc in a thrower's possession is considered part of the thrower. Although it should be avoided whenever possible, incidental contact that occurs during the follow-through (after the disc has been released) is not sufficient grounds for a foul, unless the contact constitutes harmful endangerment.

A receiving foul may be called when there is contact between opposing players who are in the process of attempting a catch, interception, or knockdown. A certain amount of incidental contact before, during, or immediately after the catching attempt is often unavoidable and is not a foul. When the disc is in the air, players must play the disc, not the opponent. A player may not move in a manner solely to prevent an opponent from taking an unoccupied position via an unoccupied path; doing so is a blocking foul. No defensive player may touch the disc while it is in the possession of an offensive player. If a defensive player initiates contact with the disc, and the offensive player loses possession as a result, it is a stripping foul. No offensive player may move in a manner that causes a defensive player guarding an offensive player to be obstructed by another player.

TERMS

The **best perspective** is the most complete viewpoint available to a player. This perspective includes the relative positions of the disc, ground, players, and line markers involved in the play.

A **brick** may be called by a player receiving a pull that initially lands out of bounds untouched by the receiving team, resulting in bringing the disc to either the closest brick mark of the receiving team's defending end zone, or the nearest spot to where the disc crossed the out-of-bounds perimeter and midway between the sidelines on the playing field proper.

Legal position is the stationary position established by a player's body, excluding extended arms and leg, that can be avoided by all opposing players when time and distance are taken into account.

The **pivot** is the point of the thrower's body in continuous contact with a single spot on the field during a thrower's possession once the thrower has come

to a stop or has attempted a throw or intentional throwing motion.

To be in **possession** of the disc, a player must have sustained contact with, and control of, a nonspinning disc, typically by catching a throw or picking up a disc after a turnover or pull.

A **pull** is the throw from one team to the other that starts play at the beginning of a half or after a goal.

OFFICIALS

Ultimate relies on a spirit of sporting behavior that places the responsibility for fair play on the players. Often officials are used and it is up to the players to adhere to the rules and to make the appropriate calls when rules are violated. Observers may be used if desired by the captains or tournament organizers, especially at more competitive levels of championship play. Observers are nonplayers whose role is to watch the action of the game carefully, tracking time limits, infracting instances of poor sportspersonship, resolving player disputes with a third-party perspective and rendering opinions as determined by event organizers on events such as inbounds or out of bounds, offsides, and disc hitting the ground or out-of-bounds area before a player attempts to catch.

MODIFICATIONS

Sometimes ultimate is played on an indoor field, such as those used in futsal or arena football or even hardwood basketball, volleyball, or handball courts. Playing the disc off the walls or ceiling may or may not be permitted. National and international governing bodies are still in the process of establishing formal rules of indoor play for championship play, so a significant amount of variation in recreational play still exists. Depending on the size of the field, games of four on four or five on five are played indoors.

Some indoor leagues have rules that speed up play. This form of ultimate is sometimes called speed-point, or no-pull rules. Following are modifications, each of which may or may not be instituted with this form of play, depending on the organizer and participating team preferences:

■ There are only two pulls: One at the beginning of the game and one after halftime, such that each team pulls once during the game.

- After a point is scored, play resumes from the point in the end zone where the point was scored. The scoring team simple drops the disc at the spot of the score so that the other team may resume play on offense.

- There is a maximum 20-second delay between the scoring of a point and the beginning of the next play.

- Players may substitute at any point in time between points without play having to stop, although the incoming player may not enter the field of play until the outgoing teammate has crossed the perimeter line.

- Each team is allowed one timeout per game.

- Timeouts cannot be called in the last 5 minutes of the game.

- In five on five, substitutions are allowed on the fly (while playing).

ORGANIZATIONS

European Flying Disc Federation
Brieger St. 8
76139 Karlsruhe
Germany
www.efdf.org

USA Ultimate
5825 Delmonico Dr., Ste. 350
Colorado Springs, CO 80919
719-219-4832
www.usaultimate.org

World Flying Disc Federation
5825 Delmonico Dr., Ste. 350
Colorado Springs, CO 80919
www.wfdf.org

60

Volleyball

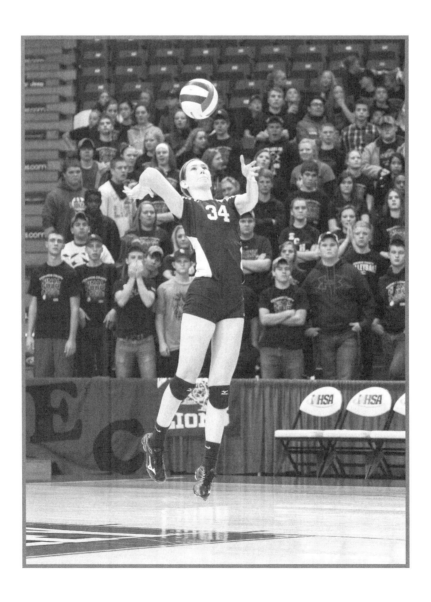

Volleyball is a popular and diverse sport with many variations, including indoor, outdoor, and beach volleyball; two-, three-, four-, or six-player teams; mixed six (coed); games to 11 points, to 15 points, or by the clock; and the rally-point system. With its high participation both competitively and recreationally for youth and adults both male and female, plus long-time global recognition, volleyball is one of the most popular sports in the world. It originally was developed as an alternative to basketball by William G. Morgan of the YMCA in Holyoke, Massachusetts, in 1895, and it has been an Olympic sport since 1964.

OVERVIEW

Objective: To score more points than the other team by hitting the ball over the net so that the opponents cannot return the ball.

Number of Players: Two, three, four, or six, depending on the type of play.

Scoring: Rally scoring is used exclusively in USA Volleyball, high school, and NCAA action; in this system, a point is scored on every play.

Games and Matches: A match is the best of three or five games. Each nondeciding game is played to 25 points using rally scoring. A game must be won by at least 2 points; there is no scoring cap. The deciding game is played to 15.

The referee blows her whistle for the first serve, which begins play. After the serve, players may move around on their sides of the court but may not step completely over the center line. (Rules allow the hand and foot to completely cross the center line and give some latitude with other body parts, such as the knee or forearm, to cross partially over the center line without creating a safety hazard.)

Players may hit the ball with any part of their bodies. A point is scored on every play; the team that scores serves the next ball.

The main body of this chapter refers to indoor, six-player rules. Modifications are noted near the end of the chapter.

COURT

The playing court is a rectangle measuring 59.0 by 29.6 feet, surrounded by a free zone, which is a minimum of 3 meters wide on all sides (see figure 60.1). It is divided into two equal parts by the center line, which runs the width of the court under the net. Attack lines are on both sides of the net. The net itself is made of mesh and is a minimum of 32 feet long and 39 inches wide, with

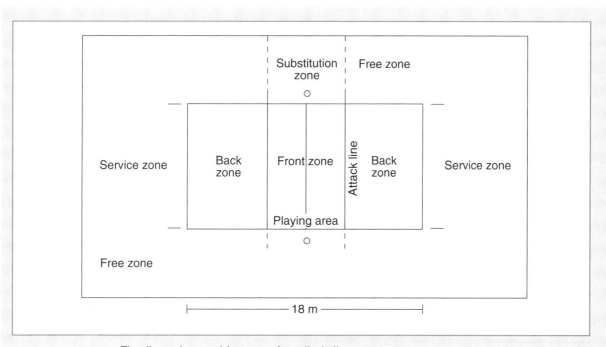

▶ **Figure 60.1** The dimensions and features of a volleyball court.

a 2-inch canvas band at the top. For men, the top of the net is 2.43 meters (7 feet, 11-5/8 inches) high; for women, it is 2.24 meters (7 feet, 4-1/8 inches) high. The top and the bottom of the net are fastened to the posts to remain taut.

Two white side bands, if used, are fastened vertically to the net directly over the sidelines; they are considered part of the net. An antenna is fastened at the outer edge of each side band and placed on opposite ends of the net.

PLAYERS

A team may consist of up to 12 players and 2 liberos. Six players are on the court at any given time: three in the front row and three in the back row (left, center, and right in both rows). Player position is determined by the position of the foot last in contact with the floor at the time the ball is served. Each front-row player must have at least part of one foot closer to the center line than both feet of the corresponding back-row player. Outside players in each row must have at least part of one foot closer to their sideline than both feet of the center player in the same row.

Once the ball is served, players may move to any position within their side of the court. When a team gains the serve, its players rotate one position clockwise. In USA Volleyball open play, a team is allowed a maximum of six substitutions per game. A starting player may leave the game and reenter once. A substitute player may not reenter a game after he is replaced, and he may be replaced only by the player he replaced. In all other USA Volleyball play, a team may substitute 12 times per game, a starting player may reenter a game an unlimited number of times but only in her previous position in the lineup, and a substitute player may enter a game an unlimited number of times.

Each team has an option to register a libero player. The libero player is restricted to playing in the back row and cannot serve, block, or attack-hit when the ball is above the height of the top of the net. The libero wears a different-colored shirt from the other team members and does not take part in normal substitutions; instead, the libero enters or leaves a game on her own while the ball is out of play and before the whistle for service. Replacements involving the libero do not count as regular substitutions. All rule sets in the United States except NCAA men's allow the libero to serve in one position in the rotation.

EQUIPMENT

The ball is spherical and bound in leather or approved synthetic materials. Its circumference is 25.6 to 26.4 inches; its weight is 9 to 10 ounces. It has 4.26 to 4.61 pounds of air pressure per square inch. Players wear jerseys, shorts, and soft or rubber-soled shoes. The libero position is permitted to wear a jersey that is a different color from that of teammates. Players' jerseys are numbered from 1 to 99. No jewelry may be worn.

RULES

Most of the basics of volleyball can be understood through its rules for serving, ball in play, net play, attacking, and blocking.

Serving

Players must follow the service order recorded on the lineup sheet. A player retains the serve until the other team wins the right to serve. A player has 8 seconds to serve once the referee whistles for service. If a player serves before the whistle, the play is canceled and the serve is repeated.

The server may serve from anywhere behind the end line. After completing the serve, the player may step or land inside the court. If the server tosses the ball and it touches the ground without touching the player, this is a service error. A service fault occurs if the ball

- touches a player of the serving team,
- fails to cross the vertical plane of the net completely through the crossing space,
- touches the antenna or any other object (including the net) outside the antenna,
- lands out of bounds, or
- passes over a screen of one or more players.

Ball in Play

The ball is in bounds when it touches any portion of the court, including the boundary lines. The ball is out of bounds when it touches the floor completely outside the boundary lines. It is also out when it touches an object outside the boundary lines; when it crosses the net outside the crossing space; or when it touches the net, rope, antenna, or post outside the antenna or side band.

The rules allow for the pursuit of a ball that crosses outside the crossing space after the first contact, provided there is minimum clearance of 2 meters beyond the court equipment on both sides of the court.

Each team has three hits, in addition to blocking, to return the ball. A hit is any contact with the ball, whether or not intentional. A player may not contact the ball twice in succession during a rally unless the first contact is a block or unless two players contact the ball simultaneously. In this case it is counted as one contact, and any player may hit the ball next. A player may not receive assistance from a teammate in trying to hit a ball, but a teammate may hold back a player who is about to cross the center line or touch the net.

Net Play

If a ball outside the crossing space has not fully crossed the vertical plane of the net, it may be played back to a teammate. A ball is "out" when it completely crosses under the net. A ball may touch the net and still be in play. A ball driven into the net may be recovered within the limits of the team's three hits.

- A serve that contacts the net and continues into the opponents' court remains in play.
- A blocker may contact the ball beyond the plane of the net but may not interfere with an opponent's play. A hitter's hands or arms may cross the net if the contact was made on his side of the net or within the net's plane.

All rule sets allow the hand and foot to completely cross the center line and allow some latitude with other body parts (e.g., a knee or forearm) to cross partially over the center line. A fault is called when there are interference or safety concerns.

USA Volleyball allows penetration into the opponents' court beyond the center line to touch the opponents' court with one or both hands or feet, provided some part of the penetrating hands and feet remains either in contact with or directly above the center line.

A player may not touch the net while in the act of playing the ball. The only exceptions are incidental contact by a player's hair or insignificant contact by a player not involved in the play. If a driven ball causes the net to touch a player, this is not a fault.

Attacking

An attack-hit is any action that directs the ball toward the opponents' court, except for serves and blocks. Front-row players may make an attack-hit when the ball is at any height. Back-row players may make an attack-hit at any height as long as they are behind the attack line at takeoff; they may land beyond the line. A back-row player may also make an attack-hit from the front zone if the ball is below the top of the net.

Blocking

Blocking is the action of a player or players close to the net to intercept the ball coming from the opponents by reaching higher than the top of the net. Only front-row players are permitted to complete a block. A block is not counted as one of the team's three hits.

In blocking, the player may place her hands and arms beyond the net, provided the action does not interfere with the opponents' play. It is not permitted to touch the ball beyond the net until an opponent has executed an attack-hit.

Consecutive contacts with the ball are permitted in blocking if the contacts are quick and continuous and made during one action. A serve cannot be blocked.

Scoring

A point is scored when

- the ball lands in bounds on the opponents' court,
- the opponents are unable to return the ball within three hits,
- the opponents hit the ball out of bounds, or
- the opponents commit a fault or foul.

If one team is penalized, the other team receives the serve and a point. If the receiving team faults, the serving team gets a point. If the serving team faults, the receiving team gets a point and the serve.

Misconduct

Misconduct is classified as unsporting conduct, rude conduct, offensive conduct, or aggression.

It may be directed at officials, players, coaches, or fans. Depending on the degree of the misconduct, a player may be warned, penalized, expelled for the rest of the game, or disqualified for the match.

TERMS

An **attack-hit** is a hit aimed into the opponents' court. All actions directing the ball toward the opponent, except a serve or block, are attack-hits.

Attack lines separate each side of the court into a front zone and a back zone. Players in the back row may attempt an attack-hit when they are behind the attack line or when they are in front of the line when the ball is lower than the top of the net.

Back-row players are the three who are situated in the back zone when the serve is made.

A **block** occurs when one or more players at the net reach higher than the top of the net and deflect the ball coming from the opponent.

A **delay** may be called by a referee when a team takes too long to substitute or otherwise delays play. The first delay results in a warning; the second results in the loss of a rally.

A **dig** is made by the player who first contacts the ball after it passes over the net (unless this player is making a block).

A **fault** results in a lost serve and a point awarded to the opposition.

A **front-row** player is one who is positioned in the front zone between the attack line and the net.

A **held ball**, which is a fault, may be called when the ball is caught or thrown.

A **hit** is any contact by a player with the ball. A player may not hit the ball two times consecutively during a play with the following exception: During a block and during the first hit of the team, the ball may contact the same player on various parts of the body consecutively, provided that the contacts occur during one action to play the ball. Also, the first hit after the block may be executed by any player, including the one who touched the ball on the block.

A **match** is won by the team that wins the most games (also called sets) in the match.

A **playing fault** is any breach of the rules by a player. A fault results in loss of the rally.

A **rally** is the exchange of hits between the teams. The team that wins the rally gets a point and the serve.

A team's **rotation order** must be kept when it gains the serve. Each time a team gains a serve, players rotate one position clockwise. Failure to do so is a fault.

Sanctions are given for various penalties. In all rule sets, a yellow card signifies a warning; a red card is a penalty for a more serious offense that results in the loss of a rally. When the referee holds up both a red card and a yellow card in one hand, the offending player is expelled from the game. When the referee holds up a red card in one hand and a yellow card in the other, the offending player is disqualified for the match. In the NCAA, there is no such thing as expulsion. The next offense after a red card penalty is disqualification.

Players of the serving team may not **screen** the opponents from seeing the server or the path of the ball. Screening includes arm waving, jumping, and moving sideways as the serve is being made. It also occurs when the server is hidden behind two or more players.

A **service** puts the ball into play. The server may move freely behind the end line when serving.

A **set** is a contact that sets up a spike. The typical order of contacts is dig, set, spike. Internationally, a game is referred to as a set.

A **sideout** occurs when the serving team does not score, and the serve goes over to the other team.

A **spike** is a hard-driven ball that is hit in an attempt to score.

A player may **tip** a ball with her fingers if the ball is cleanly hit and not caught or thrown.

OFFICIALS

The officials include the first referee, the second referee, the scorer, the assistant scorer, and two or four line judges. The first referee stands at one end of the net and has final authority over all decisions. He may overrule other officials. The second referee stands near the post outside the playing court, opposite the first referee. She signals faults, including net, center line, and attack-line violations, and assists the first referee. The second referee authorizes game interruptions, substitutions, and timeouts.

The scorer sits facing the first referee; he records points and timeouts and checks that substitutions are legal. The assistant scorer tracks the libero. Line judges stand at opposite corners of the court, closest to the right hand of each referee (if two judges are used) or at each corner (if four judges are used). They stand at the intersection of the end line and sideline and rule whether balls are in or out, signal when a ball crosses the net outside the crossing space, and indicate when a server foot-faults. Officials' signals are shown in figure 60.2.

MODIFICATIONS

The two main variations of the sport allow for coed play and for outdoor play. The net heights suggested by USA Volleyball are indicated in table 60.1.

A re-serve is no longer allowed in NCAA and USA Volleyball rules. An exception that may be used for 14-and-under play (USAV rules) allows one service tossing error for each service (within 5 seconds for the re-serve).

Twelve-and-under competition may be conducted using a lighter ball (7 to 8 ounces instead of 9 to 10 ounces).

Mixed-Six Play

The rules for mixed-six (coed) play are the same as for indoor play, except for the following:

- Males and females alternate serves and court positions.
- When the ball is played more than once by a team, at least one hit must be made by a female. A block does not count as a hit. Females may make all three hits; a male is not required to hit.

▶ **Figure 60.2** Common officials' signals in volleyball.

(continued)

▶ **Figure 60.2** *(continued)*

TABLE 60.1

Net Heights

Age groups (yr)	Females and reverse mixed 6 (ft, in.)	Males and mixed 6 (ft, in.)
70 and above	7, 2-1/8	7, 6
55 and above	7, 2-1/8	7, 9-5/8
45 and above	7, 2-1/8	7, 11-5/8
15-18 and under	7, 4-1/8	7, 11-5/8
13-14 and under	7, 4-1/8	7, 4-1/8
11-12 and under	7, 0	7, 0
10 and under	6, 6	7, 0

Adapted by permission from USA Volleyball, *2008-2009 Domestic Competition Regulations*. Available: https://www.teamusa.org/USA-Volleyball/Features/2009/November/04/Reflections-on-Net-Heights-Court-Dimensions.aspx.

- An illegally hit ball by an illegal blocker becomes a double fault, and a playover is directed.

- When only one male is in the front row, one back-row male may, after beginning in the back row, come forward off the attack line in order to block.

- No female back-row player may block.

- The net height is 2.43 meters (7 feet, 11-5/8 inches) (the same as in men's play).

Reverse Mixed-Six Play

The rules for reverse mixed-six play are the same as for mixed-six play, with the following exceptions: When only one female is in the front row, one female in the back row may be in the attack zone in order to block. No male may block or spike. Male players may contact the ball above the net and send it into the opponents' court, but the trajectory of the ball upon contact must be upward. The net height is 2.24 meters (7 feet, 4-1/8 inches) (the same as for women's play). When the ball is played more than once on a side, it must be contacted at least once by a male.

Outdoor Play

The popularity of volleyball is evidenced by outdoor participation on beaches or grass. The rules for outdoor play are the same as for indoor play, with these exceptions:

- Brightly colored boundary lines (flat bands or tape) mark the boundaries; if they move during play, play continues. If it can't be determined whether the ball was in or out, the rally is replayed. It is the players' responsibility to correct the boundary lines if they are moved.

- Attack lines are marked, but the center line is not.

- Teams may consist of two, three, four, or six players, either of the same sex or coed.

- In doubles competition, no substitutions are allowed. Rosters are as follows for other play: triples competition—five players; four-player competition—six players; six-player

competition—12 players. Unlimited substitution is allowed in triples, four-player competition, and six-player competition, as long as each player plays within her serving position during a single game.

- It is forbidden to wear any object that may cause injury to a player, such as pins, bracelets, or casts. Rubber-soled shoes may be worn on grass, but nonflexible cleats or spikes are not allowed.

- A match is won by the first team to win two games to 21 points with a 2-point advantage. The deciding game is played to 15 points with a 2-point advantage. All games are played by rally-point rules.

- In doubles, triples, and four-player competition, players may position themselves anywhere on the court, and the server may serve from anywhere beyond the end line.

- In doubles and triples play, the first contact after a hard-driven ball (a spike or block) can be held momentarily overhand with the fingers, as well as doubled with the fingers.

- In doubles and triples play, if a ball is intentionally set into the opponents' court, the shoulders of the player setting the ball must be square to the direction of the ball.

- In doubles play, if a player serves out of turn, the play is allowed, but the service order should be corrected for all subsequent rallies.

- In doubles, triples, and four-player competition, players may not "dink," or tip, an attack-hit with the fingers.

- In doubles and triples competition, a player may not make an attack-hit using an overhand set that puts the ball on a sideways trajectory with the player's shoulders.

- In six-player competition, a back-row player may not participate in a block.

- In 21-point games, the teams switch after every 7 points. In 15-point games, teams switch sides each time the total score reaches a multiple of five. In 11-point games, teams switch sides each time the total score reaches a multiple of four.

ORGANIZATIONS

Association of Volleyball Professionals
AVP Pro Beach Volleyball Tour
6100 Center Dr., 9th Floor
Los Angeles, CA 90045
310-426-8000
www.volleyball.org/avp

Fédération Internationale de Volleyball
Château les Tourelles
Edouard-Sandoz 2-4
1006 Lausanne
Switzerland
41-21-345-3535
www.fivb.org

USA Volleyball
4065 Sinton Rd., Ste. 200
Colorado Springs, CO 80907
719-228-6800
www.teamusa.org/USA-Volleyball

61

Water Polo

Chad McDermott/fotolia.com

Water polo originally drew its rules from rugby, and in the 1860s it was being played in rivers and lakes. By 1870, the sport had moved indoors, and by the late 1880s, water polo was introduced in the United States. By that time, the game had become more similar to soccer, with its passing and its caged goals. Water polo became an Olympic sport in 1900.

OVERVIEW

Objective: To score goals by putting the ball into the opponents' goal.

Number of Players: Each team has seven players in the water, a goalkeeper, and six field players.

Scoring: A player scores a goal when the entire ball passes fully over the goal line and into the goal (between the posts and under the crossbar).

Length of Game: A game consists of four 8-minute periods with 2 minutes' break within the quarters and 5 minutes' break at halftime; time stops when the referee blows the whistle. The game is restarted when a players puts the ball back into play.

To begin a game, players line up on their goal lines at least 1 meter apart and at least 1 meter from the goal posts. No more than two players may be between the goal posts, and no part of a player's body at water level may be beyond the goal line. A referee blows a whistle to begin play and tosses the ball on the half-distance line, near the edge of the field of play. Each team sprints for possession. The clock begins when a player touches the ball. Each team tries to advance the ball by passing and dribbling it to get into position to score. A team has 30 seconds to shoot at the opponents' goal.

If the score is tied at the end of four periods, a penalty shootout takes place immediately. If the game does not require a definite result (e.g., a preliminary-round game), the tie stands.

POOL

The pool has a half-distance line dividing the pool in half. The distance between the goal lines is 20 to 30 meters for men and 20 to 25 meters for women, with the width for both between 10 and 20 meters. It also has 5-meter and 2-meter lines, which are 5 meters and 2 meters from each goal line, respectively. Goal lines run the width of the pool. A reentry area is marked at each end of the pool, 2 meters from the corner, on the side opposite the official table (see figure 61.1).

Each goal consists of white, rigid goal posts, a crossbar, and a net. Goals are rectangular; they are 3 meters wide and centered between the sides of the pool.

PLAYERS

A team consists of seven players in the pool and no more than six reserves. Substitutes may enter freely between periods, before extra time, after a goal has been scored, or during a timeout. During play, a substitute may enter from the reentry area after the exiting player has entered the reentry area. If a player is bleeding, he must immediately leave the water. The game is not stopped; a substitute may immediately replace the injured player, who may return after the bleeding has stopped. Age classifications for competition include 13 and under, 15 and under, 16 to 17, 18 to 20, open, and masters.

EQUIPMENT

The ball is round, weighs between 400 and 450 grams, and has a circumference between 68 and 71 centimeters for men and between 65 and 67 centimeters for women. The two teams wear caps of contrasting colors (other than solid red or the color of the ball). Goalkeepers wear red caps. The goalkeeper's cap is numbered 1; the rest of the caps are numbered 2 through 13. Caps are fastened under the chin. If a cap comes off during play, it should be replaced at the next stop in play when that player's team has possession.

RULES

After a goal, once the players are in their respective halves of the pool, the referee whistles the ball into play. A player of the team just scored on puts the ball into play by passing to a teammate; the teammate may be forward, backward, or to the side of the passer. The clock begins when the player releases the ball.

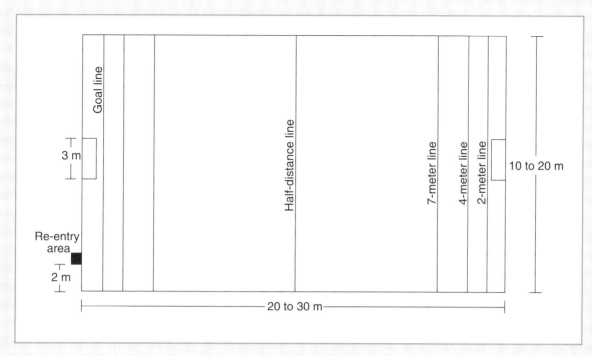

▶ **Figure 61.1** The field of play and its dimensions for water polo.

Scoring

A goal shall be scored when the entire ball has passed fully over the goal line, between the goal posts and underneath the crossbar. A team may score a goal from anywhere within the field of play, although a goalkeeper may not touch the ball beyond the half-distance line or go beyond that line herself.

A field player may score a goal with any part of his body except a clenched fist. (A goalkeeper may score a goal with a clenched fist.) At least two players, excluding the defending goalkeeper, must have intentionally touched the ball on the play for a goal to count. A player may score a goal by obtaining a goal throw or free throw from the goalkeeper and throwing the ball into the goal; it doesn't have to touch another player first.

A player may score a goal by immediately shooting from outside the 5-meter line after her team has been awarded a free throw outside 5 meters. The player may not score after putting the ball into play unless the ball has been touched intentionally by another player other than the defending goalkeeper.

A goal is legal if the 30-second clock or the period clock expires after the ball has left a player's hand but before the ball enters the goal. If the ball floats over the goal line in this circumstance, the goal is good if the ball floated over the goal because of its own momentum.

Fouls

There are three types of fouls: ordinary fouls, exclusion fouls, and penalty fouls, which result in penalty throws. Ordinary fouls are common fouls that result in a free throw. Exclusion and penalty fouls are personal fouls. A player committing three personal fouls is excluded for the remainder of the game.

Ordinary Fouls   An ordinary foul is called for

- advancing beyond the goal line at the start of a period, before the referee gives the signal to start;
- assisting a player;
- holding onto or pushing off from the goal posts or sides or ends of the pool;

- standing on the bottom of the pool while taking an active part in the game;
- holding the ball underwater while being tackled;
- striking the ball with a clenched fist (except the goalkeeper, within the 5-meter area);
- touching the ball with two hands at once (except the goalkeeper);
- impeding the movement of an opponent who is not holding the ball;
- pushing, or pushing off from, an opponent;
- being within 2 meters of the opponents' goal, except when in possession of the ball or behind the line of the ball;
- unduly delaying a free throw, corner throw, or goal throw;
- the goalkeeper's going beyond the half distance line or touching a ball beyond that line;
- maintaining possession of the ball for more than 30 seconds without shooting at the opponents' goal; or
- sending the ball out of the pool.

Exclusion Fouls   An exclusion foul results in a free throw for the team offended and in the exclusion of the player who committed the foul. This player can reenter the game at the earliest of these occurrences: when 20 seconds of playing time has elapsed; when a goal has been scored; when the excluded player's team has regained possession of the ball; or when play has stopped and then restarted, with possession in favor of the excluded player's team. An exclusion foul is called in a number of instances, including leaving the water or sitting or standing on the steps or side of the pool during play, except for injury or illness (this exception must be allowed by the referee); intentionally splashing water in an opponent's face; holding, sinking, or pulling back an opponent who does not have the ball; intentionally kicking or hitting an opponent, or trying to do so; interfering with a free throw, corner throw, or goal throw; and the goalkeeper's failing to take position for a penalty throw after being told to do so by the referee.

In addition, players are excluded for the remainder of the game for using foul language or violent or persistent foul play, for interfering with a penalty throw, for committing an act of brutality, or for refusing to obey or disrespecting an official.

When players from both teams simultaneously commit personal fouls, both players are excluded, and a neutral throw is made.

Penalty Fouls   Penalty shots are taken from the 5-meter line for any foul that occurs inside the 5-meter mark that would probably have prevented a goal. A penalty foul, resulting in a penalty throw for the team offended, is called when

- a minor foul occurs inside the 5-meter line;
- a defending player kicks or strikes an opponent within the 5-meter area;
- an excluded player intentionally interferes with the goal alignment or other aspects of play;
- or any player pulls over the goal to prevent a likely score.

One of these throws may be awarded, according to the foul: goal, corner, neutral, free, or penalty.

- Goal throw: A goal throw is awarded when the entire ball has passed the goal line, outside of the goal posts (i.e., it hasn't scored), and was last touched by an attacking team player. The throw is taken by the defending goalkeeper within the 2-meter area. If the goalkeeper is out of the water, it is taken by another defender.
- Corner throw: A corner throw is awarded when the ball has passed the goal line but has not gone between the goal posts and was last touched by a defender. The throw is taken by an attacking team player from the 2-meter mark on the side where the ball crossed the goal line. The throw may be taken by any attacking player if undue delay does not occur.
- Neutral throw: A neutral throw is awarded when players from each team commit a foul at the same time or when, at the start of a period, the ball falls into a position of definite advantage for one team. The referee throws the ball into the water or up into the air at the same lateral position where the event occurred, so that players of both teams have an equal chance to gain possession.

Players may touch the ball before it touches the water. The goalkeeper is excluded from taking a neutral throw.

▪ Free throw: A free throw is awarded for ordinary and exclusion fouls. The throw must be made so that the other players can see the ball leave the thrower's hand. The thrower may carry or dribble the ball before throwing. The ball is in play when it leaves the hand of the player passing it to another player. The throw must be taken at or behind the line of the foul.

▪ Penalty throw: A penalty throw is awarded for a penalty foul and may be taken by any player except the goalkeeper, from any point on the opponent's 5-meter line. No player other than the defending goalkeeper may be in the 5-meter area, and no player may be within 2 meters of the player taking the penalty throw. On the referee's signal, the player must immediately throw, with an uninterrupted motion, toward the goal. If the ball rebounds off the goal or the goalkeeper, it is in play, and another player does not need to touch it before a goal can be scored.

Timeouts

Each team is entitled to two timeouts of a minute each during a game. The timeout must be called by the coach of the team in possession of the ball. After a timeout has been called, the players must go to their half of the field of play until 45 seconds of the timeout has concluded and been signaled by the officials' table or by the referee. Play is resumed by a free throw at the half-distance line or at the corner, if the timeout was taken immediately before a corner throw. If the game extends into extra time, each team is permitted an additional timeout. Timeouts may be taken at any time. For example, if a team has not used any timeouts during regular time, it may use all three of its timeouts during extra time.

TERMS

The **advantage rule** allows referees not to declare a foul if, in their opinion, calling the foul would be an advantage to the offending player's team.

A **corner throw** is taken by the attacking team from the 2-meter mark on the side nearest where the ball crossed the goal line.

An **exclusion foul** results in a free throw for the team fouled and in the temporary or permanent exclusion of the offending player.

A **free throw** is awarded for ordinary and exclusion fouls.

A **goal throw** is a free throw awarded to the goalkeeper and taken within the 2-meter area.

A **neutral throw** is made by the referee to put the ball back into play after players from each team have committed simultaneous fouls or when the ball hits an overhead obstruction and rebounds into the field of play.

An **ordinary foul** results in a free throw for the offended team.

A **penalty foul** results in a penalty throw for the offended team.

A **penalty shootout** results if the score is still tied after two periods of extra time. Each team selects five shooters; these shooters take penalty throws, alternating by team. If the score is still even after all five shooters on each team have taken a penalty throw, then pairs of shooters (one from each team) shoot until one team scores and the other does not.

A **penalty throw** may be taken by any player of the team awarded the throw, except for the goalkeeper. The throw is made from the opponents' 5-meter line as a direct shot on goal.

A **personal foul** is assessed against a player who commits an exclusion or penalty foul. A player who commits three personal fouls is excluded from the game.

OFFICIALS

Games are controlled by up to eight officials: two referees, goal judges, timekeepers, and secretaries. The referee is in absolute control of the game. Goal judges assist signals on goals, corner throws, and goal throws. Timekeepers keep the time and keep track of excluded players and reentries. Secretaries maintain records of the game.

MODIFICATIONS

The following modifications are made for Junior Olympic competition (18 and under) and for masters competition (30 and over).

▪ Junior Olympic: A game lasts four 7-minute periods. Each team is allowed one 2-minute timeout per half. Substitutes may be made during a timeout. The maximum size of the field of play is 25 meters from goal line to goal line and 20 meters in width.

■ Masters: Age groups are in 5-year intervals, starting with 20 years old (20+, 25+, 30+, and so on). A team is placed in the age group of its youngest player; there are no age limits for older players playing in younger age groups. The distance between goal lines is 23.5 meters minimum, and the minimum width of the field of play is 17 meters. A game lasts four 5-minute periods. Each team receives two 1-minute timeouts.

ORGANIZATIONS

Fédération Internationale de Natation
Av. de l'Avant-Poste 4
CH-1005 Lausanne
Switzerland
41-21-310-4710
www.fina.org

USA Water Polo
2124 Main St., Ste. 210
Huntington Beach, CA 92648
714-500-5445
www.usawaterpolo.org

62

Water Skiing

Water skiing got its beginnings in the United States in 1922 when Ralph Samuelson, an 18-year-old Minnesotan, figured that if he could ski on snow, he could ski on water as well.

Competitions are held in various divisions, beginning with boys' and girls' divisions for 9 years old and younger and ending with men's and women's divisions for 85 years old and older.

OVERVIEW

Objective: To receive the highest score and to increase individual or team rank.

Scoring: Each contestant receives points in proportion to a national standard (see "Scoring").

Water skiing is a sport that combines strength, dexterity, grace, and precision at high speeds. Skiers perform in three events: jumping, slalom, and tricks. Places are determined in each event, based on scores, with the highest being best. Boys 1 and girls 1 divisions (9 years old and younger) are the only divisions that do not complete all three events. These divisions do not take part in the jumping competition.

Competitions may be held for individuals and for teams. At national tournaments, skiing order is based on seedings, with the highest-rated skier going last. At other tournaments, order may be based either on seedings or on a draw.

COURSES

Courses for the jump, slalom, and trick events are marked with buoys and have the following specifications:

A jump course has a 15-meter run-up to the ramp, which must be parallel to the course. The ramp is 3.7 to 4.3 meters wide and 6.4 to 6.7 meters long out of the water. It has an apron that extends to 8 inches below the water (see figure 62.1a).

A slalom course is 259 meters long, with buoys set up throughout (see figure 62.1b).

A trick course measures between 157.5 and 192.5 meters long by 12.0 to 18.0 meters wide, with an additional 13.5 to 16.5 meters at each end of the course. Buoys set approximately 200 meters apart mark the course.

SKIERS

Skiers compete in the following age divisions:

- Boys 1 and girls 1: 9 years old and under
- Boys 2 and girls 2: 13 and under
- Boys 3 and girls 3: 17 and under
- Men 1 and women 1: 18 to 24
- Men 2 and women 2: 25 to 34
- Men 3 and women 3: 35 to 44
- Men 4 and women 4: 45 to 54
- Men 5 and women 5: 55 to 59
- Men 6 and women 6: 60 to 64
- Men 7 and women 7: 65 to 69
- Men 8 and women 8: 70 to 74
- Men 9 and women 9: 75 to 79
- Men 10 and women 10: 80-84
- Men 11 and women 11: 85 and over
- Masters men and masters women: 35 and over
- Open men and open women: any age

Boys 1 and girls 1 divisions do not compete in jumping.

EQUIPMENT

Towboats must be able to maintain required speeds. Each is equipped with a towing pylon that has an area integrated in its design for a trick release mechanism. Towlines are 0.24 inch thick and 23 meters long. An event also should have one or two safety boats in use.

Skiers must wear approved flotation devices or suits or vests designed to provide flotation. Maximum ski width must not be greater than 35 percent of the length; skiers may use any type of foot binding and fixed fins.

In slalom and jump skis: Any type of fixed fins may be used. Devices affixed to the skis intended to control or adjust the skiing characteristics of the ski, such as wings on a fin, are allowed as long as they are fixed and do not move or change during actual skiing.

In trick skis: Skis used in the tricks event shall not have fins. Trick skis with molded rails or

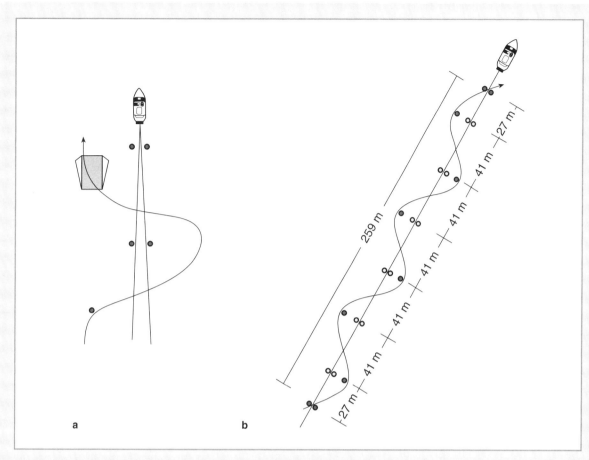

▶ **Figure 62.1**   The dimensions of the (*a*) jump and (*b*) slalom courses.

grooves less than 0.5 inch are allowed. A foot pad cemented to the ski as a place for the rear foot is also permitted.

Boat-guide buoys may be spherical, cylindrical, rectangular, or bullet shaped. Skier buoys are usually spherical, 22 to 28 centimeters in diameter, with 7 to 11 centimeters showing out of the water. Buoys are fastened to anchor lines.

RULES

This section contains the essential rules that pertain to jumping, slalom, and tricks. Scoring rules are detailed after that.

Jumping

Each contestant gets three passes through the jump course. The course begins with a 180-meter buoy and ends with 100-meter buoys.

If the towboat passes the ramp, the skier must pass or jump. If the skier passes because of hazard or interference, he is allowed another pass. A skier is considered to have passed a jump if he falls within or outside the course, or if his handle throw is not acceptable to the judges. He is considered to have made a jump when he passes over the ramp, lands, and skis to the ride-out buoys without falling. The skier must regain skiing position to be credited with a scoring jump. A skier must be on his skis within 3 minutes of a fall, or else he passes his remaining jumps.

The jumper may tell the boat driver what speed to use; the maximum speed ranges from 28 miles per hour for boys 2, girls 2, and women 6 and 7 divisions to 35 miles per hour for open men, men 1, and men 2 divisions. The jumper may tell the boat driver at what distance to pass the ramp.

The driver must drive straight and parallel to the right side of the ramp.

A jumper may petition for a reride because of unfair conditions or because the boat was going either too fast or too slow. The boat is timed in two segments to ascertain accurate speeds. A jumper may refuse to enter the course by throwing her handle before she reaches the course entry buoy. If the judges agree with her decision not to enter the course, she is not penalized. If they don't agree, the jumper is charged with a pass. If the jumper's handle is damaged after a throw, the jumper is granted 3 minutes to repair or change the handle. If the jumper is not ready to ski after 3 minutes, she may not continue that round.

Jump distances are measured from the end of the jump ramp to the point where the skier's heels reach their maximum depression in the water (usually where the plume of water rises upon landing). Distances are calculated to the nearest whole foot; a half foot or more is rounded up.

A jumper's single longest jump is his official score for the event. If two jumpers tie, then the one with the longest second jump places higher. If all three of their jumps are equal, then each tied contestant gets two more passes through the course.

Slalom

The skier skis through the entrance gate of the slalom course and must pass around the outside of the six buoys and proceed through the far-end gate. If the skier has not missed any buoys or end gates, she may continue making runs through the course until she falls or misses a buoy or gate. The sponsoring club may choose to make rules exceptions or format changes if approved by the American Water Ski Association.

A miss is defined as riding inside a buoy or outside an end gate or riding over, straddling, or grazing a buoy. A skier is not penalized for grazing a buoy. A fall inside or outside the course ends the run at that point.

Boat speeds range from a minimum and maximum of 16 and 30 miles per hour, respectively, for boys 1 and girls 1 divisions, to 30 and 36 miles per hour, respectively, for open men. Speed increases by 2 miles per hour on each pass until the maximum speed for that division is reached. A skier may select his starting speed and rope length, which ranges from 10.25 to 18.25 meters. Once maximum speed is attained, the rope length is shortened on each subsequent pass, anywhere from 2.25 meters when the rope is between 16.0 and 18.25 meters long to 0.50 meter beginning when the rope is 11.25 meters long.

The boat is driven in a straight line through the center of the course. A reride may be granted because of unfair conditions or because the boat speed is either too slow or too fast. A skier may refuse to enter the course by throwing her handle before she reaches the entry gate. If the judges agree with the skier's decision not to enter the course, the skier is not penalized. If they don't agree, the skier is given a score of zero. Once the skier enters the course, she may not refuse to enter the course on subsequent passes.

If the skier's handle is damaged after a throw, he is granted 3 minutes to repair or change the handle. If the skier is not ready to ski after 3 minutes, he may not continue that round.

Judges mark scores for each pass. Any disagreement is decided by the majority of judges before the next pass. Skiers earn full, half, or quarter points for not missing a buoy or gate. In case of a tie, the skier with the most consecutive points scored wins. If skiers are still tied after this, the skier with the fastest boat speed at the shortest rope length where the miss occurred is the winner.

Tricks

Each contestant gets two 20-second passes through the trick course. The skier may perform as many tricks as she can during each pass. A trick is any activity that occurs between two hesitations. To receive credit for tricks, a skier must perform tricks listed in the rules and return to skiing position. At larger tournaments, the skiers must turn in their declared trick lists before they compete, and they must perform their tricks in the order listed to earn points.

A pass begins when the skier makes her first move to do a surface trick after reaching the entrance buoy, when the skier crosses a wake to attempt a wake trick, or when the skier makes no movement to do a trick as she passes the second entrance buoy. A pass ends when 20 seconds have elapsed, when the skier falls, when 3 minutes have elapsed while the skier is repairing or replacing equipment, or when the skier falls twice while practicing. If the skier falls at the end of the first pass and the 20 seconds have already elapsed, it is not considered a fall.

The skier may choose the boat speed, which must be maintained within 0.5 mile per hour. The skier may request a speed change by hand signal in the 50 meters before he enters the course, but if he does this, the skier must accept whatever speed the boat attains and not ask for a reride, assuming that the speed is constant in the course.

The boat path is specified by the judges before the event; the second path is in the opposite direction of the first. The path is reasonably straight throughout the course. A skier may request a reride for unfair conditions, for boat speed that varies beyond the limit allowed, for a boat that does not follow the path, and for timing device malfunctions.

A skier may throw the handle before entering the course. The skier is not penalized for this if the judges agree with the reasoning for not entering. If the judges do not agree, the skier is charged with a fall while practicing. If a skier's handle is damaged after a throw, she may be given 3 minutes to repair it. If the skier is not ready after that time, she may not continue that round. Trick skiers may use only one line; they may not use a helper line.

When a skier executes a toe turn trick, where he is towed by one foot, the towing foot may not touch water.

Judges score each trick; if five judges are scoring, at least three must credit a skier for a trick for the skier to receive points. The American Water Ski Association recognizes more than 55 tricks, with point values ranging from 20 for a side-slide on two skis to 1,000 for a wake double flip.

If two trick skiers are tied, the skier with the highest-scoring single pass wins. If they are still tied, they get one more pass through the trick course to break the tie.

Scoring

Each event has a standard of 1,000 national overall performance standards (NOPS) points. (USA Water Ski & Wake Sports provides formulas for each event.) Each contestant receives points in proportion to the standard. For example, a trick skier with 1,130 points compared with a 2,560 NOPS would get 441 overall points: $1,130 / 2,560 \times 1,000 = 441$.

A jumper receives points in proportion to the square of her distance to the square of the NOPS distance. For example, if the NOPS standard is 150 feet, and the jumper jumps 130 feet, she scores 751 points: $[(130 \times 130) / (150 \times 150)] \times 1,000 = 751$.

Points are carried to the first decimal (one-tenth of a point), if necessary, to break a tie. If a tie still exists, the winner is the one with the highest single-event NOPS score.

In addition to the scoring, skiers are ranked in each event and overall within their age divisions. The ability levels are 3 through 8, with 8 being the highest level in each age division. Level 9 is the elite ranking level. The ranking list is continually updated.

TERMS

A **balk** occurs when a skier refuses to take a ramp in a jumping event.

A **fall** occurs when a skier loses possession of the towline, does not have at least one ski on, or does not have his weight primarily supported by one or both skis and is not able to regain skiing position.

A **handle throw** occurs when a skier refuses to enter a jump, slalom, or trick course by throwing the handle in the air before reaching the entry point. She is not penalized for this if the majority of judges agree that she had reason to refuse to enter the course.

A **pass** is registered if a skier in skiing position passes the 180-meter buoy mark on the jump course and does not make a jump, if he falls, or if his handle throw is not acceptable to the judges. Once the boat moves past the ramp, the skier must jump or pass.

A **reride** request may be made by the contestant or by a judge. A reride is allowed for unfair conditions or for faulty equipment. The reride must be taken before the next contestant starts.

A skier has **skiing position** when she has possession of the towline; is riding on the water with a ski or skis on her feet; and, supported by her ski or skis, is able to regain control.

A judgment of **unfair conditions** can result in a reride for a competitor. Unfair conditions include malfunctioning equipment, fast slalom times, slow jump times, and short trick times.

A **wake** is the area of water disturbed by the tow-boat, lying at the rope's length, with the crest of the wave as the wake's nominal boundary.

OFFICIALS

Officials include a chief judge, an assistant chief judge, and a qualifications judge as well as appointed judges, boat drivers, scorers, and safety personnel. In case of a disagreement among judges, the majority rules. An issue is settled before the next contestant begins. Judges are separated, when possible, to ensure independent opinions.

ORGANIZATIONS

USA Water Ski & Wake Sports
1251 Holy Cow Rd.
Polk City, FL 33868-8200
863-324-4341
www.usawaterski.org

International Water Ski & Wakeboard Federation
P.O. Box 564
6314 Unteräegeri
Switzerland
www.iwwfed.com

National Collegiate Water Ski Association
www.ncwsa.com

Weightlifting

MoMo Productions/Stone/Getty Images

Weightlifting got its start in the 1860s in "strong man" contests, with George Barker Windship, a physician, health reformer, and strong man, at the fore. Windship is credited with inventing the plate-loading barbell, which he patented in 1865, calling it the "Practical Graduating Dumb-Bell." In Germany, Vladislav Krayevsky, a native of Poland, founded the St. Petersburg Amateur Weightlifting Society in 1885, and a national federation was established in Germany in 1891. The first international championship was held in London in 1891, with lifters from Austria, Belgium, Germany, and the United States competing. Weightlifting became an Olympic event in 1896 but was intermittently dropped from the Games until 1920. In 1928, the three "classic" lifts—press, snatch, and jerk—were established. The press was dropped from Olympic lifting in 1976 because of controversy over what constituted a proper lift.

OVERVIEW

In weightlifting, participants execute two lifts, in this order: (1) the snatch and (2) the clean and jerk. Each participant gets three attempts at both lifts. Competitions are held in weight divisions, beginning from 45 kilograms for women and 55 kilograms for men, and beginning from 49 kilograms for women and 61 kilograms for men in Olympic competition.

In international competitions, men's and women's teams have eight members each and can have no more than two members per weight class. The Olympic Games have their own unique qualifying procedures, based on a country's placing at the world championships; a team may have as many as 7 members and does not use team scoring.

World championship events still use team scoring where scoring is based on a range of 28 points to 1 point for the top 25 placings (28 points for first, 25 points for second, 23 for third, with each additional place receiving one less point, all the way down to 1 point for 25th place). Athletes earn points for their placement in the individual lifts (snatch, clean and jerk). In the Olympic Games, medals are awarded for the total only, and there is no team scoring.

The objective is to successfully lift the most weight. As soon as the participant successfully executes the movement and becomes motionless,

the referee signals completion of the lift, and the participant may lower the barbell. The source for rules for this chapter is USA Weightlifting.

PLATFORM

All lifts take place on a platform, which is 4 meters square on each side. The platform is between 50 and 150 millimeters high; it is made of wood, plastic, or any solid material, and it has a nonslip surface. There must be a 100-centimeter area clear of obstruction surrounding the competition platform. A stretcher or backboard must be in close proximity to the competition platform in case of emergency.

ATHLETES

Athletes compete at the youth level (up to age 17), the junior level (up to and including ages 20), the senior level (ages 15 and older) and the masters level (ages 35 and older). Men and women compete in the weight categories shown in table 63.1.

Competitors must wear costumes that are one piece, close fitting, and collarless. The costumes may not cover the elbows or knees. Lifters may wear a T-shirt under the costume, but it may not cover the elbows. Similarly, they may wear leotards under or over the costume, but these may not touch the knees.

Lifters must wear weightlifting shoes, which may have a strap over the instep. The maximum height of the shoes is 130 millimeters from the top of the sole to the top of the shoe. Competitors may wear a belt, up to 120 millimeters wide, around the waist to provide support. It must be worn outside the costume.

An athlete may wear bandages, tape, or plaster on the wrists, knees, hands, fingers, and thumbs. The plasters or bandages may not be fastened to the wrist or the bar. Fingerless gloves are allowed. No bandages or similar materials may cover the elbows, the torso, the thighs, the shins, or the arms.

EQUIPMENT

The barbell consists of the bar, the discs, and the collars. For men, the bar weighs 20 kilograms and is 2,200 millimeters long, with a distance of 1,310 millimeters between the collars. Its diameter is 28 millimeters on the smooth part of the bar. For

TABLE 63.1

Weight Categories

Category	Men (kg)	Women (kg)	Youth boys (kg)	Youth girls (kg)
1	55	45	49	40
2	61	49	55	45
3	67	55	61	49
4	73	59	67	55
5	81	64	73	59
6	89	71	81	64
7	96	76	89	71
8	102	81	96+	76
9	109	87	102	81
10	+109	+87	+102	+81

Data from International Weightlifting Federation, *Technical Rules* pp 1-2. Available: http://iwf.net/doc/technical.pdf.

women, the bar weighs 15 kilograms and is 2,010 millimeters long. Its diameter is 25 millimeters, with a distance of 1,310 millimeters between the collars. See table 63.2 for disc weights and colors.

The collars, which fasten the discs to the bar, weigh 2.5 kilograms each. The bar is loaded with the heaviest weights toward the inside, and the weights must be fastened with collars.

RULES

Lots are drawn for each athlete before a competition. This determines the order of both weigh-in and lifting. Weigh-ins begin 2 hours before the competition, and they conclude 1 hour before the competition. In national and international events, athletes must compete in the weight class they registered for at the technical conference (which is held the day before competition). Athletes may try to weigh in as many times as possible during the 1-hour time frame, but once they have registered an acceptable weight, they are entered in the competition. Athletes failing to weigh in properly may not compete.

Each competitor receives three attempts in the snatch and in the clean and jerk. The best snatch is added to the best clean and jerk, and this total determines the final placings.

TABLE 63.2

Disc Weights and Colors

Weight (kg)	Color
25	Red
20	Blue
15	Yellow
10	Green
5	White
2.5	Red
2	Blue
1	Green
0.5	White

Data from International Weightlifting Federation, *Technical Rules* pp 1-2. Available: http://iwf.net/doc/technical.pdf.

When a competitor's name is called, she has 1 minute to begin her attempt. If she does not begin her attempt within 1 minute, "no lift" is ruled, and the competitor has one fewer attempts left for that lift. If a competitor is attempting two lifts in a row, she has 2 minutes between attempts.

Before each attempt, the athlete or the coach writes the weight required for the attempt. Each athlete has two changes per attempt plus an automatic 2-kilogram increase between attempts. If an athlete does not declare his next weight within the allotted time, he is given a 2-kilogram increase. Athletes may ask for and receive a 1-kilogram increase between their second and third attempts.

These rules apply to both the snatch and the clean and jerk:

- Hooking—covering the thumb joint with the fingers when gripping the bar—is allowed.

- If the competitor lifts the bar to her knees and then doesn't finish the attempt, it is a no lift.

- On the referee's signal to lower the bar, the athlete must not release the bar until it has passed his waist.

- The lifter may swing and rock her body to aid recovery while snatching or cleaning.

- A lifter may not use lubricant or any other substance on the legs.

In either lift, the athlete may not

- touch the platform with any part of the body other than the feet,

- unevenly or incompletely extend the arms to finish a lift,

- pause while extending the arms,

- finish with a press-out,

- bend and extend the arms during recovery,

- touch any area outside the platform during the lift,

- lower the bar to the platform before the referee's signal,

- drop the bar after the referee's signal,

- finish with the feet out of line and not parallel to the plane of the trunk, or

- replace the bar outside the platform.

Snatch

The lifter stands with the barbell on the platform in front of his legs. He grips the barbell, palms down, and in a continuous movement pulls the barbell from the platform to above his head, with his arms fully extended. He may not pause during the lift or touch the bar to his head while lifting it above his head.

He may either split or bend his legs while lifting the bar, and the bar may slide along his thighs and lap as he moves it upward. He may not turn over his wrists until the bar passes the top of his head. He may recover in his own time from a split or squat position. He must hold the weight motionless with his arms and legs fully extended and his feet in a line. When the referee signals that he has executed the lift, he may lower the barbell to the floor.

Clean and Jerk

This lift has two parts. For the clean, the athlete stands with the bar on the platform in front of her legs. She grips the bar, palms down, and in a continuous movement pulls the bar from the platform to her shoulders. Her elbows or upper arms may not touch her thighs or knees. She may either split or bend her legs as she executes this lift, and the bar may slide along her thighs and lap. The bar may not touch the chest before the final position. It should rest on the clavicles or on the chest above the nipples or on the fully bent arms. She returns her feet to the same line, straightens her legs, and recovers in preparation for the second part, the jerk. She and the barbell must be motionless before she begins the jerk.

When the athlete begins the jerking motion by lowering her body or bending her knees, she must complete the movement. To execute the jerk, she bends her legs and extends them and fully extends her arms vertically. She returns her feet to the same line and waits—with her arms and legs fully extended—for the referee's signal, which will come when she is motionless in this fully extended position. She may then lower the barbell to the platform.

Before the jerk, the barbell position may be adjusted for the following reasons:

a. To withdraw or "unhook" the thumbs

b. To facilitate breathing

c. To relieve pain caused by the barbell

d. To adjust the width of the grip

The barbell adjustments listed here are not considered to be an attempt at an additional jerk.

TERMS

A **barbell** is the apparatus containing the bar, the discs, and the collars.

A **clean** is the first part of the clean and jerk lift. It involves lifting the barbell from the platform to the shoulders.

Collars are used to hold the discs on the barbell.

Discs are of various weights (ranging from 0.25 kilogram to 25 kilograms) and colors.

Hooking describes the technique of covering the thumb joint with the fingers while gripping the bar.

The **jerk** is the second part of the clean and jerk lift. It involves lifting the barbell from the shoulders to above the head.

No lift is called when an athlete commits a fault during a lift or fails to begin a lift in the allotted time.

The **snatch** is a lift that involves lifting the barbell from the platform to above the head.

OFFICIALS

Referees judge the lifts. At larger competitions, a secretary is responsible for running the competition, and technical controllers assist the secretary. A timekeeper operates the competition clock.

ORGANIZATIONS

International Weightlifting Federation
H-1146 Budapest, Istvánmezei út 1-3.
Hungary
36-1-353-0530
www.iwf.net

United States All-Round Weightlifting
  Association
www.usawa.com

USA Weightlifting
1 Olympic Plaza
Colorado Springs, CO 80909
719-866-4508
http://weightlifting.teamusa.org

Wrestling

Wrestling is recognized as the world's oldest sport, with records of it dating back to the 5th century BC. It was part of the ancient Olympic Games, which began in 776 BC, and it is part of the modern Games, which began in 1896.

The two main styles of international wrestling are *Greco-Roman* and *freestyle.* In Greco-Roman, wrestlers may not attack their opponent's legs or use their own legs to trip, lift, or execute any holds. In freestyle, wrestlers may use their legs to execute holds and to defend or attack opponents.

Although the styles differ, the requirements for scoring points and for winning are the same. Near the end of the chapter is a section on National Collegiate Athletic Association (NCAA) rules.

OVERVIEW

Objective: To win by pinning the opponent's shoulders to the mat (a fall) or to win by scoring more points.

Length of Bout: Typical bouts in the men's division are three 2-minute periods with a 30-second break between periods. Cadet and junior levels consist of two 3-minute periods with a 30-second break between for championships and medal bouts. Some consolation rounds may reduce the match time to two 2-minute periods. Women's bouts range from two 2-minute periods with a 30-second break to two 3-minute periods with a 30-second break in between, depending on the level of competition.

Scoring: Wrestlers score points in a number of ways; see "Scoring" to win a match.

Wrestlers weigh in before the competition to ensure they are not over their weight limit and to match athletes according to size.

The referee calls the wrestlers to the center of the mat and makes sure that the wrestlers' bodies have no greasy or sticky substances on them, that they are not perspiring excessively, and that their fingernails are cut short. The wrestlers shake hands, and when the referee blows a whistle, the bout begins.

Both wrestlers start each period standing, in a neutral position.

The referee may warn one or both wrestlers regarding passivity (or negative wrestling), which is against the aims and spirit of wrestling. After a verbal warning, if a wrestler is still passive, the referee may stop the bout and give the wrestler a formal warning, or caution. In the event of a tied match, the athlete scoring last is awarded the win while a caution overrides all other criteria in determining the outcome of the match; if cautions are awarded, the wrestler with no cautions wins the match.

COMPETITION AREA

The mat is cushioned canvas or synthetic material with a diameter of 9 meters (see figure 64.1). The starting area is a circle in the center of the mat, 1 meter in diameter. It has a thin orange border. The central wrestling area, called the center area, is 7 meters in diameter.

The passivity zone is orange and encircles the central wrestling area. It is 1 meter wide. The protection area surrounds the passivity zone and is a minimum of 1.5 meters wide.

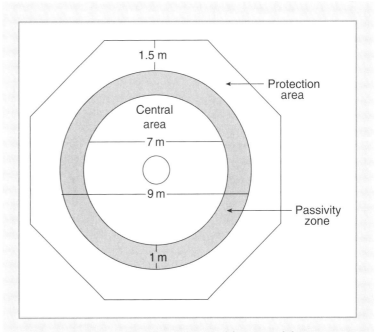

▶ **Figure 64.1** The dimensions and features of the competition area of a wrestling match.

Diagonally opposite corners of the mat are marked in red and blue to identify the corner for each athlete's coach (based on the color of the athlete's single – red or blue).

Wrestlers

Wrestlers compete in age divisions and are then categorized by weight, men's categories are as follows:

▫ Bantam (7 to 8): 8 classes from 43 to 85 pounds

▫ Intermediate (9 to 10): 12 classes from 49 to 120 pounds

▫ Novice (11 to 12): 14 classes from 58 to 160 pounds

▫ Schoolboy (13 to 14): 18 classes from 71 to 250 pounds

▫ Cadet (15 to 16): 17 classes from 88 to 285 pounds

▫ UWW cadet (14 to 16): 10 classes from 90 to 242

▫ Junior (20 years of age and under or enrolled in grades 9-12): 15 classes from 100 to 285 pounds

▫ UWW junior FS (19 to 20): 10 classes from 121 to 286 pounds

▫ UWW junior GR (19 to 20): 10 classes from 121 to 286 pounds

▫ U23 FS (19 to 23): 10 classes from 125 to 275 pounds

▫ U23 GR (19 to 23): 10 classes from 121 to 286 pounds

▫ Senior freestyle (20+): 10 classes from 125 to 275 pounds

▫ Senior Greco (20+): 10 classes from 121 to 286 pounds

▫ USA wrestling masters (25+): 6 classes from 136 to 286 pounds

Women's categories are:

▫ Intermediate (7 to 9): 10 classes from 45 to 85 pounds, plus heavyweights

▫ Novice (10 to 12): 11 classes from 60 to 118 pounds, plus heavyweights

▫ Schoolgirl (13 to 14): 12 classes from 72 to 185 pounds

▫ Cadet (15 to 16): 14 classes from 94 to 200 pounds

▫ UWW cadet (15 to 17): 10 classes from 79 to 160 pounds

▫ Junior (20 years of age and under or enrolled in grades 9-12): 14 classes from 100 to 225 pounds

▫ UWW junior (20+): 10 classes from 110 to 167 pounds

▫ U23 (19 to 23): 10 classes from 110 to 167 pounds

▫ Senior (20+): 10 classes from 110 to 167 pounds

EQUIPMENT

Wrestlers wear singlets (tight-fitting one-piece uniforms), either red or blue, corresponding to each athlete's corner of the mat. Headgear to protect the ears is prohibited in international competition but mandatory for all high school and youth USAW regional and national championships. Headgear is allowed in the United States in most levels of competition, although it must be removed upon an opponent's request unless it is worn for a certified medical reason. Wrestlers' shoes must have soft, pliable soles with ankle support, and laces must be taped to the shoes or fixed with a device to keep the shoelaces tied. A penalty point can be assessed if laces come undone. Women wrestlers must wear a sports bra. Kneepads are permissible. Except in cases of injury, bandages on wrists, arms, and ankles are not allowed.

RULES

The following sections include rules for the Greco and freestyle forms of wrestling.

Scoring

Various moves and holds are given point values. Following are examples of how wrestlers may score points.

If an athlete attempts to flee a hold in Freestyle, the referee may caution or award the opponent a point. In Greco-Roman, fleeing can be cautioned and opponents can be awarded two points. In either situation, a restart will occur and athletes will start either in the neutral (on the feet) or par terre (on the mat) positions.

Wrestlers score 2 points when they execute a regular takedown (bringing the opponent to the mat but not putting the opponent on their back, in danger of a fall).

One point may be awarded for an athlete executing a reversal (moving out from underneath an opponent and gaining control).

In FS and GR, wrestlers can score 1 point by forcing the opponent to step out of the outer circle. Referees are to allow action to continue after a step out on the edge to encourage opportunities for more points if athletes are still engaged in scoring opportunities.

Wrestlers score 2 points when they place the opponent in a position of danger by rolling the opponent across their shoulders either on the mat or by lifting them in the air and exposing their back.

Wrestlers score 4 points when they execute a takedown from the standing/neutral position, which brings the opponent to a position of danger (exposing their back) on the mat; when they raise the opponent off the mat and place them in danger.

Wrestlers score 5 points when they execute a grand amplitude hold from a standing position that places the opponent in immediate danger (on their back) and when they lift the opponent off the mat in executing a grand amplitude hold that places him in immediate danger.

In Greco-Roman, senior level athletes lifting an opponent off the mat (from the par terre position) and executing a lift/throw with grand amplitude awards the offensive wrestler 4 points. Younger ages will see the lifting action stopped by the official for safety reasons. Grand amplitude throws from par terre where the opponent lands in danger result in 5 points for the offensive wrestler. If the opponent does not land in danger, the par terre lift results in four points.

Illegal Actions and Holds

Wrestlers are not allowed to pull hair, ears, or genitals; to pinch, bite, kick, or head-butt; to strangle; to twist fingers; to use a hold that may fracture or dislocate a limb; or to act in any way to injure an opponent intentionally.

Wrestlers may not cling to the mat, talk during the bout, or grab the sole of the opponent's foot. (Grabbing the upper part of the foot or the heel is allowed.) Wrestlers may not flee a hold or flee the mat. Illegal holds include

- holding the throat;
- twisting an arm more than 90 degrees, including behind the back;
- applying a forearm lock;
- executing a three-quarter nelson or double nelson (unless executed from the side, without using the legs on any part of the opponent's body);
- stretching the opponent's spinal column;
- using two arms on an opponent's head or neck (one arm may be used);
- breaking a "bridge" by pushing in the direction of the opponent's head;
- lifting an opponent in a bridge position and throwing him to the mat; and
- holding an opponent upside down and then falling on top of her (a "header").

If a wrestler uses any of these holds, the action is void, and the wrestler is either warned or cautioned. If a defending wrestler executes an illegal hold in an attempt to prevent the attacking wrestler from executing his hold, the defending wrestler is cautioned, and his opponent is given 1 or 2 points (depending on the style of wrestling).

TERMS

A **bout** is the competition, or match, between two wrestlers.

A wrestler creates a **bridge** to support herself on her head, elbows, and feet, to keep from touching her shoulders to the mat.

Brutality is unnecessary roughness with intent to injure the opponent. A wrestler may be disqualified for such an act.

A wrestler receives a **bye** in tournament action when he has no opponent in a given round.

A **caution** may be issued for using an illegal hold, for fleeing a hold or the mat, or for refusing to take the proper starting position. A wrestler is disqualified after three cautions.

The **center circle** is 1 meter in diameter in the center of the mat. It is the starting area.

The **central area** is the middle of the mat, 7 meters across, where most of the action should take place.

A **correct hold** refers to a well-executed throw that doesn't result in a takedown or in putting the opponent in danger. On a correct throw, a wrestler may be awarded a point even though the scoring criteria are not met.

A **counter move** is one that stops or blocks an opponent's attack. A wrestler may score on a counter move.

A wrestler is in the **danger position** when the line of her shoulders or back forms an angle with the mat that's less than 90 degrees and when she resists with the upper body to avoid a fall.

A **decision** refers to a victory on points, with a margin of 1 to 5 (international) or 7 points in high school or college.

A **default** occurs when the outcome of a bout is determined by injury.

A wrestler is **disqualified** after three cautions for misconduct.

A **fall** is scored when a wrestler pins her opponent's shoulders to the mat.

Fleeing the mat/hold to elude an opponent's attack may result in a caution and a point. In the course of wrestling activity, if a wrestler steps out of bounds from the standing position, his opponent is awarded 1 or 2 points, depending on style.

A **forfeit** occurs when a wrestler fails to show for his bout.

A **grand amplitude** hold is a high, sweeping throw during which the opponent is lifted off the mat.

A **gut wrench** is a hold applied to a wrestler's torso to turn her to score points. Two points are awarded for a gut wrench when executed in the *danger position*, 1 point when not in the danger position. A wrestler can score consecutive points for executing a hold repetitively.

An **illegal hold** is one prohibited by the rules (see "Illegal Actions and Holds"). A wrestler is cautioned for an illegal hold, and the opponent may be awarded 1 or 2 points.

Par terre position occurs when one wrestler gains control and the athletes continue wrestling on the mat. Generally, the official will give the top wrestler 15 to 20 seconds to perform a successful turn. If no

progress is being made, the official will briefly stop the match and then start the wrestlers in the neutral position to continue the bout.

The **passivity zone** is the outermost part of the mat that is in bounds. When wrestlers reach the passivity zone, the referee calls, "Zone!" They must try to return to the center of the mat while not interrupting their action.

The **protection area** of the mat borders the passivity zone (see figure 64.1). It is out of bounds.

A **reversal** (1 point) is executed by a wrestler who comes out from underneath the other wrestler and gains control of his opponent. (This move is worth 2 points in folkstyle.)

A **slam** occurs when a wrestler throws an opponent down with unnecessary force without accompanying her to the mat. A slam is illegal in youth competition.

A **slip throw** is an unsuccessful attempt at a throw from either a standing position or the par terre position. Wrestling action continues after a slip, even if no points are awarded.

A **takedown** (2 points) occurs when a wrestler takes his opponent to the mat in a position not in danger.

A **technical fall** occurs when a wrestler gains an advantage of 6 or more points in any one period (15 or more points in high school and college during the course of the match).

Technical points refer to points scored for holds and moves. Penalty points may also count as technical points.

OFFICIALS

Three officials work competitions: a referee, a mat chairperson, and a judge. Referees work the mat and are in charge of the bout. Each referee wears a red cuff on the left arm and a blue cuff on the right arm and raises the appropriate arm and fingers to indicate points for the wrestlers. Referees should not wear any jewelry except wedding ring and wristwatch.

The mat chairman is the head official and settles any disagreements between the referee and the judge. The judge marks points on a score sheet, consults with the referee, and verifies and signals a fall. He may indicate a passive wrestler. Doctors and other medical attendants may declare a wrestler unfit to continue. Officials' signals are shown in figure 64.2.

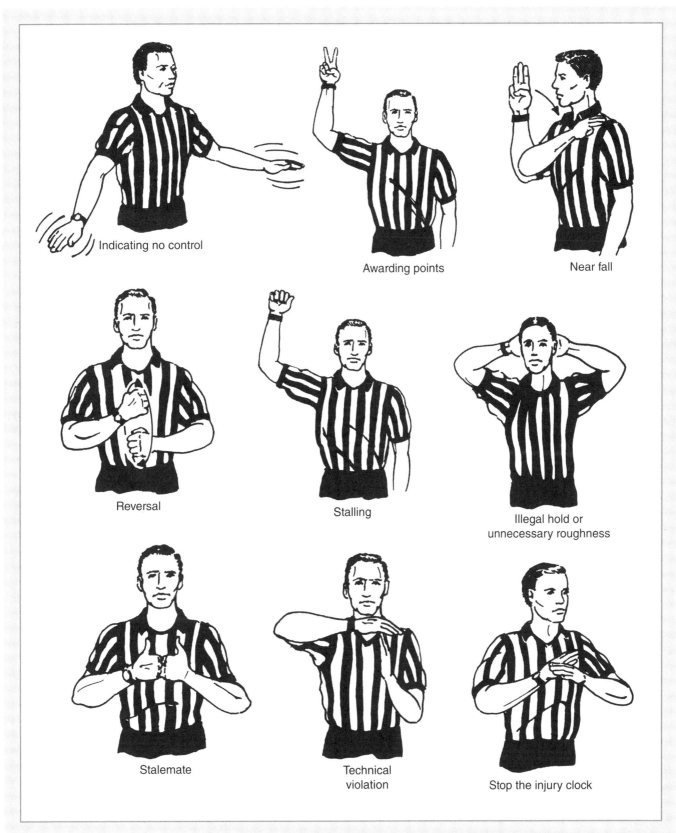

Indicating no control

Awarding points

Near fall

Reversal

Stalling

Illegal hold or
unnecessary roughness

Stalemate

Technical
violation

Stop the injury clock

▶ **Figure 64.2** Common officials' signals in wrestling.

(continued)

Unsportsmanlike conduct

Stopping the match

Out of bounds

Start the injury clock

Potentially dangerous

Neutral position

Timeout

Indicating wrestler in control

▶ **Figure 64.2** *(continued)*

MODIFICATIONS

Modifications for NCAA rules are categorized in the following sections: mat, weight classifications and rules, match length and procedures, and scoring.

Mat

The wrestling area is circular (no less than 32 feet and no greater than 42 feet in diameter). A mat area, or apron, at least 5 feet wide, encompasses the wrestling area.

At the center of the mat is a circle, 10 feet in diameter. Inside this circle are two 1-inch starting lines; they are 3 feet long and 10 inches apart. One starting line is green and located closest to the home team; the other is red and nearest the visitors.

Weight Classifications and Rules

Senior wrestlers are divided into 10 weight classifications:

Men

- 125 pounds (57.0 kilograms)
- 133 pounds (60.4 kilograms)
- 141 pounds (64.0 kilograms)
- 149 pounds (67.7 kilograms)
- 157 pounds (71.3 kilograms)
- 165 pounds (75.0 kilograms)
- 174 pounds (79.0 kilograms)
- 184 pounds (83.6 kilograms)
- 197 pounds (89.5 kilograms)
- Heavyweight 183-285 pounds (83.0-129.5 kilograms)

Data from USA Wrestling (2018). Available: http://content.themat.com/forms/Weights.pdf.

For dual, triangular, and quadrangular meets, wrestlers weigh in 1 hour before the meet. For tournaments, wrestlers weigh in each day. On the first day of competition, weigh-ins are 2 hours before the start of competition. Each day following, weigh-ins are 1 hour before the competition.

In all tournaments, wrestlers may weigh 1 pound more each day above the weight limit of the previous day (up to 2 pounds more). Wrestlers may not forfeit in one weight class and wrestle in another, or compete in more than one weight class in any meet. A wrestler may, however, weigh in at one weight and then shift to a higher weight class.

Match Length and Procedures

Matches last 76 minutes, split into three two periods. The first is 3-minutes followed by two 2 minute periods with 30-second breaks between the periods. Each match is begun with both wrestlers standing. A premeet coin toss determines which team has the choice of position (top, bottom, neutral) at the start of the second period. The winner may choose the odd- or even-numbered weight classes.

The wrestler with the choice of position may either make his choice or defer until the third period. If he defers, his opponent chooses the position to begin the second period. In a tournament, choice of position is determined for each match by a coin toss by the referee at the beginning of the second period. The other wrestler has the choice for the third period.

An injured or ill wrestler has up to 90 seconds of injury timeout throughout the match. This time is cumulative, and only the referee may call such timeouts. Timeout for excessive bleeding does not count against the wrestler's 90 seconds of injury timeout.

If the match score is tied at the end of regulation, a 1-minute sudden-victory overtime period immediately follows. Wrestlers begin in the neutral position; the first to score wins. If there is no scoring at the end of the sudden-victory period, the wrestlers then wrestle two 30-second tiebreaker periods. Choice of position is determined by the first to score in the regulation bout. The athletes wrestle the entire 30-second period, and all scoring is cumulative. At the end of the tie break, if no scoring advantage exists, wrestling resumes with an additional sudden-victory period followed by another tie breaker if no scoring occurs. At this point, riding time advantage from the tie-breaker periods determines the winner of the bout, if all else remains equal.

Scoring

As mentioned earlier, wrestlers may score by takedown, escape, and reversal. They may also score a near fall, where a wrestler has her opponent in a controlled pinning situation for at least 2 seconds (2 points) or at least 45 seconds (4 points). Points may also be awarded for an imminent score, when a wrestler is injured and action is stopped just before the successful completion of a scoring move that appeared imminent.

If a wrestler accumulates 1 minute or more of riding time advantage, he receives 1 point. Both shoulders of a wrestler must be pinned to the mat for 1 second for a fall to occur. Part of both shoulders must be in bounds. A technical fall occurs when a wrestler gains a 15-point advantage. (A time advantage cannot be counted toward a technical fall until regulation time expires.)

A major decision occurs when the margin of victory is between 8 and 14 points, inclusively. A decision is a victory with the margin less than 8 points. Individual and team scoring are as follows:

- Individual points: near fall, 2 or 4; takedown, 2; reversal, 2; escape, 1; time advantage, 1

- Team points, dual meet:

  - 6 points—fall, forfeit, default, or disqualification

  - 5 points—for a 15-point margin that includes at least one set of back points

  - 5 points—technical fall (when a 15-point margin is reached with no back points awarded)

  - 4 points—major decision

  - 3 points—decision

ORGANIZATIONS

National Wrestling Coaches Association
P.O. Box 254
Manheim, PA 17545
717-653-8009
www.nwcaonline.com

USA Wrestling
6155 Lehman Dr.
Colorado Springs, CO 80918
719-598-8181
www.TheMat.com

References

AAU Baseball. (2018). *National Championship Rule Book 2018.* [Online]. Available: https://cdn2.sportngin.com/attachments/document/0154/4787/formet-rules-nationals-2018.pdf

All About Table Tennis. (2018). Best Table Tennis Players. [Online]. Available: https://www.allabouttabletennis.com/table-tennis-players.html

American Cornhole Association. (2018). *Official Cornhole Rules for ACA Tournaments.* [Online]. Available: https://www.playcornhole.org/aca-official-rules-of-cornhole-corn-toss

American Cornhole Organization. (2016). *ACO Official Rules for the Sport of Cornhole.* [Online]. Available: https://american-cornhole.com/aco-official-rules-for-the-sport-of-cornhole

American Water Ski Association. (2018). *Official Tournament Rules.* [Online]. Available: http://www.usawaterski.org/pages/divisions/3event/AWSARuleBook.pdf

AR World Series. (2017). *Adventure Racing World Series Rules of Competition.* [Online]. Available: http://arworldseries.com/resources

Australian Football League. (2015). *Women's Participation Soars in 2015.* [Online]. Available: http://www.afl.com.au/news/2015-10-13/womens-participation-in-afl-soars-in-2015

Bocce Standards Association (2010). *Court Bocce Standard Rules for Leagues and Tournaments.* [Online]. Available: http://www.boccestandardsassociation.org

Canadian Football League. (2018). *The Official Playing Rules of the Canadian Football League 2018.* [Online]. Available: https://cfldb.ca/rulebook

Crawford, E.J. (2015). "Tennis participation on the rise in U.S." [Online]. Available: http://www.idtennis.com/news/tennis_participation_on_the_rise_in_us

Dodd, C. (1992). *The Story of World Rowing.* London, UK: Stanley Paul & Co.

Fédération Internationale de Gymnastique. (2017). *2017 – 2020 Code of Points.* [Online]. Available: http://www.fig-gymnastics.com/publicdir/rules/files/en_WAG%20CoP%202017-2020.pdf

Fédération Internationale de Ski. (2018). *The International Ski Competition Rules (ICR): Book II Cross Country.* [Online]. Available: http://www.fis-ski.com/mm/Document/documentlibrary/Cross-Country/02/95/69/ICRCrossCountry2018_clean_Neutral.pdf

Fédération Internationale de Ski. (2018). *The International Ski Competition Rules (ICR): Book IV Joint Regulations for Alpine Skiing.* [Online]. Available: http://www.fis-ski.com/mm/Document/documentlibrary/AlpineSkiing/03/29/54/ICR_2018_final_clean_Neutral.pdf

Fédération Internationale de Ski. (2017). *The International Ski Competition Rules (ICR): Book VI Joint Regulations for Snowboarding.* [Online]. Available: http://www.fis-ski.com/mm/Document/documentlibrary/Snowboard/05/56/03/SB_FIS_ICR17Snowboard_English.pdf

Federation Internationale de Volleyball. (2017). *Official Volleyball Rules, 2017-20.* [Online]. Available: http://www.fivb.org/EN/Refereeing-Rules/documents/FIVB-Volleyball_Rules_2017-2020-EN-v06.pdf

Federation of International Lacrosse. (2016). *FIL Indoor Lacrosse Rulebook 2016-19.* [Online]. Available: https://filacrosse.com/rules/

Federation of International Lacrosse. (2015). *2015-18 Women's Official Rules.* [Online]. Available: https://filacrosse.com/rules

Federation of International Lacrosse. (2017). *2017-18 Rules of Men's Field Lacrosse Rulebook.* [Online]. Available: https://filacrosse.com/rules

FIBA. (2017). *2017 Official Basketball Rules.* [Online]. Available: http://www.fiba.basketball/OBR2017/Final.pdf

Friends of Rowing History. (n.d.). [Online]. Available: http://www.rowinghistory.net

Heitner, D. (2016). "The State of the Golf Industry in 2016," in *Forbes.* [Online]. Available: https://www.forbes.com/sites/darrenheitner/2016/05/08/the-state-of-the-golf-industry-in-2016/#7919d7c633a6

International Boxing Federation. (2018). *IBF Rules Governing Boxing Contests.* [Online]. Available: http://www.ibfusbaregistration.com/ibfusba_02APR2014/images/pdfs/IBFChampionshipContestRules0518.pdf

International Brazilian Jiu-Jitsu Federation. (2018). *Rule Book.* [Online]. Available: http://ibjjf.com/wp-content/uploads/2018/06/Rules_Book_IBJJF_v5.0_en-US.pdf

International Canoe Federation. (2017). *Canoe Freestyle Competition Rules 2017.* [Online]. Available: https://www.canoeicf.com/sites/default/files/canoe_freestyle_rules_2017.pdf

International Canoe Federation. (2017). *Canoe Slalom Competition Rules 2017.* [Online]. Available: https://www.canoeicf.com/sites/default/files/canoe_slalom_competition_rules_2017_rev_csl_final_inclcslx_4.pdf

International Canoe Federation. (2017). *Wildwater Canoeing Competition Rules 2017.* [Online]. Available: https://www.canoeicf.com/sites/default/files/wildwater_canoeing_rules_2017docx_0.pdf

International Cheer Union. (2017). *International Cheer Union Rules and Regulations 2017-2019.* [Online]. Available: http://cheerunion.org.ismmedia.com/ISM3/std-content/repos/Top/docs/ICU_TeamCheer_Rules_2018.pdf

International Cricket Council. (2017). *Rules and Regulations.* [Online]. Available: https://www.icc-cricket.com/about/cricket/rules-and-regulations/playing-conditions

International Federation of Sport Climbing. (2015). *Rules 2015.*

[Online]. Available: http://climbingcanada.ca/wp-content/uploads/2016/01/IFSC-Rules_2015_V1.1-12.pdf

International Football Association Board. (2017). *Laws of the Game 2017/18*. [Online]. Available: https://ussoccer.app.box.com/s/xx3byxqgodqtl1h15865/file/185132971909

International Gymnastics Federation. (2017). *Code of Pointage 2017*. [Online]. Available: http://www.fig-gymnastics.com/publicdir/rules/files/en_MAG%20CoP%202017%20-%202020.pdf

International Handball Federation. (2016). *Rules of the Game.* [Online]. Available: http://www.ihf.info/files/Uploads/NewsAttachments/0_New-Rules%20of%20the%20Game_GB.pdf

International Hockey Federation. (2017). *Rules of Hockey.* [Online]. Available: http://www.fih.ch/media/12236728/fih-rules-of-hockey-2017.pdf

International Ice Hockey Federation. (2018). IIHF Official Rule Book, 2018-2022. [Online]. Available: http://www.iihf.com/fileadmin/user_upload/PDF/Sport/IIHF_Official_Rule_Book_2018.pdf

International Judo Federation. (2018). *Explanation of the IJF Referee & Coach Seminar.* [Online]. Available: https://www.teamusa.org/usa-judo/rules/2018-ijf-rules

International KungFu Federation. (2005, updated 2010). *Rules and Regulations.* [Online]. Available: http://www.internationalkungfu.com

International Netball Federation. (2018). *International Rules of Netball.* [Online]. Available: http://netball.org/wp-content/uploads/2018/06/INF-Rules-of-Netball-2018-Edition-text-correction.pdf

International Shooting Sport Federation. (2017). *Official Statutes, Rules, and Regulations.* [Online]. Available: https://www.issf-sports.org/documents/rules/2017/ISSFRuleBook2017-2ndPrintV1.1-ENG.pdf

International Skating Union. (2016). *Special Regulations and Technical Rules, Speed Skating and Short Track Speed Skating 2016.* [Online]. Available: https://www.isu.org/isu-statutes-constitution-regulations-technical

International Surfing Association. (2017). *ISA Rulebook & Contest Administration Manual.* [Online]. Available: http://www.isasurf.org/downloads/ISA_Rulebook_Feb17.pdf

International Table Tennis Foundation. (2017). *International Table Tennis Foundation Handbook.* [Online]. Available: https://d3mjm6zw6cr45s.cloudfront.net/2016/12/2017_ITTF_Handbook.pdf

Jacques, T.D. (1994). *Australian Football: Steps to Success.* Champaign, IL: Human Kinetics.

Kistler, B. (1988). *Hit it!: Your Complete Guide to Water Skiing.* Champaign, IL: Human Kinetics.

Little League Baseball and Softball. (2018). *Rules, Regulations, and Policies.* [Online]. Available: https://www.littleleague.org/playing-rules/rules-regulations-policies

Lord's. (2017). *Summary of New Laws of Cricket Released.* April 11, 2017. [Online]. Available: https://www.lords.org/news/2017/april/summary-of-new-laws-of-cricket-released

National Football League. (2017). 2017 Official Playing Rules of the National Football League. [Online]. Available: https://operations.nfl.com/media/2725/2017-playing-rules.pdf

National Horseshoe Pitchers Association. (2016). The Official Rules/Regulations, Guidelines, Specifications for the Sport of Horseshoe Pitching. [Online]. Available: http://www.horseshoepitching.com/wp-content/uploads/2018/03/completebook.pdf

National Ski Areas Association. (2017). *Table 3: Estimated U.S. Snowsports Visits by Region, 1978/79-2017/18 (in millions).* [Online]. Available: http://www.nsaa.org/media/303945/visits.pdf

National Sporting Goods Association. (2016). *Golf: Participation by Total vs. Frequent.* [Online]. http://www.sportsmarketanalytics.com/research.aspx?subRID=199

National Sporting Goods Association. (2017). *Snowboarding: Participation by Total vs. Frequent.* [Online]. Available: http://www.sportsmarketanalytics.com/research.aspx?subRID=385

Netball Australia. (n.d). *What is Netball?* [Online]. Available: https://netball.com.au/our-game/what-is-netball

Office of the Commissioner of Baseball. (2017). *Official Baseball Rules.* [Online]. Available: http://mlb.mlb.com/documents/0/4/0/224919040/2017_Official_Baseball_Rules_dbt69t59.pdf

RRC Associates. (2016). *Estimated U.S. Snowsports Visits by Region, 1978/79-2016/17 (in millions),* in *Kottke National End of Season Survey, 2016-17.* [Online]. Available: http://www.nsaa.org/media/303945/visits.pdf

Sports & Fitness Industry Association. (2016). *Martial arts participation report, 2016.* [Online]. Available: https://www.sfia.org/reports/426_Martial-Arts-Participation-Report-2016

Sports & Fitness Industry Association. (2015). *Table Tennis Participation Report 2015.* [Online]. Available: https://www.sfia.org/reports/360_Table-Tennis-Participation-Report-2015

Statista. (2017). *Estimated number of skier/snowboard visits in the U.S. from 2000/01 to 2017/18 (in millions).* [Online]. Available: https://www.statista.com/statistics/206544/estimated-number-of-skier-visits-in-the-us-since-2000

Statista. (2016). *Number of participants in badminton in the United States from 2006 to 2016 (in millions).* [Online]. Available: https://www.statista.com/statistics/191754/participants-in-badminton-in-the-us-since-2006

Statista. (2016). *Number of participants in bowling in the United States from 2006 to 2016 (in millions).* [Online]. Available: https://www.statista.com/statistics/191898/participants-in-bowling-in-the-us-since-2006

Statista. (2016). *Number of participants in table tennis in the United States from 2006 to 2016 (in millions).* [Online]. Available: https://www.statista.com/statistics/191959/participants-in-table-tennis-in-the-us-since-2006

Statista. (2016). *Number of participants in tennis in the United States from 2006 to 2016 (in millions).* [Online]. Available: https://www.statista.com/statistics/191966/participants-in-tennis-in-the-us-since-2006

Statista. (2017). *Number of participants in triathlons in the United States from 2006 to 2017 (in millions).* [Online]. Available:

https://www.statista.com/statistics/191339/participants-in-triathlons-in-the-us-since-2006

Statista. (2016). *Number of participants in ultimate frisbee in the United States from 2006 to 2016 (in millions)*. [Online]. Available: https://www.statista.com/statistics/191967/participants-in-ultimate-frisbee-in-the-us-since-2006

Statista. (2018). *Share of people who played basketball in the United States in 2018, by age*. [Online]. Available: https://www.statista.com/statistics/227414/number-of-basketball-players-usa

The Croquet Association. (2018). *Garden Golf Croquet Rules*. [Online]. Available: https://www.croquet.org.uk/?p=games/garden/rules/GardenGolfRules

United States All-Round Weightlifting Association. (2017). *Official Rule Book, 10th Edition*. [Online]. Available: http://usawa.com/wp-content/uploads/2010/05/RULEBOOK-10th-Edition.pdf

United States Bowling Congress. (2017). *2017-2018 Playing Rules and Commonly Asked Questions*. [Online]. Available: http://usbcongress.http.internapcdn.net/usbcongress/bowl/rulebook/2017-2018Rulebook.pdf

United States Croquet Association. (2018). *Rules*. [Online]. Available: http://www.croquetamerica.com/croquet/rules

USA Badminton. (2018). *General Competition Regulations*. [Online]. Available: http://system.bwf.website/documents/folder_1_81/Regulations/GCR/Part%20III%20Section%201A%20-%20General%20Competition%20Regulations%20-%20August%202017.pdf

USA BMX (2018). *2018 Rule Book: The Official Rules of BMX USA/BMX Canada*. [Online]. Available: https://www.usabmx.com/site/sections/78

USA Climbing. (2018). *Rulebook*. [Online]. Available: http://www.usaclimbing.org/Assets/USA+Climbing/USA+Climbing+Digital+Assets/Documents/2017-2018+USA+Climbing+Rulebook.pdf

USA Cycling. (2018). *Rule Book 2018*. [Online]. Available: https://s3.amazonaws.com/imm-usac-uat-bucket-16e9mh-4tuo6kc/documents/Rules-Policies/USACycling_Rule-Book_2018_03.pdf

USA Fencing. (2018). *2018 USA Fencing Rulebook*. [Online]. Available: https://www.usafencing.org/usa-fencing-rule-book

US Equestrian. (2018). *2018 USEF Rulebook*. [Online]. Available: https://www.usef.org/compete/resources-forms/rules-regulations/rulebook

US Figure Skating. (2018). *The 2019 Official US Figure Skating Rulebook*. [Online]. Available: http://www.usfsa.org/story?id=84114

US Golf Association. (2018). *Rules and Decisions*. [Online]. Available: http://www.usga.org/content/usga/home-page/rules/rules-and-decisions.html#!rule-01

US Rowing. (2018). *Rules of Rowing*. [Online]. Available: http://www.usrowing.org/rules-of-rowing

US Ski & Snowboard. (2018). *2018 Alpine Competition Guide*. [Online]. Available: https://usskiandsnowboard.org/sites/default/files/files-resources/files/2017-10/2018_alp_comp_guide.pdf

US Squash. (2018). Squash Facts. [Online]. Available: https://www.ussquash.com/squash-facts

US Synchronized Swimming. (2018). US Synchronized Swimming Rules. [Online]. Available: https://www.teamusa.org/usa-synchronized-swimming/resources/usa-synchro-rulebook

USA Gymnastics. (2018). *Men's Rules and Policies*. [Online]. Available: https://usagym.org/pages/men/pages/rules_policies.html

USA Gymnastics. (2018). *2017-18 Women's Program Rules and Policies*. [Online]. Available: https://usagym.org/PDFs/Women/Rules/Rules%20and%20Policies/2017_2018_w_rulespolicies_0522.pdf

USA Gymnastics. (2018). *Rhythmic Rules and Policies*. [Online]. Available: https://usagym.org/pages/rhythmic/pages/rules_policies.html

USA Karate. (2017). *Federation Rules of Kata and Kobudo Competition*. [Online]. Available: https://www.teamusa.org/USA-Karate/Events/Rules-of-Competition

USA Karate. (2017). *Federation Rules of Kumite Competition*. [Online]. Available: https://www.teamusa.org/USA-Karate/Events/Rules-of-Competition

USA Pickleball Association and International Federation of Pickleball. (2018). *USAPA and IFP Official Tournament Rulebook*. [Online]. Available: http://ifpickleball.org/wp-content/uploads/2017/07/IFP-Booklet-PBrules.pdf

USA Racquetball. (2015). *Official Rules of Racquetball*. [Online]. Available: https://www.teamusa.org/usa-racquetball/rules

US Squash. (n.d.). *Squash Facts*. [Online]. Available: https://www.ussquash.com/squash-facts

USA Swimming. (2017). *Rulebook 2017*. [Online]. Available: https://www.usaswimming.org/docs/default-source/rules-regulations/2017-rulebook.pdf

USA Taekwondo. (2017). *Kyorugi Competition Rules & Interpretation*. [Online]. Available: https://www.teamusa.org/usa-taekwondo/v2-events/competition-rules

USA Triathlon. (2017). *USA Triathlon Competitive Rules*. [Online]. Available: https://www.teamusa.org/USA-Triathlon/About/Multisport/Competitive-Rules

USA Ultimate. (2017). *11th Edition Rules*. [Online]. Available: http://www.usaultimate.org/resources/officiating/rules/default.aspx

USA Ultimate. (2015). "About Ultimate." [Online]. Available: https://www.usaultimate.org/about

USA Water Polo. (2015). *USA Water Polo Rules, 2015-2018*. [Online]. Available: http://www.usawaterpolo.org/resources/rules-ethics.html

World Archery Foundation. (2018). *Sport Rules, Book 3*. [Online]. Available: https://worldarchery.org/rulebook/article/3

World Archery Foundation. (2018). *Sport Rules, Book 4*. [Online]. Available: https://worldarchery.org/rulebook/article/3137

World Baseball & Softball Confederation. (2018). 2018-21 Official Rules of Softball. [Online]. Available: http://www.wbsc.org/wp-content/uploads/ENGLISH-2018-2021-Slow-Pitch-Softball-Playing-Rules-A4-1.pdf

World Curling Federation. (2017). *The Rules of Curling and Rules of Competition*. [Online]. Available: http://www.worldcurling.org/rules-and-regulations-downloads

World Freestyle Skateboard Association. (2018.) *Contest Guidelines*. [Online]. Available: http://www.wfsafreestyle.org/resources/guidelines.pdf

World Paddle Association. (2018). *2018 Event Rules & Guidelines*. [Online]. Available: https://worldpaddleassociation.com/wp-content/uploads/2018/02/2018-WPA-Event-Rules-Guidelines_1_1_18.pdf

World Rugby. (2015). *A Beginner's Guide to Rugby Union*. [Online]. Available: http://passport.worldrugby.org/beginners_guide/downloads/Beginners_Guide_2015_EN.pdf

World Rugby. (2015). "More women are playing rugby than ever before." [Online]. Available: https://www.worldrugby.org/news/60275

World Rugby. (2016). Player numbers. [Online]. Available: https://www.worldrugby.org/development/player-numbers?lang=en

World Squash Federation. (2014). *World Squash Singles Rules*. [Online]. Available: http://www.worldsquash.org/ws/wp-content/uploads/2017/06/170620_Rules-of-Singles-Squash-2014-V2014-04.pdf

About the Authors

Human Kinetics has been providing the world authoritative information related to physical activity since 1974. That information takes the form of textbooks and their ancillaries, consumer books, journals, online courses, software, and audiovisual products. The information touches the lives of millions of people worldwide who are interested in some form of physical activity. Those people include college students and professors, personal trainers, rehabilitation specialists, athletes, coaches, physical educators, nutritionists, parents, and sedentary people who want to become active.

Myles Schrag is the founder of Adina Publishing and a former acquisitions and developmental editor at Human Kinetics. He has been involved in sport throughout his life as a participant, fan, coach, and parent. His career also includes experience as a freelance writer, book reviewer, and newspaper editor. His sports writing, youth coaching experience, and all-around interest in sport and physical activity make him uniquely qualified to author this book.

Find more outstanding resources at

www.HumanKinetics.com

In the **U.S.** call 1-800-747-4457
Canada 1-800-465-7301
U.K./Europe +44 (0) 113 255 5665
International 1-217-351-5076

eBook
available at
HumanKinetics.com

HUMAN KINETICS